**Fifty Years of
Russian Prose**

Volume 2

Alexander
Solzhenitsyn

**Fifty Years of
Russian Prose:**

From Pasternak to
Solzhenitsyn

Edited by
Krystyna Pomorska

Volume 2

The MIT Press
Cambridge,
Massachusetts,
and London,
England

Set in Lumitype Optima
Printed by The Apine Press Inc.
Bound in the United States of America by The Colonial Press Inc.

Second printing, first MIT Press paperback edition, October 1973

"Levers," "A Light in the Window," and "A Trip Home" reprinted by
permission of Walter Vickery and Hugh McLean; "Matryona's Home"
reprinted by permission of Holt, Rinehart and Winston, Inc., New York,
and George Weidenfeld & Nicolson Limited, London; For the Good of
the Cause reprinted by permission of Frederick A. Praeger, Inc., New
York, and The Pall Mall Press Ltd., London; "Good-bye Schoolboy!,"
previously published as "Lots of Luck, Kid," reprinted by permission
of Little, Brown and Company, Boston; Seryozha, previously published
as A Summer to Remember and Time Walked, reprinted by permission
of A. S. Barnes & Company, Inc., Cranbury, New Jersey, and The Harvill
Press Ltd., London.

ISBN 0-262-16038-2 (hardcover)
ISBN 0-262-66020-2 (paperback)
Library of Congress catalog card number: 70-122263

Contents

**Fifty Years of
Russian Prose**

Volume 2

Acknowledgment   I extend my sincere thanks to Mrs. Elsie Bowen for her editorial help in preparing this volume.

Krystyna Pomorska

After almost three decades, during which the scheme of
Socialist Realism made literary plots totally predictable and
therefore unliterary and dreary, a new revival of art came to
Russia. Its way was prepared by several noteworthy events.

In 1953 the journal *Novy Mir* published an article by
Pomerantsev entitled "On Honesty in Literature," in which the
doctrine of Socialist Realism was revised for the first time.
Shortly after there appeared a novel by Vera Panova, *Seasons
of the Year*, depicting the crude conflicts within two families—
not of a political but of a moral nature. The conclusion of the
story is unusual: the son of excellent comrades turns out to be
bad, whereas a sinister character happens to have excellent and
worthy children. To an uninitiated person this might seem to
suggest an obvious and elementary truth, but in the given
situation it was quite a revolutionary idea.

After the appearance of Ehrenburg's important novel *The
Thaw* (1954), the literary and intellectual ferment progressed
even faster. This book constituted a polemic not only against
some important doctrines but also against the very scheme of
the novel, obligatory in the code of Socialist Realism. Naturally,
it stimulated a vivid debate, followed two years later by fresh
discussion, this time on Dudintsev's famous book, *Not by Bread
Alone*.

The year 1956, rightly called "the year of protest and freedom," saw two more intellectual events. At the assembly of
the Moscow section of the Soviet Writers Union, Dudintsev
was sharply attacked for his novel, which accused the bureaucracy and defended the freedom of the individual to display
his creative abilities. Dudintsev's retort was brilliant and
courageous. His example was followed by several other writers
of the section. For the first time since 1934 no one present
spoke in terms of self-accusation and repentance.

The almanac *Literary Moscow* (Vol. 2) brought out in the same
year an impressive collection of prose and poetry by both
older and younger writers. Some hitherto forbidden names,
such as Tsvetaeva, appeared in it; certain young people brought
in new ideas and cast a new light on contemporary life and its
problems.

In our anthology the stories by Yashin, Nagibin, and Zhdanov
have been taken from *Literary Moscow*. All three of these,
"Levers," "A Light in the Window," and "A Trip Home,"
are of great informative value and contain remarkably strong
implications. They reveal capital sins in the management of
collective farms: the role of the bureaucracy in hampering
real initiative; the impracticability of the schedules imposed
on farmers by the central authorities; and the resultant lies

and hypocrisy. Some of the accusations pertain to the whole situation, such as the all-powerful fear that rules even the smallest communities. The most dangerous symptom is the gap between the party officials and the people. Hence the direct conclusion that class differentiation still exists. This is shown most vividly in Nagibin's story "A Light in the Window."

The writer whose talent and courage equal that of Tolstoy and Dostoevsky is Nobel Laureate (1970) Alexander Solzhenitsyn. His fame in the world began with the publication of his staggering narrative, *One Day in the Life of Ivan Denisovich* (1962), about a prisoner in a concentration camp in Stalin's Russia.

The literature on concentration camps, both Russian and German, is rich and abundant. Even the best examples, however, display a feature that became almost obligatory in this genre: the accumulation of horrors in their most striking and explicit form. Solzhenitsyn employs the opposite means: he avoids the dramatic, he does not present any overt conflict. Hour by hour the account develops, slowly and quietly. At the end it turns out that Ivan Denisovich's day in the camp was quite successful. Such a conclusion can be drawn thanks to a particular view on human nature, already so well shown by Dostoevsky: man's ability to adapt to *any* conditions. Ivan Denisovich Shukhov is fully aware of this ability and cultivates it, beginning with the purely physiological functions, as he decides "not to tease" his stomach but to proceed very cautiously with food, and ending with the great virtue of not developing hostility of any kind to anyone. This is the adaptability and at the same time the goodness of the simple Russian man. It reminds us of the Tolstoyan principle of nonresistance to evil. Consequently, Shukhov becomes, indeed, comparable to Platon Karataev, Tolstoy's symbol of a Russian peasant, with his complex simplicity and outstanding mediocrity.

We find a further continuation of the Russian classical tradition in Solzhenitsyn's story "Matryona's Home." The author's choice of his main character is eloquent: an "insignificant" person, a woman, who is sick, untidy, and strikingly inefficient. But she is gentle, meek, totally without possessiveness. Such people are the truly righteous ones, "without whom no village can stand. . . . Nor our whole land." This is the religious message of the story, and it is reminiscent of Tolstoy, Dostoevsky, and Turgenev.

The critics reproached Solzhenitsyn for having chosen a "nontypical" collective farm, a "nontypical" problem, and a "nontypical" heroine. Where, they asked, are the traces of progress in the Soviet villages? These critics obviously missed the main point of Solzhenitsyn's writings, in which the interest is focused on silent, quiet, primordial Russia. That is why he pursues every vestige of such a Russia, everything old, unchanged, "regressive," "nontypical." Hence his love of old customs and local, unwritten laws, as shown in his story "Zakhar Kalita," published in *Novy Mir* (1966). His predilection for various local dialects also derives from this concern.

His interest in things unchanged—"as before, so now"—leads Solzhenitsyn to indicate similar features in human nature and human relations. He concludes that very little has altered in the character of the "new man": people are still eager to appropriate another's goods—"before they stole from the landlord, today from the kolkhoz." Possessiveness and petty ambition are still alive, disguised only superficially under the label of "collectivism." This is the theme of the story "For the Good of the Cause." The righteous are still as rare as in all other epochs, and only they can save the world.

"An Incident at Krechetovka Station" (originally published in *Novy Mir*, 1963) stands out among Solzhenitsyn's writings by virtue of both its message and its construction. The notorious image of the informer appears here in a new key. Ordinarily such a character has been presented as a one-dimensional person with the traits of a fanatic, a frightening and repulsive image. Certain abnormal features have often been ascribed to this type: sometimes psychopathological or cynically perverted.

No such feature is to be seen in Zotov. He is highly self-disciplined, a typical Spartan Communist who deserves the reader's full sympathy. His entirely human reflexes, sentiments, and attachments are shown in his attitude toward other people, his high moral principles in rejecting all fraud and dishonesty. His high principles even alienate him from the community. A devoted Communist, he tries hard to extend his knowledge of Marxism in a rather remarkable way: to read *Capital* in extenso was not a widespread practice among average Party members.

A genuine idealist, Zotov hands over an innocent man *in spite of* his full sympathy for him, according to his best understanding of his duty. The denunciation does not come easily to him; he struggles with himself and attempts to save the man until the very last moment, when Tveritinov loses his chance by mere ignorance, which proves fatal. So as to illumine the image of Zotov further, we are shown his diametrical opposite: the political officer who proceeds according to a routine of cynicism and cruelty.

Such is Solzhenitsyn's answer to the ever-puzzling question of the "brainwashed" man. It is presented with total honesty, with a knowledge of human psychology, and with the simplicity that only great art can achieve.

Another aspect of "An Incident at Krechetovka Station" is its interesting depiction of the rear line, about which we have only scant information. In this respect the story is an extension of the war or, rather, the antiwar literature that developed vividly after 1953.

One of its best representatives is Bulat Okudzhava, who is first and foremost a singer and a poet. A large number of his songs, which he performs to the accompaniment of his guitar, are devoted to the problems of war, its supporters and opposers, and, above all, to unmasking a myth, a false image of war. The same is true of his charming prose piece "Good-bye, Schoolboy!," written in the form of a soldier's diary, which may be considered autobiographical. Okudzhava belongs to the generation that volunteered "to fight for the Motherland," not having reached draft age when the war began. Heroic, disillusioned, and decimated in battles, this same generation today offers us new and vivid talents in literature, film, painting, and sculpture as well as in modern scholarship.

There are several recurrent motifs in Okudzhava's poetry and prose, which may be summarized as follows: soldiers invariably go to war; their women are left behind. On their return they find their lives ruined beyond repair. They lack the necessary courage to fight back. For to be a hero in war does not imply courage in civil life. According to Okudzhava, this is the reason why people generally like soldiering: it frees them of responsibility for their conduct and decision. The woman in Okudzhava's poetry always belongs to someone else, and the lyrical hero is left alone with his unreturned love and his melancholy.

All these motifs are to be found in the two tales included in this volume. In particular, the second, "Promoxys" (published in the journal Youth in 1966), displays both the content and the poetics of Okudzhava's verses. Its definitely lyrical, slightly fantastic tone, its poetically attuned hero with his symbolic (and autobiographical) guitar and his reckless ventures—all these elements echo Bulat Okudzhava the poet.

Besides social and political themes—that of war with its various repercussions on people's lives, presented boldly and in a new light by the younger generation and, to an extent, by the older and middle-aged writers—there has also developed a remarkable stream of literature about children, one with a special eloquence. Since it was regarded as too intimate, too "private" and insignificant to satisfy the demands that Socialist

Realism imposed on a writer, this genre had little chance of
survival before the period of the "thaw."

We present here two of the best stories of this type. *Seryozha*,
the first, is from the pen of an older writer, Vera Panova,
whose important role in the revival of Soviet literature was
noted in our opening remarks. The second was written by Yury
Nagibin, whose name became known when his writings first
appeared in *Literary Moscow* in 1956.

Seryozha—now internationally known thanks to the film
based on it—is deeply rooted in traditional Russian literature
about children. To see the adult world exclusively through the
eyes of a child has been a device familiar to Russian readers
for at least a century. Saltykov-Shchedrin, Tolstoy, and Chekhov,
as well as Sologub, Gorky, Andrey Bely, and Pasternak, have
used it. *Seryozha* is written in a classical, quiet tone; it lacks the
experimental touch of Bely and Pasternak, but it does carry a
feature seemingly universal in literature on children: it shows
the natural alienation of the child among grown-ups, the child's
innate disposition toward poetry, and his capacity—much
stronger than an adult's—for love.

A point of special interest in Panova's story is that Seryozha's
microworld faithfully reflects all the aspects of the larger reality.
It shows how pedagogical discipline may be too rigid and therefore harmful, and how much it can hurt, how easily a mere game
can turn into cruelty and oppression. Yet the story is not at all
overloaded with philosophical issues. On the contrary, its touch
is extremely light, and its charm resides mainly in this.

In Nagibin's "The Fourth Daddy," the focus falls more on
the adults than on the child, who is the principal character
in the story and whose point of view is expressed through
quasi-indirect speech. Thus little Sasha serves as a filter
through which the true picture of other personages is presented.
This is so not only because his point of view dominates the
narrative but also because the turn of the story depends on
him: Baykov becomes disillusioned with Fenichka after she
had maltreated the little boy.

The main interests of Nagibin and Kazakov are very similar.
Both choose "marginal" themes: neglected people, events
that seem insignificant on the surface, provincial towns, abandoned, remote places. Kazakov continues Chekhov's tradition
and emphasizes it. Paustovsky and Prishvin are also among his
literary antecedents, and to these two he dedicated a number
of stories, especially those devoted to nature.

The critics have often accused Kazakov of "wasting his talent
on trifles," of writing about the trivialities of life, and of being
blind to its grandeur. By an odd coincidence, it is almost a century

ago that Chekhov was accused of the same shortcomings.

Kazakov's "On the Island" belongs to his best and most characteristic prose. Its leitmotif—boredom, from which the only salvation could be spontaneous and unexpected love— is a classic in Russian literature. The value of life lies in a deeply moving experience, not in peace and serenity. This once again will remind the reader of Paustovsky. In "Rain at Dawn," what Kuzmin envies in Bashilov is his strong emotion of love, despite its unhappy turn. The structure of the story also follows a pattern in Paustovsky: an incidental meeting and a compulsory parting, time delimited and marked by the signal from the vessel—these dramatic points create the basic compositional units of both pieces. Both stories are permeated by a familiar symbolism. The signal from the boat and the vessel itself serve as metaphors of human destiny.

What is happiness? This is the question that preoccupies Zabavin and Gustya, as it does many of the characters created by Pushkin, Turgenev, and Chekhov. The answer is given in the same spirit as the reply once given by Chekhov: happiness is an illusive and fluctuating notion; therefore people tend to seek it in the past or in the future, but rarely see it in the present. The charm of the past lies in its elusiveness and the mirage of the future in people's imaginations. They make plans founded on the hope that it may be possible to make life correspond to one's dreams. Gustya, for example, imagines her coming happiness in a big city, which she contrasts with the remote and boring place where she lives at present. This illusionary opposition of the big center to the far province is a direct echo of Chekhov, especially in *The Three Sisters*. The melancholy cry of the three heroines, "To Moscow, to Moscow," has become symbolic, almost proverbial, in Russian culture.

The decade of Russian literature represented here may be viewed as sharply opposed to all the articles of the code of Socialist Realism. The first and essential issue of that code was the idea of a positive hero. The development of this category —from a revolutionary to a toiler on behalf of the State— is worthy of note.

At the end of the thirties and the beginning of the forties, the positive hero reached the final crisis of his *raison d'être*, because he turned out to be totally limited in his choices. A decision had to be made for the sake of a happy ending, a compulsory feature of Socialist Realism, since it provided literature with an optimistic and edifying tone. There was, however, but one choice, and this was wholly predictable within the framework of the ideology. A hero either comes to a decision by himself, or he is instructed by the Party. Thus he finds himself bound either by obedience to or criticism from the higher authorities, who are in possession of the final truth. And so a hero became his contrary: deprived of free will and of a free choice of action, he lacked anything heroic in his behavior. His destiny now was entirely predictable, and this in turn drained the plot of any interest, for all suspense had been deleted.

We noted that in the stories by Kazakov, Okudzhava, Nagibin, and others there is no trace of such a one-sided view. On the contrary, all questions are left open. Instead of an optimistic ending in which all problems are solved, the reader is faced with a bitter-sweet dénouement, often melancholic or even tragic. In place of a notorious "strong" character, we have simple people, with all their imperfections and vices, for which they are not punished but are left to choose their own destinies.

Broadly speaking, we observe the revival of the short form— a story, short narrative, or novella—whereas the preceding period, with its emphasis on the monumental, favored large novels with an epic and heroic cast. Children in their own particular world, neglected or unknown, and handicapped people again appear in the pages of Russian literature, as they did during the epoch of Pushkin and Lermontov, Dostoevsky and Chekhov.

Krystyna Pomorska
Ossabaw Island, Georgia
January 1971

One evening in the administration building of the collective farm the kerosene lamp was burning, and the battery radio crackling as usual. The radio was playing marches, but you could hardly hear them. Four men were sitting and talking at a square pine table. Just as at big meetings, there was so much tobacco smoke in the room that the lamp barely flickered. Even the radio seemed to be crackling because of the smoke. There was a large clay jar for cigaret butts standing on the table, and it was already full. Every now and then a fire would break out in the jar from one of the butts thrown there, and then the bearded Tsipyshev, who was in charge of the animals on the farm, would cover the jar with a piece of glass which had broken off the table top. And every time this happened, someone would make the same joke: "If you burn off your beard, the cows won't be afraid of you any more!"

To this Tsipyshev invariably replied: "If they're not afraid, maybe they'll give more milk." And everyone laughed.

They knocked the ashes from their cigarets onto the floor or the windowsills and threw only the butts into the jar.

They had sat there talking for a long time, without hurrying, talking a little bit about everything, and confidentially, without reservations, like good old friends.

In the dim light you could just make out on the log walls various posters and slogans hung there at random, along with a list of the members of the collective farm, indicating by the month how many work days each one had earned, a fragment of an old wall newspaper, and a blackboard divided into two equal parts by a white line: on one half was written in chalk the word "black" and on the other "red."

"You know, the co-op got some more sugar a few days ago," said the warehouseman Shchukin, the youngest of the group. From his clothes you could tell that he had been to a city school: he was wearing a shirt and tie, and a fountain pen and comb protruded from the breast pocket of his jacket.

"Somebody told on him, is that it?" slyly asked the third person at the table, a man with his left arm missing, corpulent and a bit flabby, with a dilapidated raincoat that looked as if he had worn it at the front flung over his shoulders.

"Nobody told on him. Mikola himself sent a woman to my house with a couple of kilograms. He said we'd settle for it later."

"And you took it?"

"Sure I did. If you don't take it when you can, you'll spend your life without sugar. You would have taken it, too."

"But he won't send *you* any, Pyotr Kuzmich." Tsipyshev laughed behind his beard, squinting sideways at the one-armed

man. "He's got a grudge against you. But Seryoga ia a pal of his,"
he said, turning to Shchukin. "Seryoga did not kick him out of
the warehouse, even though he took over his job."

Until quite recently Shchukin had been a rank-and-file
collective farmer. When he joined the Party about a month ago,
he had started hinting that all the leading positions in the collective farm should be held by Communists, and that now it
was awkward for him not to get some sort of promotion. People
agreed with him. They recalled that the farm's warehouseman
had been reprimanded several times for pilfering; and so they
assigned Shchukin to the warehouse. At the next general meeting no one objected to this decision. Shchukin bought himself
a fountain pen and began wearing a tie. His predecessor went to
work for the co-op. He was the person they had been discussing.

"What if I did take it?" Shchukin said after some thought.
"Where is there any justice, anyway? Where does the sugar go
to, and the soap, and everything?" After saying this he took out
his comb and began smoothing his thick, young, unruly hair.

At this the fourth man spoke up: "What do you need with
justice? You're a warehouseman now!"

The fourth man was middle-aged, prematurely gray, pale,
and apparently not in very good health. He smoked incessantly,
more than anyone else, and coughed a great deal. When he
stretched out his hand toward the jar to throw away a cigaret
butt that was burning his fingers, you could see his big thick
nails and the earth under them — not dirt, but earth. He was the
field-work brigade leader Ivan Konoplev. He had the reputation
of being a fair-minded but ill-tempered fellow He spoke little,
but when he did, his words had a bite to them. Still, as a rule
nobody took offense at his cutting remarks; apparently people
did not feel any personal animosity in them. Shchukin was not
offended either.

The one-armed man, whom everyone called by his first name
and patronymic, Pyotr Kuzmich, replied: "Well, as for justice,
we do need it. It's what holds us all together. But, friends, there
is still something I don't understand. I can't understand what is
going on in our rayon.* First they issue a statement that the plan
should be drawn up from below, that the kolkhoz should decide what is profitable to plant and what isn't. But when we
do it, they don't approve our plan. This is the third time now
that it's been returned for corrections. Apparently they col-
lected all the kolkhoz plans, added them up, and found they
didn't agree with the rayon plan. And the rayon plan is given
from above. There's not much room for discussion there. It's

*Rayon — here, a district.

like the scythe that hits the stone: the sparks fly, but there's no
sense to it. Again there is nothing left of our plan. There's
justice for you! They don't trust us."

"In our rayon, justice is only elected to honorary presidiums
so that it won't feel slighted and won't open its mouth," said the
pale Konoplev, throwing a cigaret butt into the jar.

Shchukin too put in a word: "Justice is only needed at meetings, on holidays, like criticism and self-criticism. It's of no use
in real life, isn't that right?"

An expression of cautiousness and of some feeling of
embarrassment suddenly crossed Tsipyshev's face, as if he had
become displeased with this confidential conversation.

"All right, hack away, but look out where the chips may
fall," he said harshly to Shchukin, but immediately changed his
tone, as if regretting his rudeness. "Justice, brother, is justice.
And if somebody put you on an honorary presidium, you too
wouldn't be able to see the ground any more," he said, and
burst out laughing, blowing out his moustache and beard.

Tsipyshev's beard grew not merely on his chin, but also on
his cheeks and in back of his ears, and merging with his reddish
eyebrows, it overhung his eyes; and when he laughed his whole
face and beard laughed too, and his eyes twinkled from somewhere in the depths of all this hair.

"A few days ago I went to the rayon committee and saw the
big man himself," Pyotr Kuzmich continued, referring in this
way to the first secretary of the rayon committee." 'And what,'
I said, 'are you doing to us? The kolkhoz members won't agree
to change the plan a third time, and they'll be offended. We
need flax. The best land should be given over to flax. We've
already experimented with rabbits and with grass-crop rotation. We wore out a lot of people to no purpose. There was no
grain, and to the state's loss. Let's take,' I said, 'say, ten or
twenty hectares at the most to start with, not a hundred or a
thousand. When we get used to it we will increase the amount
ourselves, we'll be asking for more. Let's not try to do it all at
once.' 'No,' he says, 'it has to be at once. We must overfulfill
the plan, and we must promote innovations actively.' 'Actively
is a fine word,' I said, 'but this is the North: there aren't many
people here, and the earth demands its own. People have to be
persuaded. As Lenin said, we must actively try to persuade
people.' But he says: 'So you go ahead and persuade them!
We persuaded you before, when we organized the collective
farms; now you persuade the others, uphold the Party line.
You,' he says, 'are our levers in the village now.' While he
was talking, he waved his arms as if to say that things weren't so
nice for him, either. But he's too inflexible. He doesn't under-

stand what the Party wants, he's afraid of understanding."

"A red-hot atmosphere," Shchukin said as if in explanation of his statement, and once again reached for his comb.

"Things won't be so nice. Anyway, he won't last long here," Tsipyshev said. "He didn't take the right attitude here. He's too strict. He doesn't listen to people, but decides everything himself. For him people are only levers. And the way I see it, friends, this is just what 'bureaucracy' means. Let's say we go there to a meeting. Well, he ought to talk to us like a man, straight from the shoulder. But no, he can't get along without acting tough, he always sticks to this toughness of his. He looks everybody over condescendingly and then growls: 'Let us begin, comrades! Is everybody present?' Well, everybody's heart sinks: we sit and wait to be raked over the coals. If he would only tell us frankly what is wrong—people will move mountains if you talk to them straight. But that's something he can't do."

"He thinks that the Party will lose its authority if he talks simply, like a human being. He knows very well that in the kolkhoz we get a hundred grams per work day, but he keeps on saying the same thing: every year the value of the work day rises and prosperity increases. There are no cows left in our kolkhoz, but he says: every year animal husbandry in the collective farms is expanding and growing stronger. If only he would say, there are such and such reasons why you're not living too well, but we're going to live better. If he would say that, people would be more willing to buckle down to work."

"A red-hot atmosphere!" Shchukin said again, as if concluding Pyotr Kuzmich's impassioned speech.

Ivan Konoplev was finishing another cigaret; he was nervous and seemed eager to say something—probably something sharp and cutting. But a severe fit of asthmatic coughing suddenly gripped him and made him get up from the table. By the entrance Konoplev lifted up a broom and spent a long time spitting into the corner. Meanwhile the cattleman, Tsipyshev, scolded him sympathetically: "You must have changed your tobacco again. Don't smoke anything but the cheapest tobacco, with only stems in it, and you'll feel better."

Feeling somewhat relieved, but still bent over, Konoplev raised his head and said hoarsely: "Our rayon chiefs have forgotten how to talk to peasants: they are ashamed to. They understand what needs to be done, but they're afraid to take the leap. What business is it of theirs to persuade? They are counting on us levers. They see houses in the village all shut up, but they don't want to talk about it aloud. All they care about is that the figures in their accounts should be in round numbers. And as for real people, who cares about them? What are they left with?" And Konoplev once again began coughing painfully.

"All right, all right, keep still, or you'll cough your soul right out of your body." Tsipyshev got up from behind the table and started toward the door, where Konoplev was. "Wait a bit, Ivan, and we'll wangle you some travel order through the rayon committee. You'll take a trip to the seashore for the fresh air, and at the same time you'll take a look at how people live there, you'll study them a bit and tell us about it. You'll bring us back some extra cheer."

Konoplev waved away impatiently, as if to say: "Sit down, what are you wandering over here for? Go away!" But because of his coughing he couldn't say a word. Tsipyshev went back to the table.

"His wife will write him such a set of travel orders that he won't know what hit him," said Shchukin. "She keeps a close eye on him. He can cough and smoke and drink as much as he wants, but she won't let him go a step away from her."

"Our air is as good as it is at the seashore," Pyotr Kuzmich observed dreamily. "Air is one thing we do have! In the old days to cure a cough people used to go to work for a tar or resin distillery. A man would live in the pine woods for three or four weeks, collecting this resin from little cups into barrels, and before you knew it he would have earned some money and found it easier to breathe at the same time. Do they buy up this resin anywhere nowadays? For some reason I haven't heard anything about it. They used to make a kind of turpentine out of it, and the resin for violinists. I'll bet they play without resin now."

"They've replaced it with plastic. Look here!" Shchukin held up his comb. "It's made of plastic, too."

No one looked at Shchukin's comb.

"Look, boys, our lamp is going completely out," said Tsipyshev, lifting his beard upward.

Konoplev replied from the doorway: "You would go out too if you didn't have any air. A lamp needs air too."

For the last time Konoplev rustled the dry broom and came back to the table. His face was pale, and he was breathing heavily. "This is the way I see things," he said. "As long as they have no confidence in the ordinary peasant in the collective farms, things won't be really right, we'll have a lot to put up with. They keep writing that a new kind of man has appeared. It's true, he has! The collective farms have transformed the peasant. It's true, they have! The peasant is really a different man. All right! Then this peasant must be trusted. He has a mind too."

"The wolves haven't eaten it," Tsipyshev agreed slyly.

"That's it! So they shouldn't just teach us, they should listen to us too. But everything comes down from above, always from above. The plans are sent down from above, the kolkhoz chairmen come from above, and so does the size of the harvest. They haven't got time to persuade people, and why should they, it's easier without! All they have to do is pass the word down, know what's happening, and make recommendations. As for educational work, they've given that up: it's too much trouble. The reading rooms and clubs exist only on paper, and there is no one to give lectures and reports. The only thing left is the campaigns for various supplies and collections—the five-day campaigns, the ten-day, the month-long ones."

Konoplev stopped for breath, and Pyotr Kuzmich took advantage of this to get in a word: "Sometimes things happen this way. When you can't get a wedge in somewhere, you blame it on the wood; you say the wood is rotten. Try and disagree with them in the rayon center. They say they're giving advice, recommendations, but it isn't advice, it's an order. If you don't carry it out, it means you have let the reins slip out of your hands. And if the collective farmers don't agree, it means you have failed politically."

"Why failed?" Konoplev almost shouted. "Aren't we working for the same cause? Are our interests any different?"

"Well, the rayon committee too doesn't exactly get a pat on the back if something goes wrong. They have demands made on them too, God knows.

"God knows indeed!" fumed Konoplev. "Next to us, in Gruzdikhin rayon, things are different. My brother-in-law was here a few days ago and told me that their chairmen don't shake in their boots every time they are ordered to report to the rayon center. There isn't any of this fear. The secretary comes to the kolkhoz without any fanfare and talks with people without reading from notes."

The radio on the shelf in the front corner began to sound louder. It was still crackling and hissing like an exhausted fire extinguisher, but now through all the hissing and static it was no longer music that one heard, but a voice talking hesitantly and in a northern accent. They were broadcasting letters from people in the virgin lands. Some fellow was telling about his feats of labor in the Altay region. The four men began to listen.

"They call us all Muscovites, even though we come from various towns. We get along together well and don't let anyone push us around. Last year we got an extraordinary harvest. You walked into a wheat field as if it was planted with reeds. Even the

old men didn't remember grain like this. There wasn't any place
to put the grain; that was the trouble."

The boy was speaking to his dear mamma, but he talked as if
he had never called her that before. He was obviously micro-
phone shy.

"Just listen to that," said Pyotr Kuzmich. "Even there they have
their troubles: nowhere to put the grain." He waved his hand
in the direction of the radio, and his tarpaulin raincoat slipped
off his armless left shoulder.

"Everybody can't go off to the Altay!" growled Konoplev, and
started coughing again. He got up from the table, took the jar
with the cigaret butts in both hands, and went toward the doorway. There he kicked back the broom with his foot and emptied
the butts into the corner.

Then it was discovered that during this whole conversation
there had been a fifth person in the room. From behind the big
tile stove there came an imperious old woman's cry. "Where do
you think you're dumping those butts, you old carcass? You're
not the one who has to clean up in here. I just got through
cleaning the floor, and now you've made a mess of it again!"

Taken by surprise, the peasants started and exchanged
glances.

"Are you still here, Marfa? What do you want?"

"What do I want! I'm keeping track of you. If you set fire to
this office, they'll try me for it. That broom is dry, and if, God
forbid, there were a sudden spark. . . ."

"You go on home now."

"When it's time to go, I'll go."

The friends' conversation was cut short. It seemed as if they
felt guilty toward one another for some reason. For a moment
you could hear the noise of the wind in the street outside and
a girl singing a long way off. Sergey Shchukin turned off the
radio, and the voices of the virgin-land pioneers fell silent
abruptly.

Again they began tearing off bits of newspaper, pulling it out
little by little from beneath the broken table top and rolling
themselves homemade cigarets. For a long time they smoked
in silence. When they began exchanging short remarks again,
they talked in phrases, about nothing in particular and concern-
ing nobody in particular. About the weather—the weather is
lousy, the kind that makes your bones ache. About the newspapers—there are different kinds: when you roll a cigaret
out of some of them, they are so bitter that you can't even taste
the tobacco. Then something about what had happened the day
before—somebody should have gone somewhere, but didn't.
Then something about the next day; somebody had to get up

early because for once his old woman was going to make pancakes. They were empty phrases, and even they were uttered somehow quietly, in subdued tones, with constant glances to one side and the other and at the stove, as if it was not the office charwoman Marfa who was hiding there but a stranger, an unknown person of whom they had to be wary. Tsipyshev grew serious, stopped talking and smiling, and only asked three times or so, without addressing anyone in particular: "Why is that schoolteacher so late? It's time to start the Party meeting."

Shchukin was the only one who behaved rather queerly: he couldn't sit still, his stool kept squeaking, and his mischievous and sly young eyes had a gleam in them. He looked challengingly at everyone. Shchukin seemed to have seen something that no one else had seen yet, and therefore he felt superior to the others. Finally he couldn't restrain himself and burst into guffaws.

"Whew, that damned woman has given us a scare!" Shchukin said, roaring with laughter.

Pyotr Kuzmich and Konoplev exchanged glances and also burst out laughing.

"She really did, the she-devil! Suddenly she bellows out from behind the stove. . . . Well, I thought . . . " Ivan Konoplev had trouble finishing his sentence. "Well, I thought that the big man had come and caught us redhanded."

"We were as scared as boys caught in their neighbor's bean patch."

Laughter released the tension and restored the men to their normal state of feeling.

"What are we so afraid of, fellows?" said Pyotr Kuzmich suddenly in a thoughtful and somewhat mournful voice. "We've got to the point where we're even afraid of ourselves."

But this time Tsipyshev did not smile. He hadn't seemed to notice it when both Konoplev and Pyotr Kuzmich had started laughing, but he looked sternly, like a superior officer, at Sergey Shchukin.

"You're too young to make fun of such things. When you've lived as long as we have . . . "

But Shchukin was not to be squelched, especially as Pyotr Kuzmich and Konoplev were clearly on his side. They gave him encouraging winks and went on laughing.

"That's how scared we are," said Konoplev.

Behind the stove Marfa was silent.

Two lads of Komsomol age burst into the office.

"What do you want?" said Tsipyshev, turning his whole body toward them.

"We want to listen to the radio."

"You can't. There's going to be a Party meeting here right now."

"Where can we go? There are a lot of us here."

"You can go where you like."

Saying this, Tsipyshev glanced at his friends, as if he wanted to find out whether they approved of his behavior. Pyotr Kuzmich did not approve of it. "Look here, fellows," he said to the young boys. "We'll polish off this Party meeting, have a talk, and then you can take over the field."

Finally the schoolteacher, Akulina Semyonovna, arrived, a short young woman, almost a little girl, looking tired. She unwound her gray wool scarf and took it off her head, then buried herself in the corner under the wooden shelf where the radio was. When she came in, Tsipyshev became more animated. But he expressed this animation by addressing the teacher in an exaggeratedly strict and authoritarian tone.

"Akulina Semyonovna, why do you keep us all waiting?"

Akulina Semyonovna looked guiltily at Tsipyshev, at Pyotr Kuzmich, and then at the jar with the cigaret butts and at the lamp, and lowered her eyes.

"I—I got delayed in the school. Look, Pyotr Kuzmich," she said to the one-armed man, "I would like to settle one thing before the beginning of the meeting. There is no firewood in the school."

"We'll talk about business later," Tsipyshev interrupted her. "Now we must hold our meeting. The rayon committee has been insisting for a long time that we hold two meetings a month, and we can't even get together and agree on the minutes for one of them. How are we going to account for it?"

At this Ivan Konoplev gave a snort, and for a brief moment Tsipyshev again seemed to feel awkward and unsure of himself. He looked timidly around as if apologizing for what he had said. But everyone kept still. Then Tsipyshev's voice took on real firmness and authority. What had happened? His beard was straightened out and grew longer, his eyes became stern and lost the lively twinkle that had gleamed in them a few minutes before during the unaffected friendly conversation. Tsipyshev now addressed the charwoman Marfa in a peremptory tone. "Marfa, you get out of here! We're going to have a Party meeting here. We're going to be talking."

Even Marfa seemed to sense the change that had taken place; she made no attempt to argue and didn't even grumble. "Go ahead and talk. I understand. I'm going."

When the door had closed quietly behind the subdued Marfa, Tsipyshev stood up and repeated the same words that the secretary of the rayon Party committee always said on similar occasions and even in the same dry, severe, and seemingly conspiratorial voice that the secretary used at the beginning of meetings.

"Let's get started, comrades! Is everyone present?"

When he said this it was as if he had turned the switch of some magic machine. Everything in the room began to change, so much so that it became unrecognizable: people, things, and even the air seemed to be transformed.

Shchukin and Konoplev moved noiselessly back from the table. Pyotr Kuzmich remained seated where he was, but he folded up the raincoat, which had half slipped from his shoulders, and put it to one side on the bench. Akulina Semyonovna, the schoolteacher, shrank still farther into the corner under the radio. Everyone's face became set, tense, and bored, as if they had prepared themselves to perform an extremely familiar but nevertheless solemn and important ceremony. Everything ordinary and natural disappeared, and the scene seemed to shift to another world, a more complicated world, to which these unaffected, warmhearted people had not yet fully grown accustomed or come to understand.

"Is everyone present?" Tsipyshev repeated, looking around at the people in the room as if there were at least several dozen of them there.

Yet, as we already know, there were only five of them all told. The herdsman Stepan Tsipyshev turned out to be the secretary of the Party organization. On the recommendation of the rayon committee, he had been recently elected secretary. Flattered by this, Tsipyshev was trying to carry out his duties as best he could, and being inexperienced, without knowing it he began imitating the "rayon boss" in everything. To be sure, he sometimes made fun of himself, but every directive from on high he carried out so zealously and so literally—for fear he might make a mistake—that at times things would have gone better if he hadn't tried to fit all the spokes into the wheel. The zonal instructor of the rayon committee, who had been present at Tsipyshev's election, had joked that Comrade Tsipyshev had many virtues, but that he had a few defects as well and that his chief defect was his beard. Tsipyshev had taken this joke seriously, as a directive, and had made up his mind that he would certainly remove the beard and all other hair from his face; but so far there had not been an appropriate occasion for doing this.

Pyotr Kuzmich Kudryavtsev, the one-armed man, proved to be the chairman of the kolkhoz. Ivan Konoplev, as we know, was a field-work brigade leader. Sergey Shchukin was the warehouseman. When Shchukin had been made warehouseman, his predecessor had been stricken from the Party rolls at the same time as he was transferred to work in the co-op; since then there had been no rank-and-file collective farmers in the Party organization. Akulina Semyonovna was a full-fledged member of the intelligentsia, though she was no outsider, but had been born in the village. She was completely dependent on the kolkhoz administration.

"According to the agenda, I first turn over the floor to the chairman of our kolkhoz, Pyotr Kuzmich."

Pyotr Kuzmich Kudryavtsev stood up. Tsipyshev sat down. The Party meeting had begun.

And the meeting was marked by just what these members of the Party organization, including the secretary himself, had just been talking about and criticizing with such frankness and perspicacity—official routine, bureaucracy, and pedantry of word and deed.

"Comrades!" said the chairman of the kolkhoz. "The rayon committee and the rayon executive committee have not approved our production plan. I believe there are certain things we have not taken into account and have allowed to drift. This is unbecoming of us. We have not carried out explanatory work among the masses and have not convinced them. And people must be persuaded, comrades. We here are the levers of the Party in the kolkhoz village. This has been pointed out to us in the rayon committee and the rayon executive committee."

The schoolteacher, with careful, stealthy movements of her hands, so as not to disturb anyone, again tied her kerchief on her head. Her face could no longer be seen, and no one could tell what she was thinking about.

But Shchukin began to smile again. He took his fountain pen out of his pocket, spun it in his hands, then took out his comb, looked through it at the lamp, blew lightly on its teeth, and put it back without using it on his hair. His face grew broader and broader, and a sly, mocking twinkle began to sparkle in his eyes. It looked as if Shchukin might burst out laughing any minute. But he did not do so; he only poked Konoplev in the side and whispered: "Did you see what is happening? Do you recognize him now?"

Konoplev smiled too, but wryly and unpleasantly. "All right, now, don't hinder him from saying his say. That's the way it has to be. Pyotr Kuzmich is speaking officially now. That's the way it is in the rayon committee, that's the way it is here. As the priest is, so is the parish."

"And what about justice?"

"Justice—it will make itself known. Soon it will even reach us; it will come like thunder."

"But we'll come to the end of our rope."

"No, we won't."

And Konoplev reached for the jar on the table, pulled it toward him, and went on smoking, smoking. He didn't dare cough and held himself in, even though everything in his chest was clattering and whistling.

Pyotr Kuzmich Kudryavtsev did not talk long. The gist of his speech was that the rayon would begin to doubt the militance of the Party organization unless the kolkhoz plan for crop rotation was corrected immediately and unconditionally according to the specifications of the rayon committee and the rayon executive committee. With this all those who took part in the discussion agreed. It was impossible to do otherwise.

Those who took part in the discussion were Akulina Semyonovna, Shchukin, and Konoplev. No differences of opinion were revealed, just as there had been none during the friendly conversation before the beginning of the Party meeting; to be sure, the agreement and unanimity were now manifested in a different way—one might even say, exactly in reverse.

Tsipyshev was satisfied by the solidarity of the Communists and took the floor himself on the second question. Once the zonal secretary of the rayon committee had called attention to the fact that political education work in the kolkhoz was inadequately developed. He had accordingly presented a memorandum on this subject to the first secretary of the rayon committee.

"We are not encouraging the better elements, comrades," Tsipyshev said in this connection. "We are not punishing the laggards; there is no competition. Take a look at our red-and-black board: the picture is clear. We must lead the masses, comrades! This is what I think: we should select several projects for awards and pick one or two persons for each project. And a few people should be fined so that things will be balanced on both sides. We will be commended by the rayon committee."

The meeting unanimously decided to select five persons for awards and three for fines. The only discussion was about which projects should be used for the awards and which for punishments.

They did not have time to compose a single resolution, for Marfa came back to clean up the office and lock up. Pyotr Kuzmich proposed that the drawing up of resolutions be left to the secretary.

"You know how to write it up," he whispered, pleased that the meeting had come to an end. "In an atmosphere of great enthusiasm for work, there is spreading over the whole kolkhoz—"

"Over the whole country . . . " Shchukin prompted him.

They quickly got ready to go home, and it looked as if everyone had a feeling of having done his duty and yet at the same time a certain embarrassment and dissatisfaction with himself. But on the porch there was already a tramping of boots. A lot of young people appeared at the door.

"Have we come at the right time?" asked one of the two boys who had been in the office before.

"Right on time," replied Pyotr Kuzmich. "Just right. Come in, boys, all of you."

A draft of cool air from the street filled the room. The lamp burned brighter, stools were moved around. A window was opened.

"It's awfully smoky in here," clamored the girls.

When the young people appeared, Akulina Semyonovna straightened up and took off her kerchief. These were people of her own age, and with them she felt freer. Sergey Shchukin too began circulating; he tightened his necktie and attached himself to the girls' company.

The radio was turned on. Unexpectedly, it emitted loud, clear tones. The announcer was giving a report on the preparations for the Twentieth Party Congress. Everyone listened to it.

Pyotr Kuzmich seemed to soften up. As he was going out, he said to Akulina Semyonovna: "Don't worry, there will be some wood. I'll take care of it."

And Tsipyshev came up to Sergey Shchukin and squeezed his arm above the elbow. "Are you staying here?"

"Yes."

"Well, watch out that nothing . . . "

When Kudryavtsev, the collective-farm chairman, and Konoplev, the field-work brigade leader, emerged from the office into the dark, muddy street, they resumed their conversation about life, about everyday doings, work—the same conversation that had been going on before the meeting.

"Now let's see what the Twentieth Congress will say!" they kept repeating. And once again they were clean, warm-hearted, straightforward people—people, and not levers.

1956

A Light in the Window

Yury Nagibin

The little bridge over the deep gully that lay between the rest home and the highway collapsed late in March. And on top of that the ice on the river broke up, destroying the road across the ice—the last link with the outside world. Deliveries of supplies to the rest home stopped. Emergency stores kept the home going for a few days, but eventually they were exhausted. A few cans, some sugar, vegetable oil, and dried vegetables remained in the pantry. Then the director, Vasily Petrovich, decided to slaughter his own pig to feed the vacationers.

The slaughtering was done by the chief cook himself—a former army cook, middle-aged and tough as iron—while Vasily Petrovich helped. It turned out to be not so easy. The enormous, immobile Mashka, who had been overfed on warm, greasy kitchen slops till she weighed over 400 pounds, took to flight like a bird when the slaughterers crossed the threshold of her pen. She had evidently guessed what they had come for, even though the chef hid the knife behind his back. They had a terrible time throwing her. First in turn and then together Vasily Petrovich and the chef sprawled out on the dirty floor boards, trying to get hold of Mashka's legs. But with an agility inspired by her fear of death, the heavy sow, almost blinded by fat, kept slipping out of their clutching hands and dashing about the pen with heartrending squeals. Finally they managed to throw her onto her back. The chef took the long knife and, with a neatly calculated movement, plunged the thin, narrow blade under the sow's left leg and pulled the knife sharply toward himself.

First Mashka was singed till she became like brown wax, then skinned and cut up; the dark clots of blood were scooped out with spoons. Vasily Petrovich worked as though in a dream. He had killed pigs many times, but now this simple, ordinary business seemed to him an act of the most brutal cruelty against a warm, breathing, defenseless creature. He could not forget the desperate reproach in Mashka's half-blind, amber-colored, narrow eyes. No pig he had slaughtered for his own use had ever looked at him like that.

But the deed was done. The vacationers consumed Mashka with the same unfailing appetite with which they devoured all the other courses served them. Nor did Vasily Petrovich expect any thanks. He found a sort of bitter satisfaction in the very fact that his selfless action was doomed to oblivion. But events proved otherwise. The eyes of the members of the rest-home staff, when they looked at the director, reflected something that had not been in them before. Vasily Petrovich did not notice this at once, and when he did notice it, he did not at first understand the faint but warm light that shone from the

eyes of the charwomen, waitresses, nurses, and other employees. Nonrecognition has a melancholy joy of its own, but
the approval of one's associates, even a silent approval, bestows
much greater happiness on a man. A certain bounciness appeared in the gait of this rotund, heavy-set, rolypoly director.

Only one person did not appreciate the modest good deed of
Vasily Petrovich: Nastya, the charwoman of the annex building.
In her black sunken eyes the director missed the familiar, heart-
warming glow. And her approval would have been especially
pleasing to him: there was a delicate and complicated relation-
ship between Nastya and the director. . . .

When Vasily Petrovich had first taken charge of the rest
home, he and the former director had made the rounds of all
the outbuildings and land, and all the residential premises of
the main buildings and the annex. When this was done, the
former director took him to a neat one-story bungalow with a
glassed-in porch.

"In this bungalow . . . "

Breaking off, he moved ahead, opened the spring lock on
the door, which was lined with felt and oilcloth, and gestured to
Vasily Petrovich to follow him. They entered a roomy hall smelling of dry pinewood, from which Vasily Petrovich could see a
spacious three-room apartment worthy of Moscow or Leningrad, while on his right an open door disclosed the dull green
cloth of a billiard table.

In the first room—the living room—a television set stood on
a polished oak table; soft sofas lined the walls; in the center of
the room, an oval table covered with a heavy fringed tablecloth was surrounded by massive armchairs, which seemed to
be made of lead. Over the table a crystal chandelier glittered in
the dull reflected light. The two doors leading to the other
rooms gave a glimpse of the starchy coolness of well-stuffed
pillows in the bedroom and the corner of a desk and the edge
of a thick rug.

Vasily Petrovich, overwhelmed by this magnificence, remained silent.

"This is our special untouchable reserve," said the former
director with playful pride. "We kept it in case he himself were
to come."

"Well, I doubt that he himself would come here . . . " Vasily
Petrovich murmured with a forced smile. Not once during his
long life of hotel management had he ever had any dealings
with the higher authorities and therefore he would not admit
that such things were possible.

"You know, I wouldn't be too sure," concluded the former

director in the same special, vaguely playful tone which he had assumed when they had crossed the threshold of the sanctuary. "So be on your guard."

This advice had gone to Vasily Petrovich's very heart. He actually had been on his guard all the time lest the arrival of an exalted guest from the ministry catch him unaware. He assigned to the apartment the charwoman of the annex building, Nastya. Every day she had to clean the deserted rooms, scrub the untrodden floors, change the flowers in the vase, which shed their fragrance in vain, brush the green cloth of the billiard table, the pile of which seemed to be growing like a neglected lawn. Part of the responsibility fell also on the porter, Stepan: he had to chop off the ice on the steps, remove the snow piled up under the windows, have a ready supply of birch logs in case the high personage might want to enjoy the play of flames in the fireplace.

In short, everything was done to make a spur-of-the-moment guest feel that he had been eagerly awaited and that everything had been provided for his coming with great care.

And yet these rooms were a source of constant inner anxiety to Vasily Petrovich. As a manager he had difficulty reconciling himself to the fact that a splendid apartment stood vacant, uselessly wasting money and work. At times he became irked in a very human way at the prohibition laid upon these rooms. He could not forget for a long time the faces of two newlyweds who had come to the rest home right at the peak of the July season: they had been assigned to separate dormitory rooms. He had almost faltered then, imagining what bliss a private apartment would have brought them. But he had controlled himself, and the young people had gone off to different buildings, exchanging a look as if they were parting for life.

Vasily Petrovich did not feel any better when a famous stonemason, who had worked on the rest home itself, came to stay. The stonemason came with his wife and three irrepressible sons; even in a two-room suite the old couple never had a minute's rest from the stormy high spirits of their unruly offspring.

The new director listened sadly to the rattle of the balls on the broken-down public billiard tables, while a magnificent table stood useless and without purpose in the vacant apartment; the same sickly feeling came to him when he saw the waitresses with their faces glued to the windows of the television room—the cramped viewing hall could hardly hold the vacationers. The girls pushed each other and quarreled, trying to catch the fleeting images distorted by the window glass, and all the while a splendid television set was going to waste in the cottage.

All this depressed Vasily Petrovich to the point that he found it intolerable to bear the burden of his sorrows alone. He began to share them with the charwoman Nastya; he was sure that this taciturn, reserved woman with her dark, deep-set eyes would not give him away. He told her about the newlyweds and about the stonemason, but each time what he saw clearly in Nastya's dark eyes was not sympathy but censure. This made him feel even more distressed, but still he complained to her again and again about each recurring episode of this kind with the dim hope that someday she would at last understand him. But when he realized that even his sacrificial act, his little feat of martyrdom, had not extinguished the piercing reproachful light in Nastya's deep and excessively steady gaze, he knew he must bear his cross alone.

Vasily Petrovich did not understand Nastya. And it was no easy thing to understand this quiet, somewhat deaf, reserved woman with a strange, ugly, and yet attractive face. Of course, Nastya was homely; yet if anyone said: "But you know, she has something," everyone was ready to agree. People only needed this kind of prompting to make them recognize suddenly Nastya's latent, rather wild charm. It is hard to say where this charm came from: perhaps from her shy, very youthful (though Nastya was long past thirty), oddly deep and penetrating gaze; perhaps in the proud carriage of her head; perhaps in something else. This second image of Nastya was ephemeral; it faded quickly, leaving after it a feeling of puzzlement; then once again there reappeared a homely woman of undetermined age with a pale, weather-beaten face and big, work-worn hands. Many years before, Nastya's strange and fleeting charm had attracted a young trainer from the horse farm, but the war came and Nastya was no sooner a bride than she became a widow. She had developed a grudge against life, and whereas the director wanted to be thought good, Nastya feared more than anything else that someone might suspect her of being kind.

She fiercely protected her rights: to do the rooms between nine and ten o'clock in the morning—not a minute sooner, and not a minute later; to bring hot water for shaving at eight-thirty sharp. She did not have to make the beds: this was supposed to be done by the vacationers themselves. Whenever someone tried to demand extra services, she flung in his face: "It is not my duty!" But it somehow turned out that Nastya did make the beds, brought hot water three times a day, and performed many other services which were not her duty. She avenged herself for this in her own way, by refusing categorically to take the

ten- and twenty-five-ruble notes which people pressed on her
as they were leaving. At such times her face became so cross
that the vacationers, murmuring apologies awkwardly, tried to
hide the wads of money which had grown damp in their hands.

Nastya's entire life changed when she was assigned as charwoman for the special building. At first she took the director's
order as a gross infringement of her rights, and even the
ominous word "himself" did not impress her at all. But she
was enraptured by the magnificent furnishings of the rooms and
suddenly lost all desire to protest. After that the whole purpose
of her existence became focused on these rooms.

Nastya gave herself up to her new job with all the passion
of her unexpended heart. Gradually her mind created a marvelous, fairylike picture of the person who was to come and reign
over all this grandeur. She believed that he was an extraordinary man, unlike anyone else, because so much effort was
expended on his behalf, and even though he remained unseen,
he caused people to think of him every day and every hour. And
Nastya was never so happy as when she was taking care of the
rooms which were to receive him. But she did not neglect her
former duties. Unfailingly conscientious as usual, she cleaned
both floors of the annex, swept the floors, emptied the ash trays,
scrubbed the bathtub and wash stands till they shone like glass,
changed the water in the carafes, shook out the scatter rugs,
and even made the beds, grumbling to herself. But none of this
touched her heart; it was all part of everyday life, a life which
could have been dispensed with. But, on the other hand, she
lived fully, passionately, tremblingly when the turn of the
sacred chambers came. Here ordinary drudgery became
creative work. One can simply wash a window, or one can
perform a miracle; make the panes so transparent, so shining,
so sunny that they seem to draw into the room the blueness of
the sky, the whiteness of the snow, and the greenness of the
pines; the walls vanish and the room becomes part of the open
spaces. It is one thing to tidy up a room, and another when, in
the whole expanse of a room, each object finds the perfect
place for itself; to place the cabinet not quite straight but
slightly at an angle, to pull the television set a bit forward, to
move the flowers from the whatnot to the center of the oval
table— and everything becomes different; instead of mere
orderliness— beauty.

Almost every passing day brought Nastya a small discovery,
and the director, who from time to time inspected the vacant
premises, felt something which he could hardly define. He did
not notice any changes; everything seemed to be as it was; but
for some reason the sight of these rooms gave him, every time,

new happiness and an ever growing sense of security.

Nastya considered blasphemous the very idea that these rooms might be occupied by some chance person. The waverings of the director outraged her; nobody could dare to cross the threshold of this house except *himself*. . . .

But days, weeks, and months went by, and nobody came. A year passed, and another quickly started rolling by after it; still the rooms remained as before, vacant and cold, unwarmed by human presence. The objects continued to gleam with a cleanliness appreciated by no one; the blind and mute television set continued to stare blankly with its whitish eye; the balls on the greensward of the billiard table seemed to have lost the knack of rolling and were growing fatter and rounder; the beautiful mirror in its carved frame did not reflect a single human face except the swarthy face of Nastya with its tautly drawn skin and black deep-set eyes; no head drugged with sleepiness touched the tight, cool starch of the pillows.

Vain expectation, wasted effort, and ardor expended to no purpose gradually aroused in Nastya a feeling of hatred. She had been deceived. It was not the director—what did she care about him!—who had deceived her; it was the one for whom she had been waiting with such passionate impatience.

But to think that the long-awaited guest had not come meant that she was still awaiting him; and Nastya could not, would not, wait any longer. She stopped touching or moving anything in rooms, and it seemed to Vasily Petrovich that Nastya had begun to neglect her duties. He passed his hand over the top of the television set and over the arms of the chairs, but found no speck of dust anywhere; he touched the windowpanes with his finger and the finger squeaked on the cleanly washed and carefully wiped surface; he stamped on the scatter rugs trying in vain to raise even a small cloud of dust. There was nothing he could find fault with. And yet something was lacking, and Vasily Petrovich frowned in discontent.

Meanwhile, Nastya's contempt for the invisible tenant grew and finally mastered her whole being. It now seemed to her that a gross injustice was being perpetrated in assigning to him these large rooms full of light and air and all these beautiful and useful articles.

One night Vasily Petrovich was returning home after a lonely late walk. He loved this hour near midnight, when the entire rest home and all the surrounding buildings were deep in sleep; and when he no longer felt the constant pressure of people's importunate demands; when he could no longer be bothered by the vacationers, or the housekeeper-nurse, or the chef, or the bookkeeper, or the warehouseman, or the gardener, or a

sudden inspector from the Ministry, or a telephone call from
the kolkhozes, which always wanted something from him, or his
wife, who could never get it into her head that he was the director and not the owner of the rest home. True, he was not often
able to enjoy even this simple happiness; usually weariness laid
him flat as soon as the working day was over.

The night had wrapped the rest home and its grounds in darkness, through which the greenish light of the new moon barely
filtered. In this greenish darkness everything seemed elegant,
orderly, appropriate, necessary, and beautiful—even the high
piles of snow along the paths and walks, their tops turned to
solid ice, even the plaster deer, which looked unbearably
ugly in the daylight, resembling a sheep dog with horns tacked
on as a joke.

It was a time when he could think of everything clearly and
calmly: that the most difficult things in life were behind; that
now he could fall asleep slowly and pleasantly in the warmth
of his bed, without fear that he would be got up during the
night; that the spirit of mutual understanding and trust among
people was increasing; that without fear of ill-wishers, he could
try wholeheartedly to make the lives of his vacationers more
agreeable, more satisfying, more peaceful and gay, and his own
life into the bargain.

Vasily Petrovich turned at the corner of the house and suddenly froze, throwing his head back and a little to one side, like
a horse that had run against a fence; there were lights in the
windows of the vacant cottage. More exactly, there were lights
in the den, the bedroom, and the billiard room, where he
could hear the dry, brittle crack of balls. The living room was
dark, but there was music there, and when Vasily Petrovich
overcame his momentary numbness and took a step forward,
he saw on the wall facing the living room windows a fluttering,
pale-lilac reflection, and he realized that the television set had
been turned on.

A strange feeling went through Vasily Petrovich. For an in-
stant he fancied that the furniture had got tired of being useless
and had revolted. It had started living a life of its own without
the aid of man: the lamps had flashed on, the balls had begun
rolling over the green field of the billiard table, the television
set had come alive to the joy of the armchairs, the whatnots,
the table, and the sofas. But this queer feeling immediately gave
way to another, which was more sober but just as exciting: it
had happened! . . . The event he had expected with such trepi-
dation for over a year and had almost stopped expecting—it
had happened. The highly placed guest had deliberately arrived
when the director was absent, when nobody was expecting him,

and in some mysterious, incomprehensible way had found the
rooms set aside for him, penetrated into them without a key,
and with his masterly, confident authority had animated the
inanimate.

But this thought, too, did not stay in Vasily Petrovich's mind
for more than a flash and was crowded out by anxious perplexity; no, this could not have happened. . . .

Standing for some reason on tiptoe and moving stealthily, he
stepped from the path into the wet, loose snow and went up to
the window.

In front of the television set, on the screen of which glimmered a bluish spot crisscrossed by fast-moving thin lines, sat
the charwoman Nastya with her large hands folded on her
knees. To her right, eyes and mouth wide open, crouched
Klavka, the ten-year-old daughter of the porter, Stepan, while
on the other side Klavka's younger brother was sleeping sweetly
in a large armchair. Through a crack in the door he could see
Stepan toiling at the billiard table, lit up by the two chandeliers;
he was jabbing clumsily with the cue at the balls.

Nastya had violated the interdiction! Openly, brazenly, she
had entered this charmed world, set herself up as its rightful
mistress, and brought Stepan into it. Vasily Petrovich felt, with
a strange sinking feeling, that what he was now witnessing was
something very good, very right, and very necessary. But at the
same moment he raised his hand and knocked at the windows
so sharply and roughly that the glass rattled. . . .

And then Vasily Petrovich shouted, threatened, and stamped
his feet, carried away, intoxicated by his own screaming. He expended as much effort as if he thought that his furious indignation would reach the ears of the one whose rights had been so
crudely disregarded. Whether *he* heard him or not, the violators
remained deaf to the director's rage. Leading the children by
the hand, they walked past the director with calm and severe
dignity.

And seeing their stern, almost solemn faces, Vasily Petrovich
suddenly stopped short and fell silent, listening with surprise to
a strange, new, unfamiliar feeling that was rising and growing
inside him, penetrating to his very finger tips—a feeling of unbearable disgust with himself.

1956

A Trip Home

Nikolay Zhdanov

Returning to his office after a long, wearisome meeting, Pavel Alekseyevich Varygin began sorting the official papers that had accumulated in his absence and that his secretary, Nonna Andreyevna, handed to him in a calico-covered folder. He glanced over several questionnaires and started on the telegrams, which were usually sent from outlying areas and dealt with various reminders and problems. While reading, he marked the telegrams with a blue pencil and laid them aside one after another. Now only one was left, for some reason unopened: probably Nonna Andreyevna had been careless. Varygin himself tore off the paper band and unfolded the sheet.

"Marya Semyonovna died Wednesday, twenty-fourth. Funeral Saturday," he read.

He left for the country the same night, on an inconvenient train, which necessitated changing twice on the way. The express ran only every other day, and that would have meant waiting another whole day.

Varygin's wife said good-bye to him at the door of their apartment. She kissed him on the cheek with a mournful face and said she thought she would not say anything to the children, as they had not yet received their grades for this quarter.

"Do as you please," he replied. But as he walked down the stairs in the yellow light of the bulbs, he thought: "For her it is just a vexatious annoyance, nothing more."

In the railroad car he sat near the window and looked out through the dim pane at the grayish strip of land and the dark silhouettes of trees flying past.

Varygin had seen his mother for the last time about six years ago. She had come from the collective farm for some "millets," as his wife, who had a somewhat ironic attitude toward his village relatives, had later said.

It now seemed to him that those six years had gone by without his noticing them at all. One fall he had planned a trip to the country, but his doctors had advised him to take a rest cure for his heart trouble, and he had gone to Kislovodsk instead.

Sometimes, very seldom, he received letters from his mother. They were dictated by her and written in a childish handwriting, usually on a sheet torn out of a school notebook.

"We are living not too well, but we don't complain," his mother reported. He felt saddened, but then reminded himself that his mother had never lived too well and that therefore the phrase "We are living and don't complain" sounded on the whole quite optimistic.

It took the train more than twenty-four hours to reach the station of Dvoriki. The sluggish November dawn had not yet chased away the gray shadows of the night. They clung

to the low, cold sky and hid under the station shed, where
mounds of potatoes, probably awaiting shipment, lay covered
with matting.

He remembered from his childhood that immediately back
of the station there began a low, marshy wood, stretching for
about eight versts. Beyond it were the villages, all of them with
similar names: Lozhkino, Derevlyovo, Kashino, Korkino,
Lapshino, Pirogovo, and finally his village, Tyurino. But he did
not see any wood. Varygin set out on foot through a swampy
depression along a fence of blackened poles.

On either side rose regular stacks of peat. They evidently
were extracting peat here now. Beyond the depression there
was a highway, which hadn't been there in the old days, either.
Varygin was picked up by a truck going his way, rode as far as
Lapshino, and walked from there to Tyurino.

He learned that his mother had already been taken to the
cemetery. This he heard at the first cottage from a middle-aged
woman in a well-washed soldier's blouse, who was carrying
water from the well in wooden pails.

"And who might you be?" she asked, glancing at Varygin's
good, heavy cloth coat.

"Her son," he said.

The woman put the pails down on the ground and looked at
Varygin again.

"Konstantin? Really?" she asked. "I am Anastasiya Derevlyova,
don't you remember?"

"My brother, Konstantin, died long ago. I am Pavel," he
explained.

"That's just what I was saying, that Konstantin was dead,"
the woman answered quickly. "My daughter-in-law keeps
insisting, no matter what you say to her. But can you find your
way to the cemetery? You've probably forgotten how to find
your way around here. Klashka!" she shouted to a little girl
gathering the cabbage leaves that had been left on the ground
after the harvest. "Run along and show him the way to the
cemetery—straight across the field."

Following the girl, who ran ahead of him, he strode over
the field, already frozen hard but not yet covered with snow.
He stumbled heavily at the uneven places, trying not to pant,
and kept wiping the perspiration from his face.

They rounded a field of winter crops and on a crooked log
crossed a tiny brook that looped among some bushes. Further
on, the bank rose in a sloping hillock, and against the gray
sky Varygin saw an old wooden church and cemetery crosses
among sparse, leafless trees. He remembered this old church
and this brook. But now they were considerably smaller than

they used to be. He also remembered the pits full of water
they were now walking past. People used to soak reeds in
these pits, and boys said that goblins hid in them.

The cemetery had no fence around it. They saw from a distance that there was someone standing on the church porch.

"Uncle, I'll go back now, all right?" the girl said, slowing
down. "There is the midwife, your lodger. She might tell the
teacher that I've been to church! I'll go back, all right?"

"All right, you can go," Varygin said.

When he came closer, a young woman ran down the wood-
en church steps to meet him. Her face, rosy from the frosty air,
was wet with tears and at the same time glowing with health.

"We had begun to think you weren't coming," she said
when Varygin told her who he was. "We expected you on the
night express and went to the station to meet you. We didn't
know what to do. You see, perhaps you will be angry—I am an
unbeliever, too—but Marya Semyonovna insisted on being
buried in the old way, as a Christian."

Taking off his fur cap and without adjusting the hair that
had clung to his forehead, Varygin passed in under the dark
archway. Inside, three or four figures were standing in the dim
light cast by a few meager candles.

The midwife followed him in and stood near the door. He
moved nearer. Suddenly he saw the dark face of his mother,
small as a child's, lit up by yellow candlelight. He stopped
and stood motionless, seeing only this face in front of him.

A priest with sparse gray hair and a thin cartilaginous forehead was chanting a prayer. He seemed to be addressing only
the mother, who lay motionless, her thin, bloodless lips pressed
together. Out of the darkness loomed the flat countenances
of the saints painted on the altar screen. There was an odor of
incense, and this smell, combined with the Church Slavic
words the priest was intoning in the gloom, reminded Varygin
of his childhood, when he used to go with his mother to this
church and even sang in the choir. All this seemed so long ago
that it might never have happened at all. Once the priest came
quite close, and Varygin got a whiff of garlic from his worn old
vestments.

When the funeral service was over, the women who had
been hidden in the darkness closed the coffin, lifted it, and
carried it off.

Varygin came out of the church with the others and helped
carry the coffin over the faded grass between the wooden
crosses. He came to himself only when his mother had already
been buried.

Then he made his way back over the crooked log across the

tiny brook, from which rose a thin mist resembling incense,
and walked again over the hard field. It seemed to him that he
had just returned from a world he thought had long since
ceased to exist.

When they had returned to the village and came to the house,
the midwife ran ahead up to the porch and, fishing the key out
of her pocket, opened the door. Varygin remembered the porch
and the door with the iron handle. Only the gate by the house
was different. It was a new one, and as he passed he saw a sign
on it: "Midwife's Office."

Varygin crossed the threshold. On the left, a white stove rose
to the ceiling. In the corner on the right stood a wide wooden
basin and over it a clay jug— probably the same ones that had
been there in his childhood. He had completely forgotten
them, but now he remembered them well.

The ceiling had become much lower than it used to be. But
the dark hewn beams, slightly sagging in the middle, were the
same, he could vouch for that. Here were the old iron hooks
for the cradles: one, two, three. His father had lived here with
his brothers. There had been three sisters-in-law in the house,
and each had rocked her own cradle. In one of them he,
Varygin, had begun his growth.

"I mostly stay in the other part of the house," the midwife
said. "I have an office for my patients there. Marya Semyonovna
stayed here. There is her bed, and the towel is hanging just
as it was."

Varygin looked at the towel, gray with age, and again, and not
for the first time, the thought that his mother had been in need
stabbed him painfully.

He took off his coat and cap and wearily sank onto a stool.
He wanted to lay his head down on the table and drop off into
forgetfulness. Long ago the whole family used to have their
meals at this table. In the corner, under the wooden ikon, his
father had sat. Varygin remembered the smell of cabbage soup
and warm bread with cabbage leaves clinging to the bottom
crust. His mother often washed the table with hot water and
scraped it with a knife with a broken handle. This knot there,
with its dark center, had always seemed to him like the eye of a
horse. Now the boards of the table had yellowed and cracked
and the "eye" had turned black and crumbled.

A stack of copybooks lay on the table. "Oblast Courses in
Midwifery. Notes of A. Antonova," he read. He had seen this
painstaking childish writing on the letters he sometimes
received from his mother.

A. Antonova brought in an armful of firewood, lit the stove,
and put on a kettle. Then she removed the copybooks, took a

clean towel from a suitcase under the shelf, wiped out a cup, and poured a cup of tea for Varygin.

"I have to hurry off to Lapshino. I have a delivery there," she said. "So please excuse me."

He did not want any tea. He sat there alone, motionless. During his childhood this house had been seething with life, but now this life had all vanished. It seemed strange that only these walls and he, Varygin, remained. But he too had nothing to do here and ought to leave. He did not want to think about leaving. He simply didn't want to move. Was there some place to lie down? He turned his head to look around.

On the bench in the corner, leaning foolishly to one side, stood an old samovar, no longer used, with a broken faucet. It seemed to be grinning slyly and winking at the bench as if to say: "Aha! You too have become broken down on the road! So lie down next to me, brother!"

Varygin pressed both hands on the table to help himself up, and the table too seemed to wink at him with its horse's eye: "So you have come back, in spite of everything!"

Varygin walked over to the bed and lay down.

When he opened his eyes, the cold red strip of sunset was burning, out beyond the fence. It was reflected in the window-pane. He suddenly thought that he had fallen asleep on his mother's bed, where she had died. He got up and sat down at the table. Opposite him, on the wall, hung his overcoat; his cap lay on the bench. Beyond it, in the corner, stood the samovar, serious and sullen, as if offended at something.

Near by, probably back of the wall, someone was crying in a shrill, nervous voice: "They are not behaving like Communists, that's why I'm making a noise. If you want to know, nobody is going to push us village machine operators around. What is it, anyway, is it according to the law? People should know if things are not done properly!"

"They will go into it at the rayon executive committee," replied a reserved, remonstrating voice. "You had better go now. I told you he was resting."

The voices moved away. Apparently the disputants had gone out the gate.

Then a little later a board creaked on the porch and a stooped figure in a sheepskin coat appeared in the doorway.

"Are you awake?" came out of the dark. The switch clicked, and an electric light bulb came on over the table. Varygin saw a skinny old man looking at him with small, jolly eyes.

"And who are you?" Varygin asked.

"I? I am Ilya Moshkaryov. I'm a watchman now, but I used to be a blacksmith. It's because of sickness that I've become a watchman. Right here, at the smithy. That's where I keep watch."

He sat down on a stool by the table.

"I've brought some firewood for Antonina Vasilyevna. I saw that you were asleep. She must have gone to Lapshino: Zoya Sinyukhina is having another baby there."

"Who was that shouting out there?" Varygin asked, nodding toward the wall.

"Pelageya Komkova, the wife of the combine operator, a refueler. They used to be here with us in the artel, but now they are on the M.T.S. payroll. She kept holding on to her membership in the kolkhoz, but only as a formality, so that her personal plot would not be taken from her. They have two-fifths of a hectare. Now she has been taken off this list. The reason is that in the whole year she only earned twelve work days. You could hardly keep her in the kolkhoz for that! Their private plot is being taken away from them, and so she is screaming that the machine operators are being mistreated. She came to complain to you. Who can possibly injure her! The very idea!"

"Aren't they entitled to a plot?"

"They are. According to the law they get fifteen-hundredths of a hectare, but not out of kolkhoz land. It's going to be marked off separately, on wasteland. This was decided by the village Soviet at a formal session."

He was silent for a moment and then began again. "So you came to bury your mother? The last duty. You showed respect for the aged. Thank you for not forgetting. I was assigned to work on peat and couldn't make it to the funeral."

The old man stretched out one leg and, bending backward, pulled a quarter-liter bottle of vodka out of his trouser pocket. The bottle was almost full.

"Here," he continued, becoming more animated. "If you're not too important to drink with a working man, let's drink to your mother's memory. Don't get the idea that I'm a drinking man. My niece, Marya Skornyakova, got married today to Pyotr Dezhurov, from the flax plant. They're having a celebration, but I couldn't get Semyonovna out of my head. So I grabbed up a quarter bottle and left. To each his own."

He rubbed his hands as though they were cold, looked on top of the shelf, carefully lifted down two cups, one after the other, and poured a little into each.

"Your father and I used to be great friends. Now I hear that you're one of the leaders. That's the way things are: some people go one way and some another. But actually we are all alike. Will you have some?" he asked, passing the cup. "Wait a minute, I have something we can eat with it."

He thrust his left hand into his pocket, brought out a dark, knobby pickle, wiped off the tobacco crumbs sticking to it, and broke it in two.

The vodka burned Varygin's mouth. He puckered his face at the sight of the pickle and refused. The blacksmith also took a drink and ate his half of the pickle.

"So-o-o," he said with satisfaction, screwing up his cunning eyes under their bushy, faded eyebrows. "So you are the leaders; we are the producers. That's how it is, heh-heh. Shall we finish up what is left?"

He carelessly joggled the half-full bottle in his hand, and they drank again.

"For some it's a funeral, and for others a wedding. That's the way it is, heh-heh!" said the old man.

Varygin felt a warmth in his chest, and his spirits rose for the first time in three days.

"But how did my mother live? Fairly well, or—how?" he asked.

"Well, she had her ups and downs. She lived the way everybody else did."

"But, still . . . Well, what about food, for instance?"

"Well, there was nothing to complain about. Our own grain does not last longer than the spring, so we go to Lapshino, to the village co-op. Some people even go to the town. The village Soviet paid rent to her for the house. They set up the midwife's office here. Thirty-five a month. She didn't need much. Sometimes she had white bread and enjoyed some factory tea. This year they brought in some sugar several times, and she had some too. No, there is nothing to complain about."

Wheels rattled on the frozen road outside the gate. A cart passed the house, and you could hear the clumping and noisy snorting of the horse.

Then an accordion sounded somewhere close by, a gay crowd walked past the house, and a strident girlish voice sang, half yelling:

Over the spring wheat field
Over the rayon co-op
Over the courses for beekeepers,
I am parting from you.

"That's our people having themselves a good time," said the blacksmith. "Shouldn't I go out and get some more?" He stood up, pushed the empty bottle into his pocket, and vanished without saying good-bye.

Varygin also got up, put on his overcoat, and went outside. It was already quite dark, and cold stars shone in the cloudless sky. He walked up and down near the gate, shivered from the cold, and looked at his watch. The luminous green hands

showed only 7:10. He remembered that the express left late at
night, and the few hours remaining before he could leave
seemed long and tiresome.

The accordion was playing at the outskirts of the village,
and he could hear the sounds of voices, girls' squeals, and
laughter. Varygin turned around and went toward the house.
Derevlyova, the soldier's wife, was waiting for him on the porch.
She was still wearing the soldier's blouse, but now had a heavy
woolen shawl wrapped around her head and shoulders.

"I came to make you some tea," she said in a singsong voice,
following him into the cottage. "Antonina Vasilyevna is worry-
ing about you. She sent a messenger from Lapshino. She can't
come herself: Zoya is slow to give birth and is holding her up."

She started a fire in the front of the stove and set the teapot
to boil.

"It is too bad that Semyonovna did not live to see you. How
happy the old soul would have been!" Varygin heard her say.

"Did she expect me to come?" he asked.

"She didn't say anything about it this year. But the other
summer, when you had promised to come, she really did look
forward to it very much. She used to say: 'It will be today,
today!' Then she became silent. But she was not angry, no. She
understood that it is not so easy for such a busy man to get away.
Out of all our village people you have gone the farthest. And
Afanasy Beryozin from Korkino—he's a general somewhere
in transportation."

She scalded the tea, put the cup on the table near him, and
sat down.

"It's only that we haven't much to brag about. There are only
women in this kolkhoz. We do what we can, but not much
comes of it. In the kolkhoz named 'Struggle' people got four
kilos of grain apiece, while we—" she made a hopeless gesture.
"Things are not going right with us," she said apologetically.
Probably she was embarrassed to speak to a man of Varygin's
prominence and importance about the lack of achievements
of their kolkhoz.

"This is what I wanted to ask you," she went on, untying her
shawl. "Is it right, what they are doing to us? This year we
planted seventy-four hectares of hemp. No sooner had it
started to bloom than the spring grains were ripe. We wanted to
reap the grain and leave it in sheaves, but they told us to thresh
it and bring it in right away: procurements. So you see what
happened? It's thirty-nine versts from here to the grain-
collection station. There are two ferries, and then you have to
wait at the grain elevator. Yet if you don't pick the hemp on
time, it's not good for anything. But the agents keep pestering

us. 'Bring in the grain!' 'Is it possible,' we said, 'that our government can't wait seven days?' We would have delivered our quota. We would have brought in the grain as soon as we were through with the hemp. Nothing doing! You can't get anywhere with them! And there's no one to appeal to. By the time we had carried the grain to the elevator and threshed it, we had missed the time for harvesting the hemp crop. The hemp we had not finished reaping had fallen to the ground. True, we were credited with delivering the grain: in fact, we were listed among the first to deliver. But again we had no bread for ourselves. So you tell me: is it right? Or isn't it?"

"She thinks that this is all within my power," Varygin thought distractedly, trying to remember what he knew about hemp. But he couldn't think of anything.

"This is a political problem," he said aloud. "The state must always come first. Everything depends on the level of consciousness of the masses."

He felt he was not saying the right thing and fell silent. But Derevlyova listened to him with an expression of satisfaction on her face. "That's just what I think—a political problem," she chimed in readily, apparently pleased that the conversation was acquiring real depth. "That is true. You put it very well. Our masses still lack consciousness."

The noise of a motorcycle came from the darkness outside.

"She must have come," said Derevlyova. "Probably the M.T.S. engineer brought her. He comes every Saturday. And she is always busy. Oh, the midwife doesn't know where her luck lies."

Antonina Vasilyevna came in first. Following directly behind her was a tow-headed young man with a weather-beaten face and prominent cheekbones.

"Well, how are you doing?" she asked briskly. Her melancholy mood of the morning seemed to have disappeared without a trace.

She washed her hands, sat down by the table, opened a package of sandwiches apparently bought somewhere in a restaurant, and, offering them around, began telling about the nice strong girl Sinyukhina had given birth to.

She made a pleasant picture with her milk-white arms, bare to the firm elbows, the gentle, feminine movements with which she swept the strands of wet hair behind her pink ears, and her brightly flushed fresh cheeks. As she talked she did not once look at the engineer, but she must have been continually aware that his eyes were fixed on her.

"No, she knows where her luck is," Varygin decided, looking at the girl, whose eyes were shining despite all the anxieties and worries of the day. He remembered his shapeless wife, always disgruntled about something, and the way she overfed the children, as a result of which at eleven Gena already had a paunch and Sveta looked like her aunt with her childish face and heavy, thick legs. He thought: "This engineer is a lucky fellow." If, long ago, life had taken another turn and he, Varygin, had remained in the village, he would now probably still be a strong and healthy man, and the skin on his face would have been firm and swarthy, like the engineer's. But the past cannot be changed—nor the future either, apparently. Perhaps if a young woman with arms as white as these and a beautiful, supple, strong body would consent to love him, nothing would come of it anyway.

"Have you been here long, in this area?" he asked.

"It's time for me to get away!" She gave a laugh, but there was a hard glint in her eyes. "Everyone is eager to get away from here, from the villages into the towns, and the nearer the center, the better. Things are more civilized there, and there's more to eat. But they say we are needed here more."

She looked at the engineer as if asking for his support.

"Yes, there is lots of work here," said the engineer. "Out of the nineteen collective farms in our rayon, more than half are below par. Their crops are poor, their income is negligible. The people work unwillingly and eat badly." Without looking, he took a cigaret out of the field bag at his side and lit it nervously.

"Why so?" Varygin asked.

The engineer shrugged. "You should know better than we do. Nobody wants to work without pay."

The midwife silently touched the engineer's hand. He got up from the table and began walking up and down the room.

Varygin sat with his back against the wall and chewed his sandwich. He had eaten nothing since morning. He thought the engineer was looking at him in an unfriendly way.

"Aren't you spreading it on a bit thick?" he asked hoarsely. "At first I thought you were an optimist."

The engineer went over to the corner and threw his cigaret into the basin.

"Optimism," he said, coming back, "is a much more complicated thing than it looks. The village would be a lot better off if there were fewer dispensers of official cheer. We have to grit our teeth and surmount the difficulties we face, not try to gloss them over. Take our M.T.S., for instance. There is so much latent potential there—but nobody really cares. Come over tomorrow: you'll see for yourself."

"I'm leaving today on the express. Urgent business!" Varygin said, and looked at his watch.

The engineer also looked at his watch. The enthusiasm he

had just shown disappeared at once. "So I'll be going, Tonya," he said.

She went out into the passage with him. Varygin heard them whispering about something on the porch.

"It's probably time for me to go, too," Varygin said when she returned.

"Wait. There is still plenty of time. Mitya will tell them to send a car from the M.T.S." Looking around at Derevlyova, who was quickly washing the dishes in the corner, she began speaking with embarrassment about the house. What was to be done with it? Did he want to break her lease, or perhaps was he thinking of selling it, or were things to remain as before?

"Let everything remain as it was," Varygin said.

Some of his mother's belongings remained in the chest of drawers. He took two old family photographs from the bottom of the top drawer.

He felt that he had neither the desire nor the strength to go into all this, or into what the engineer had said, or into what he himself had seen here in a day.

"So please make the necessary arrangements yourself," he said, and pushed the drawer back.

The car came much sooner than he expected. The midwife went with him so that he would not have to bother about buying a ticket himself.

The road to Lapshino was horrible, but later, when the car came out onto the highway and with a soft rustling of tires began to speed along the gray ribbon lit up by the moonlike glow of the headlights, Varygin gradually recovered his usual calm, and the aftertaste remaining from his meeting with the engineer disappeared of itself.

"Of course," he thought. "The local Party organs are not yet adequately staffed. Sometimes they work clumsily and crudely and cite objective factors only to cover up their own ineptitude. But we cannot straighten things out everywhere at once. We can correct and prompt them from above, but they must do the work themselves. Themselves!

"Yes, themselves. That's right," he thought again a minute later and was angry with himself for not having said so to the engineer.

They arrived at Dvoriki almost an hour before the train came and, after buying a ticket, sat down in the buffet.

The midwife, embarrassed, clumsily drank the port he offered her and kept glancing around as if afraid of something.

"Why don't you come with me? You could be my secretary," Varygin said jokingly.

She choked, spilled some wine on the oilcloth, and blushed so deeply that Varygin too felt uncomfortable.

In the train, while getting ready for bed in the half-dark compartment, where the other passengers were already asleep, he reminded himself with relief that the disturbing and unpleasant experiences of the last few days had already been left behind, and he thought with pleasure about how tomorrow he would come to his warm, well-furnished office and would sit down in his comfortable chair at his desk.

However, some feeling of guilt remained with Varygin for a long time. He couldn't get to sleep. Through heavy drowsiness his imagination conjured up images of the wooden crosses against the gray sky, the familiar house, the long plank bench against the wall, and in the corner the old samovar, tilted sideways. His mother was sitting at the smoothly planed table; her face was small and dark, just as it had been in the church. She moved toward him and asked him, just as Derevlyova, the soldier's wife, had asked him, with hope and expectation: "Is it right or isn't it, what they have done with us?"

1956

An Incident at
Krechetovka Station

Alexander
Solzhenitsyn

"Hallo! Is that the dispatcher?"

"Go ahead."

"Who is that? Dyachikhin?"

"Go ahead."

"Not 'go ahead'—is that Dyachikhin?"

"(Get those tank cars off No 7. Push them on to No 3.) Yes, this is Dyachikhin."

"This is Lieutenant Zotov, assistant to the C.O., Military Transport Command. Listen, what have you been doing over there? Why haven't you sent Train 677 off to Lipetsk yet? (What, Valya?)"

"(. . . Seventy-eight . . . .)"

"Train 678."

"We've nothing to pull it with."

"What d'you mean, nothing?"

"There's no engine. (What, Varnakov? Varnakov, out on No. 6. You see those four flat cars with the coal? Switch them over there.)"

"Listen, what do you mean, there's no engine? Through the window here I can see six in a row."

"They're doing a lineup."

"What's a lineup?"

"Coupling engines. The ones from the 'graveyard.' For evacuation."

"All right, then. You've got two switch engines on the go."

"(Comrade Lieutenant, fact is, I saw three switch engines!)"

"The man in charge of the convoy's with me now, setting me right: *three* switch engines. Give us one!"

"I can't."

"What d'you mean, you can't? D'you realize the importance of this cargo? We shouldn't delay it by so much as a minute. Whereas you. . . ."

"(Run it over the mound, then.)"

"Only a bit longer, and you'll have held it up half a day!"

"Oh, not as much as half a day."

"What've you got there, a dispatcher's center or a nursery school? What are those toddlers yelling about?"

"We're crowded out in here. (Comrades, how often do you have to be told? Clear the room.) I can't send anything. I've even got army cargoes I can't move."

"*In this train* we've got the stored blood! Hospital supplies! D'you get that?"

"I get it all right. (Varnakov! Get a move on over to the water-tower and take these ten.)"

"Listen! If you haven't dispatched this train in half an hour, I'll report it to the authorities—it'll be no joke, you'll have to answer for it.''

"(Vasil Vasilich! Give *me* the phone. . . .)''

"Here's the military dispatcher.''

"Nikolay Petrovich? This is Podshebyakina. Listen, what's happening over there at the depot? Only the train for the Medical C.O.'s been made up so far.''

"Here's what you do, comrade sergeant: go to the brake van and if, in forty minutes. . . . No, if they haven't dispatched you by six-thirty, come and report.''

"Report, very well! Have I permission to go?''

"You have.''

The sergeant in charge of the convoy stood smartly to attention, then, bringing his hand down from his cap with the first step, went out.

Lieutenant Zotov adjusted the spectacles that gave a severe expression to his not-at-all severe countenance, glanced at the military dispatcher, Podshebyakina, a girl in a railroad employee's uniform who stood fidgeting with her fair, abundant curls as she spoke down the antiquated mouthpiece of the antiquated telephone, and walked out of her small office into his own—equally small—from which there was no further egress.

The offices of the military transport command were on the first floor in the corner of the building. Above this floor, and also at the corner, there was a damaged drainpipe; a thick stream of water beat noisily on the wall outside and, with the gusting of the wind, was carried away to spill down either the left-side window and over the platform or the right-side window onto a deserted alleyway. Following the sharp October frosts, when morning had found the whole station covered with rime, the last few days had been wet and cold; rain had been falling uninterruptedly since the day before, so that you began to wonder where in the sky such a quantity of water could possibly have been stored.

Conversely, the rain brought with it some form of order: no longer was there that aimless chatter so typical of people, that constant swarming of civilians on the platforms and over the tracks that disturbed the proper appearance and function of the station. Everyone was taking shelter, no one attempted to crawl on hands and knees under the cars or to climb the steps, local inhabitants no longer ran up with pails of boiled potatoes, and people riding the freight trains no longer loitered between the cars, bearing on their shoulders and under their arms cloth, garments, and knitted things such as you see in the Flea Market. This practice of trading sorely troubled Lieutenant Zotov: it really should not be allowed, yet it could

not be forbidden, because supplies for the evacuees had
not been released.

Only those legitimately employed in the station had not been
driven away by the rain. From the window a sentry could be
seen standing on the platform beside certain crated supplies—
he was soaked to the skin by the driving rain. He stood motionless, not even attempting to shake off the wet. On Track No. 3
a switch engine was shunting tank cars, and a switchman in
hooded oilskins was waving a flag at it. The dark and dwarfish
figure of the foreman went along the train that stood on Track
No. 2, ducking down to peer under every car.

This was rain that fell with lashing, slanting strokes; obeying
the persistent wind, it struck against the tops and sides of freight
trains, the breastwork of engines; it whipped the bent red iron
ribs of about twenty skeleton coaches (the casing had been
burned off during an air raid somewhere, but the rolling parts
had survived this and had been towed back to the rear). The
rain poured over four artillery guns that stood uncovered on
their flat cars; blending with the prevailing half-light, it clamped
grayly down on the foremost green circle of the signal and on
the crimson sparks that flashed in all directions from the stacks
of heated freight cars. The asphalt on Platform No. 1 was wholly
awash with bubbling water that had had no time to drain itself
away; even in the half-light, the rails gleamed in this water and
the dark brown fill of the permanent way itself quivered in
those undrying puddles.

No sound came from any part but the shuddering pull of the
earth and the subdued whistling of the switchman—for train
whistles had been forbidden since the first day of the war.

But the rain blasted down the damaged drainpipe.

Outside the other window, in the deserted alley by the
warehouse fence, grew a young oak tree. Disheveled and
drenched, it had held on to its dark leaves, but today the last
of these had blown away.

There was no gazing out of the window. There had to be the
pulling of paper shades over windows for camouflage, lighting
of lamps, sitting down and getting to work. There was a great
deal to catch up with before the next shift came on duty at nine
o'clock that evening.

Zotov, though, had not pulled down the shade; he took off
his officer's cap with the green band which, during duty hours
and even indoors, always sat firmly on his head, he took off his
spectacles and slowly rubbed his fingers over eyes that were
weary with conveying the code numbers of convoys from one
penciled ledger to the other. No, it was not weariness that
stole over him, but a clawing anguish of spirit at the day's

growing dark before time.

This was not anguish for his wife, left with an unborn child far away in German-occupied Belorussia. It was not anguish for days gone by, for Zotov did not have much past to recall. It was not for possessions lost, because he had had none, nor did he wish any.

What Zotov did have was an oppressed feeling, a need for release, because the war could be conducted to the point of savagery beyond reason. According to Informburo bulletins, it was not possible to define the front line; it was disputable whether it lay at Kharkov or Kaluga. But among the railroad employees it was well known that no more trains were being sent beyond Uzlov in the direction of Tula, and that over the Elets they were probably backed up as far as Verkhov. Here and there bombers had penetrated as far as the Ryazan-Voronezh line, dropped a few bombs, some of which had fallen on Krechetovka. Ten days before two crazed German soldiers on motorcycles had rushed through Krechetovka, firing their machine guns as they went. One of them was cut down, the other sped off, but everybody at the station had been alarmed by the firing, and the head of the rescue and evacuation squad had had a tank car loaded with explosive towed away to a safe distance. They had sent for a salvage train, which was now in its third day of service.

It was not Krechetovka that was in Zotov's mind, but rather why the war had taken this particular turn. Not only had there been no revolution in all Europe, not only had we not shed even a little of our blood in invading it or in resisting any combination of aggressors, but now it had all come about. For how much longer? Whatever he did during the day, when he lay down at night, Zotov's only thought was, "How much longer?" When he was off duty, lying in his room, he would invariably wake up with the radio signing on at six o'clock in the morning. Yet out of the radio's black mouth came no hope, only communiqués about troop displacements from Vyazma to Volokolamsk that gave him heartache: were they about to surrender Moscow as well? Zotov was afraid to ask this, not only out loud, but even to himself—but he thought about it constantly, though he tried not to.

As a matter of fact, this gloomy question was not the ultimate one. The surrender of Moscow was not the worst thing that could happen; Moscow had yielded before—to Napoleon. The burning question would then be: what next? Supposing they pushed on as far as the Urals?

Vasya Zotov reproached himself with what he considered the sin of letting these disturbing thoughts pass through his mind. It was an offense, an act of reprobation in the face of the almighty, the omniscient Father and Master, who was always at his post, who would foresee all things, take all necessary steps, and let nothing stand in his way.

Railwaymen came from Moscow with monstrous, outlandish tales of factory managers' taking flight, of the destruction of offices and stores, and again the silent anguish gripped Zotov's heart.

Recently, on his way to this post, Zotov had spent two days at command headquarters. There had been a mess party, and a thin lieutenant, face pale, hair unruly, had read his own poems, words with no regard for the censor, coming from the heart. Vasya had not then known that these verses would stick in his memory, but later he found them surfacing in his mind. And now, whether walking in Krechetovka, or traveling by train to the Railroad Network Central Command, or riding in a farm cart to the rural Soviet where he had been assigned the duty of training the local lads and the physically unfit—Zotov went over these words again and again, as if they were his own:

Our burning villages and our smoking towns . . .
And one thought alone that goads and
goads us to fury: but when? But when? When
are we going to counter their offensive?
And then, again:
If Lenin's life work were to crumble now,
would there by any reason for me to go on living?

Since the first day of the war Zotov had not for one moment sought his own safety. His life was unimportant, meaning only: how far can I serve the Revolution? However, much as he had begged them to send him to the front line, he had been appointed to the Rail Transport Command.

To keep himself safe was meaningless. Neither for his wife's sake nor that of the child about to be born was it imperative to keep safe. If the Germans reached Baikal, and Zotov by some miracle were left alive, he had resolved to make his way on foot through Kyakhta to China or India or across the ocean—but his only reason for going would be to join up with the military units being formed to make an armed reentry into Europe and Russia.

And so he stood in the twilight with the driving, scourging rain, the wind buffeting the windows, and, to steel himself, repeated that young lieutenant's lines.

The blacker the darkness in the office, the clearer shone the cherry-red window of the stove and the mass of undefined light behind the glass portion of the door to the neighboring office, where the military dispatcher for the N.K.P.S. was sitting with her lamp burning.

Though she did not officially depend on the Transport
Officer on duty, she could not in fact get along without him,
because it was not her business to know what either the
contents or the destination of the rolling stock might be. Her
job was to familiarize herself with the numbers on the cars. The
lists of these numbers were drawn up and brought to her by the
checker, "Aunt" Frossy, who had just come in and was noisily
stamping her feet.

"Oh, what torrents of rain!" she complained. "Torrents!
But it seems to be letting up, bit by bit."

"Don't forget to write in No. 765, Aunt Frossy," said Valya
Podshebyakina.

"All right, I will. Hand over the lamp." The door was
neither heavy nor tightly closed, and Zotov could hear what
they were saying.

"Things are looking up, I'm getting some coal," said Aunt
Frossy. "Now I'm not afraid of anything. I can feed my kids
entirely on potatoes. But over at Dasha Melentyeva's, you can't
so much as dig for them. Just try shoveling that mud!"

"Going to freeze up good and proper, wouldn't you say? How
cold it's getting."

"We'll have the winter on us early this year. Oh, to think of
a war like this and winter getting here early as well. . . . How
many potatoes have you dug up?"

Zotov sighed and began to pull the paper shades down over
the windows, carefully straightening the edges so as not to let
any ray of light shine out.

This was what he could not understand, what roused in him
a sense of outrage, even loneliness. All these working people
around him appeared to listen to the bulletins with the same
fatalistic air as himself, and, as they turned away from the
loudspeakers, they evinced the same silent anxiety. But Zotov
could see the difference: these people depended on other
additional considerations. Apart from the news from the
front, they had among other things potatoes to pull out of the
earth, cows to milk, wood to saw, windows to tape. Now and
again they would talk of these things, which took far more of
their attention than did the news from the front.

Silly old woman! She'd got herself some coal, and now had
"nothing more to be afraid of." Not even Guderian's tanks?

The wind tossed the young tree beside the warehouse and
jingled the small panes in Zotov's window.

Zotov pulled down the last shade, switched on the light. Suddenly the room, swept clean though bare, had a feeling of
comfort, a kind of security, where you could bravely turn your
thoughts to anything.

Directly under the lamp in the middle of the room stood the
table intended for the commander's deputy; behind it and
near the stove stood a safe, by the window, an old oak station
bench intended to seat three, on its back the name of the railroad had been carved in large letters. A man could stretch
out on that bench at night, but this happened only rarely, owing
to the pressure of work. There were also a couple of common
chairs. Between the windows hung a colored portrait of
Kaganovich in a railroad uniform. Previously in that place there
had been a map showing connecting routes, but the commanding transport officer had ordered it taken down, as people came
into this room, and, should the enemy be concealed among
them, he would be able to inform himself as to what route
went where.

From the adjoining room:

"I traded for stockings," Aunt Frossy was boasting. "I got a
pair of silk ones for five potato cakes. There may not be any
more stockings till the end of the war. Tell your mother to get
a move on—she ought to cook up something and take it down
to the heated cars. They simply tear it out of your hands.
Grunka Mostryukova went down the other day, got a wonderful sort of shirt for women, a nightdress, so they say, with
vents—no, listen to this—let in at such places. . . . well, it was
too funny. They all went over to her house and watched her try
it on—they laughed till their sides ached. . . . You can get soap,
too, and cheap. Soap's in short supply now, can't buy it at the
store. Tell your mother to look sharp!"

"Well, I don't know, Aunt Frossy. . . ."

"Don't tell me you don't need any stockings?"

"Oh, yes, I do, and badly, but I don't know—I'd feel ashamed
taking from evacuees. . . ."

"It's just those displaced people you should take from! They
carry dress lengths, they carry suits, they carry soap—loaded
with things, they are, as if they were going to the fair! And
some of them have such faces! Boiled fowl, now, that's what
you give 'em, they ask only for that. Some of them—no, folk
have seen them—they've whole packages of hundred-ruble
notes tied with string, boxes full. So, I ask you, did they rob a
bank? But money's the only thing we don't need, so they can
take *that* on down the line!"

"Yes, well, what about those tenants of yours?"

"Now don't go comparing them with the others. The poor
wretches haven't a rag to their backs—came from Kiev with
just what they managed to pick up at a moment's notice, it's a
wonder they got here at all. Polinka got a position at the Post
Office, they don't give her much of a wage, but what does she

want with wages? I took her old mother in, opened my cellar to
her—'There you are,' I told her, 'take some potatoes and
sauerkraut as well, and as for your room, I'll not ask you to pay
me anything.' I've always been sorry for the poor, you know,
Valyusha—as for the rich, they'd better not expect any hand-
outs from me!''

There were two telephones on Zotov's desk: one for the
track—an old handle-operated model in a yellow wooden box,
an exact replica of the one used by the military dispatcher—
and the other (a field model with a buzzer) connecting him to
the captain's office and to the guardroom for the ration distri-
bution. The soldiers at the ration center constituted the sole
military strength of the Krechetovka command. Even so their
principal task was to stand guard only over the supplies.
They kept themselves warm, and the guardroom neat and
clean: at the present moment a bucket of large pieces of
anthracite stood, "just in case," before the stove stoked to
the bursting point.

The track telephone rang. Having already got the better of
his twilight moment of weakness, Zotov sprang to the receiver,
putting his cap on with his free hand, and began shouting. He
always shouted when it was a long-distance call, sometimes
because the connection was poor, but more often out of
habit.

This call was from Bogoyavlenskaya to ascertain what track
schedules he had or had not received. The track schedules—
orders from the command post up the line about what convoy
was going where—were usually telegraphed in. Just one hour
earlier Zotov had taken some of these orders to the telegraph-
ist and received others from her in return. His duty was then
quickly to make out which convoys should be grouped with
which and at what station, and to instruct the military dispatcher
as to what cars to couple. And then he had to draw up and send
out a fresh set of schedules, retain copies of these for himself,
and pinpoint the movements on a diagram.

No sooner did Zotov put down the receiver than he leaped
to his chair. Poring shortsightedly over his desk, he applied
himself to the schedules. However, he was somewhat disturbed by what was going on in the room next door. A man had
entered, stamping his boots, and his shoulder bag full of iron
had been thrown down on the floor. Aunt Frossy asked him
whether the rain was stopping. He muttered some reply and
(presumably) sat down.

It was true that the rain did not seem to be tearing out of the
damaged pipe so forcefully, but the wind had grown stronger
and was rattling the window.

"What did you say, old man?" Valya Podshebyakina raised her voice.

"I said, 'beginning to get colder,'" replied the old man, still muttering.

"Is your hearing good, Gavrila Nikitich?" Aunt Frossy was shouting.

"It's all right," answered the old man. "Only, something keeps crackling in my ear."

"So how can you attend to the cars, granddad? You have to keep giving them a good, firm tap."

"Can see them, anyway."

"You don't know it, Valya, but he's from around here, from Krechetovka, name's Kordubaylo. All the wagon masters in all the stations learned their trade from him. Ten years before the war he retired to his small corner, but now he's come out of it, as you see."

Again and yet again Aunt Frossy started up a conversation. The chatter began to annoy Zotov, and he was just going in to chase her out, when in the room they began to talk further about what happened yesterday with a convoy of stragglers.

Zotov knew about the incident through his replacement, who, like him, was an assistant to the Military Transport C.O., and to whom it had fallen the evening before to take emergency measures, as the Krechetovka station had no halting place for transported convicts. Yesterday morning two convoys had run alongside each other into the station; thirty cars of stragglers were being pulled from Shchigr via Otrozhka, and for these thirty cars of desperate men there were only five N.K.V.D. agents as escorts, who, of course, could do nothing with them. The other convoy had come from Rtishchev and was loaded with flour. The flour was being carried partly in sealed cars, partly on half-cars, in bags. Suddenly the stragglers took united action and attacked the half-cars, climbed right on top of them and started opening the bags with their knives, pouring the flour into their mess tins and turning their field tunics into bags for it. Two guards from the escort accompanying the flour had been posted, one at the head, one at the foot of the train, on the track itself. The guard at the head, still hardly more than a boy, shouted at them not to touch the flour, but none paid any heed, and he received no help from inside the heated cars. So he lifted his gun to his shoulder, fired, and with that one shot hit one straggler on the top of the wagon in the head.

Zotov listened hard to their conversation—they hadn't got it right, had got hold of the wrong end of the stick. He could not help going in to set them right. Opening the door, he stood on the threshold looking at the four through his round spectacles.

To the right of the door the slender Valya was sitting at her desk spread with registers and plans made up of multicolored squares. Against the window with its blue paper camouflage stood a bench on which Aunt Frossy had seated herself. She was no longer young, was fat, had that authoritative air encountered in Russian women used to managing by themselves both at work and at home. To wear while on duty she had been issued a raincoat of some sturdy, grayish green material, which now clung sopping wet to the wall, while she sat in her soaking boots and in her worn black civilian coat, trimming the candle from a four-sided lantern.

The door leading into the office bore a pink poster of the sort found everywhere in Krechetovka: "Beware of Spotted Fever." The color was the same dire pink as the rash accompanying spotted fever or the scorched iron skeletons of railroad cars after an air raid.

Not far from the door, so as not to track in mud yet as close to the stove as he could get, old Kordubaylo was sitting on the floor, his back against the wall. At his side was his old leather bag of heavy tools, laid so as not to be in anyone's way, and his mittens, all dirty with tar. The old man must have sat down the moment he arrived, without shaking off the rain or taking off his outdoor clothes, for his boots and cape were streaming water onto the floor. Clutched between his knees was an unlit lantern of the type Aunt Frossy used. Under his cape the old man wore a dirty black peajacket with a rather grimy brown belt. His hood had been thrown back and an old— very old— railroad worker's cap was jammed down on his still hairy head. That cap somehow offended the eye. The small lamp lighted only his bluish nose and thick lips. Kordubaylo now wetted a cigaret paper torn from a newspaper, lighted up, and smoked. His untidy beard still had dark hairs among the gray.

"Well, what else could he have done?" Valya was arguing, rapping her little pencil. "He was the sentry on duty."

"Yes, that's right," said the old man, nodding and dropping red-hot cinders of shag tobacco on the floor and the lantern lid. "That's right. Everyone has to eat."

"What are you driving at?" asked the girl with a frown. "Who do you mean, 'everyone?'"

"Well, us, at least, and you," muttered Kordubaylo.

"You *are* an old silly! And do you think they are starving? They get the same rations as the public. Or do you think they don't get any rations in transit?"

"Well, you're right," agreed the old man. Again the burning bits fell from his cigaret this time onto his knee and his jacket.

"Look out, you'll burn yourself, Gavrila Nikitich!" Aunt Frossy warned him.

The old man looked down with complete indifference at the tobacco plates dying on his damp, thick-wadded trousers. When all were out, he half raised his curly gray head in its cap.

"You girls ever eaten raw flour and water for your midday meal? "

"Why raw?" said Aunt Frossy, puzzled. "I usually put water with it, knead it, and bake it."

The old man smacked his lips together and said, but not all at once—his words never came out all at once, but seemed to take their time, hobbling forward on crutches from their source: "Means you don't know what hunger is, my dears."

Then Lieutenant Zotov crossed the threshold and interrupted. "Listen, old man, what's a sworn oath—you got any idea?" Zotov carefully stressed all his vowels.

The old man looked at the lieutenant with a troubled air. Though the old man was not tall, his boots were big and heavy, saturated with water, and foul with patches of sludge.

"What else?" he grumbled. "Sworn my own personal oath five times up to now."

"And who did you swear your oath to? Tsar Mikoloshka?"

The old man shook his head. "Goes further back than that."

"What? You mean Alexander III?"

The old man appeared dismayed. Chomping, he went on smoking.

"Well, and now we swear allegiance to the people. Tell me, what's the difference?"

The old man dropped more embers on his knee.

"And whose is the flour? Doesn't that belong to the people?" said Valya, losing her temper, tossing back her bright, forward-falling hair. "Where were they carrying the flour? Who for? For the Germans or what?"

"Well, you're right there." The old man saw nothing to argue over in that. "But those fellows weren't Germans either—they were our own people."

He smoked his homemade cigaret to the end, then stubbed it out on the lid of his lantern.

"Well, that's a smart old man for you. And what's the law of the State—you any idea? If each of us just takes whatever he likes—I take, you take—how are we going to win the war?"

"And why did they have to slit open the sacks?" protested Valya indignantly. "What was that for? Do our people behave like that?"

"They could have been sewn up again," Kordubaylo got out, wiping his nose on his hand.

"Did they have to rip them open like that? And throw the flour out? All over the track?" cried Aunt Frossy heatedly. "How

many did they rip open and empty, Comrade Lieutenant? How
many children could have been fed with it all?"

"Well, you're right," said the old man. "With rain like this
the rest of it must have got soaked on the half-cars."

"Oh, what's the use of talking to him?" said Zotov, annoyed
with himself for taking part in this squalid argument that got
nowhere. "You shouldn't make so much noise in here! People
can't work!"

Aunt Frossy had already cleaned the mantel and now she lit
the candle inside the lantern. She rose to take down her stiff,
battered raincoat.

"Here, Valyusha, sharpen my pencil for me. I'm just going
to write in No. 765."

Zotov went back into his office.

That business yesterday could have been worse, on the
whole. On seeing their fellow straggler killed, the others left
the flour bags and threw themselves yelling on the young
sentry. They tore his rifle away from him—it appeared he had
given it up without a struggle—and began to beat him.
They would have pulverized him, if the corporal of the guard
had not arrived in time. He pretended to arrest the sentry and
led him away.

When all the stragglers were at last borne away, each command post did its utmost to send them on at once. The night
before yet another convoy of the sort had come in, No. 245413,
on its way from Pavelets to Archeda. Zotov had met it and
escorted it out as fast as possible. The convoy had stopped at
Krechetovka for only twenty minutes; the stragglers were asleep
and did not come out. In large numbers, stragglers are terrible,
an ugly mob. They are not a military unit, they are not armed,
but there is a feeling of yesterday's army about them, for they
are the same fellows who made a stand somewhere near
Bobruysk in July, or near Kiev in August, or near Orel in
September.

Zotov was intimidated by them—probably for the same
reason that made the young sentry yield his gun to them without
firing another shot. Zotov was ashamed to command a post at
the rear. He envied the stragglers and would take at least some
of their misdeeds onto his own shoulders, if only to feel that
he also had to his credit action under fire with its shells and
flares. All the young men in Vasya Zotov's graduating class, all
his friends, were at the front.

And he was here.

Therefore all the greater was his perseverance in doing his
work, not only to keep abreast of it while on duty, but also to
make time for still more tasks; all the more did he contrive to

complete his assignments with perfect thoroughness and
efficiency, particularly at a time like this, the twenty-fourth
anniversary of the Revolution. It was the most cherished public
holiday of the year, a feast of joy, in spite of the weather that
usually prevailed, but this time it only tore at the heart.

Apart from his regular tasks, one chore on Zotov's agenda
for the past week had come up while he himself was on duty.
There had been an air raid on the station, and the Germans had
done a fair job of destroying a convoy of army cargoes that
contained food rations. If the convoy had been utterly destroyed, the matter would have ended there and then. Happily,
however, a large part had been left intact. Now Zotov had been
ordered to draw up a complete list in quadruplicate of those
shipments rendered completely useless (these had to be
entered on the list with their destinations, and replacements
had to be ordered), which were forty to eighty percent useless
(a separate decision would be taken as to how to use these),
also those that were ten to forty percent useless (these had
to be sent on to their destination either as they were or with
partial substitution), and finally those undamaged. The job
became all the more complicated, as, even though the cargoes
from the bombed convoy were now in the freight sheds, it had
been impossible to send them there at once; unidentified
persons had been seen loitering around the station, and there
might have been some looting. Besides, to establish the percentage of usefulness demanded the considered opinion of
experts (who had come from Michurinsk and Voronezh for the
purpose) and the continual shifting of the crates when there
were not enough loaders to do this work.

Any idiot can drop a bomb, but just try clearing up the mess
it makes!

Anyhow, Zotov loved absolute accuracy in all forms of work.
Consequently he had already drawn up the greater part of the
lists; he had a chance of finishing them today, and he hoped to
send the whole off within the week.

Even this kind of work had now become part of his current
agenda. So Zotov had found even more work for himself. Here
he was, a highly qualified man with a bent for systematization,
working as a responsible officer and thus acquiring useful
experience. Now he could clearly see what had been wrong
with the system of mobilization at the outbreak of the war, and
what had gone amiss in organizing the supervision of military
convoys. He could also see a large number of needed improve-
ments, of varying degrees of importance, that might be applied
to the running of the command posts. Therefore, wasn't it his
solemn duty to note all the observations he could, work on

them, and submit them as a report to the People's Commissariat? Even if his work did not prove useful in this war, might it
not be important in the next?

For this kind of work also time and strength had to be
mustered, however much the captain and the others at the key
command post might snicker when he explained to them. (They
were very short-sighted fellows, anyway.)

He had to get on with the business in hand! Zotov rubbed his
hands with their calloused palms and thick stubby fingers. He
picked up an indelible pencil and ran through several sheets,
written in a clear, round hand, verifying the complex, even
fractional, figures on cargoes, convoys, and carloads. There
could be no slips in this work, otherwise it was like showing the
target to the artillery. In his concentration, his forehead creased
into a mesh of short lines and he pushed out his lower lip.

Podshebyakina knocked on the glass panel of the door: "May
I come in, Vasily Vasilich?" Without waiting, she came in with a
check sheet in her hand. As a rule she wasn't supposed to enter
his office. Any problem could be settled on the threshold, or
inside the other office, but since he was usually on duty with
her more than once a day, he did not like to tell her not to
enter. Therefore, having just written down a number, he made
it appear that he had just chanced to cover the list of cyphers he
was making with a blank sheet of paper.

"Vasily Vasilich, I've got into rather a fix here. Here, look."
There was no other chair, so Valya leaned over the table, pushing the check sheet with its crooked lines of uneven figures
over to Zotov. "Look, in convoy No. 446 there was supposed to
be a car No. 57831. Well, what's become of it?"

"I'll tell you in just a moment." He pulled out a drawer,
picked the appropriate ledger out of the three lying there,
opened it (but not in such a way as to let her look at it) and at
once declared: "No. 57831—destination Pachelma."

"Uh-huh." Valya wrote in "Pach," but did not leave. She
sucked the end of her pencil and looked at her check sheet,
still leaning over his table.

"Look how you've written the 'ch,' it's not legible," Zotov
reproved her. "You'll be reading it as 'v' and sending that car
off to Pavelets."

"No, I won't," replied Valya equably. "Don't try and find
fault, Vasily Vasilich."

She looked up at him from under a curl. But she corrected
the 'ch'.

"Now here's another thing," she hesitated, and stuck her
pencil back in her mouth. Her wealth of curls fell over her
forehead into her eyes, but she didn't brush them back. They

were so clean, probably soft as well, that Zotov imagined how nice it would be to stroke them. "Another thing: flat car No. 10510."

"Light?"

"No, heavy."

"Not very likely."

"Why not?"

"There must be a digit missing."

"So now what am I going to do?" She pushed back her hair. Her eyelashes were very blonde.

"Well, you'll have to find it, won't you? You ought to be more careful, Valya. Is it the same convoy?"

"Uh-huh."

Looking in the ledger, Zotov checked the numbers.

Valya looked at the lieutenant, with his ridiculous jutting ears, his potato nose, and his pale blue eyes with their fleck of gray—his spectacles emphasized them. He was inclined to find fault at work, that Vasily Vasilich, but he was not a bad sort on the whole. What she particularly liked about him was that he never stepped out of line, he was truly a kind man.

"Ugh!" said Zotov, irritably. "Whipping's too good for you. It isn't o-five, it's o-o-five. You *are* a dimwit!"

"Two o's?" said Valya, astonished and wrote in another zero.

"You graduated from the senior class in high school, didn't you? Aren't you ashamed of yourself?"

"Oh, come on, Vasily Vasilich, what's high school got to do with it? And what's its destination?"

"Kirsanov."

"Uh-huh." Valya wrote it in.

Still she didn't leave. In this position, leaning on the desk beside him, she turned pensive. With one finger she began to fidget a small splinter of wood broken off the writing surface, pushing it until it again found its niche.

His eyes roamed involuntarily over the girl's breasts, now evident in this leaning posture, though they were hidden as a rule under the heavy service shirt of her railroad employee's uniform.

"Off duty soon," said Valya, pushing out her lips. They looked very fresh, pale pink.

"Until you're off duty, there's work to be done!" frowned Zotov, taking his eyes off the girl.

"You'll be going back to your old woman's, yes?"

"Where else?"

"You never go visiting."

"A fine time to think about visiting!"

"And what's so fine at that old woman's place? She hasn't so much as a campbed. You sleep on a chest."

"How do you know?"

"People know those things, they talk."

"This isn't a time for spoiling oneself with soft beds, Valichka, and still less in may case. I feel too ashamed not to be out at the front."

"What an idea! Don't you do your job? What's there to be ashamed of? You'll be in the trenches, too, that's certain. And how long will you have to live then? Meanwhile, you should live here as decently as you can."

Zotov took his cap off, rubbed his forehead where it had been pinched by the cap (a little too small for him, but he hadn't found a bigger one in the stores).

Valya had been idly drawing a long tail like a fancy monogram in one corner of the check sheet. "Why did you leave the Avdeyevs? Their place was better, anyhow."

"Because I left, and that's all there is to it." (Might the Avdeyev business have got around the town?)

Valya made the tail longer and longer. Neither spoke.

Valya glanced at his round head out of the corner of her eye. If he took off the spectacles, it would be a child's head; his thin blonde hair stood up here and there in little curls, like question marks.

"And you never go to the cinema. You certainly must have some pretty interesting books. At least, lend me something to read."

Zotov got up. The flush had not left his face. "How do you know I have any books?"

"I guessed."

"I haven't any books. They're back at home."

"You're mean with your books, that's all."

"But I tell you, I haven't any. How could I have brought them along? A soldier only has his duffle bag, he's not allowed to carry any more."

"Then come to our house and take some of ours to read."

"You've a lot of them?"

"A shelf full."

"What kind?"

"Well, let me see: there's *The Iron Foundry, Prince Serebryany* and others."

"Have you read them all?"

"Some of them." And suddenly she raised her head, looked him straight in the eye and, breathing jerkily, got out: "Vasily Vasilich! Why don't you— move over to our place? We've got Vovka's room free— you can have it. It's got a stove, it's heated. Mamma'll cook for you. What pleasure can it be for you, staying on at that old woman's?"

Valya saw that the lieutenant was hesitating, about to agree. And why not agree, the funny fellow! All the army denied they were married, he was the only one who declared he was. All the army were billeted in the town with good families, well heated, well looked after. Now that her father and brother were away at the war, Valya wanted a man living at her own house. Then they could come back together after curfew late at night in the blacked-out town, maybe even arm-in-arm through the muddy streets, and afterward have a cheerful supper together, exchanging jokes and stories.

It cannot be said that Zotov fearlessly looked back at the girl who had openly invited him to her home. She was only three years younger than he, so that if she called him by his given name and patronymic and addressed him in the formal plural, it was not because of the difference in their ages but out of respect for his lieutenant's flashes. He realized that it would not end with tasty dishes in exchange for his dry rations, and with stove heat. This disturbed him. All the same, the desire was on him now to fondle her accessible blonde curls.

But . . . it was quite impossible.

He pulled at his collar with the red flashes within their green knots, though it was not too tight, and adjusted his spectacles.

"No, Valya, I shan't go anywhere else. Anyway, we've work to do, and here we've been chattering all this time."

And he put on his green cap, which lent a great severity to his defenseless face with its turned-up nose.

The girl looked up at him once more and said hesitantly: "All right, just as you like, Vasily Vasilich."

She breathed a sigh. In a manner that seemed not so youthful, she straightened with some difficulty from her leaning position and, dropping her hand that held the checklist, went out.

He blinked helplessly. Perhaps she would come back once more, and if she asked him again and insisted, he would give in. But she did not come back.

Vasya could not explain to anyone why he went on living with the old woman and her three granddaughters in the ill-heated house, sleeping on an uncomfortable chest. In the great, harsh topsy-turvy truth of the year 1941, he had already been laughed at once or twice, when he declared aloud that he loved his wife and meant to stay true to her all through the war, and that he could be absolutely certain, besides, of her fidelity to him. Good fellows all, his down-to-earth friends teased him in an amicable fashion that also had a ferocity in it, they slapped him on the shoulder and advised him not to depart too far from reality. Since then he had never voiced his faith again, only he was very bored, especially when he lay awake in the black night, thinking of her far away, under German rule, and expecting his child.

It was not because of his wife, however, that he had just refused Valya, it was because of Polina.

And not even Polina, but . . .

Polina, a young woman from Kiev with dark hair cut short and a smooth, pale face, lived at Aunt Frossy's and worked at the post office. Whenever he had time, Vasya would go to the post office and read the recent newspapers that would pile up for a number of days because of arriving late. In this way one could read all the papers at once, not just one or two. Obviously, the post office was not a reading room and no one was obliged to provide him with papers, but Polina understood him and laid out all the newspapers at the end of the counter, where he would stand reading them in the cold. For Polina as for Zotov, the war was not the turning of an irreversible wheel, but the whole of life, the future in its entirety, and in order to divine that future she, too, would unfold the papers with anxious hands, and she, too, would seek in them grains of sand that might show her how the war was going. They would read side by side, pointing out the important items to each other as they came across them. For them the newspapers took the place of the letters they no longer received. Polina assiduously read through every item in the military communiqués, trying to guess where her husband would be. On Zotov's advice, she would, wrinkling her unlined forehead, even go through the articles on infantry tactics or tank warfare in the *Red Star*. As for Ilya Ehrenburg's articles, Vasya excitedly read these aloud to her. And there were certain papers he got from Polina that hadn't yet been sent out, from which he cut articles to keep.

Polina, her child, and her mother—he loved them with a love that rarely comes to those in the depth of despair. He gave his sugar ration to her little boy. But never once, as they turned the pages of the newspapers, did he dare to touch her white hand—not because of her husband nor his wife, but because of the secret anguish that had made them one.

Polina became the person closest to him at Krechetovka— no, in all that part of the front she was the eye of his conscience, his fidelity—how could he set up house at Valya's? What would Polina think of him? But even without Polina—without Polina he could take no comfort from the presence of any woman—now when there was a danger that everything he held dear would crumble.

It would somewhat have embarrassed him to admit to Valya— as to the lieutenant who relieved him on duty—that he did have something to read in the evenings and that he had a book, only one, which he had snatched out of some library during all the comings-and-goings of the past year and which went with him in his duffle bag.

This book (it was blue) was the first plump volume of Marx's *Capital*, printed on coarse yellowing paper dating from the thirties. During all his five years as a student he had dreamed of reading this beloved book, and he had taken it out of the Institute library more than once and tried to make a summary of it, keeping it for the whole term, even the whole year—but he never had enough time, he was inundated with social obligations, meetings, examinations. Without completing even one line of his summary, he returned the book when he went off on his study tour in June. And even when they attended the course on political economy—the most appropriate time for reading *Capital*—the professor dissuaded them from reading it: "You'll drown in it." He told the students to cleave to Lapiduce's manual and to their class notes. When it came down to it, they were barely able to do that much.

Now, in this hole, in the fall of 1941 and in the burning light of his immense inward anguish, Vasya Zotov found time for *Capital*. This was what he did in his time off duty, away from the noise and away from the tasks of the Party district committee. At the Avdeyevs' apartment, in a little room embellished with philodendra and aloes, he would sit at a shaky little table in the light of a kerosene lamp (the Diesel-powered dynamo could not supply all the houses in the community), smoothing the paper, reading a passage through once to get the general idea of it, a second time to mark the notable parts, and a third to summarize it so as to store it securely in his head. The gloomier the communiqués from the front, the greater his determination as he immersed himself in the thick blue book. Vasya believed that once he had assimilated the first volume and had got it all clear and ordered in his head, he would become invulnerable, irresistible, in any battle of ideas.

However, there had not been many such evenings or off-duty hours, and he had set only a few lines down on paper when he was disturbed by Antonina Ivanovna.

She too was a lodger at the Avdeyevs', having come from Liski to be—with no trouble at all—manager of a canteen at Krechetovka. A keen business woman, she was so active that there was little idling under her management. At her canteen (Zotov later heard), in exchange for one ruble, they would wet the bottom of a clay porringer with hot, gray, nonfat water with a few strands of macaroni floating in it. If some did not care to drink straight out of the porringer, they demanded another ruble as security for the use of a cracked wooden spoon. In the evening Antonina Ivanovna herself would ask the Avdeyevs about putting on the samovar and set out bread and butter on her landlord's table. She was in fact no more than twenty-five, but she had the air of a woman of consequence, white-fleshed, well-fed. She always greeted the lieutenant politely. He would make some absentminded reply. For a long time, indeed, he confused her with a relative of his landlady's who had lately arrived. Bent over his book, he neither saw nor heard her as, on her return from work, she passed his room on the way to her own room, back to the landlord's part of the house, and then once more to her own room.

Once she came into his room, unexpectedly, and asked, "Why are you always reading, Comrade Lieutenant?" He closed both his book and notebook and made some evasive answer. Another time she asked: "Don't you think it terrible that I don't bolt my door at night?" Zotov replied, "What's there to be afraid of? I'm here, and I've even got a gun." A few days later, as he was sitting over his book, he sensed that she had left off going to and fro in the small passage. He looked around, and was stupefied at what he saw: she was right inside his room, on his divan, already lying down, her hair spread out on the pillow, the cover failing to conceal her impudent white shoulders. He was rooted to the spot, staring at her, not knowing what to do. "Am I in your way here?" she asked ironically. Vasya stood up, all power of comprehension gone. He even took a stride toward her, but the sight of this well-fed criminal had no attraction for him—on the contrary, it repelled him.

He could say nothing to her. His aversion strangled him. He turned again to his books, closed *Capital* with a slam, found the strength from somewhere to put it back in his bag, and ran to where his cap and cape were hanging on a hook. Picking up the heavy strap of his pistol and holding it in his hand without buckling it on, he fled from the house as fast as his legs would carry him.

He went out into a darkness made blacker by the cloudy sky as much as by the camouflaged windows. A cold autumn wind, like today's, laden with rain, was ripping and flailing. Staggering through puddles, potholes, and mud, Vasya made his way to the station without once realizing that he was still holding the strap with the pistol. The sense of his powerlessness against the affront so gnawed him that he all but cried, running crazily down the black embankment.

From that moment on life was no longer livable at the Avdeyevs'. Not only did Antonina Ivanovna cease speaking to him, but she now began to bring some mug or other home with her—a civilian, but dressed in boots and a tunic, as the spirit of the times demanded. Zotov tried to go on with his reading—she did not close her door on purpose, so that all the time he could hear them giggling together and her yelping and sighing. At that point he left for the half-deaf old woman's, where he had only a chest and a blanket to sleep on.

Now he felt that the gossip about his departure had circulated all over Krechetovka. Could Polina have heard it? What a disgrace if she had. . . .

These thoughts distracted him from his work. He picked up his indelible pencil and forced himself to study the route schedule. In his clear round handwriting, he again began to copy the numbers of convoys and cargoes from one sheet to another, at the same time making a carbon copy of the new routes. He would have finished this job if there had not been a knotty point about the dividing up of a large convoy from Kamyshin. In such matters only the C.O. could decide. Zotov rang the outside line, took off the receiver, and listened. He rang again and waited a longer time. And then again, at great length. No reply meant the captain was not in his office. Perhaps he was resting at home after supper. He would be sure to come before the railroad employees went off duty, to hear the report.

Behind the door Podshebyakina would now and again ring the station dispatcher. Aunt Frossy came and went. Then the heavy tread of two pairs of boots was heard. There was a knock on the door, which was ajar, and someone demanded in sonorous tones: "Permission for us to enter!"

Without either waiting for or hearing the permission, they came in. The first, tall as a grenadier, lithe, and pink faced with cold, came right into the middle of the room and, clicking his heels, announced: "Chief of convoy escort number 9505 Sergeant Gaydukov! Thirty-eight cars, Pullman type, all present and correct, ready to proceed!"

He wore a new winter cap, a handsome long cape, officer's style, with a wide leather belt and a star-shaped buckle, and well-polished boots.

From behind him the second man—stockily built, with a face darkly tanned—came gingerly forward as if in fear of trespassing, not drawing too far away from the door. Almost reluctantly he lifted five fingers of one hand to his Budyonny type of cap with ear flaps lowered but not buttoned. He did not spring to attention, but slowly he said: "Chief of convoy escort 71–628 Lance Sergeant Dygin. Four sixteen-ton cars."

His soldier's cape, held by a narrow belt of coarse webbing, had one wing crumpled and one irreparably ripped as if it had been caught in a machine. His disgraceful boots had worn, broken fastenings. Sergeant Dygin's face, especially the eyebrows and jaws, was not unlike Chkalov's, not the brave young Chkalov who had recently been killed, but someone who had lived a long time and had had a few knocks.

"Excellent! Very pleased to see you!" said Zotov, rising.

Owing to his rank and the kind of work he did, he was not in the least obliged to rise and greet any sergeants who came in. But the fact was, he was always happy to see them, he set himself to do what had to be done with each as well as he could. The C.O.'s assistant had no subordinates, and it was only to those who came, whether for five minutes or forty-eight hours, that Zotov could demonstrate his responsibilities as an officer and his administrative skill.

"I know, I know, your itineraries have already come." He picked these up from his desk and looked them over. "And here 95–505, 71–280." Conscientiously, he raised his eyes to the two sergeants.

Their caps and capes were damp, but only slightly, as from a spatter of raindrops.

"Why, you're dry! Has the rain stopped, then?"

"Off and on," smiled the well-built Gaydukov, nodding, seeming to hold himself not so much at attention as at ease. "North wind's blowing up."

He was about nineteen, but he had that precocious look of valor which, like a sunburn, stays on a face that comes from the front.

(It was just that straight-from-the-front look on their faces that had made Zotov get up from his desk.)

The station commander's assistant had little business with this. In any case, talk of what was in the shipments was discouraged, as they might be convoying sealed cars loaded with nailed crates, unaware of what they were carrying. They did, however, have a great deal of business with the station command regarding their itineraries, and they settled in his office with a satisfied and also a dissatisfied look.

Gaydukov wanted to find out if the commander would turn out to be some creep of a rear-line rat and if he would take his time about surveying his convoy and shipments.

It was not that he had misgivings about the latter; he not only kept watch over it, he was even fond of it. It consisted of some hundreds of horses, thoroughbreds, dispatched under the care of a sensible guard, who had loaded sufficient quantities of compressed hay and oats onto the same convoy, foreseeing that there would be no supplies available along the route. Gaydukov had grown up in the country and had had a passion for horses since he was small; he would turn to them as to friends, freely and from no obligation helping the soldiers on duty to water, feed, and groom them. When he pulled back the door and climbed the hanging wire ladder, carrying the bat type lantern in his hand, all sixteen horses in the wagon stalls, chestnuts, roans, and grays, turned their long, intelligent muzzles toward him. Some rested their heads on their neighbors' backs and looked at him with their great, sad, unwavering eyes, twitching their ears with concern, as if asking not only for hay but also to be told what that crate was that creaked and jerked and why and where it was being carried. Gaydukov went from one to the other, edging past their warm buttocks, fondling their manes. When he had no soldiers with him, he stroked them until they snorted and spoke to them. It was a greater hardship for them to go to the front than for men: they needed the front like a wooden leg.

What Gaydukov now feared was that the commander (his deputy seemed to be the lenient sort, not suspicious) would take a look at his heated freight car. Though the soldiers in Gaydukov's convoy were for the most part new recruits, he himself had already served at the front and had been wounded the previous July near the Dnieper, kept two months in a hospital, where he'd worked in the stores, and then sent back to the front. Because of all this, he knew the regulations and how to get around them. These twenty men, no more than youths, were escorting the horses only in an auxiliary capacity, for, as soon as the cargo had been delivered, they would be taken back into some division or other. In a few days' time all that new equipment might very well be encrusted with the slimy clay of the trenches. Even to be in the trenches would be better than hiding behind small mounds of earth to protect head and shoulders against German mortar fire. German mortars had bothered Gaydukov more than anything else that summer. But now the idea was for them to spend these last days warmly, amicably, happily.

In their enormous half-car, two cast-iron stoves burned uninterruptedly, fed with large lumps of coal got from other convoys. Their convoy was let through quickly, they had never been held back anywhere, and besides, they managed to stop once every twenty-four hours to feed and water the horses, and once every three days they turned in their ration cards for food. Even when the train was going at full speed, people would beg to be taken aboard. Though the regulations strictly forbade civilians to ride in the same part of the train as the escort, Gaydukov and his helper (who had taken from him something of his 'I'll-fix-it' style) could not bear to see people standing frozen on the autumn roads and running madly up and down the rails. They did not take anyone who asked onto the train, but several they did not refuse. They took a knowing inspector aboard for a liter of liquor; another time, a red-haired old man for a quantity of cider. Some they took on in exchange for suet, others they took on for nothing, but especially they could not bear to refuse—they would reach down their arms to them—young women, young girls, all going somewhere for some reason or other. Now, in the warmth of the noisy half-car, the red-haired old man was mumbling something about World War I, and how there was no reason why he shouldn't have been given the Cross of St. George, while only one of the girls, that Touch-me-not, was sitting by the stove, ruffling her feathers like an owl. The others had taken off their coats long before because of the heat, then their padded jackets, and even their blouses. One of them now sat in nothing but a red under-shirt—as a matter of fact, she herself was red in the face as well—and was washing the boys' shirts; as one of them helped her wring out the linen, she struck at him with a wet, twisted shirt when he tried to sneak up too close to her. There were two doing the boys' cooking, oiling the dry army rations with home-made lard. Yet another was mending the boys' clothes. As soon as they left the station they would have supper and sit round the stove, singing to the rough lurching of the car as it sped along, and then, without much sorting out as to who would keep watch and who would sleep (they would all have to water the horses, anyway), they would stretch out on planks of unplaned wood and get what sleep they could. Neither the young married women they had on board today, who, like those they had had the day before, had just seen their husbands off to war, nor the girls would stay up but would lie in the shadows out of the lantern light in the soldiers' arms.

Anyhow, who wouldn't pity the soldier on his way to the front? These might well be the last days of his life.

What Gaydukov really wanted from the commander of this station was permission to leave as quickly as possible. But he needed to work out the itinerary, so as to find out where to set down his passengers and where he was going himself—what sector would he be fighting in now? Would he pass by his home on the way?

"A-all right, then!" said the lieutenant, scrutinizing the itineraries. "Weren't you moved along together? Didn't they hook you together only a while back?"

"Yes, a few stations back."

Fixing his spectacled eyes on the paper, the lieutenant thrust his lips out. "And why did they send you here?" he asked the wizened version of Chkalov. "Were you at Penza?"

"Yes, we were," answered Dygin hoarsely.

"So why the devil did they send you around Ryazhsk? You can't help wondering at the things they do, the crackpots."

"So do we go on together from here?" asked Gaydukov. (On the way here he had got Dygin to tell him what his destination was; now he wanted to find out his own.)

"Yes, as far as Gryazi."

"And after that?"

"That's for the army to know," Zotov replied, pleasantly emphasizing his vowels. He turned and, peering through his glasses, looked the tall sergeant over from head to foot.

"Well, anyway, we go through Kastornaya, don't we?" fished Gaydukov, leaning toward the lieutenant.

"You probably go that way," Zotov would have liked to reply, but he allowed his lips only a faint smile, so that Gaydukov understood that they would be going through Kastornaya.

"Do we leave as soon as it gets dark?"

"Yes. No reason to keep you here."

"Well . . . *I'm* not going," said Dygin through clenched teeth, his manner assertive and hostile.

"Just *you*? Do you feel all right?"

"None of our escort can go."

"What are you driving at? I mean . . . I don't understand you. Why can't you?"

"Because we're not just dogs!" said Dygin, as if dredging up the words out of his chest; his eyeballs rolled madly under their lids.

"Think what you're saying!" said Zotov, frowning and drawing himself up. "Be more careful, Lance Sergeant!"

Just at that moment he noticed that one of the green triangles of the lance sergeant's insignia, which should have been firmly pressed into the storm collar of Dygin's cape, was hanging by one hook, while there was none at all on the other side, but only a triangular patch with a hole in the middle. The lowered earflaps of his Budyonny-type of cap hung burdocklike onto his chest.

Dygin stared malevolently from under his cap: "Because we . . ." he said in the hoarse voice of someone who has caught cold. "It's the eleventh day—we haven't had anything to eat. . . ."

"What?" said the lieutenant, starting back; his spectacles fell off one ear, he caught them and hooked them back on again. "Not possible!"

"That's what I said. It just happened like that."

"Haven't you any ration cards?"

"We couldn't eat them, could we?"

"But how is it you're alive?"

"Because we're alive, that's all."

"How is it you're alive!" the empty speciousness of this
spectacled man's question brought Dygin's rage to boiling
point: he saw there would be no help for him at Krechetovka.
"How is it you're alive!" Not because of something in himself
but out of hunger and exasperation, his jaw tightened and his
hollow eyes pierced the pale assistant to the station commander
in his warm, clean room. A week before they had ferreted out
some beetroots at a station along the way—they managed to
salvage two sackfuls out of a heap of refuse. For a whole week
all they could manage was to boil the beetroots in their mess
cans, boil them and eat them. Already they were beginning to
feel sick at the thought, their innards rejected them. Night
before last, the convoy having stopped at Aleksandro-Nevskoe,
Dygin took one look at his frostbitten soldiers—reservists, all
older than he, who himself was not young—made up his mind
and got to his feet. The wind swirled under the cars and whirled
through the cracked boards. Somehow or other he had to find
food for them, however little. Off he went into the darkness.
Returning an hour and a half later, he threw three loaves of
bread on the plank bed. One soldier sitting close by was
astounded: "Why, one of them's white!" "Is it?" said Dygin,
casting them an indifferent glance, "I hadn't noticed." But now
was not the time to tell this lieutenant about that. "How is it
you're alive?!" The four of them had been together for ten
days, going on and on, like men in the desert. Their load consisted of twenty thousand trenching spades, packed in factory
grease; it came from Gorky and was going to Tbilisi. This much
Dygin could guess from the stations they went through. But
every other shipment seemed to be more urgent than their own
damned load lying in its hardening grease. Even the lowest rank
of dispatcher seemed to be in a position to uncouple their four
cars and leave them in a siding at any old whistle stop. Their
ration cards had entitled them to take on supplies for three days
at Gorky and for three more days at Saransk, but from that time
on they had never been able to find a ration center open. Having stood this discomfort so far, they might even have been
ready to endure another five days of it, if they could be certain
that they would receive their whole supply for the last fifteen
days. But their bellies rumbled and their souls groaned at the
law that prevailed in all ration centers: no back-dated rations
issued. The days past were so much water over the dam.

"But why weren't you issued with rations?" wound up the
lieutenant.

"Well, what about you—you going to give us any?" said
Dygin, with tightened jaw.

He had been about to jump into the car—a soldier had told him that there was a ration center at this station. But it was already dark, and army food regulations made it pointless to batter on that window now.

Sergeant Gaydukov forgot the brisk manner he had used with the lieutenant and turned to Dygin. His long hand patted the other's shoulder. "Lit-tle bro-therr! Why didn't you tell me? We'd have let you have some right away!"

Dygin did not stir under the hand on his shoulder nor turn. He went on looking at the lieutenant with the same lifeless stare. He was disgusted with himself and his own clumsiness at the expense of his close comrades—for the entire eleven days they had not asked either civilians nor military for food, knowing there was none to spare in times like these. No one so much as demanded to look at their uncoupled, abandoned cars. They had no tobacco left. As the sides of the converted car were cracked, they had nailed three or four planks over the crevices, so that it was dark in there even during the day. And so, in utter despair, sitting through the long waits that might last one or two days, they would range themselves around the unglowing stove and try to boil beetroots in their mess cans, silently prodding them with their knives.

Gaydukov sprang to attention.

"Permission to leave, Comrade Lieutenant?"

"Granted."

And he bounded out, eager to give out grain and tobacco to the soldiers. They hadn't taken anything from that tearful old woman for letting her get on the train—so now it wouldn't hurt her to give something to the boys. That inspector would hand out something from his chest—he was obliged to.

"Well, it's now seven o'clock," mused the lieutenant. "The ration center's closed."

"They always are. Only open from ten till five. I was standing in line at Penza, and then they started shouting the echelon was moving. They went through Morshansk in the night. *And* Ryazhsk—in the night."

"Wait, wait a bit!" fussed the lieutenant. "I'm not going to leave things in this state." He lifted the receiver off the telephone and cranked repeatedly. No reply.

He cranked again, three times.

No reply.

"What the devil!" He cranked three times. "Is that you, Guskov?"

"Yes, Comrade Lieutenant."

"Why isn't there a man on the telephone over there?"

"He went out for a moment. I've got some soured milk here,

Comrade Lieutenant—shall I bring you some?"

"Rubbish—I don't need any."

(It wasn't because of Dygin that he said this. He constantly refused Guskov's offers to bring him this or that—on principle. Also in the interests of good order—otherwise, there would be no getting them to do any work. In fact, in his report to the captain, Zotov had gone so far as to state that Guskov was a slacker.)

"Guskov! Here's what's come up. There's a convoy arrived— four men—haven't had any rations for eleven days."

Guskov whistled at his end of the wire.

"What have they lived on—air?"

"It looks like it. We have to help them. Now listen, you've got to fetch Chichishev and Samorukov and have them issue these men with rations."

"Where am I to find them? No easy job."

"Where? In their billets, of course."

"There's mud up to your knees outside, and besides it's as dark as . . ."

"Chichishev lives near here."

"And what about Samorukov? Other side of the tracks he lives. He won't go for love or money, Comrade Lieutenant."

"Chichishev will go."

Chichishev, the pay clerk, had been brought in from the army reserve and given a sergeant's stripes, though there was nothing of the army accountant about him, rather, he had the air of an ordinary payroll official, no longer young, called away from his regular employment. He could not even talk without doing accounts. He would ask, "What's the time? Five?" And count off five beads on his abacus. Or he would say musingly, "When a man's on his own"—click! one bead ran along the row—"his life's a burden. He has"—a second bead, click! after the first—"to marry." Chichishev was very hard in dealing with a line of soldiers shouting and thrusting their ration cards at him, their hands groping through the little open square in his window grid. He shouted back at them, pushed their hands away, and would even close the little square. But if he had actually to go out into the crowd or if the command forced a way through into his little room, he would sink his round head between his narrow shoulders, call the men "brother," and stamp their cards. Willing alacrity was the keynote of his behavior toward his superiors; he never dared refuse anyone with flashes on his collar. The ration center was not under the orders of the station command, but Chichishev would not refuse, Zotov told himself.

"Samorukov certainly won't go," Guskov repeated.

Samorukov also paid heed to his superiors but not to lieutenants, whom he looked on with contempt. A well-fed, well set-up fellow, he was only storekeeper and clerk at the ration center, but carried on as though he wore an officer's insignia. He arrived at the center each time with an air of considerable importance and always a quarter of an hour late, examined the seals, unlocked the padlocks, raised the grids and fastened them, doing all this with an expression of condescension on his apathetic, plump face. And whatever the number of Red Army men hurrying to get to their trains, singly or in their units, or hospital cases pressing up to the grids, abusing and struggling with one another in their efforts to get closer, Samorukov would calmly roll up his sleeves to the elbows, revealing the plump arms of a pork butcher, and with an air of finding fault, examine Chichishev's stamp on the torn and crumpled cards. Then, just as calmly, he would weigh out the rations (he was known to cheat over the weight), without caring in the least whether the men would have time to get back to their trains or not. He had picked out his remote billet on purpose so as not to be disturbed when off duty, selecting a peasant's holding with a vegetable garden and a cow.

At the thought of Samorukov something rose in Zotov's gullet. He looked with the same detestation on such persons as he did on Fascists, for they constituted no less of a threat. He did not understand why Stalin did not issue an order to have Samorukov and his kind shot on the spot, outside the ration center, in full view of the people.

No, Samorukov won't go, Zotov agreed in thought. And because he stood both in anger and in fear before him, Zotov would never have given an order that affected him, had not these unoffending men been without food for no more than three or five days. But—eleven!

"Here's what you do, Guskov, don't send an enlisted man, go yourself. And don't say anything about four starving men, say it's an urgent call from the captain and I passed it on, understand? And I'll settle with him!"

Guskov did not speak.

"Well, let's hear from you! You've had your orders, say 'Heard and understood!' and off you go."

"But did you ask the captain?"

"What's that to you? I'll take the responsibility. The captain's out, can't reach him now."

"The captain'd never give an order like that," reasoned Guskov. "There isn't any regulation about breaking the seals at night, and all for two crumbs of bread and three herrings."

This was true.

"And what's the hurry?" mused Guskov. "They can wait till
ten tomorrow morning. It's only one night. They can sleep on
their bellies, keep their backs warm."

"But their echelon's leaving now. It's an express—uncoup-
ling them would be an awful pity. It's not their fault they got
into this mess. Their shipment's expected, needed up the line."

"But if their echelon's leaving now, Samorukov wouldn't
have time to get here, anyway. It would take an hour and a
half, at least, to get here through the mud, even with a lantern.
Two hours."

Guskov certainly had a reasonable way of putting things.

Still with his jaws clenched, in his Budyonny-type of cap with
its lowered earflaps, tanned almost black by the sun, Dygin
stood staring at the receiver so as not to lose what was being
said at the other end.

"Another day lost," he said dazedly, shaking his head.

Zotov sighed and put his finger down on the buzzer so that
Guskov should not hear.

"What can we do about it, brother? There's nothing more to
be done about it today. You could go on to Gryazi with this
echelon—it's a good one, you'll be there by morning."

He might have persuaded him, had not Dygin already sensed
the weakness in this lieutenant.

"I won't go. Arrest me. I won't go."

Someone rapped on the glass of the door. A well-built
civilian was standing there in a wide, woolen cap with dark gray
speckles. His polite salute seemed to ask for permission to come
in, but no one paid any heed.

"Well, come in then!" called Zotov, holding down the buzzer. "(All right, Guskov, you can hang up, I'll think about it.)"

The man outside the door had not understood Zotov; he now
opened the door a little and again asked:

"May I come in?"

Zotov was astonished at his voice—a rich, noble, but modest
bass. He was dressed in a heavy rust-colored, nonmilitary
jacket, with long front flaps and shortened sleeves, and on his
feet were Red Army snow boots, bound with puttees. In one
hand he held a grease-stained Red Army duffel bag of middling
size. With the other hand he lifted his ponderous cap as he
entered and greeted them.

"Good evening."

"Evening."

"Will you be so good as to tell me," the newcomer very
politely asked, bearing himself with confidence as if he were
not strangely but altogether correctly dressed, "who is in
command here?"

"The deputy commander on duty. Myself."

"Then it's probably you I have to see."

He looked for a place to put down his speckled cap—it also seemed to have coal smuts all over it; finding none, he held it pressed under the elbow of the other arm; with the hand thus freed he began unfastening his cloth collar, an absent look in his eye. His collar entirely lacked a backing, or more precisely, it had been torn away, and a woolen muffler encircled the bare neck beneath. Having unbuttoned the collar, he then uncovered the inner layers, revealing a Red Army summer uniform, faded and stained, and set about unfastening his tunic pocket.

"Wait a moment, wait a moment," said Zotov, turning his back on him. "Now, here's what." Blinking, he now addressed the surly Dygin, who stood rooted to the spot. "Here's what it's in my power to do: I can have you uncoupled now. At ten tomorrow you'll be issued with rations."

"Thank you," said Dygin, tears blurring his eyes.

"Don't thank me, you may not like the arrangement. You're on a very good train for the moment. I don't know what else I've got to couple you to."

"We've been on the go for the last two weeks. Twenty-four hours more or less won't matter," said Dygin, life returning to him. "I know my shipment."

"No, no," said Zotov, raising his finger and shaking it at him. "Neither you nor I have the right to judge." He looked askance at the newcomer, drew nearer to Dygin and, in tones scarcely audible but retaining the carefully pronounced vowels, said: "As you already know what your shipment is, you should also know how many troops dig themselves in with those entrenching tools you're carrying. Two divisions. Digging trenches means saving lives. Twenty thousand trenching spades means twenty thousand Red Army men saved. Am I right?"

Again Zotov looked askance at the stranger, who, realizing that he was in the way, went over to the wall, turned his back and with his free hand, began closing—no, not closing but warming—his ears.

"What, you frozen?" said Zotov out loud, with a mocking smile. The other turned, and said amiably: "Just go out and you'll see how terribly cold it's got. There's a fierce wind blowing. *And* it's wet, to top it all!"

It was true: the wind was howling, rubbing itself against the corner of the building and drumming on the loose pane in the right-hand window behind the shade. And again the water was moaning as it gushed out of the drainpipe.

This strange, unshaven being had a very sweet, heart-melting
smile. He had not had his head shaved to the scalp; though
short and somewhat sparse, his graying, silver-shot hair fell
softly over his broad head.

There was an air about him that was neither civilian nor
military.

"Here," he was holding a scrap of paper with writing on it,
"here's my. . . . "

"Rightaway, rightaway!" Zotov took the paper without looking at it. "And—sit down, you can sit there, on that chair. . . ."
Throwing another glance at the other's ludicrous jacket, he
turned to the table, picked up a list of cyphers and the checklist, locked them in his strongbox, nodded at Dygin, and took
him off to see the military dispatcher.

She was explaining something over the telephone, and Aunt
Frossy was crouching over the stove, drying herself off. Zotov
went to Podshebyakina and gripped her hand—the hand holding the receiver.

"Valyusha . . . ."

The young woman turned vivaciously and looked at him with
delighted surprise—she thought his taking hold of her hand
meant that he was making advances; but she went on with her
telephone call.

"Number one thousand two's going through now, it's not one
of ours. Take it on to Tambov station, Petrovich."

"Valyusha! Send Aunt Frossy right away and have her either
write in those four cars or tell the couplers direct which they
are—this lance sergeant will go with her—and have the dispatcher uncouple them and run them on to a siding till tomorrow."

Still in her crouching position, Aunt Frossy turned her large
severe face to the lieutenant and moved her lips.

"Very well, Vasily Vasilich," said Valya, smiling. Although
there was no need, she kept hold of the receiver for as long as
he did not withdraw his hand. "I'll send her at once."

"And have the four cars sent out with the first locomotive
available. Do the best you can."

"Very good, Vasily Vasilich," said Valya, a smile of joy on
her face.

"That's all!" the lieutenant told Dygin.

Aunt Frossy blew out her breath like a bellows and, groaning,
got to her feet.

Without a word Dygin lifted his hand to his brow and held
it there. With his ears protruding under the flaps of his cap,
there was nothing very martial about him.

"Just drafted? Inducted from the workers' reserve, right?"

"Right. . . ." Dygin was gazing at the lieutenant with gratitude in his eyes.

"Fix those triangles," said Zotov, pointing at his empty collar.

"Haven't any. They fell off and broke."

"And either button down your earflaps or roll them up, understand?"

"Where's he to roll them to?" Aunt Frossy, now wearing her raincoat, showed her teeth. "Roll up that trashy stuff! Come on, my lad!"

"That's right, off you go now! Tomorrow another lieutenant'll be here, be sure he puts you on your way."

Zotov went back into his office. Four months earlier he himself had not known how to tie the flaps, and raising the hand to return a salute had seemed to him quite laughable and absurd.

As Zotov came in, the stranger did not completely rise off his chair, but made a movement intimating that he would readily get to his feet if need be. His small bag now lay on the floor, under his speckled cap.

"Don't get up, don't get up!" Zotov sat down at the table. "Now, what's all this?"

He unfolded the paper.

"I . . . got left by the train. . . ." The other smiled guiltily.

Zotov read down the paper—a list of stragglers from the military commander at Ryazhsk—and, looking at the stranger, began to ask him the usual official questions:

"Your family name?"

"Tveritinov."

"And your given name and patronymic?"

"Igor Dementyevich."

"Are you over fifty?"

"No, forty-nine."

"What was your echelon number?"

"I've no idea."

"What, didn't they tell you the number?"

"No, they didn't."

"Well, what's it written down here for? Did you make it up?"

(It was No. 245412, the echelon from Archedinsk that Zotov had checked out the night before.)

"No. I told them at Ryazhsk where it had come from and when, so probably the commander guessed it."

"Where were you left behind?"

"At Skopino."

"How did it happen?"

"Well, to be quite frank," the same deprecating smile touched Tveritinov's large mouth, "I went . . . to trade some things. . . .

for food . . . and the train pulled out. There's no loudspeaker or bell or whistle these days, they just leave without any noise at all."

"When was this?"

"Day before yesterday."

"And there wasn't any chance of your running and catching it?"

"There didn't seem to be. I mean, how could I have? It was raining on the platform and the wind was blowing terribly hard and you had to go up one of those little ladders to get into the car—anyway, they don't let you into the sealed cars, they tell you you haven't the right or there's no more room in there. At one time I saw a passenger train, what a sight, conductors standing in pairs on the steps and—you know—fighting off the people as soon as they tried to hang onto the bars. Once the freight trains have pulled out, it's too late to get a seat, and when they uncouple the locomotive, you haven't any idea what direction they'll take next. They haven't got any sort of board on the side with words painted on it like 'Mineral Water—Moscow.' You can't ask any questions, or you're taken for a spy, and then I'm improperly dressed, too. . . . But it's risky for any of us to ask questions, in any case."

"Well, naturally, in war time."

"And even before the war."

"I didn't notice."

"It was." Tveritinov's eyes were almost slits. "After 1937."

"What's 1937?" asked Zotov, astonished. "And what happened in 1937? The Spanish Civil War?"

"Oh no." Again the guilty smile and lowered eyelids.

His muffler had come adrift from his collar, the ends flapped about his belt.

"Well, why aren't you in a proper uniform? Where's your army cape?"

"I've never been able to get one. They never issued me any," Tveritinov smiled.

"But where did you get that outfit?"

"Some good-hearted people gave it to me."

"We-ell, all right," said Zotov hesitantly. "But I must say you got here quickly enough. Only yesterday morning you were with the C.O. at Ryazhsk and this evening you're already here. How did you manage it?"

With his large, soft, trusting eyes Tveritinov looked right into Zotov's face. His way of speaking was exceptionally agreeable to Zotov's ear; his trick of hesitating if he thought that his interlocutor was about to reply, his trick of refraining from gestures but carrying his words forward with unobtrusive movements of his fingers.

"I had a most uncommon stroke of luck. I was just getting off a half-car somewhere along the line. These last couple of days I've grown very familiar with railroad terms. 'Half-car'— I thought that must be a sort of car with half a roof, or something. I had climbed up a little stepladder, but when I looked inside there was a kind of ravine with spikes on the sides and nowhere to sit or lean against. There had been coal in it and there were great clouds of dust blowing up and around as it went along. I stood it as long as I could. It was raining as well."

"In that case, what was your stroke of luck?" Zotov burst out laughing. "I don't see it. So that's how you got so filthy!"

As he laughed, the sides of his mouth were furrowed by two long laughter lines that rose to his snub nose.

"It came when I'd just got off the half-car and was brushing off the dust and washing. I saw them coupling a southbound locomotive onto a train. I ran all along the train, but there wasn't one heated car, and all the doors were sealed. Then I suddenly saw a messmate of mine come out and obey the call of nature and get back onto a cold open car. With me behind him. And there—what do you think?—was a car loaded with cotton-wool blankets."

"And not sealed?"

"No! Because, you see, the covers had been all tied up at first in packages of five or ten, but then a lot of packages had come undone and you could just sink down into them. And there were some people already sleeping there."

"Ay-ay-ay!"

"I wrapped myself up in two or three comforters and I had such a good, sweet sleep—I must have slept the clock round. Were we still going or had we stopped? I didn't know! And besides, it was the third day I hadn't been issued with rations— so I slept and slept and forgot the whole war, the whole jamboree. I was even dreaming of my family."

His unshaven, crumpled face lit up.

"Hold on!" Zotov started out of his chair. "That was the train you came in with—how long ago?"

"Only a few minutes—how many? I came to see you at once."

Zotov hurled himself at the door, jerked it open, and leaped out:

"Valya! Valya! That train that stopped here on the way to Balashov, number one thousand and—what was it?"

"One thousand two."

"Is it still here?"

"It's left."

"Sure?"

"Certain."

"Oh, hell!" He clutched his head. "We sit here like a damned
lot of bureaucrats trading papers, not seeing past the ends of
our noses—we're not worth our salt. Look, get me Michurinsk-
Uralsky on the line."

He hurried back into his room and asked Tveritinov: "You
don't happen to remember the number of the car?"

"No," said Tveritinov, smiling.

"Was it a two- or a four-wheeler?"

"I don't follow you."

"How is it you don't? Was it small or large? How many tons?"

"As they used to say in the Civil War, 'forty men, eight
horses.'"

"That sounds like sixteen tons. And no escort?"

"There didn't seem to be."

"Vasily Vasilich!" called Valya. "The military dispatcher's on
the line. D'you want to speak to the C.O.?"

"Well, maybe not the C.O., it might not be a military shipment."

"Then will you let me explain to them?"

"Yes, please do, Valichka. Those blankets may have merely
been evacuee supplies, I don't know. They should check carefully till they find that car and see if they can make out who put
it on—and tell them to seal it—they know what to do, anyhow."

"Right, Vasily Vasilich!"

"And thanks, Valichka. You're an invaluable worker."

Valya smiled at him, the curls falling over her forehead.

"Hallo? Michurinsk-Uralsky?"

Zotov closed the door and, still much disturbed, crossed the
room, striking the back of one hand against the other.

"There's so much work you can't begin to deal with it all,"
he said, again giving particular stress to his vowels. "And they
never give you an assistant. Those blankets could be stolen, or
something. There're probably a number missing already."

He took a few more strides, then sat down. He removed his
spectacles to clean them with a scrap of cloth. At once his face
lost its air of consequence and ready common sense and
became childlike, its openness protected only by the green cap.

Tveritinov waited patiently. His eyes ran sadly over the shades,
the colored portrait of Kagonovich in his railroad man's uniform, the stove, coal bucket and shovel. In this heated office,
Tveritinov's soot-marked cloth collar began to constrict him. He
threw it open to the shoulder and took off his scarf. The lieutenant put his glasses back on and again glanced over the list
of stragglers. In point of fact, the list was not a properly drawn-
up document. It consisted of the soldier's own testimony, which
might well be the truth but might also be a lie. Regulations
demanded that extreme caution be exercised in the matter of

stragglers, even more so when they came in on their own. Tveritinov could not prove that he had stayed behind at Skopino only. Could he have stayed behind at Pavelets, too? And used this time to have gone on a special mission to Moscow or somewhere?

On the other hand, it was true he had lost no time in getting here.

Yet what proof was there that he had come off precisely that train?

"So you were nice and warm on your journey?"

"I was indeed. I wouldn't have minded going on with the same train."

"Why did you get off, then?"

"To report to you. That's what I was ordered to do at Ryazhsk."

All the features of Tveritinov's large head were well defined: a high, wide forehead, thick, heavy eyebrows, and a big nose. His chin and cheeks were covered with a gray stubble.

"How did you find out this was Krechetovka?"

"There was a Georgian next to me—he told me."

"A soldier? What rank?"

"I don't know. He only raised his head from the blankets."

Tveritinov's answers had taken on a note of regret, as if each reply cost him a little more.

"So that's how it was." Zotov laid aside the list of stragglers. "What other papers have you?"

"Well, none at all, really," answered Tveritinov with a sad smile. "Where was I to get any?"

"You mean . . . not one?"

"When we were surrounded, we destroyed all our papers on purpose."

"But when you got back across the Soviet lines, shouldn't they have given you some sort of identity card to keep with you?"

"No, nothing. They made a list of our names, divided us up into groups of forty, and sent us on our way."

Of course, that must be it. As long as he did not lag behind, he was a member of a group of forty and so had no need of papers.

In spite of being involuntarily drawn to this cultured man with his fine head, Zotov must still have some material proof of his story.

"But you must have kept something! Some paper or other in your pockets?"

"Well, only some photographs. Seven of them."

"Let me see them." The lieutenant was not ordering but pleading with him.

Tveritinov's eyebrows rose a little. Again he smiled that indescribably lost smile and from the same pocket of his tunic (the other could not be fastened as it was buttonless) he took out a flat

packet of thick paper in an orange wrapper. Laying it on his
knee, he unfolded it and disclosed two photographs, roughly
four inches by five. He looked at them, one after the other, and
then got up to hand them to the lieutenant—but it was not far
from his chair to the table, and so Zotov leant forward and took
them. He looked at them while Tveritinov still kept the unfolded
wrapper on his knee, craning his neck and trying to see them
too from where he was sitting.

One of the photographs—taken in a sunny garden, almost
certainly in early spring, for the leaves were not properly open and
you could see through the foliage of the trees—showed a young
girl of about fourteen in a gray striped dress caught in at the waist.
Her long thin neck rose from her open collar, and her face was thin
and drawn—although unmoving for this photograph, it still had an
air of being caught in a startled moment. There was something
immature, unfinished about the photograph so that its effect was
not of gaiety but of melancholy.

Zotov liked the look of the young girl. His lips relaxed into a
smile. "What's her name?" he asked softly.

Tveritinov was sitting with his eyes closed. "Lyalya," he
answered in an even quieter voice.

Then he opened his eyes and said, "Irene."

"When was this taken?"

"This year."

"Where?"

"Near Moscow."

Half a year—six months—had passed since that moment
when he had called, "Lyalinka! Don't move!" and clicked the
shutter, but since then tens of thousands of artillery cannon had
thundered, and millions of black fountains had ripped out of
the earth, and millions of men had turned in a hellish kind of
carousel, some on foot to Lithuania and some by train to
Irkutsk. And now at this station, where a cold wind had frozen
rain and snow alike, where trains stood motionless, where
people went on crowding without respite by day and sleeping
on rows of blackened boards at night—how could anyone
believe that anywhere in the world the little garden, the young
girl, the striped dress, could still exist?

In the other photograph a woman and a little boy were sitting
on a sofa looking at a big book with pictures entirely filling the
page. The mother was thin, too, and drawn, she was almost
certainly tall, and the little boy, who must be about seven, had
a well-formed little face with an intelligent, a very intelligent
expression, turned not on the book but on his mother, who
was explaining something to him. His eyes were as large as
his father's.

The whole family were people of cultured background, it was plain. Zotov had never frequented such people but the slight impressions gleaned from the Tretyakov Gallery, the theater, and his own reading had enabled him to conceive of the existence of such families. From those two photographs alone Zotov could sense their atmosphere of intelligent intimacy. As he handed the photographs back, he observed: "You're feeling the heat in here. Take off your jacket."

"Yes, I am," agreed Tveritinov, and took off his cloth jacket. He found himself at a loss where to put it.

"Put it on the bench," Zotov advised him, and even made a gesture as if to put it there himself.

Now the medley of patches, rents, and ill-matched buttons that made up Tveritinov's summer uniform was revealed as well as his unsure touch with his puttees, their free ends sliding out and hanging loose. His entire dress seemed to make a mockery of his large graying head.

Zotov could not restrain his liking for this self-possessed man, he had had this liking from the outset.

"What is it you do, if I may ask?" he inquired respectfully.

Wistfully folding the photographs inside their orange wrapping, Tveritinov replied with a smile: "Actor."

"Not really?" Zotov was surprised. "Why didn't I realize it at once? You look like one, very much so."

(Anything less like one at the present moment. . . !)

"I'm sure you must be famous?"

"No."

"What places have you played in?"

"At the Drama Theater in Moscow."

"I've only gone once in Moscow to the Moscow Art Theater, when we went on an excursion. But at Ivanov now, I went quite often to the theater there. Have you seen the new theater at Ivanov?"

"No."

"From the outside it isn't much, like a gray box made of reinforced concrete, but the inside is really something! I certainly like going to the theater, it's not only an amusement, it's an education, too, don't you think?"

(It was true that there was still work to be done on the papers dealing with the burnt-out train, but in any event this would take two full days. It was gratifying to meet a great actor and spend a few minutes talking with him!)

"What parts have you played?"

"A good many," Tveritinov smiled a joyless smile. "You lose count after so many years."

"Yes, but at least, give us an example?"

"Well, Lieutenant Colonel Vershinin, Doctor Rank. . . ."

"Hm-m . . ." (Zotov did not recall what plays these were in.)

"Were you in any of Gorky's plays?"

"Oh yes, of course."

"I like Gorky's plays better than anything. I like Gorky in
general. He's our most intelligent writer, he's the most humane,
the greatest, wouldn't you agree?"

Tveritinov knit his brows in an effort to reply but found none
to make and so remained silent.

"I'm sure I know your name. Aren't you famous?"

Zotov was flushed with pleasure at his conversation.

"If I were famous," Tveritinov sketched a hand-spreading
gesture, "I wouldn't be here."

"How's that? Oh, yes, you wouldn't have been mobilized."

"We weren't mobilized. We went as volunteers— in the
National Guard. We enlisted."

"But then the famous ones would have enlisted as well?"

"Everybody enlisted, from the best-known directors down.
But after a bit someone drew a line: those above the line stayed
and those below it went off to war."

"Did you get any army training?"

"A few days of it. Bayonet assaults. We used walking sticks.
And throwing grenades. Wooden ones."

Tveritinov's eyes were fixed on the floor so intently that they
seemed turned to glass.

"Yes, but after that they must have issued you with rifles?"

"Yes, when we were already on the move they did hand out a
few, dated from 1891. We went on foot to Vyazma. And when
we got there, we found ourselves in the thick of it all."

"Many killed?"

"I think so, but more were taken prisoner. A few of us joined
up with some stragglers and they got us out. Now I find I can't
figure out where the front was. Have you a map?"

"No, I haven't, and the news bulletins are far from clear,
but I can tell you this: Sebastopol and a bit more is in our hands,
and Taganrog, and we're holding the Don basin. But they've
taken Orel and Kursk."

"Oy-oy-oy! And what about the Moscow sector?"

"Well, there's quite some confusion about the Moscow
sector. The location reports are already talking about the
suburbs. And Leningrad's cut off, anyhow."

Zotov's brow and eye sockets had melded into a single line
of suffering.

"And I can't even get near the front!"

"You've still time."

"Not if the war only lasts a year."

"Were you a student?"

"I was! As a matter of fact we were defending our theses just
as the war began ... 'defending,' what a word! ... We had to be
ready by December. They told us to bring whatever we had in
the way of plans, estimates, and go ahead." Zotov felt himself
committed, his tongue loosened, carried away by an urge to tell
everything at once. "The whole thing had taken five years. We
started at the Institute during Franco's rebellion! Then Austria
capitulated, and Czechoslovakia. ... Then World War II broke
out. Then war with Finland! Hitler invaded France, and Greece,
Yugoslavia. ... How could we concentrate on textile machines?
But it wasn't so much that as, after the thesis, they started sending students off for courses at the School of Motor and Mechanical Engineering, and I was kept back because of my eyes—I'm
very nearsighted. Well, I went and pestered them every single
day at the Recruiting Office. I'd accrued five years' useful
experience since 1937 ... and all I could get out of them was,
they sent me off to the Quartermasters' School. So!—on my
way there I went through Moscow and managed to get inside
the People's Commissariat. I got to see an old colonel. He was
in a terrible hurry, already strapping up his briefcase. Anyhow,
I was an engineer, I didn't want to be a quartermaster. 'Show
me your diploma!' But I didn't have it with me. 'All right, I'll ask
you one question; if you can answer it, it'll mean you're an
engineer: what's a crankshaft?' So, as we walked along, I recited: 'It's a shaft attached to a rotating axis which is itself joined
at right angles.' He crossed out 'Quartermaster' and wrote in
'School of Transport.' And then he rushed off with his briefcase. I was happy as a dog with two tails! But when I got to
the School of Transport, there was no recruitment, only
courses for commanders. So the crankshaft had been no good
to me, either!"

Vasya knew that this was no time for talking over things past,
but the opportunity occurred so rarely for pouring out his heart
to an intelligent, attentive listener.

"You smoke, don't you?" Vasya recalled. "Please go ahead
and smoke." (He squinted at the list of stragglers.) "Igor
Dementyevich. Here's some tobacco and cigaret papers; they
issue these, but I don't smoke."

He took a package, barely opened, of light tobacco from his
drawer and handed it to Igor Dementyevich.

"I do smoke," admitted Igor Dementyevich, and his face lit
up with anticipation. He got up to take the package but, before
rolling the cigaret, stood there simply smelling the tobacco; he
gave a faint moan of pleasure. Then he read the label on the
package and nodded: "Armenian," he said.

He rolled himself a fat cigaret, moistened and sealed it with his lips, and Vasya struck a match for him.

"What about those cotton-wool blankets—anybody smoking there?" asked Zotov.

"I didn't notice," answered Igor Dementyevich, leaning back in pure bliss. "Shouldn't think anyone had any."

He drew on the cigaret, eyes narrowed against the smoke.

"You remember what had been going on those years?" Eagerly Vasya began talking again. "The Spanish Civil War. The Fascists were holding the university towns. And the International Brigade—remember Guadalajara, Jarama, Teruel? Could we get in to help? We demanded instruction in Spanish—but they taught us German instead. I got hold of a grammar and a dictionary, I simply neglected my tests and exams and studied Spanish. I felt that the whole situation was such that we must join in, as good revolutionaries we couldn't just stand by and watch. But there was nothing about it in the newspapers. How could I get there? Of course, you could simply go to Odessa and get on a boat—but this would be considered childish, and there were the frontier guards besides. And there was I, running to the heads of the recruiting centers, from the fourth to the third, to the second, to the first divisions: 'Send me to Spain!' They laughed at me: 'What are you, crazy? None of our people are there, what would you do if you went?' (You know, I can see how much you like to smoke, so please take the whole package. I only keep them to offer around. And I've got more at home. No, please put them in your bag, now fasten it, then I'll believe they're in. Now, tobacco—it's like a railroad pass, it'll be useful to you on the journey.) And suddenly, you see, I read in the *Red Star*—I read all the papers from cover to cover—where it quoted a French journalist, and one of the things he said was, 'Germany and the U.S.S.R. look on Spain as an out-and-out testing ground.' I got a copy of the issue at the library, waited another three days to see if the editors would refute it. They didn't. So I went to the head of the recruiting center himself and said, 'Here, read this. There's been no refutation, that means that we must be fighting there. So I'm begging you to send me to Spain, even as a simple rifleman.' At that the head of the recruiting center actually thumped the table. 'Don't you tell me what to do! Who sent you here? We'll have him up before the Board. Dismissed!'"

Vasya burst out laughing as he recalled this. Again the laughter lines drew themselves on his face. He had begun to feel very much at ease with this actor and wanted to tell him more, about how some Spanish sailors had come into port and how he had answered them in Spanish, and to ask him what it

was like to be surrounded, and talk generally of the progress of
the war with this cultured, intelligent man.

But Podshebyakina half-opened the door.

"Vasily Vasilich! The dispatcher's asking if you've anything
else for the 794? Otherwise, we'll clear it."

Zotov looked at his schedule: "Which one is that? The one
for Povorino?"

"Yes."

"It's already here?"

"In ten minutes it will be."

"We have a few shipments of our own for it. What others
are there?"

"There are some industrial shipments and a few converted
cars for passengers."

"Oh good, splendid! Igor Dementyevich, I'll get you a seat
on this one. It's an excellent train for you, you won't even have
to get off. No, Valichka, all my shipments go onto that one. Run
them onto the siding. But have them bring it in closer—on No.
1 or No. 2 Track, tell them."

"Very well, Vasily Vasilich."

"Did you pass on all that about the blankets?"

"Yes, all of it, just as you said, Vasily Vasilich."

She went out.

"I'm only sorry I haven't anything to give you to eat, there
isn't so much as a cracker in this drawer."

Zotov pulled the drawer out as if to prove to himself that
there was no cracker inside. But his ration had been as usual,
and the bread brought him when he came on duty he had eaten
during the morning. "Haven't you had anything to eat since you
got left behind?"

"Don't concern yourself about me, please, Vasily Vasilich."
Tveritinov placed his spread fingers on the bosom of his grimy
shirt with its ill-matched buttons. "You have warmed me,
literally and figuratively. You are a kind man. I particularly
appreciate it in these hard times. Now will you be so good as to
explain to me where I'm to go now and what I'm to do?"

Gratified, Zotov explained: "First, you'll be going to Gryazi
station. What a pity I haven't a map. Do you know where
that is?"

"Not really . . . I've heard of it, I think."

"It's a very well-known station! If you get to Gryazi during
the day, have your paper with you. I'm writing a note on it
about your being here with me—go to the army C.O. and
he'll give you an order on the Ration Center—you'll get two
days' rations."

"I'm very grateful to you."

"And if you get there at night, stay in your seat, don't get
off, hang on to that train. Suppose you'd stayed tucked up in
your covers and hadn't awakened, you'd have been marched
off! From Gryazi your train'll go to Povorino, but don't get
down there unless it's to go to the Ration Center—then
you'll go on as far as Archeda. At Archeda you'll be put on
train No. 245413."

With this, Zotov gave Tveritinov the paper with the stragglers'
names on it. Pushing the paper into his tunic pocket—the one
that still had a flap he could button—Tveritinov asked:

"Archeda? Never heard of that. Where is it?"

"You could say it was just outside Stalingrad."

"Outside Stalingrad," nodded Tveritinov. But his forehead
wrinkled. Half-absently, he made an effort and asked: "Pardon
me . . . Stalingrad . . . What was it called before?"

Then—all was in splinters, ice-cold, inside Zotov. How could
this be? A Soviet citizen who didn't know Stalingrad? No, it
was utterly impossible, utterly! Inconceivable!

But he was able to control himself. He got up. Adjusted his
spectacles. Almost calmly, he said: "It was called Tsaritsyn
before."

(That means he isn't a straggler! He's on a secret mission! An
agent! Probably a White Russian émigré, that's why he has
such fine manners.)

"Oh, of course. Tsaritsyn, of course. The siege of Tsaritsyn."

(Could he be an officer in disguise? Yes, that's why he asked
for a map. And then he had that irregular uniform on.)

That enemy word, "officer," which had long since disappeared from Russian speech, was like a bayonet stab to Zotov.

(What a foolish mistake he'd made! What a foolish mistake!
Now it was up to him to keep calm and proceed with extreme
caution. But what action should he take? What was he to do?)

Zotov pressed insistently on the field telephone buzzer. He
held the receiver to his ear, praying that the captain would pick
up the receiver at his end.

But the captain did not reply.

"I do feel rather ashamed, though, Vasily Vasilich, taking all
your tobacco like this."

"It's nothing. Don't mention it," answered Zotov.

"Well, anyway, if you'll allow me, I'll just have another. Or
would you like me to go outside?"

(Go outside? So that was it! He could see his scheme had gone
amiss and was trying to get away!)

"No, no, have your smoke here. I like the smell of it."

(Think up a plan—but what? What could he contrive?)

He pressed the telephone buzzer three times. Someone

picked up the receiver.

"Guardroom here."

"This is Zotov."

"I'm listening, Comrade Lieutenant."

"Where's Guskov?"

"He went out, Comrade Lieutenant."

"Where did he go? What's he mean by going out? See to it he's back at his post in five minutes."

(He was out after some woman, the no-good. . . .)

"Heard and understood! I'll see to it!"

(What was to be done now?)

Zotov took a sheet of paper and, placing it so that Tveritinov should not see, wrote in large letters: "Valya! Come into my office and say that No. 794 will be an hour late."

He folded the paper, went to the door and standing there with his hand held out toward her, said:

"Comrade Podshebyakina. Come and take this. It's about that shipment."

"Which one, Vasily Vasilich?"

"The number's written here."

Surprised, Podshebyakina got up and took the paper. Zotov went straight back into his office.

Tveritinov was already putting on his outer clothes. "We won't miss the train?" he said, good will in his smile.

"No, they'll call us."

Zotov walked across the room, not looking at Tveritinov. He straightened the folds of his field shirt under the back of his belt and switched the pistol hanging behind to his right side. Settled his cap on his head. There was absolutely nothing he could find to do or say.

And to dissemble was not in Zotov's nature.

If only Tveritinov would say something, but he maintained a discreet silence.

Outside the window the water's fitful murmur could be heard as it ran out of the pipe and spattered in the wind.

The lieutenant stopped by a corner of the table and studied his fingers.

(If the change in him was not to be apparent, he must face Tveritinov with the same look as before, but he could not bring himself to do this.)

"There'll be a holiday in a few days' time!" he said guardedly.

(Now ask, ask! "What holiday?" Then there'll be no doubt at all about it.)

But the visitor answered: "Ye-e-s."

The lieutenant threw a glance at him, but he went on nodding as he smoked. "It'd be worth finding out if there's to be a parade in Red Square."

(A *parade*! He wasn't thinking what he was saying, simply playing for time.)

There was a knock on the door.

"May I come in, Vasily Vasilich?" Valya put her head round the door. Seeing her, Tveritinov reached for his duffel bag.

"No. 794's been held up. It'll be coming in late."

"Oh, de-ar! What a shame!" (The jarringly false note in his voice was most hateful to him.) "Very well, Comrade Podshebyakina."

Valya withdrew.

Outside the window—quite close, on Track No. 1—the long-drawn-out exhaling of a locomotive was heard, dropping in pitch as it drew to a stop and the ground ceased to tremble.

"What should I do?" wondered Zotov out loud. "I must go to the Ration Center."

"I'll go out, too, I'll go wherever you wish, of course," said Tveritinov willingly, smiling and rising to his feet, the duffel bag already in his arms.

Zotov took down his cape.

"Why should you freeze out there? You couldn't get into the waiting room, the floor's covered with sleeping people. Don't you want to come with me to the Ration Center?"

This sounded rather more convincing and, conscious of turning red, he added: "Maybe . . . I'll . . . find a way of getting you something to eat . . . there."

No doubt at all that Tveritinov was pleased at that! He said, beaming with joy: "That would be the height of goodness on your part. I didn't dare ask you."

Zotov turned his back and cast his eye over his desk, made sure of the lock on the safe, put out the light. "Well, let's go!"

Closing the door, he said to Valya: "If the telegraph office wants me, I'll soon be back."

In his incongruous jacket and loosely flapping puttees, Tveritinov went out in front of him.

They walked along a small dark corridor lit by a little blue lantern and out onto the platform. Through the blackness of the night with its indistinguishable sky, there fell an eddy of heavy wet flakes, far from white and made of neither rain nor snow.

Right on Track No. 1 stood the train. It was very black, rather blacker than the sky, so that you had to guess at the outlines of its roofs and cars. On the left where the locomotive was, clusters of red-hot cinders falling in bursts of flame spread over the rails and were quickly borne away to the side. Further on and higher up, a solitary round green light seemed to hang from nowhere. On the right somewhere toward the rear of the train, sparkling jets of fire flashed in and out under the cars. Beside these live sparks, shadowy figures—for the most part old women—hastened along the platform; their breath came labored because of the shapeless, overwhelming loads they bore. Children, some tearful, some silent, dragged along behind them. Two persons bumped into Zotov as they puffed on, carrying an enormous trunk between them. Behind them, another came along the platform, teeth grinding, pulling a two-wheeled cart loaded with an object heavier still. (It was precisely at this time—when traveling was sheer torture—precisely now, that everyone brought their children, their grand-mothers, with them, struggling with baggage they could not even lift, baskets the size of daybeds, and trunks as big as linen closets.)

If there had been no cinders flying under the locomotive, no signals, no sparks from the stacks of converted cars, and no muted lights flashing like fireflies along distant tracks, it would have been hard to believe that there were numerous transport echelons standing cheek-by-jowl here, and that this was a station, not some dense forest or level plain going through those leisurely annual changes that are a gentle preparation for winter.

But the ear could hear the clank of chains, the switchman's whistle, the panting of the two locomotives, the tread and turmoil of fretting passengers.

"Here we are!" cried Zotov, reaching the narrow passage-way that ran beside the platform.

He had a small lantern with honeycombed glass, which he held so as to throw light on his feet and show Tveritinov the way.

"Oh! I nearly got my cap blown off!" complained Tveritinov.

The lieutenant walked on in silence.

"Snow it may be, but something's slipping under my collar," he added. He didn't even have a collar.

"There'll be some mud here," warned the lieutenant.

And they walked into the most slushy, smacking mud imaginable. Not a dry spot that foot could find.

"Halt! Who goes there?" came a sentry's deafening shout from close by.

Tveritinov quivered violently.

"Lieutenant Zotov!"

In mud up to their ankles and, where it was thickest, pulling their feet out with difficulty, they went around a wing of the ration center and up on the landing at the other side. Vigorous-ly they stamped their feet and brushed the wet snow from their shoulders. Lighting the ins and outs with his lantern, the

lieutenant took Tveritinov into a general room with a bare
table flanked by two benches (here the army personnel at the
ration center took their meals and otherwise spent their time).
They looked a long time for a cord to tie onto the lantern, for
simply placing it on the table caused a poor and uneven light
to fall on this room with its walls and floors of unpainted
wooden planks. The corners were left in complete darkness.

The guardroom door opened. A soldier appeared at the
door, electric light behind him, darkness before.

"Where's Guskov?" asked Zotov severely.

"Halt! Who goes there?" shouted the strident voice outside.

Feet pounded the landing, Guskov came in and, hurrying
beside him, a Red Army man.

"Present, Comrade Lieutenant." Guskov's hand made a
rough approximation of a salute. Even in the dimness Zotov
could guess at the sulky set of Guskov's face (which always
bore an expression of near insolence) at being dragged out
on a trivial pretext by a lieutenant whose orders he almost did
not have to obey.

Abruptly raising his voice, Zotov hurled the angry question:
"Sergeant Guskov! How many men on your watch here?"

Guskov was not so much frightened as surprised (Zotov
never shouted). He answered meekly: "Two, but as you
know, they. . . ."

"I *don't* know! If their names are on the roster, you should
have them here on the spot."

Again Guskov's mouth set.

"Red Army Private Bobnev! Arm yourself and mount
guard!"

The soldier Guskov had brought with him stamped noisily
as he marched around his superior, and went off into the
adjoining room.

"And you come with me to the command post!"

Then it was that Guskov realized something was amiss.

The Red Army man returned carrying a rifle with fixed
bayonet, took a few precise steps in full view, and took up a
sentry's stance beside the door.

(At that moment Zotov was seized with hesitation. He could
not think what to say.)

"You . . . I," said Zotov in a very quiet voice, timidly raising
his eyes to Tveritinov's. "I'll just go and attend to another
matter." He was pronouncing his vowels very distinctly now.
"You sit down here, please, and wait. Wait."

Tveritinov's head in its wide cap, combining with his agitated
shadow on the wall and ceiling, looked ridiculous, unearthly.
The scarf with its jutting knot encircled his neck.

"Are you leaving me here? But, Vasily Vasilich, if I stay here, I'll miss the train! Let me go out on the platform."

"No, no, you're staying here," said Zotov, hurrying toward the door.

And Tveritinov understood.

"You're *arresting* me?" he cried. "But why, Comrade Lieutenant? Let me catch up with my echelon!"

And making the same gesture he had already used to express thanks, he placed his hand on his chest, the five fingers spread like a fan. He made two quick strides after the lieutenant but the sentry promptly threw his bayoneted rifle across his path.

Zotov could not help casting one more glance behind him and for the last time in his life saw in the lantern's pale gleam that face, the despairing face of Lear on the verge of the realm of death.

"What have you done! What have you done!" cried Tveritinov in a voice that tolled like a bell. "You can never make amends for this!"

He threw up his hands. The one holding his duffel bag flew out of his sleeve, and so he seemed to swell until, large as his dark winged shadow, his head became one with the ceiling.

"Don't worry, don't worry," Zotov bade him, as his foot felt for the threshold. "There's just one little matter I must clear up."

He went out, Guskov behind him.

Going through the military dispatcher's office, the lieutenant said: "Hold back the train."

In his own office he sat down at his desk and wrote:

Central Operations, N.K.V.D.
The bearer of this is a detained straggler calling himself Tveritinov, Igor Dementyevich, who claims to have been left behind by train No. 245413 at Skopino. In conversation with me. . . .

"Get yourself ready," he said to Guskov. "Take another man with you and escort the straggler to Central Operations."

Several days went by, and the holidays were over. But Zotov's mind could not free itself of this man with his haunting smile and the little snapshot of his daughter in a striped dress.

Everything seemed to have been done as it should have.

Should, and yet should not have been done.

He had to be sure, either that the other had in fact been a spy in disguise or that he had been freed a long time since. Zotov telephoned to the key post at the Central Operations Command.

"Look, I sent you a detained straggler—November 1st—

named Tveritinov. Can you tell me what became of the case?"

"We're looking into it!" the stern reply came back along the wire. "And *you* look, Zotov: there are some pretty vague entries in those lists you made of the shipment that was eighty percent burned. It's a very serious matter—someone may have been filling his pockets."

So all winter long Zotov went on working at Krechetovka Station as assistant to the C.O. He was more than once drawn to the telephone to ask what had happened, but was afraid of rousing suspicion.

One day an investigator chanced to come from Central Operations on business. Trying to appear casual, Zotov asked him: "D'you happen to remember a man called Tveritinov? I sent him to you last fall."

"Why do you ask?" said the investigator with a deep frown.

"Oh, no reason. Just interested to know . . . how it turned out."

"We'll see about your Tveritinov. We don't allow slip-ups in our work."

For the rest of his life, however, Zotov could not forget that man.

1963

Matryona's Home

Alexander
Solzhenitsyn

A hundred and fifteen miles from Moscow trains were still slowing down to a crawl a good six months after it happened. Passengers stood glued to the windows or went out to stand by the doors. Was the line under repair, or what? Would the train be late?

It was all right. Past the crossing the train picked up speed again and the passengers went back to their seats.

Only the engine drivers knew what it was all about.

The engine drivers and I.

In the summer of 1953 I was coming back from the hot and dusty desert, just following my nose—so long as it led me back to European Russia. Nobody waited or wanted me at my particular place, because I was a little matter of ten years overdue. I just wanted to get to the central belt, away from the great heats, close to the leafy muttering of forests. I wanted to efface myself, to lose myself in deepest Russia . . . if it was still anywhere to be found.

A year earlier I should have been lucky to get a job carrying a hod this side of the Urals. They wouldn't have taken me as an electrician on a decent construction job. And I had an itch to teach. Those who knew told me that it was a waste of money buying a ticket, that I should have a journey for nothing.

But things were beginning to move. When I went up the stairs of the N—— Regional Education Department and asked for the Personnel Section, I was surprised to find Personnel sitting behind a glass partition, like in a chemist's shop, instead of the usual black leather-padded door. I went timidly up to the window, bowed, and asked, "Please, do you need any mathematicians somewhere where the trains don't run? I should like to settle there for good."

They passed every dot and comma in my documents through a fine comb, went from one room to another, made telephone calls. It was something out of the ordinary for them too—people always wanted the towns, the bigger the better. And lo and behold, they found just the place for me—Vysokoe Polye. The very sound of it gladdened my heart.

Vysokoe Polye did not belie its name. It stood on rising ground, with gentle hollows and other little hills around it. It was enclosed by an unbroken ring of forest. There was a pool behind a weir. Just the place where I wouldn't mind living and dying. I spent a long time sitting on a stump in a coppice and wishing with all my heart that I didn't need breakfast and dinner every day but could just stay here and listen to the branches brushing against the roof in the night, with not a wireless anywhere to be heard and the whole world silent.

Alas, nobody baked bread in Vysokoe Polye. There was nothing edible on sale. The whole village lugged its victuals in sacks from the big town.

I went back to the Personnel Section and raised my voice in prayer at the little window. At first they wouldn't even talk to me. But then they started going from one room to another, made a telephone call, scratched with their pens, and stamped on my orders the word "Torfoprodukt".*

Torfoprodukt? Turgenev never knew that you can put words like that together in Russian.

On the station building at Torfoprodukt, an antiquated temporary hut of gray wood, hung a stern notice, BOARD TRAINS ONLY FROM THE PASSENGERS' HALL. A further message had been scratched on the boards with a nail, *And Without Tickets*. And by the booking office, with the same melancholy wit, somebody had carved for all time the words, *No Tickets*. It was only later that I fully appreciated the meaning of these addenda. Getting to Torfoprodukt was easy. But not getting away.

Here too, deep and trackless forests had once stood and were still standing after the Revolution. Then they were chopped down by the peat cutters and the neighboring kolkhoz. Its chairman, Shashkov, had razed quite a few hectares of timber and sold it at a good profit down in the Odessa region.

The workers' settlement sprawled untidily among the peat bogs—monotonous shacks from the thirties, and little houses with carved façades and glass verandas, put up in the fifties. But inside these houses I could see no partitions reaching up to the ceilings, so there was no hope of renting a room with four real walls.

Over the settlement hung smoke from the factory chimney. Little locomotives ran this way and that along narrow-gauge railway lines, giving out more thick smoke and piercing whistles, pulling loads of dirty brown peat in slabs and briquettes. I could safely assume that in the evening a loudspeaker would be crying its heart out over the door of the club and there would be drunks roaming the streets and, sooner or later, sticking knives in each other.

This was what my dream about a quiet corner of Russia had brought me to—when I could have stayed where I was and lived in an adobe hut looking out on the desert, with a fresh breeze at night and only the starry dome of the sky overhead.

I couldn't sleep on the station bench, and as soon as it started getting light I went for another stroll round the settlement. This

*Peat-product

time I saw a tiny marketplace. Only one woman stood there at that early hour, selling milk, and I took a bottle and started drinking it on the spot.

I was struck by the way she talked. Instead of a normal speaking voice, she used an ingratiating singsong, and her words were the ones I was longing to hear when I left Asia for this place.

"Drink, and God bless you. You must be a stranger round here?"

"And where are you from?" I asked, feeling more cheerful.

I learnt that the peat workings weren't the only thing, that over the railway lines there was a hill, and over the hill a village, that this village was Talnovo, and it had been there ages ago, when the "gipsy woman" lived in the big house and the wild woods stood all round. And farther on there was a whole countryside full of villages— Chaslitsy, Ovintsy, Spudni, Shevertni, Shestimirovo, deeper and deeper into the woods, farther and farther from the railway, up towards the lakes.

The names were like a soothing breeze to me. They held a promise of backwoods Russia. I asked my new acquaintance to take me to Talnovo after the market was over and find a house for me to lodge in.

It appeared that I was a lodger worth having: in addition to my rent, the school offered a truckload of peat for the winter to whoever took me. The woman's ingratiating smile gave way to a thoughtful frown. She had no room herself, because she and her husband were "keeping" her aged mother, so she took me first to one lot of relatives then to another. But there wasn't a separate room to be had and both places were crowded and noisy.

We had come to a dammed-up stream that was short of water and had a little bridge over it. No other place in all the village took my fancy as this did: there were two or three willows, a lopsided house, ducks swimming on the pond, geese shaking themselves as they stepped out of the water.

"Well, perhaps we might just call on Matryona," said my guide, who was getting tired of me by now. "Only it isn't so neat and cozylike in her house, neglects things she does. She's unwell."

Matryona's house stood quite near by. Its row of four windows looked out on the cold, homely landscape, the two slopes of the roof were covered with shingles, and a little attic window was decorated in the old Russian style. But the shingles were rotting, the beam-ends of the house and the once mighty gates had turned gray with age, and there were gaps in the little shelter over the gate.

The small gate was fastened, but instead of knocking my companion just put her hand under and turned the catch, a simple device to prevent animals from straying. The yard was not covered, but there was a lot under the roof of the house. As you went through the outer door a short flight of steps rose to a roomy landing, which was open, to the roof high overhead. To the left, other steps led up to the top room, which was a separate structure with no stove, and yet another flight led down to the basement. To the right lay the house proper, with its attic and its cellar.

It had been built a long time ago, built sturdily, to house a big family, and now one lonely woman of nearly sixty lived in it.

When I went into the cottage she was lying on the Russian stove under a heap of those indeterminate dingy rags which are so precious to a working man or woman.

The spacious room, and especially the best part near the windows, was full of rubber plants in pots and tubs standing on stools and benches. They peopled the householder's loneliness like a speechless but living crowd. They had been allowed to run wild, and they took up all the scanty light on the north side. In what was left of the light, and half-hidden by the stovepipe, the mistress of the house looked yellow and weak. You could see from her clouded eyes that illness had drained all the strength out of her.

While we talked she lay on the stove face downward, without a pillow, her head toward the door, and I stood looking up at her. She showed no pleasure at getting a lodger, just complained about the wicked disease she had. She was just getting over an attack; it didn't come upon her every month, but when it did, "It hangs on two or three days so as I shan't manage to get up and wait on you. I've room and to spare, you can live here if you like."

Then she went over the list of other housewives with whom I should be quieter and cozier and wanted me to make the round of them. But I had already seen that I was destined to settle in this dimly lit house with the tarnished mirror, in which you couldn't see yourself, and the two garish posters (one advertising books, the other about the harvest), bought for a ruble each to brighten up the walls.

Matryona Vasilyevna made me go off round the village again, and when I called on her the second time she kept trying to put me off, "We're not clever, we can't cook, I don't know how we shall suit. . . ." But this time she was on her feet when I got there, and I thought I saw a glimmer of pleasure in her eyes to see me back. We reached an agreement about the rent and the load of peat which the school would deliver.

Later on I found out that, year in year out, it was a long time
since Matryona Vasilyevna had earned a single ruble. She
didn't get a pension. Her relatives gave her very little help. In
the kolkhoz she had worked not for money but for credits;
the marks recording her labor days in her well-thumbed
workbook.

So I moved in with Matryona Vasilyevna. We didn't divide the
room. Her bed was in the corner between the door and the
stove, and I unfolded my camp bed by one window and pushed
Matryona's beloved rubber plants out of the light to make room
for a little table by another. The village had electric light, laid
on back in the twenties, from Shatury. The newspapers were
writing about "Ilyich's little lamps," but the peasants talked
wide-eyed about "Tsar Light."

Some of the better-off people in the village might not have
thought Matryona's house much of a home, but it kept us snug
enough that autumn and winter. The roof still held the rain out,
and the freezing winds could not blow the warmth of the stove
away all at once, though it was cold by morning, especially
when the wind blew on the shabby side.

In addition to Matryona and myself, a cat, some mice, and
some cockroaches lived in the house.

The cat was no longer young, and was gammy-legged as well.
Matryona had taken her in out of pity, and she had stayed. She
walked on all four feet but with a heavy limp: one of her feet
was sore and she favored it. When she jumped from the stove
she didn't land with the soft sound a cat usually makes, but with
a heavy thud as three of her feet struck the floor at once—such
a heavy thud that until I got used to it, it gave me a start. This
was because she stuck three feet out together to save the fourth.

It wasn't because the cat couldn't deal with them that there
were mice in the cottage: she would pounce into the corner like
lightning and come back with a mouse between her teeth. But
the mice were usually out of reach because somebody, back in
the good old days, had stuck embossed wallpaper of a greenish
color on Matryona's walls, and not just one layer of it but five.
The layers held together all right, but in many places the whole
lot had come away from the wall, giving the room a sort of inner
skin. Between the timber of the walls and the skin of wallpaper
the mice had made themselves runs where they impudently
scampered about, running at times right up to the ceiling. The
cat followed their scamperings with angry eyes, but couldn't
get at them.

Sometimes the cat ate cockroaches as well, but they made her
sick. The only thing the cockroaches respected was the partition
which screened the mouth of the Russian stove and the kitchen

from the best part of the room.

They did not creep into the best room. But the kitchen at night swarmed with them, and if I went in late in the evening for a drink of water and switched on the light the whole floor, the big bench, and even the wall would be one rustling brown mass. From time to time I brought home some borax from the school laboratory and we mixed it with dough to poison them. There would be fewer cockroaches for a while, but Matryona was afraid that we might poison the cat as well. We stopped putting down poison and the cockroaches multiplied anew.

At night, when Matryona was already asleep and I was working at my table, the occasional rapid scamper of mice behind the wallpaper would be drowned in the sustained and ceaseless rustling of cockroaches behind the screen, like the sound of the sea in the distance. But I got used to it because there was nothing evil in it, nothing dishonest. Rustling was life to them.

I even got used to the crude beauty on the poster, forever reaching out from the wall to offer me Belinsky, Panferov, and a pile of other books— but never saying a word. I got used to everything in Matryona's cottage.

Matryona got up at four or five o'clock in the morning. Her wall clock was twenty-seven years old and had been bought in the village shop. It was always fast, but Matryona didn't worry about that—just so long as it didn't lose and make her late in the morning. She switched on the light behind the kitchen screen and moving quietly, considerately, doing her best not to make a noise, she lit the stove, went to milk the goat (all the livestock she had was this one dirty-white goat with twisted horns), fetched water and boiled it in three iron pots: one for me, one for herself, and one for the goat. She fetched potatoes from the cellar, picking out the littlest for the goat, little ones for herself and egg-sized ones for me. There were no big ones, because her garden was sandy, had not been manured since the war, and was always planted with potatoes, potatoes, and potatoes again, so that it wouldn't grow big ones.

I scarcely heard her about her morning tasks. I slept late, woke up in the wintry daylight, stretched a bit, and stuck my head out from under my blanket and my sheepskin. These, together with the prisoner's jerkin round my legs and a sack stuffed with straw underneath me, kept me warm in bed even on nights when the cold wind rattled our wobbly windows from the north. When I heard the discreet noises on the other side of the screen I spoke to her, slowly and deliberately:

"Good morning, Matryona Vasilyevna!"

And every time the same good-natured words came to me

from behind the screen. They began with a warm, throaty gurgle, the sort of sound grandmothers make in fairy tales.

"M-m-m . . . same to you too!"

And after a little while, "Your breakfast's ready for you now."

She didn't announce what was for breakfast, but it was easy to guess: taters in their jackets or tatty soup (as everybody in the village called it), or barley gruel (no other grain could be bought in Torfoprodukt that year, and even the barley you had to fight for, because it was the cheapest and people bought it up by the sack to fatten their pigs on it). It wasn't always salted as it should be, it was often slightly burnt, it furred the palate and the gums, and it gave me heartburn.

But Matryona wasn't to blame: there was no butter in Torfoprodukt either, margarine was desperately short, and only mixed cooking fat was plentiful, and when I got to know it, I saw that the Russian stove was not convenient for cooking: the cook cannot see the pots and they are not heated evenly all round. I suppose the stove came down to our ancestors from the Stone Age, because you can stoke it up once before daylight, and food and water, mash and swill will keep warm in it all day long. And it keeps you warm while you sleep.

I ate everything that was cooked for me without demur, patiently putting aside anything uncalled-for that I came across: a hair, a bit of peat, a cockroach's leg. I hadn't the heart to find fault with Matryona. After all, she had warned me herself.

"We aren't clever, we can't cook—I don't know how we shall suit. . . ."

"Thank you," I said quite sincerely.

"What for? For what is your own?" she answered, disarming me with a radiant smile. And, with a guileless look of her faded blue eyes, she would ask, "And what shall I cook you for just now?"

For just now meant for supper. I ate twice a day, like at the front. What could I order for just now? It would have to be one of the same old things, taters or tater soup.

I resigned myself to it, because I had learned by now not to look for the meaning of life in food. More important to me was the smile on her roundish face, which I tried in vain to catch when at last I had earned enough to buy a camera. As soon as she saw the cold eye of the lens upon her, Matryona assumed a strained or else an exaggeratedly severe expression.

Just once I did manage to get a snap of her looking through the window into the street and smiling at something.

Matryona had a lot of worries that winter. Her neighbors put it into her head to try and get a pension. She was all alone in the world, and when she began to be seriously ill she had been dismissed from the kolkhoz as well. Injustices had piled up, one on top of another. She was ill, but was not regarded as a disabled person. She had worked for a quarter of a century in the kolkhoz, but it was a kolkhoz and not a factory, so she was not entitled to a pension for herself. She could only try and get one for her husband, for the loss of her breadwinner. But she had had no husband for twelve years now, not since the beginning of the war, and it wasn't easy to obtain all the particulars from different places about his length of service and how much he had earned. What a bother it was getting those forms through! Getting somebody to certify that he'd earned, say, three hundred roubles a month; that she lived alone and nobody helped her; what year she was born in. Then all this had to be taken to the Pension Office. And taken somewhere else to get all the mistakes corrected. And taken back again. Then you had to find out whether they would give you a pension.

To make it all more difficult the Pension Office was twelve miles east of Talnovo, the Rural Council Offices six miles to the west, the Factory District Council an hour's walk to the north. They made her run around from office to office for two months on end, to get an *i* dotted or a *t* crossed. Every trip took a day. She goes down to the Rural District Council— and the secretary isn't there today. Secretaries of rural councils often aren't here today. So come again tomorrow. Tomorrow the secretary is in, but he hasn't got his rubber stamp. So come again the next day. And the day after that back she goes yet again, because all her papers are pinned together and some cockeyed clerk has signed the wrong one.

"They shove me around, Ignatich," she used to complain to me after these fruitless excursions. "Worn out with it I am."

But she soon brightened up. I found that she had a sure means of putting herself in a good humor. She worked. She would grab a shovel and go off to pull potatoes. Or she would tuck a sack under her arm and go after peat. Or take a wicker basket and look for berries deep in the woods. When she'd been bending her back to bushes instead of office desks for a while, and her shoulders were aching from a heavy load, Matryona would come back cheerful, at peace with the world and smiling her nice smile.

"I'm on to a good thing now, Ignatich. I know where to go for it (peat she meant), a lovely place it is."

"But surely my peat is enough, Matryona Vasilyevna? There's a whole truckload of it."

"Pooh! Your peat! As much again, and then as much again, that might be enough. When the winter gets really stiff and the wind's battling at the windows, it blows the heat out of the house faster than you can make the stove up. Last year we got heaps and heaps of it. I'd have had three loads in by now. But they're out to catch us. They've summoned one woman from our village already."

That's how it was. The frightening breath of winter was already in the air. There were forests all round, and no fuel to be had anywhere. Excavators roared away in the bogs, but there was no peat on sale to the villagers. It was delivered, free, to the bosses and to the people round the bosses, and teachers, doctors, and workers got a load each. The people of Talnovo were not supposed to get any peat, and they weren't supposed to ask about it. The chairman of the kolkhoz walked about the village looking people in the eye while he gave his orders or stood chatting and talked about anything you liked except fuel. He was stocked up. Who said anything about winter coming?

So just as in the old days they used to steal the squire's wood, now they pinched peat from the trust. The women went in parties of five or ten so that they would be less frightened. They went in the daytime. The peat cut during the summer had been stacked up all over the place to dry. That's the good thing about peat, it can't be carted off as soon as it's cut. It lies around drying till autumn, or, if the roads are bad, till the snow starts falling. This was when the women used to come and take it. They could get six peats in a sack if it was damp, or ten if it was dry. A sackful weighed about half a hundredweight and it sometimes had to be carried over two miles. This was enough to make the stove up once. There were two hundred days in the winter. The Russian stove had to be lit in the mornings, and the "Dutch" stove in the evenings.

"Why beat about the bush?" said Matryona angrily to someone invisible. "Since there've been no more horses, what you can't have around yourself you haven't got. My back never heals up. Winter you're pulling sledges, summer it's bundles on your back, it's God's truth I'm telling you."

The women went more than once in a day. On good days Matryona brought six sacks home. She piled my peat up where it could be seen and hid her own under the passageway, boarding up the hole every night.

"If they don't just happen to think of it, the devils will never find it in their born days," said Matryona smiling and wiping the sweat from her brow.

What could the peat trust do? Its establishment didn't run to a watchman for every bog. I suppose they had to show a rich haul in their returns, and then write off so much for crumbling, so much washed away by the rain. Sometimes they would take it into their heads to put out patrols and try to catch the women as they came into the village. The women would drop their sacks and scatter. Or somebody would inform and there would be a house-to-house search. They would draw up a report on the stolen peat and threaten a court action. The women would stop fetching peat and stumps which the tractors unearthed in the out with sledges in the middle of the night.

When I had seen a little more of Matryona I noticed that, apart from cooking and looking after the house, she had quite a lot of other jobs to do every day. She kept all her jobs, and the proper times for them, in her head and always knew when she woke up in the morning how her day would be occupied. Apart from fetching peat and stumps which the tractors unearthed in the bogs, apart from the cranberries which she put to soak in big jars for the winter ("Give your teeth an edge, Ignatich," she used to say when she offered me some), apart from digging potatoes and all the coming and going to do with her pension, she had to get hay from somewhere for her one and only dirty-white goat.

"Why don't you keep a cow, Matryona?"

Matryona stood there in her grubby apron, by the opening in the kitchen screen, facing my table, and explained to me.

"Oh, Ignatich, there's enough milk from the goat for me. And if I started keeping a cow she'd eat me out of house and home in no time. You can't cut the grass by the railway track, because it belongs to the railway, and you can't cut any in the woods, because it belongs to the foresters, and they won't let me have any at the kolkhoz because I'm not a member any more, they reckon. And those who are members have to work there every day till the white flies swarm and make their own hay when there's snow on the ground—what's the good of grass like that? In the old days they used to be sweating to get the hay in at midsummer, between the end of June and the end of July, while the grass was sweet and juicy."

So it meant a lot of work for Matryona to gather enough hay for one skinny little goat. She took her sickle and a sack and went off early in the morning to places where she knew there was grass growing—round the edges of fields, on the roadside, on hummocks in the bog. When she had stuffed her sack with heavy fresh grass she dragged it home and spread it out in her yard to dry. From a sackfull of grass she got one forkload of dry hay.

The farm had a new chairman, sent down from the town not long ago, and the first thing he did was to cut down the garden plots for those who were not fit to work. He left Matryona a

third of an acre of sand—when there was over a thousand
square yards just lying idle on the other side of the fence. Yet
when they were short of working hands, when the women dug
in their heels and wouldn't budge, the chairman's wife would
come to see Matryona. She was from the town as well, a determined woman whose short gray coat and intimidating glare
gave her a somewhat military appearance. She walked into the
house without so much as a good morning and looked sternly
at Matryona. Matryona was uneasy.

"Well now, Comrade Vasilyevna," said the chairman's wife,
drawing out her words. "You will have to help the kolkhoz!
You will have to go and help cart manure out tomorrow!"

A little smile of forgiveness wrinkled Matryona's face—as
though she understood the embarrassment which the chairman's wife must feel at not being able to pay her for her work.

"Well—er," she droned. "I'm not well, of course, and I'm not
attached to you any more . . . ," then she hurried to correct
herself, "What time should I come then?"

"And bring your own fork!" the chairman's wife instructed
her. Her stiff skirt crackled as she walked away.

"Think of that!" grumbled Matryona as the door closed.
"Bring your own fork! They've got neither forks nor shovels
at the kolkhoz. And I don't have a man who'll put a handle
on for me!"

She went on thinking about it out loud all evening.

"What's the good of talking, Ignatich. I must help, of course.
Only the way they work it's all a waste of time—don't know
whether they're coming or going. The women stand propped
up on their shovels and waiting for the factory whistle to blow
twelve o'clock. Or else they get on to adding up who's earned
what and who's turned up for work and who hasn't. Now what I
call work, there isn't a sound out of anybody, only—oh dear,
dear—dinner time's soon rolled round—what, getting dark
already."

In the morning she went off with her fork.

But it wasn't just the kolkhoz—any distant relative, or just a
neighbor, could come to Matryona of an evening and say,
"Come and give me a hand tomorrow, Matryona. We'll finish
pulling the potatoes."

Matryona couldn't say no. She gave up what she should be
doing next and went to help her neighbor, and when she came
back she would say without a trace of envy, "Ah, you should see
the size of her potatoes, Ignatich! It was a joy to dig them up.
I didn't want to leave the allotment, God's truth I didn't."

Needless to say, not a garden could be plowed without

Matryona's help. The women of Talnovo had got it neatly
worked out that it was a longer and harder job for one woman
to dig her garden with a spade than for six of them to put themselves in harness and plow six gardens. So they sent for Matryona
to help them.

"Well—did you pay her?" I asked sometimes.

"She won't take money. You have to try and hide it on her
when she's not looking."

Matryona had yet another troublesome chore when her turn
came to feed the herdsmen. One of them was a hefty deaf mute,
the other a boy who was never without a cigaret in his drooling
mouth. Matryona's turn came round only every six weeks, but
it put her to great expense. She went to the shop to buy canned
fish and was lavish with sugar and butter, things she never ate
herself. It seems that the housewives showed off in this way,
trying to outdo one another in feeding the herdsmen.

"You've got to be careful with tailors and herdsmen,"
Matryona explained. "They'll spread your name all round the
village if something doesn't suit them."

And every now and then attacks of serious illness broke in on
this life that was already crammed with troubles. Matryona
would be off her feet for a day or two, lying flat out on the
stove. She didn't complain and didn't groan, but she hardly
stirred either. On these days Masha, Matryona's closest friend
from her earliest years, would come to look after the goat and
light the stove. Matryona herself ate nothing, drank nothing,
asked for nothing. To call in the doctor from the clinic at the
settlement would have seemed strange in Talnovo and would
have given the neighbors something to talk about—what does
she think she is, a lady? They did call her in once, and she
arrived in a real temper and told Matryona to come down to the
clinic when she was on her feet again. Matryona went, although
she didn't really want to; they took specimens and sent them off
to the district hospital—and that's the last anybody heard about
it. Matryona was partly to blame herself.

But there was work waiting to be done, and Matryona soon
started getting up again, moving slowly at first and then as
briskly as ever.

"You never saw me in the old days, Ignatich. I'd lift any sack
you liked, I didn't think a hundredweight was too heavy. My
father-in-law used to say, 'Matryona, you'll break your back.'
And my brother-in-law didn't have to come and help me lift
on the cart. Our horse was a warhorse, a big strong one."

"What do you mean, a warhorse?"

"They took ours for the war and gave us this one instead—
he'd been wounded. But he turned out a bit spirited. Once he

bolted with the sledge right into the lake, the men folk hopped out of the way, but I grabbed the bridle, as true as I'm here, and stopped him. Full of oats that horse was. They liked to feed their horses well in our village. If a horse feels his oats he doesn't know what heavy means."

But Matryona was a long way from being fearless. She was afraid of fire, afraid of "the lightning," and most of all she was for some reason afraid of trains.

"When I had to go to Cherusti, the train came up from Nechaevka way with its great big eyes popping out and the rails humming away—put me in a regular fever. My knees started knocking. God's truth I'm telling you!" Matryona raised her shoulders as though she surprised herself.

"Maybe it's because they won't give people tickets, Matryona Vasilyevna?"

"At the window? They try to shove only first-class tickets on to you. And the train was starting to move. We dashed about all over the place, 'Give us tickets for pity's sake.'"

"The men folk had climbed on top of the carriages. Then we found a door that wasn't locked and shoved straight in without tickets—and all the carriages were empty, they were all empty, you could stretch out on the seat if you wanted to. Why they wouldn't give us tickets, the hardhearted parasites, I don't know. . . ."

Still, before winter came, Matryona's affairs were in a better state than ever before. They started paying her at last a pension of eighty rubles. Besides this she got just over one hundred from the school and me.

Some of her neighbors began to be envious.

"Hm! Matryona can live forever now! If she had any more money, she wouldn't know what to do with it at her age."

Matryona had some new felt boots made. She bought a new jerkin. And she had an overcoat made out of the worn-out railwayman's greatcoat given to her by the engine driver from Cherusti who had married Kira, her foster daughter. The hump-backed village tailor put a padded lining under the cloth and it made a marvelous coat, such as Matryona had never worn before in all her sixty years.

In the middle of winter Matryona sewed two hundred rubles into the lining of this coat for her funeral. This made her quite cheerful.

"Now my mind's a bit easier, Ignatich."

December went by, January went by—and in those two months Matryona's illness held off. She started going over to Masha's house more often in the evening, to sit chewing sun-

flower seeds with her. She herself didn't invite guests in the
evening out of consideration for my work. Once, on the feast
of the Epiphany, I came back from school and found a party
going on and was introduced to Matryona's three sisters, who
called her "nan-nan" or "nanny" because she was the oldest.
Until then not much had been heard of the sisters in our cottage—perhaps they were afraid that Matryona might ask them
for help.

But one ominous event cast a shadow on the holiday for
Matryona. She went to the church three miles away for the
blessing of the water and put her pot down among the others.
When the blessing was over, the women went rushing and
jostling to get their pots back again. There were a lot of women
in front of Matryona and when she got there her pot was missing, and no other vessel had been left behind. The pot had
vanished as though the devil had run off with it.

Matryona went round the worshipers asking them, "Have
any of you girls accidentally mistook somebody else's holy
water? In a pot?"

Nobody owned up. There had been some boys there, and
boys got up to mischief sometimes. Matryona came home sad.

No one could say that Matryona was a devout believer. If anything, she was a heathen, and her strongest beliefs were super-
stitious: you mustn't go into the garden on the fast of St. John
or there would be no harvest next year. A blizzard meant that
somebody had hanged himself. If you pinched your foot in the
door, you could expect a guest. All the time I lived with her
I didn't once see her say her prayers or even cross herself. But,
whatever job she was doing, she began with a "God bless us,"
and she never failed to say "God bless you," when I set out for
school. Perhaps she did say her prayers, but on the quiet, either
because she was shy or because she didn't want to embarrass
me. There were ikons on the walls. Ordinary days they were left
in darkness, but for the vigil of a great feast, or on the morning
of a holiday, Matryona would light the little lamp.

She had fewer sins on her conscience than her gammy-legged
cat. The cat did kill mice.

Now that her life was running more smoothly, Matryona
started listening more carefully to my radio. (I had, of course,
installed a speaker, or as Matryona called it, a peeker.)

When they announced on the radio that some new machine
had been invented, I heard Matryona grumbling out in the
kitchen, "New ones all the time, nothing but new ones. People
don't want to work with the old ones any more, where are
we going to store them all?"

There was a program about the seeding of clouds from airplanes. Matryona, listening up on the stove, shook her head, "Oh, dear, dear, dear, they'll do away with one of the two—summer or winter."

Once Shalyapin was singing Russian folk songs. Matryona stood listening for a long time before she gave her emphatic verdict, "Queer singing, not our sort of singing."

"You can't mean that, Matryona Vasilyevna—just listen to him."

She listened a bit longer and pursed her lips, "No, it's wrong. It isn't our sort of tune, and he's tricky with his voice."

She made up for this another time. They were broadcasting some of Glinka's songs. After half a dozen of these drawing-room ballads, Matryona suddenly came from behind the screen clutching her apron, with a flush on her face and a film of tears over her dim eyes.

"That's our sort of singing," she said in a whisper.

2

So Matryona and I got used to each other and took each other for granted. She never pestered me with questions about myself. I don't know whether she was lacking in normal female curiosity or just tactful, but she never once asked if I had been married. All the Talnovo women kept at her to find out about me. Her answer was, "You want to know—you ask him. All I know is he's from distant parts."

And when I got round to telling her that I had spent a lot of time in prison, she said nothing but just nodded, as though she had already suspected it.

And I thought of Matryona only as the helpless old woman she was now and didn't try to rake up her past, didn't even suspect that there was anything to be found there.

I knew that Matryona had got married before the Revolution and had come to live in the house I now shared with her, and she had gone "to the stove" immediately. (She had no mother-in-law and no older sister-in-law, so it was her job to put the pots in the oven on the very first morning of her married life.) I knew that she had had six children and that they had all died very young, so that there were never two of them alive at once. Then there was a sort of foster daughter, Kira. Matryona's husband had not come back from the last war. She received no notification of his death. Men from the village who had served in the same company said that he might have been taken prisoner, or he might have been killed and his body not found. In the eight years that had gone by since the war Matryona had decided that he was not alive. It was a good thing that she thought so. If he was still alive he was probably in Brazil or Australia and married again. The village of Talnovo and the Russian language would be fading from his memory.

One day when I got back from school, I found a guest in the house. A tall, dark man, with his hat on his lap, was sitting on a chair which Matryona had moved up to the Dutch stove in the middle of the room. His face was completely surrounded by bushy black hair with hardly a trace of gray in it. His thick black moustache ran into his full black beard, so that his mouth could hardly be seen. Black side-whiskers merged with the black locks which hung down from his crown, leaving only the tips of his ears visible; his broad black eyebrows met in a wide double span. But the front of his head as far as the crown was a spacious bald dome. His whole appearance made an impression of wisdom and dignity. He sat squarely on his chair, with his hands folded on his stick, and his stick resting vertically on the floor, in an attitude of patient expectation, and he obviously hadn't much to say to Matryona, who was busy behind the screen.

When I came in, he eased his majestic head round toward me and suddenly addressed me, "Schoolmaster, I can't see you very well. My son goes to your school. Grigoryev, Antoshka."

There was no need for him to say any more. However strongly inclined I felt to help this worthy old man, I knew and dismissed in advance all the pointless things he was going to say. Antoshka Grigoryev was a plump, red-faced lad in 8-D who looked like a cat that's swallowed the cream. He seemed to think that he came to school for a rest and sat at his desk with a lazy smile on his face. Needless to say, he never did his homework. But the worst of it was that he had been put up into the next class from year to year because our district, and indeed the whole region and the neighboring region were famous for the high percentage of passes they obtained; the school had to make an effort to keep its record up. So Antoshka had got it clear in his mind that however much the teachers threatened him they would promote him in the end, and there was no need for him to learn anything. He just laughed at us. There he sat in the eighth class, and he hadn't even mastered his decimals and didn't know one triangle from another. In the first two terms of the school year I had kept him firmly below the passing line and the same treatment awaited him in the third.

But now this half-blind old man, who should have been Antoshka's grandfather rather than his father, had come to humble himself before me—how could I tell him that the school had been deceiving him for years, and that I couldn't go on deceiving him, because I didn't want to ruin the whole class, to become a liar and a fake, to start despising my work and my profession.

For the time being I patiently explained that his son had been very slack, that he told lies at school and at home, that his record book must be checked frequently, and that we must both take him severely in hand.

"Severe as you like, Schoolmaster," he assured me, "I beat him every week now. And I've got a heavy hand."

While we were talking I remembered that Matryona had once interceded for Antoshka Grigoryev, but I hadn't asked what relation of hers he was and I had refused to do what she wanted. Matryona was standing in the kitchen doorway like a mute suppliant on this occasion too. When Faddey Mironovich left, saying that he would call on me to see how things were going, I asked her, "I can't make out what relation this Antoshka is to you, Matryona Vasilyevna."

"My brother-in-law's son," said Matryona shortly, and went out to milk the goat.

When I'd worked it out, I realized that this determined old man with the black hair was the brother of the missing husband.

The long evening went by, and Matryona didn't bring up the subject again. But late at night, when I had stopped thinking about the old man and was working in a silence broken only by the rustling of the cockroaches and the heavy tick of the wall-clock, Matryona suddenly spoke from her dark corner, "You know, Ignatich, I nearly married him once."

I had forgotten that Matryona was in the room. I hadn't heard a sound from her—and suddenly her voice came out of the darkness, as agitated as if the old man were still trying to win her.

I could see that Matryona had been thinking about nothing else all evening.

She got up from her wretched rag bed and walked slowly toward me, as though she were following her own words. I sat back in my chair and caught my first glimpse of a quite different Matryona.

There was no overhead light in our big room with its forest of rubber plants. The table lamp cast a ring of light round my exercise books, and when I tore my eyes from it the rest of the room seemed to be half-dark and faintly tinged with pink. I thought I could see the same pinkish glow in her usually sallow cheeks.

"He was the first one who came courting me, before Efim did—he was his brother—the older one—I was nineteen and Faddey was twenty-three. They lived in this very same house. Their house it was. Their father built it."

I looked round the room automatically. Instead of the old gray house rotting under the faded green skin of wallpaper

where the mice had their playground, I suddenly saw new tim-
full smell of pine tar.

"Well, and what happened then?"

"That summer we went to sit in the woods together," she
whispered. "There used to be a woods where the stable yard
is now. They chopped it down. I was just going to marry him,
Ignatich. Then the German war started. They took Faddey into
the army."

She let fall these few words—and suddenly the blue and
white and yellow July of the year 1914 burst into flower before
my eyes: the sky still peaceful, the floating clouds, the people
sweating to get the ripe corn in. I imagined them side by side,
the black-haired Hercules with a scythe over his shoulder, and
the red-faced girl clasping a sheaf. And there was singing out
under the open sky, such songs as nobody can sing nowadays,
with all the machines in the fields.

"He went to the war—and vanished. For three years I kept
to myself and waited. Never a sign of life did he give."

Matryona's round face looked out at me from an elderly
threadbare headscarf. As she stood there in the gentle reflected light from my lamp, her face seemed to lose its slovenly
workday wrinkles, and she was a scared young girl again with a
frightening decision to make.

Yes . . . I could see it. The trees shed their leaves, the snow
fell and melted. They plowed and sowed and reaped again.
Again the tree shed their leaves, and the snow fell. There was a
revolution. Then another revolution. And the whole world was
turned upside down.

"Their mother died and Efim came to court me." You wanted
to come to our house," he says, "so come." He was a year
younger than me, Efim was. It's a saying with us—sensible girls
get married after Michaelmas, and silly ones at midsummer.
They were shorthanded. I got married. . . . The wedding was on
St. Peter's day, and then about St. Nicholas' day in the winter he
came back—Faddey, I mean, from being a prisoner in Hungary."

Matryona covered her eyes.

I said nothing.

She turned toward the door as though somebody were
standing there. "He stood there at the door. What a scream I
let out! I wanted to throw myself at his feet! . . . but I couldn't.
'If it wasn't my own brother,' he says, 'I'd take my ax to the
both of you.'"

I shuddered. Matryona's despair, or her terror, conjured up
a vivid picture of him standing in the dark doorway and raising
his ax to her.

But she quieted down and went on with her story in a sing-song voice, leaning on a chairback, "Oh dear, dear me, the poor dear man! There were so many girls in the village—but he wouldn't marry. I'll look for one with the same name as you, a second Matryona, he said. And that's what he did—fetched himself a Matryona from Lipovka. They built themselves a house of their own and they're still living in it. You pass their place every day on your way to school."

So that was it. I realized that I had seen the other Matryona quite often. I didn't like her. She was always coming to my Matryona to complain about her husband—he beat her, he was stingy, he was working her to death. She would weep and weep, and her voice always had a tearful note in it. As it turned out, my Matryona had nothing to regret, with Faddey beating his Matryona every day of his life and being so tightfisted.

"Mine never beat me once," said Matryona of Efim. "He'd pitch into another man in the street, but me he never hit once. Well, there was one time—I quarreled with my sister-in-law and he cracked me on the forehead with a spoon. I jumped up from the table and shouted at them, 'Hope it sticks in your gullets, you idle lot of beggars, hope you choke!' I said. And off I went into the woods. He never touched me any more."

Faddey didn't seem to have any cause for regret either. The other Matryona had borne him six children (my Antoshka was one of them, the littlest, the runt) and they had all lived, whereas the children of Matryona and Efim had died, every one of them, before they reached the age of three months, without any illness.

"One daughter, Elena, was born and was alive when they washed her, and then she died right after. . . . My wedding was on St. Peter's day, and it was St. Peter's day I buried my sixth, Alexander."

The whole village decided that there was a curse on Matryona.

Matryona still nodded emphatic belief when she talked about it. "There was a *course* on me. They took me to a woman who used to be a nun to get cured, she set me off coughing and waited for the *course* to jump out of me like a frog. Only nothing jumped out."

And the years had run by like running water. In 1941 they didn't take Faddey into the army because of his poor sight, but they took Efim. And what had happened to the elder brother in the First World War happened to the younger in the Second—he vanished without a trace. Only he never came back at all. The once noisy cottage was deserted, it grew old and rotten, and Matryona, all alone in the world, grew old in it.

So she begged from the other Matryona, the cruelly beaten Matryona, a child of her womb (or was it a drop of Faddey's blood?), the youngest daughter, Kira.

For ten years she brought the girl up in her own house, in place of the children who had not lived. Then, not long before I arrived, she had married her off to a young engine driver from Cherusti. The only help she got from anywhere came in dribs and drabs from Cherusti: a bit of sugar from time to time, or some of the fat when they killed a pig.

Sick and suffering, and feeling that death was not far off, Matryona had made known her will: the top room, which was a separate frame joined by tie beams to the rest of the house, should go to Kira when she died. She said nothing about the house itself. Her three sisters had their eyes on it too.

That evening Matryona opened her heart to me. And, as often happens, no sooner were the hidden springs of her life revealed to me than I saw them in motion.

Kira arrived from Cherusti. Old Faddey was very worried. To get and keep a plot of land in Cherusti the young couple had to put up some sort of building. Matryona's top room would do very well. There was nothing else they could put up, because there was no timber to be had anywhere. It wasn't Kira herself so much, and it wasn't her husband, but old Faddey who was consumed with eagerness for them to get their hands on the plot at Cherusti.

He became a frequent visitor, laying down the law to Matryona and insisting that she should hand over the top room right away, before she died. On these occasions I saw a different Faddey. He was no longer an old man propped up by a stick, whom a push or a harsh word would bowl over. Although he was slightly bent by backache, he was still a fine figure; in his sixties he had kept the vigorous black hair of a young man; he was hot and urgent.

Matryona had not slept for two nights. It wasn't easy for her to make up her mind. She didn't grudge them the top room, which was standing there idle, any more than she ever grudged her labor or her belongings. And the top room was willed to Kira in any case. But the thought of breaking up the roof she had lived under for forty years was torture to her. Even I, a mere lodger, found it painful to think of them stripping away boards and wrenching out beams. For Matryona it was the end of everything.

But the people who were so insistent knew that she would let them break up her house before she died.

So Faddey and his sons and sons-in-law came along one February morning, the blows of five axes were heard and boards creaked and cracked as they were wrenched out. Faddey's eyes twinkled busily. Although his back wasn't quite straight yet, he scrambled nimbly up under the rafters and bustled about down below, shouting at his assistants. He and his father had built this house when he was a lad, a long time ago. The top room had been put up for him, the oldest son, to move into with his bride. And now he was furiously taking it apart, board by board, to carry it out of somebody else's yard.

After numbering the beam ends and the ceiling boards, they dismantled the top room and the storeroom underneath it. The living room and what was left of the landing they boarded up with a thin wall of deal. They did nothing about the cracks in the wall. It was plain to see that they were wreckers, not builders, and that they did not expect Matryona to be living there very long.

While the men were busy wrecking, the woman were getting the drink ready for moving day—vodka would cost too much. Kira brought forty pounds of sugar from the Moscow region, and Matryona carried the sugar and some bottles to the distiller under cover of night.

The timbers were carried out and stacked in front of the gates, and the engine-driver son-in-law went off to Cherusti for the tractor.

But the very same day a blizzard, or "a blower," as Matryona once called it, began. It howled and whirled for two days and nights and buried the road under enormous drifts. Then, no sooner had they made the road passable and a couple of trucks had gone by, than it got suddenly warmer. Within a day everything was thawing out, damp mist hung in the air and rivulets gurgled as they burrowed into the snow, and you could get stuck up to the top of your jackboots.

Two weeks passed before the tractor could get at the dismantled top room. All this time Matryona went around like someone lost. What particularly upset her was that her three sisters came, with one voice called her a fool for giving the top room away, said they didn't want to see her any more, and went off. At about the same time the lame cat strayed and was seen no more. It was just one thing after another. This was another blow to Matryona.

At last the frost got a grip on the slushy road. A sunny day came along, and everybody felt more cheerful. Matryona had had a lucky dream the night before. In the morning she heard that I wanted to take a photograph of somebody at an old-fashioned handloom. (There were looms still standing in two cottages in the village; they wove coarse rugs on them.) She smiled shyly and said, "You just wait a day or two, Ignatich,

I'll just send off the top room there and I'll put my loom up, I've still got it, you know, and then you can snap me. Honest to God!"

She was obviously attracted by the idea of posing in an old-fashioned setting. The red frosty sun tinged the window of the curtailed passageway with a faint pink, and this reflected light warmed Matryona's face. People who are at ease with their consciences always have nice faces.

Coming back from school before dusk I saw some movement near our house. A big new tractor-drawn sledge was already fully loaded, and there was no room for a lot of the timbers, so old Faddey's family and the helpers they had called in had nearly finished knocking together another homemade sledge. They were all working like madmen, in the frenzy that comes upon people when there is a smell of good money in the air or when they are looking forward to some treat. They were shouting at one another and arguing.

They could not agree on whether the sledges should be hauled separately or both together. One of Faddey's sons (the lame one) and the engine-driver son-in-law reasoned that the sledges couldn't both be taken at once because the tractor wouldn't be able to pull them. The man in charge of the tractor, a hefty fat-faced fellow who was very sure of himself, said hoarsely that he knew best, he was the driver, and he would take both at once. His motives were obvious: according to the agreement, the engine driver was paying him for the removal of the upper room, not for the number of trips he had to make. He could never have made two trips in a night—twenty-five kilometers each way, and one return journey. And by morning he had to get the tractor back in the garage from which he had sneaked it out for this job on the side.

Old Faddey was impatient to get the top room moved that day, and at a nod from him his lads gave in. To the stout sledge in front they hitched the one they had knocked together in such a hurry.

Matryona was running about among the men, fussing and helping them to heave the beams on the sledge. Suddenly I noticed that she was wearing my jacket and had dirtied the sleeves on the frozen mud round the beams. I was annoyed and told her so. That jacket held memories for me: it had kept me warm in the bad years.

This was the first time that I was ever angry with Matryona Vasilyevna.

Matryona was taken aback. "Oh dear, dear me," she said. "My poor head. I picked it up in a rush, you see, and never thought about it being yours. I'm sorry, Ignatich."

And she took it off and hung it up to dry.

The loading was finished, and all the men who had been working, about ten of them, clattered past my table and dived under the curtain into the kitchen. I could hear the muffled rattle of glasses and, from time to time, the clink of a bottle, the voices got louder and louder, the boasting more reckless. The biggest braggart was the tractor driver. The stink of hooch floated in to me. But they didn't go on drinking long. It was getting dark and they had to hurry. They began to leave. The tractor driver came out first, looking pleased with himself and fierce. The engine-driver son-in-law, Faddey's lame son, and one of his nephews were going to Cherusti. The others went off home. Faddey was flourishing his stick, trying to overtake somebody and put him right about something. The lame son paused at my table to light up and suddenly started telling me how he loved Aunt Matryona, and that he had got married not long ago, and his wife had just had a son. Then they shouted for him and he went out. The tractor set up a roar outside.

After all the others had gone, Matryona dashed out from behind the screen. She looked after them, anxiously shaking her head. She had put on her jacket and her headscarf. As she was going through the door, she said to me, "Why ever couldn't they hire two? If one tractor had cracked up, the other would have pulled them. What'll happen now, God only knows!"

She ran out after the others.

After the boozing and the arguments and all the coming and going, it was quieter than ever in the deserted cottage, and very chilly because the door had been opened so many times. I got into my jacket and sat down to mark exercise books. The noise of the tractor died away in the distance.

An hour went by. And another. And a third. Matryona still hadn't come back, but I wasn't surprised. When she had seen the sledge off, she must have gone round to her friend Masha.

Another hour went by. And yet another. Darkness, and with it a deep silence had descended on the village. I couldn't understand at the time why it was so quiet. Later, I found out that it was because all evening not a single train had gone along the line five hundred yards from the house. No sound was coming from my radio, and I noticed that the mice were wilder than ever. Their scampering and scratching and squeaking behind the wallpaper was getting noisier and more defiant all the time.

I woke up. It was one o'clock in the morning, and Matryona still hadn't come home.

Suddenly I heard several people talking loudly. They were still a long way off, but something told me that they were coming to our house. And sure enough, I heard soon afterward a heavy knock at the gate. A commanding voice, strange to me, yelled out an order to open up. I went out into the pitch darkness with a torch. The whole village was asleep, there was no light in the windows, and the snow had started melting in the last week so that it gave no reflected light. I turned the catch and let them in. Four men in greatcoats went on toward the house. It's a very unpleasant thing to be visited at night by noisy people in greatcoats.

When we got into the light though, I saw that two of them were wearing railway uniforms. The older of the two, a fat man with the same sort of face as the tractor driver, asked, "Where's the woman of the house?"

"I don't know."

"This is the place the tractor with a sledge came from?"

"This is it."

"Had they been drinking before they left?"

All four of them were looking around, screwing up their eyes in the dim light from the table lamp. I realized that they had either made an arrest or wanted to make one.

"What's happened then?"

"Answer the question!"

"But . . ."

"Were they drunk when they went?"

"Were they drinking here?"

Had there been a murder? Or hadn't they been able to move the top room? The men in greatcoats had me off balance. But one thing was certain: Matryona could do time for making hooch.

I stepped back to stand between them and the kitchen door. "I honestly didn't notice. I didn't see anything." (I really hadn't seen anything—only heard.) I made what was supposed to be a helpless gesture, drawing attention to the state of the cottage: a table lamp shining peacefully on books and exercises, a crowd of frightened rubber plants, the austere couch of a recluse, not a sign of debauchery.

They had already seen for themselves, to their annoyance, that there had been no drinking in that room. They turned to leave, telling each other this wasn't where the drinking had been then, but it would be a good thing to put in that it was. I saw them out and tried to discover what had happened. It was only at the gate that one of them growled. "They've all been cut to bits. Can't find all the pieces."

"That's a detail. The nine o'clock express nearly went off the rails. That would have been something." And they walked briskly away.

I went back to the hut in a daze. Who were "they"? What

did "all of them" mean? And where was Matryona?

I moved the curtain aside and went into the kitchen. The stink of hooch rose and hit me. It was a deserted battlefield: a huddle of stools and benches, empty bottles lying around, one bottle half-full, glasses, the remains of pickled herring, onion, and sliced fat pork.

Everything was deathly still. Just cockroaches creeping unperturbed about the field of battle.

They had said something about the nine o'clock express. Why? Perhaps I should have shown them all this? I began to wonder whether I had done right. But what a damnable way to behave—keeping their explanations for official persons only.

Suddenly the small gate creaked. I hurried out on to the landing. "Matryona Vasilyevna?"

The yard door opened, and Matryona's friend Masha came in, swaying and wringing her hands. "Matryona—our Matryona, Ignatich—"

I sat her down, and through her tears she told me the story.

The approach to the crossing was a steep rise. There was no barrier. The tractor and the first sledge went over, but the towrope broke and the second sledge, the homemade one, got stuck on the crossing and started falling apart—the wood Faddey had given them to make the second sledge was no good. They towed the first sledge out of the way and went back for the second. They were fixing the towrope—the tractor driver and Faddey's lame son, and Matryona (heaven knows what brought her there) were with them, between the tractor and the sledge. What help did she think she could be to the men? She was forever meddling in men's work. Hadn't a bolting horse nearly tipped her into the lake once, through a hole in the ice? Why did she have to go to the damned crossing? She had handed over the top room and owed nothing to anybody. The engine driver kept a lookout in case the train from Cherusti rushed up on them. Its headlamps would be visible a long way off. But two engines coupled together came from the other direction, from our station, backing without lights. Why they were without lights nobody knows. When an engine is backing, coal dust blows into the driver's eyes from the tender and he can't see very well. The two engines flew into them and crushed the three people between the tractor and the sledge to pulp. The tractor was wrecked, the sledge was matchwood, the rails were buckled, and both engines turned over.

"But how was it they didn't hear the engines coming?"

"The tractor engine was making such a din."

"What about the bodies?"

"They won't let anybody in. They've roped them off."

"What was that somebody was telling me about the express?"

"The nine o'clock express goes through our station at a good clip and on to the crossing. But the two drivers weren't hurt when their engines crashed, they jumped out and ran back along the line waving their hands, and they managed to stop the train. The nephew was hurt by a beam as well. He's hiding at Klavka's now so that they won't know he was at the crossing. If they find out they'll drag him in as a witness. . . . 'Don't know lies up, and do know gets tied up.' Kira's husband didn't get a scratch. He tried to hang himself, they had to cut him down. It's all because of me, he says, my aunty's killed and my brother. Now he's gone and given himself up. But the madhouse is where he'll be going, not prison. Oh, Matryona, my dearest Matryona. . . ."

Matryona was gone. Someone close to me had been killed. And on her last day I had scolded her for wearing my jacket.

The lovingly drawn red and yellow woman in the book advertisement smiled happily on.

Old Masha sat there weeping a little longer. Then she got up to go. And suddenly she asked me, "Ignatich, you remember, Matryona had a gray shawl. She meant it to go to my Tanya when she died, didn't she?"

She looked at me hopefully in the half-darkness—surely I hadn't forgotten?

No, I remembered. "She said so, yes."

"Well, listen, maybe you could let me take it with me now. The family will be swarming in tomorrow and I'll never get it then." And she gave me another hopeful, imploring look. She had been Matryona's friend for half a century, the only one in the village who truly loved her.

No doubt she was right.

"Of course—take it."

She opened the chest, took out the shawl, tucked it under her coat, and went out.

The mice had gone mad. They were running furiously up and down the walls, and you could almost see the green wallpaper rippling and rolling over their backs.

In the morning I had had to go to school. The time was three o'clock. The only thing to do was to lock up and go to bed.

Lock up, because Matryona would not be coming.

I lay down, leaving the light on. The mice were squeaking, almost moaning, racing and running. My mind was weary and wandering, and I couldn't rid myself of an uneasy feeling that an invisible Matryona was flitting about and saying good-bye to her home.

And suddenly I imagined Faddey standing there, young and black-haired, in the dark patch by the door, with his ax uplifted. "If it wasn't my own brother, I'd chop the both of you to bits."

The threat had lain around for forty years, like an old broad sword in a corner, and in the end it had struck its blow.

3

When it was light the women went to the crossing and brought back all that was left of Matryona on a hand sledge with a dirty sack over it. They threw off the sack to wash her. There was just a mess . . . no feet, only half a body, no left hand. One woman said, "The Lord has left her her right hand. She'll be able to say her prayers where she's going."

Then the whole crowd of rubber plants were carried out of the cottage—these plants that Matryona had loved so much that once when smoke woke her up in the night she didn't rush to save her house but to tip the plants onto the floor in case they were suffocated. The women swept the floor clean. They hung a wide towel of old homespun over Matryona's dim mirror. They took down the jolly posters. They moved my table out of the way. Under the icons, near the windows, they stood a rough unadorned coffin on a row of stools.

In the coffin lay Matryona. Her body, mangled and lifeless, was covered with a clean sheet. Her head was swathed in a white kerchief. Her face was almost undamaged, peaceful, more alive than dead.

The villagers came to pay their last respects. The women even brought their small children to take a look at the dead. And if anyone raised a lament, all the women, even those who had looked in out of idle curiosity, always joined in, wailing where they stood by the door or the wall, as though they were providing a choral accompaniment. The men stood stiff and silent with their caps off.

The formal lamentation had to be performed by the women of Matryona's family. I observed that the lament followed a coldly calculated, age-old ritual. The more distant relatives went up to the coffin for a short while and made low wailing noises over it. Those who considered themselves closer kin to the dead woman began their lament in the doorway and when they got as far as the coffin, bowed down and roared out their grief right in the face of the departed. Every lamenter made up her own melody. And expressed her own thoughts and feelings.

I realized that a lament for the dead is not just a lament, but a kind of politics. Matryona's three sisters swooped, took possession of the cottage, the goat, and the stove, locked up the chest, ripped the two hundred rubles for the funeral out of the coat lining, and drummed it into everybody who came that only they were near relatives. Their lament over the coffin went like this, "*Oh, nanny, nanny! Oh nan-nan!* All we had in the world was you! You could have lived in peace and quiet, you could. And we should always have been kind and loving to you. Now your top room's been the death of you. Finished you off, it has, the cursed thing! Oh, why did you have to take it down? Why didn't you listen to us?"

Thus the sisters' laments were indictments of Matryona's husband's family: they shouldn't have made her take the top room down. (There was an underlying meaning, too: you've taken the top room, all right, but we won't let you have the house itself!)

Matryona's husband's family, her sisters-in-law, Efim and Faddey's sisters, and the various nieces lamented like this, "*Oh poor auntie, poor auntie!* Why didn't you take better care of yourself! Now they're angry with us for sure. Our own dear Matryona you were, and it's your own fault! The top room is nothing to do with it. Oh why did you go where death was waiting for you? Nobody asked you to go there. And what a way to die! Oh why didn't you listen to us?" (Their answer to the others showed through these laments: we are not to blame for her death, and the house we'll talk about later.)

But the "second" Matryona, a coarse, broad-faced woman, the substitute Matryona whom Faddey had married so long ago for the sake of her name, got out of step with family policy, wailing and sobbing over the coffin in her simplicity, "*Oh my poor dear sister!* You won't be angry with me, will you now? Oh-oh-oh! How we used to talk and talk, you and me! Forgive a poor miserable woman! You've gone to be with your dear mother, and you'll come for me some day, for sure! Oh-oh-oh-oh! . . . "

At every "oh-oh-oh" it was as though she were giving up the ghost. She writhed and gasped, with her breast against the side of the coffin. When her lament went beyond the ritual prescription, the women, as though acknowledging its success, all started saying, "Come away now, come away."

Matryona came away, but back she went again, sobbing with even greater abandon. Then an ancient woman came out of a corner, put her hand on Matryona's shoulder, and said, "There are two riddles in this world: how I was born, I don't remember, how I shall die, I don't know."

And Matryona fell silent at once, and all the others were silent, so that there was an unbroken hush.

But the old woman herself, who was much older than all the other old women there and didn't seem to belong to Matryona at all, after a while started wailing, "Oh, my poor sick Matryona!

Oh my poor Vasilyevna! Oh what a weary thing it is to be seeing you into your grave!"

There was one who didn't follow the ritual, but wept straight-forwardly, in the fashion of our age, which has had plenty of practice at it. This was Matryona's unfortunate foster daughter, Kira, from Cherusti, for whom the top room had been taken down and moved. Her ringlets were pitifully out of curl. Her eyes looked red and bloodshot. She didn't notice that her head-scarf was slipping off out in the frosty air and that her arm hadn't found the sleeve of her coat. She walked in a stupor from her foster mother's coffin in one house to her brother's in another. They were afraid she would lose her mind, because her husband had to go for trial as well.

It looked as if her husband was doubly at fault: not only had he been moving the top room, but as an engine driver, he knew the regulations about unprotected crossings and should have gone down to the station to warn them about the tractor. There were a thousand people on the Urals express that night, peace-fully sleeping in the upper and lower berths of their dimly lit carriages, and all those lives were nearly cut short. All because of a few greedy people, wanting to get their hands on a plot of land, or not wanting to make a second trip with a tractor.

All because of the top room, which had been under a curse ever since Faddey's hands had started itching to take it down.

The tractor driver was already beyond human justice. And the railway authorities were also at fault, both because a busy cross-ing was unguarded and because the coupled engines were traveling without lights. That was why they had tried at first to blame it all on the drink, and then to keep the case out of court.

The rails and the track were so twisted and torn that for three days, while the coffins were still in the house, no trains ran—they were diverted onto another line. All Friday, Saturday, and Sunday, from the end of the investigation until the funeral, the work of repairing the line went on day and night. The repair gang was frozen, and they made fires to warm themselves and to light their work at night, using the boards and beams from the second sledge, which were there for the taking, scattered around the crossing.

The first sledge just stood there, undamaged and still loaded, a little way beyond the crossing.

One sledge, tantalizingly ready to be towed away, and the other perhaps still to be plucked from the flames—that was what harrowed the soul of black-bearded Faddey all day Friday and all day Saturday. His daughter was going out of her mind, his son-in-law had a criminal charge hanging over him, in his own house lay the son he had killed, and along the street the woman he had killed and whom he had once loved. But Faddey stood by the coffins, clutching his beard, only for a short time, and went away again. His high forehead was clouded by painful thoughts, but what he was thinking about was how to save the timbers of the top room from the flames and from Matryona's scheming sisters.

Going over the people of Talnovo in my mind, I realized that Faddey was not the only one like that.

Property, the people's property, or my property, is strangely called our "goods." If you lose your goods, people think you disgrace yourself and make yourself look foolish.

Faddey dashed about, never stopping to sit down, from the settlement to the station, from one official to another, there he stood with his bent back, leaning heavily on his stick, and begged them all to take pity on an old man and give him permission to recover the top room.

Somebody gave permission. And Faddey gathered together his surviving sons, sons-in-law, and nephews, got horses from the kolkhoz and from the other side of the wrecked crossing, by a roundabout way that led through three villages, brought the remnants of the top room home to his yard. He finished the job in the early hours of Sunday morning.

On Sunday afternoon they were buried. The two coffins met in the middle of the village, and the relatives argued about which of them should go first. Then they put them side by side on an open sledge, the aunt and the nephew, and carried the dead over the damp snow, with a gloomy February sky above, to the churchyard two villages away. There was an unkind wind, so the priest and the deacon waited inside the church and didn't come out to Talnovo to meet them.

A crowd of people walked slowly behind the coffins, singing in chorus. Outside the village they fell back.

When Sunday came the women were still fussing around the house. An old woman mumbled psalms by the coffin, Matryona's sisters flitted about, popping things into the oven, and the air round the mouth of the stove trembled with the heat of red-hot peats, those Matryona had carried in a sack from a distant bog. They were making unappetizing pies with poor flour.

When the funeral was over and it was already getting on toward evening, they gathered for the wake. Tables were put together to make a long one, which hid the place where the coffin had stood in the morning. To start with, they all stood round the table, and an old man, the husband of a sister-in-law, said the Lord's Prayer. Then they poured everybody a little honey and warm water, just enough to cover the bottom of the bowl. We spooned it up without bread or anything, in memory of the dead. Then we ate something and drank vodka and the conversation became more animated. Before the jelly they all stood up and sang "Eternal remembrance" (they explained to me that it had to be sung before the jelly). There was more drinking. By now they were talking louder than ever, and not about Matryona at all. The sister-in-law's husband started boasting, "Did you notice, brother Christians, that they took the funeral service slowly today? That's because Father Mikhail noticed me. He knows I know the service. Other times, it's saints defend us, homeward wend us, and that's all."

At last the supper was over. They all rose again. They sang "Worthy Is She." Then again, with a triple repetition of "Eternal Remembrance." But the voices were hoarse and out of tune, their faces drunken, and nobody put any feeling into this "eternal memory."

Then most of the guests went away, and only the near relatives were left. They pulled out their cigarets and lit up, there were jokes and laughter. There was some mention of Matryona's husband and his disappearance. The sister-in-law's husband, striking himself on the chest, assured me and the cobbler who was married to one of Matryona's sisters, "He was dead, Efim was dead! What could stop him coming back if he wasn't? If I knew they were going to hang me when I got to the old place, I'd come back just the same!"

The cobbler nodded in agreement. He was a deserter and had never left the old place. All through the war he was hiding in his mother's cellar.

The stern and silent old woman who was more ancient than all the ancients was staying the night and sat high up on the stove. She looked down in mute disapproval on the indecently animated youngsters of fifty and sixty.

But the unhappy foster daughter, who had grown up within these walls, went away behind the kitchen screen to cry.

Faddey didn't come to Matryona's wake—perhaps because he was holding a wake for his son. But twice in the next few days he walked angrily into the house for discussions with Matryona's sisters and the deserting cobbler.

The argument was about the house. Should it go to one of the sister or to the foster daughter? They were on the verge of taking it to court, but they made peace because they realized that the court would hand over the house to neither side, but to the Rural District Council. A bargain was struck. One sister took the goat, the cobbler and his wife got the house, and to make up Faddey's share, since he had "nursed every bit of timber here in his arms," in addition to the top room which had

already been carried away, they let him have the shed which
had housed the goat and the whole of the inner fence between
the yard and the garden.

Once again the insatiable old man got the better of sickness
and pain and became young and active. Once again he gathered together his surviving sons and sons-in-law, they dismantled
the shed and the fence, he hauled the timbers himself, sledge
by sledge, and only toward the end did he have Antoshka of
8-D, who didn't slack this time, to help him.

They boarded Matryona's house up till the spring, and I moved
in with one of her sisters-in-law, not far away. This sister-in-law
on several occasions came out with some recollection of Matryona and made me see the dead woman in a new light. "Efim
didn't love her. He used to say, 'I like to dress in an educated
way, but she dresses any old way, like they do in the country.'
Well then, he thinks, if she doesn't want anything, he might as
well drink whatever's to spare. One time I went with him to the
town to work, and he got himself a madam there and never
wanted to come back to Matryona."

Everything she said about Matryona was disapproving. She
was slovenly, she made no effort to get a few things about her.
She wasn't the saving kind. She didn't even keep a pig, because
she didn't like fattening them up for some reason. And the silly
woman helped other people without pay. (What brought
Matryona to mind this time was that the garden needed plow-
ing, and she couldn't find enough helpers to pull the plow.)

Matryona's sister-in-law admitted that she was warmhearted
and straightforward, but pitied and despised her for it.

It was only then, after these disapproving comments from
her sister-in-law, that a true likeness of Matryona formed before
my eyes, and I understood her as I never had when I lived side
by side with her.

Of course! Every house in the village kept a pig. But she
didn't. What can be easier than fattening a greedy piglet that
cares for nothing in the world but food! You warm his swill
three times a day, you live for him—then you cut his throat and
you have some fat.

But she had none.

She made no effort to get things round her. She didn't
struggle and strain to buy things and then care for them more
than life itself.

She didn't go all out after fine clothes. Clothes, that beautify
what is ugly and evil.

She was misunderstood and abandoned even by her husband.
She had lost six children, but not her sociable ways. She was

a stranger to her sisters and sisters-in-law, a ridiculous creature who stupidly worked for others without pay. She didn't accumulate property against the day she died. A dirty-white goat, a gammy-legged cat, some rubber plants. . . .

We had all lived side by side with her and had never understood that she was the righteous one without whom, as the proverb says, no village can stand.

Nor any city.

Nor our whole land.

1963

1

"Fayina, who's got the schedule for the electrical classes?"

"What do you want it for if you've got radio?"

"Please reduce the noise here by about twenty decibels. There's a new comrade here—I want it for him."

"I'm sorry. What subject are you going to be giving here?"

"Generators—and power-transmission theory."

"There's so much noise, you can't hear a thing! And they call themselves teachers! The schedule is over there in the corner. Go have a look."

"Susanna! How are you?"

"Lydia, my dear! How well you look! Where did you spend the summer?"

"A good question. I spent all of July on the building site!"

"On the building site? But didn't you have a vacation?"

"Not really. Three weeks instead of eight. But I didn't really mind. *You* look a bit pale to me."

"Grigory! What have you got down for the electricians? You mean you've scheduled only two days?"

"But none of the other departments have fixed their classes past September second. It's all provisional. Comrades—who's that leaving? Comrades! Listen! Quiet! I repeat—Fyodor Mikheyevich asked you not to go away."

"But where is he?"

"In the new building. He'll be right back. Then we can talk about the business of moving."

"Well, it better be settled soon. We've already got out-of-town students coming in. Do we have to find them places to live or will the dormitory be ready?"

"God knows! It's dragged on so long. Why on earth can't we ever get anything done on time?"

"I'm getting two rooms in the new building, Marya Dyomi-dovna, and that'll do me fine! Electrical engineering in one and measurements in the other."

"So am I. I've got one room for electronics and another for insulating materials and lighting."

"Well, I'm really glad, for your sake. What you have now isn't a laboratory. It's a dumping ground for broken glass."

"All this stuff lying around in crates in the corridor and the cellar—it's a nightmare! But with the shelves we've put up in the new building there'll be a place for everything: ignitrons, thyratrons, and what have you. It'll be great."

"Vitaly, stop smoking! If you want to smoke you should ask the ladies."

"Let me introduce our new engineering teacher, Anatoly Germanovich. This is Susanna Samoylovna. She is head of our mathematics department."

Don't be funny. What do you mean, head of the department?"

"Well, head of the examination board, then. Isn't that the same thing? Except you don't get paid for it. Oh, and you must meet someone else— Lydia Georgyevna. She's one of the most important people around here."

"Important! I'm probably the least important. As a matter of fact, before you know it you'll be more important."

"I bet you only say that because I'm wearing glasses."

"No. Because you're an engineer and a specialist. But they could easily do without me. I'm quite superfluous."

"What do you teach?"

"Russian language. And literature."

"You can tell from Lydia Georgyevna's smile that she doesn't feel at all superfluous. In the first place, she's in charge of our youth organization."

"Really? Did the students elect you?"

"No, the Party Bureau assigned me to the Komsomol Committee."

"Come on now, Lydia, no false modesty. The kids asked for you and nobody else. And they've done it now for four years in a row."

"I'll go further than that. I'd say that Lydia Georgyevna deserves most of the credit for getting the new building put up."

"You're making fun of me."

"I don't quite understand. Who built this new building of yours? Was it the Trust or did you do it yourselves?"

"We did it together. But that's a long story."

"Let's hear it, Lydia. We've got nothing else to do while we're waiting."

"Well, it was like this. The Trust told us it didn't have enough money this year for all its jobs and it would take another couple of years to get ours done. So we asked: Can we help? And they said: Okay. If you do, you can have the building by the first of September. We jumped at the chance. We called a general meeting of the Komsomol . . . ."

"But where could you hold a meeting here?"

"Well, we managed in the corridors and on the stairs, and we had loudspeakers in the classrooms. That was the best we could do. Anyway, we got a meeting together and put the question to them. And the answer was: Yes. So we split up into work groups. At first we put a teacher in charge of each group. But the boys said that wasn't necessary—they could manage on their own. We were worried about the fourteen- and fifteen-year-olds, though. We were afraid one of them might get caught under a crane or fall or something. But we kept an eye on them."

"Wasn't it chaos?"

"We did our best to make it work. The foreman in charge told us a week ahead how many hands he would need, what kind, and when. So we set up a sort of headquarters and decided who was to do what. The kids worked every day — some before classes and some after. And a lot of them worked on Sundays too. They decided that everybody should put in at least two weeks' work during the summer vacation. Of course we tried to fix it so that out-of-town students could do their share either at the start or the end of the summer. But even if they were needed in the middle they showed up."

"Amazing!"

"Not at all. What was amazing was that it was all done without any kind of pressure. You wouldn't have recognized those kids. The people from the Trust just couldn't believe it. They said: We can't keep up with them, we just can't."

"Incredible."

"You don't believe me? Ask anybody you like."

"It's not that I don't believe you. I suppose enthusiasm is natural, and a good thing too. But the trouble is that in this country the word has become hackneyed. It's abused all the time—take the radio, for instance. What *I* hear constantly at the factory is: 'What's in it for me? What does the job pay? Let's have it in writing.' And nobody raises an eyebrow—'incentives' and all that."

"And that's not all. They took a copy of the architect's plan and made a scale model of it. Then they carried it at the head of the May Day parade."

"Lydia Georgyevna is giving you the romantic side. But to really understand it you have to hear the practical side. This school's been in existence for seven years and all this time we've been stuck out here near the railroad. A while ago they added a one-story wing for workshops and gave us another small building about half a mile from here, but even that didn't help much. And then Fyodor Mikheyevich managed to get hold of some land right in town where we could build. There were some shacks on it that had to be pulled down first."

"That didn't take long, did it?"

"No. They dug two holes with power shovels and put in the foundations for the school building and the dormitory. They got as far as building one story and then everything came to a stop. For the next three years there was never any money. During all those changes in Moscow we were always over-looked—whether they split up the ministries or amalgamated them, we were always ignored. And the snow and rain didn't help either. But now they've set up these economic councils and the one we come under gave us some money on the first of June last year, and—"

"Dusya, open the window. These men! They really filled the room with smoke!"

"Do we have to go outside every time we want to smoke?"

"Well, that's not what the teachers' room is for."

"What jobs did *you* do on the building site?"

"Oh, all sorts of things, like digging the ditches for the boiler room."

"As a matter of fact, we dug *all* the ditches. For the electric mains, and .... *And* we filled them all in again."

"And unloaded bricks from the trucks and stacked them in the hoist. And we cleared the earth out of the foundations."

"And we removed all the trash, brought up all the stuff for the central heating and the flooring, and then we did a lot of cleaning up and scrubbing."

"So actually the builders only had to send skilled men, no laborers?"

"As a matter of fact, we even trained some of the boys and girls to do skilled jobs. We had two teams of learners: plasterers and painters. They were really good at it. It was a pleasure watching them."

"Where's that singing coming from? Outside?"

We're sick and tired of darkness and gloom
We'll put TV in every room
With diodes, triodes, and tetrodes, too
We'll make bigger and better tubes for you!

"Without even looking I can tell that it's one of the third-year classes."

"They're good, aren't they? I'd like to get a look at them. Can we see them from the window?"

"Come over here. Maryanna Kazimirovna, could you just move your chair a little?"

"Don't you believe it! The latest fashion is the 'barrel' line. Haven't you seen it? It's fitted in the waist, then it widens, then it narrows again, and then tapers down to mid-calf."

"I know another lake a little further away. You ought to see the carp I've caught there!"

"Lydia, watch where you're going. There are people sitting here."

"Here we are, Anatoly Germanovich. Just lean out. See that bunch of boys and girls?"

In airplanes, sputniks, and everywhere
Our vacuum tubes have found their place
Here on earth and up in space
Electronics sets the pace!

"They sure are enthusiastic. You can see they really mean it."

"They're so proud of that song: 'The Electronics Anthem.'
They wrote it themselves and they do it so well. They even won
the second prize in a local contest. Look! Only the girls are singing. The boys just stood there like this in the contest too, but
they do come in on the chorus at the top of their voices."

"I'll tell you why I'm watching them like this. You see, I'm
rather nervous because I'm used to teaching grown-ups. I once
gave a lecture—'The Progress of Science and Technology'—
at my son's school, and I nearly died of embarrassment. No
matter what I did, I couldn't get them to pay attention. The
principal pounded the table, but not even he could make them
listen. My son told me afterward that they locked the cloak-
room and nobody was allowed to go home. He said they often
do that when there are visiting delegations or special events. So,
to get even, the kids just keep talking."

"But you can't compare that with a technical school. Things
are quite different here. We don't have any of those types with
more money than brains who are just passing their time. And
the principal here has greater powers because of scholarships
and dormitory places. . . . Though actually we've never had a
dormitory in our seven years and they have to get private ac-
commodations."

"Does the school pay for them?"

"The school gives them thirty rubles each—that's the stand-
ard rate and it's supposed to be enough. But a bed costs a
hundred rubles a month—a hundred and fifty for something a
little better. So some of them rent one bed for two. And they
live like that for years. Of course they're fed up. You seemed a
bit skeptical about our enthusiasm. There's nothing to be
skeptical about. We are just tired of living badly. We want to
live well! Isn't that why people did voluntary work on Sundays
in Lenin's time?"

"True."

"Well, that's what we've been doing. There they are. Look
out the window."

. . . bigger and better tubes for you!

"How far is it from here into town?"

"About half a mile."

"But they still have to walk that half a mile. And a lot of them
have to do it twice a day each way. And although it's summer
and we haven't had any rain for three days, we're still knee-
deep in mud. We just can't ever dress up. We have to wear
boots all the time. Long after the streets in town are nice and
dry we still get absolutely filthy."

. . . up in space

"So we had a meeting and talked things over: How much longer were we supposed to go on suffering? You should see the miserable little holes where we have classes. And there's no room for social activities. I think that's what bothers the students most of all."

. . . sets the pace!

"Lydia Georgyevna! Ma'am!"

"Here I am!"

"We must see you. Can you spare a moment?"

"I'll be right there. . . . Excuse me."

"He really scored a great goal—with his back to the goal post and over the head, from the penalty line—right under the crossbar."

"This can't be your hat! That style went out ages ago. The hats they're wearing now look like flower pots upside down."

"Maryanna Kazimirovna, can I bother you for a moment? . . ."

". . . I'm hoping to get part of the basement for a rifle range. I've already told the boys."

". . . I'm not leaving, Grigory Lavrentyevich. I'll be outside, on the stairs. . . ."

2

"Now who wanted to see me? Hello! How are you? It's so good to see all of you!"

"Congratulations, ma'am!"

"And congratulations to you." Lydia raised her hand and waved to them. "You've really earned it! Good for you and welcome back! In our new building!"

"Hooray!!!"

"Who's that over there trying so hard to keep out of my sight? Lina? You've cut your hair! Why? It was so lovely."

"Nobody wears long hair any more."

"The things you girls will do just to be in style."

Lydia, wearing a blue-green tailored suit and a black blouse, looked neat and trim. She had a friendly, open face. Standing on the landing outside the teachers' room, she studied the young people crowding around her from the narrow passage and staircase. Usually there wasn't much light here, but on this sunny day there was enough to see the details of the students' clothes. There were scarves, kerchiefs, blouses, dresses, and cowboy shirts of every color and shade—white, yellow, pink, red, blue, green, and brown—dots and designs, stripes and checks, and plain solid colors.

The girls and the boys tried not to stand too close to one another. Pressed together in their own group, they rested their chins on the shoulders of those in front, craning their necks so as to see better. They all had happy, shining faces, and there was a buzz of excitement as they looked expectantly at Lydia.

She looked around and noticed that most of the girls had changed their hair styles during the summer. There were still a few who had old-fashioned braids tied with colored ribbons, and a few with simple center parts or not quite so simple curls brushed to one side. But most of them had those seemingly un-cared for, casual, untidy, but by no means artless hairdos, from pure blond to jet black. And the boys—the short and the tall, the fat and the thin—all wore gaudy, open-necked shirts. Some had their hair brushed forward, others wore it carefully brushed back or had crew cuts.

None of the very young students were here. But even the oldest were not yet beyond that tender, impressionable age at which the best in them could be brought out. Their faces mir-rored that special eagerness.

The minute Lydia came out of the room she was over-whelmed by those trusting eyes and smiles. It was the supreme reward of the teacher: students crowding around you eagerly like this.

They could not have said what it was they saw in her. It was just that, being young, they responded to everything genuine. You only had to take one look at her to know that she meant what she said. And they had gotten to know and like her even more during those months on the building site when she came, not dressed up, but in working clothes and a kerchief. She had never tried to order them around. She would never have asked anyone to do something she would not do herself. She had scrubbed, raked, and carried things together with the girls.

And although she was nearly thirty and married and had a two-year-old daughter, all the students called her Lydia, though not to her face, and the boys were only too proud to run errands for her. She always accompanied her instructions with a slight but commanding gesture, sometimes—and this was a sign of great trust—with a light tap on the shoulder.

"When are we going to move, Lydia Georgyevna?"

"Yes, when?"

"Come now, we've waited so long, surely we can wait another twenty minutes. The principal will be back any minute."

"But why haven't we moved already?"

"Oh, a few little things still have to be done there."

"Always the same old story."

"We could put the finishing touches on ourselves if they'd just let us in."

A well-built youth from the Komsomol Committee in a red-and-brown checked shirt, the one who had called Lydia out of the teachers' room, said to her: "But we must discuss the details of the move. Who is going to be responsible for what?"

"Well, I thought of doing it like this. . . ."

"Quiet, you guys!"

"My idea is to have a couple of trucks move the machinery and the heavy stuff. I'm sure we are quite capable of carrying the rest ourselves, like ants. After all, how far is it? What do you think the distance is?"

"About a mile."

"It's fifteen hundred yards—I measured it."

"What did you measure it with?"

"With the gadget on my bike."

"Must we really have those trucks if it takes a week to get them? There are nine hundred of us. Couldn't we get all the stuff moved in a day ourselves?"

"Of *course* we can!"

"Sure!"

"Let's start right away. Then we can use this place as a dorm."

"The sooner the better, before we get rain."

"Now tell me, Igor"—Lydia tapped the young man in the red-and-brown shirt on the chest (like a general taking a medal from his pocket and firmly pinning it on a soldier)—"who's here from the Committee?"

"Practically everybody. Some of them are outside."

"All right, then. All of you get together right away, split up into groups, and make a list of them—but legibly, please! Put down the number of people in each group and decide who will take on which laboratories and which classrooms, depending on the weight of the equipment. And, as far as possible, organize yourselves by classes, but be sure that nobody takes on more than he can manage. When that's done, we'll show the plan to the principal, get it approved, and then put a teacher in charge of each group."

"Very good, ma'am," said Igor, standing at attention. "And this is the last time we'll have to meet in a corridor. Over there we'll have our own room. Hey, Committee members! Where should we meet?"

"Let's all go outside," Lydia proposed. "That way we'll see Fyodor Mikheyevich as soon as he gets back."

They made their way noisily down the stairs and out to the street, leaving the staircase empty.

Outside, on the lot in front of the school, with its scattered, stunted trees, another couple of hundred young people were waiting. The third-year students from the vacuum-tube department were still standing around in a huddle, and the girls, arm in arm and looking at each other, were still singing:

The younger ones were playing tag. Whenever anyone was caught, they let him have it between the shoulders.

"Why are you hitting me on the back like that?" a plump little girl asked indignantly.

"Not on the back, on the backside!" retorted a young man with a cap pulled down on his forehead and a deflated volley ball tucked in his belt. But when he saw Lydia Georgyevna shaking a finger at him he sniggered and ran off.

There were even younger students, just turned fourteen, standing around in groups. They were neatly dressed and rather shy, taking in everything very carefully.

Some of the boys had brought their bicycles and were giving the girls rides on the handlebars.

Fluffy white clouds looking like whipped cream sailed across the sky. At times they hid the sun.

"As long as it doesn't rain," the girls said wistfully.

Three fourth-year students from the radio department—two girls and a boy—were talking together in a separate group. The girls' blouses were of a simple striped material, but the boy's bright yellow shirt had wild designs of palm trees, ships, and sail-boats. Lydia was struck by this contrast, and something that had been puzzling her for a long time went through her mind. In her youth, her older brothers and the boys of her own age dressed rather simply, even drably; it was the girls who went in for bold colors and styles, as was only natural. But for some time now a great rivalry had been going on: boys had begun to dress with greater care and even more gaudily and colorfully than girls, wearing loudly colored socks, as though it was not up to *them* to do the courting but to be courted. And the girls seemed to take them by the arm more often than they did the girls. Lydia was vaguely troubled by this odd behavior, because she feared that the boys were losing something of great importance to them.

"Well, Valery," she asked the young man in the yellow shirt with the sailboats, "do you think you got any wiser during the vacation?"

Valery smiled smugly: "Of course not! I got stupider."

"And doesn't that bother you? The girls won't think very much of you."

"Yes, they will!"

Judging by the expressions of the two girls, he had every reason for his self-confidence.

"What did you read during the summer?"

"Practically nothing, ma'am, Valery replied as smugly as ever. He was not, it seemed, very eager to pursue the conversation.

"But why?" Lydia asked, rather put out. "Why did I waste my time teaching you?"

"Because it was in the syllabus, I guess," Valery shot back.

"If we read books, where would we find time for movies and TV?" the two girls burst in. "There's always something on TV."

Other fourth-year students gathered around.

Lydia frowned. Her thick, fair hair was pulled straight back, exposing her high forehead, on which both her disappointment and perplexity could be clearly seen.

"Of course, it's not for me, a teacher in a school where you learn about television sets, to try to turn you against TV. Watch it by all means, but not all the time! And besides, there's no comparison. A show on TV isn't lasting. It's just for a day."

"But it's interesting and alive!" the young people insisted. "And then there's dancing. . . ."

"And ski jumping!"

"And motorcycling!"

"Books last for centuries!" Lydia said curtly but with a smile.

"Books last only one day, too," said a very serious young man. He was so round-shouldered he almost looked hunchbacked.

"Whatever gave you that idea?" Lydia asked indignantly.

"Just go to my bookstore," the round-shouldered boy said, "and you'll see how many novels are gathering dust in the windows. The shelves are piled high with them. Come back a year later, and they are still there. There's a bookstore on the block where I live and I know. After a while they pack them up and cart them away. A driver told me they are pulped and made into paper again. What was the point of printing them in the first place?"

In their second year, these boys had been her students. They had never said things like this. They had worked so well and gotten such good marks.

A discussion like this couldn't really be carried on while standing in a doorway amid all this commotion. But Lydia didn't want to drop it. That would have been a mistake.

"Well, you better have another look and see what *kind* of books are made into pulp!"

"I have looked, and I'll tell you if you like." The boy stood his ground. He wrinkled his forehead shrewdly. "Some of them were highly praised in the newspapers."

But the others were all talking at the same time, drowning out his voice. Anikin, the top student of his class—a husky fellow with a camera slung over his shoulder—pushed his way to the front. (They always listened to him.)

"Lydia Georgyevna, let's be frank. At the beginning of the

vacation you gave us a terribly long list of books, not one of them less than five hundred pages. How long does it take to read a book like that? Two months? And it's always an epic, a trilogy — 'to be continued.' Who do they publish them for?"

"For the critics," came the answer.

"To make money."

"Maybe that's it," Anikin agreed. "Because technicians— and that's most of us in this country— must read technical literature and special journals to keep posted. Otherwise they'd get kicked out of their jobs, and rightly so."

"Right!" shouted the boys. "And when do we have time to read the sports magazines?"

"And what about movie magazines?"

"To my way of thinking," Anikin said impatiently, "authors who in this day and age write such long things really have a lot of nerve! We always have to find the most economical solutions when we design a circuit. When I sat in on the orals last year, the examiners kept on interrupting with questions like: 'Couldn't this be made shorter? Or simpler? Or cheaper?' Look at the sort of thing they write in the *Literary Gazette*. 'The characters,' they say, 'are too stereotyped and the plot is disjointed, but the ideas are just great!' That's like someone here saying: 'There's no current, the whole thing doesn't work, but the condensers are perfect.' Why don't they just say: 'This novel could have been one-tenth as long, and that one isn't worth reading.'"

"Well, I agree, some things could be shorter," Lydia said promptly.

The group of students surrounding her, which had steadily grown, howled with pleasure. That's what they liked about her: she never lied, and if she said she agreed, she meant it.

"But don't forget, books are a record of the people of our time, people like you and me, and about all the great things we have accomplished!"

"Memoirs are the thing nowadays," a boy with glasses and a funny-looking crew cut called out from the back. "Anyone who has reached the age of fifty or so goes and writes his memoirs— all about how he was born and got married. Any dope can write that kind of stuff."

"It all depends on *how* they are written," Lydia called back. "As long as they also write about the times they live in."

"But the kind of nonsense they put down," the boy said indignantly. "'I caught a chill while strolling in the garden.' 'I came to the city and there were no rooms to be had in the hotel. . . .'"

The others pushed him aside and shut him up.

"About keeping things short, I'd like to say something."
Another student raised his hand.

"I want to say something about the classics." Still another
one raised his hand.

Lydia, seeing all their eager faces, smiled happily. She didn't
care how excited they got or how they baited her. People who
argue are open to persuasion. What she feared most of all in
young people was indifference.

"Go ahead," she said to the first one, the one who wanted to
speak about the need for precision in writing.

This was Chursanov, a boy with unruly hair, wearing a gray
shirt with a turned and mended collar. His father was dead, and
his mother, who worked as a caretaker, had other, younger
children. That's why he had to quit regular school at fourteen
and switch to a technical school. He hadn't been getting very
good marks in Russian, but ever since he was little he had been
putting together radio receivers. Here at the school they
thought he was brilliant at it. He could find faulty connections
without even looking at a diagram, as though he sensed them.

"Listen," Chursanov called out shrilly, "Anikin's right. Time
is short. We can't afford to waste it. So what do I do? I just don't
read novels and things at all."

They all roared with laughter.

"But you said you wanted to say something about keeping
things short."

"So I do," Chursanov said in a tone of surprise. "When I'm
at home, I turn on the radio. There's the news or a talk or something and at the same time I'm getting dressed or eating or fixing
something. That's how I save time."

There was more laughter.

"What are you cackling about?" Chursanov asked, taken
aback.

"There's really nothing to laugh about," Marta Pochtyonnykh
came to his aid. She was a big, round-faced, rather plain-looking
girl with thick black braids open at the ends. "Don't you agree,
ma'am? It all depends on the book. It's all right if it tells you
something you can't find anywhere else. But if all there's in it
is something you can hear on the radio or read in the papers,
then what's the point? Things are shorter and livelier in the
newspapers."

"And they get things right. They don't make mistakes," somebody else called out.

"But what about the way things are said—the style?" a girl
with a fresh complexion asked coyly.

"What do you mean, style? What's wrong with the style in
the papers?"

"Lit-er-ary style, I mean," she answered, nodding her head at every syllable for emphasis.

"What do you mean by that?" Chursanov asked with a puzzled look. "People falling in love and all that? Is that what you mean?"

"Of course style is important," Lydia said heatedly. She put her hand to her breast as though there was nothing of which she was more convinced. "You see, a book must go into the psychological aspect of things."

She was hemmed in by them on all sides, but not all of them could hear her, and they were talking and shouting to one another. Her face was flushed.

"You just wait!" she said, trying to calm the rebels. "I won't let you get away with it. We're going to have a big auditorium in the new building, so in September we'll have a debate." She gripped Anikin and Marta firmly by the shoulders. "I'll get all of you up on the platform, everybody who's had something to say today, and then. . . ."

"Here he comes, here he comes!" The shout of the younger students was taken up by the older ones. One after the other, the young ones broke away, running faster and faster. The older ones got out of their way and turned to look after them. Teachers and students stuck their heads out of the second-story windows.

The school's battered pickup truck, lurching, bumping, and splashing mud, was approaching from the direction of the town. The principal and his driver could be seen through the windshield of the cab being pitched from side to side. The students who had been the first to rush forward noticed that, for some reason or other, the principal looked anything but happy.

And their shouting ceased.

They ran alongside the truck until it came to a stop. Fyodor Mikheyevich, a short, stocky man in a plain, worn blue suit, bareheaded, with graying hair, climbed down from the cab and looked around. He had to get to the doorway, but his way was blocked by the young people crowding in on him from both sides, watching and waiting. Some of the more impatient ones started to ask questions:

"What's the news, sir?"

"When will it be?"

Then, louder, from the back of the crowd:

"Are we moving?"

"When do we move?"

Once again he looked over the dozens of expectant, questioning faces. It was obvious that he would not be able to put off

answering them until he got upstairs. He'd have to do so right
there and then. "When?" "When do we move?" The youngsters
had been asking these questions all spring and summer. But at
that time the principal and homeroom teachers had been able
to brush off all such questions with a smile, saying: "It all depends on you. On how you work." But now Fyodor could do
nothing but sigh and, not concealing his irritation, he said:

"We shall have to wait a little longer, comrades. The builders
haven't quite finished yet."

His voice always sounded a little hoarse, as though he
had a cold.

A murmur was heard among the students. "More waiting."
"Still not ready." "And the term begins the day after tomorrow,
September first." "So now we'll have to go back to furnished
rooms again."

The boy in the bright yellow shirt with the sailboats on it
smirked and said to his girl friends:

"What did I tell you? Always the same old story. And mark
my words, that's not the end of it."

They began to shout questions:

"But can't we finish it ourselves?"

The principal smiled and said:

"I see you want to do everything yourselves now! But I'm
afraid that's not possible."

The girls standing in front tried hard to make him change
his mind: "But, sir, can't we move in anyway? What still has
to be done?"

The principal, a heavy-set man with a high forehead, looked
at them in some embarrassment:

"Come now, girls, surely I don't have to give you all the
details! First of all, the floors are still not dry in spots. . . ."

"Then we won't walk on them! We'll put boards across
them!"

"Then a lot of windows still don't have catches."

"That doesn't matter, it's still warm enough."

"The central heating hasn't been tested yet."

"That's nothing. That can wait till winter."

"Oh, and a lot of other little things. . . ."

Fyodor gestured helplessly. His forehead was a mass of
wrinkles. How could he explain to them all the formalities involved in taking over the building? A deed of transfer had to be
signed by the builders and by the other contracting party. The
builder was ready to sign and hand over the building right away.
And Fyodor was now so pressed for time that he too would
have signed right away if only the school were the other contracting party. But this was impossible from a legal point of view,

because the school had no one competent to make the required
survey. Therefore the building office of the local relay factory had placed the contract on the school's behalf. The plant was in no hurry to sign for the building before it was quite ready, especially since it meant infringing on the regulations. Khabalygin, the manager of the plant, had been promising Fyodor all summer long that he would sign for the building in August, come what may. But recently he had been saying: "Nothing doing, comrades. We won't sign the deed before they've put in the last screw." And technically he was right.

The girls went on plaintively:

"Oh, we *do* so want to move. Our hearts are set on it so."

"*Why* are you so set on it?" Chursanov shouted at them. He was standing on slightly higher ground than the others. "Whatever happens we've got to put in a month on a kolkhoz. Who cares which building we go from—this one or the other?"

"Oh, yes, the kolkhoz!" They suddenly remembered. Working on the building site all summer they had forgotten about the farm work.

"We won't be going this year," Lydia called out from the back. It was only now that the principal noticed her.

"Why aren't we going? Why not?" they asked her.

"You should read the local paper, my friends. Then you'd know why."

"I bet we'll go anyway."

The principal pushed his way through the crowd and moved toward the door. Lydia caught up with him on the stairway, which was just wide enough for two people.

"Fyodor Mikheyevich! But they *will* let us have it in September, won't they?"

"Yes, they will," he replied absently.

"We've worked out a wonderful plan for moving everything over between lunch on Saturday and Monday morning, so as not to interfere with schoolwork. We're going to split up into groups. The Commitee is arranging it now."

"Very good," the principal nodded, lost in his own thoughts. What worried him was that only a few trifling details remained to be done and that Khabalygin, who must have seen this two or three weeks ago, could easily have speeded things up and signed for the building. It almost looked as though Khabalygin was dragging his feet.

"On a quite different matter, Fyodor Mikheyevich: we've discussed the case of Engalychev in the Committee. He has given us his word and we're prepared to answer for him. So please restore his stipend on September first." Lydia looked at him pleadingly.

"You're always sticking up for them, aren't you?" The principal shook his head and looked at her with his pale-blue eyes. "And what if he does it again?"

"No, no, he won't," she assured him. They had reached the top of the stairs and could see the other teachers and the school secretary.

"I hope you're right."

He went into his cramped office and sent for his assistant and the department heads. He just wanted their assurance that they were ready to start the new school year, come what may, and that they had already prepared everything without having to be told.

In all his years at the school, Fyodor had tried to run things to keep everything going with a minimum of intervention on his part. He had finished his studies before the war and couldn't possibly keep up with all the latest developments in his rapidly changing field or with the specialists working under him. He was a modest man without personal ambition, and he had his own ideas about leadership. His idea of a leader was a man who, instead of following his own whims, settled things fairly by bringing together people who trusted one another and could work together harmoniously.

Fayina, the school secretary, came into the office. Very independent, and no longer young, she was wearing a colored kerchief tied under her chin. Its loose ends trailed behind her like a pennant as she walked. She handed the principal a diploma that needed his signature and opened a bottle of India ink.

"What's this?" Fyodor asked blankly.

"Gomozina's diploma. You remember, she couldn't take the exam because she was ill."

"Yes, of course."

He tried the pen and dipped it in the ink. Then he clasped his right wrist firmly in his left hand. And then he signed.

When he was wounded for the second time—that was in Transylvania—not only did his broken collarbone fail to heal properly, he also suffered severe shock. It had affected his hearing and his hands shook, so he always signed important papers in this manner.

3

An hour and a half later the crowd had gone. Those teachers who had to prepare experiments remained behind with their lab assistants. Students were thronging the school office to register their addresses. Lydia and the Committee members drew up their moving plan and got it approved by the principal and the department heads.

The principal was still sitting with the dean of students when Fayina, her kerchief flying, burst into the office and announced dramatically that two limousines were coming from the town, apparently heading for the school. The principal looked out of the window and saw that two cars—one blue-green, the other gray—were indeed approaching.

There could be no doubt about it. Some bigwigs coming to visit the school. He should really go down to meet them. But he wasn't expecting anybody important, so he stayed where he was —at the open window on the second floor.

Big, white clouds were swirling across the sky.

The cars drew up to the entrance and out stepped five men in fedoras—two of them in the kind of green ones worn by the higher-ups in this town, the three others in light-colored ones. Fyodor immediately recognized the first man. It was Vsevolod Khabalygin, manager of the relay factory and hence nominally the "proprietor" of the new school building. He was a real big shot. By comparison Fyodor was a nobody, but Khabalygin had always been friendly toward him. Twice that morning Fyodor had tried to reach Khabalygin on the phone. He wanted to ask him to relent and let his building office sign for the new school and draw up a list of the work still to be done, but on both occasions he had been told that Khabalygin was out.

Fyodor had a sudden thought. Turning to the dean, who was standing there as tall and thin as a rail, he said:

"Grisha, maybe it's a commission to speed things up. Wouldn't that be great?"

And he hurried out to meet the visitors. The stern, brisk dean, of whom the students were very much afraid, followed after him.

But Fyodor had only got as far as the first-floor landing when he saw the visitors coming up the stairs, one after the other. First came Khabalygin. He was a short man, still under sixty, but overweight. He had passed the 250-pound mark long ago, and he was suffering as a result. His hair was graying at the temples.

"Ah—good." He stretched out his hand approvingly toward the principal. And as he reached the landing, he turned and said: "This is a Comrade from our Ministry in Moscow."

The Comrade from the Ministry was a good deal younger than Khabalygin, but he was also putting on weight. He permitted Fyodor to hold the tips of three smooth, dainty fingers for a moment and then moved on.

Actually, for two years "our" Ministry had had nothing to do with the school, which now was under the local Economic Council.

"I tried to get you on the phone twice today," Fyodor said to Khabalygin with a smile of pleasure and reached out to take him by the arm. "I was going to ask you...."

"And here," Khabalygin went on, "is a Comrade from the Department of...." He mentioned the department by name, but in his confusion Fyodor didn't catch it.

The Comrade from the Department was young, well built, good-looking, and very well dressed.

"And this," Khabalygin continued, "is the Head of the Electronics Section from...." Khabalygin said where from, but while speaking he resumed climbing the stairs, so again Fyodor failed to catch the name.

The Head of the Electronics Section was a short, dark, polite man with a small black moustache.

And finally there was the Supervisor of the Industrial Department of the District Party Committee, whom Fyodor knew well. They exchanged greetings.

Not one of the five men was carrying anything.

The dean was standing stony faced, straight as a soldier, next to the banister at the top of the landing. Some of them nodded to him; others didn't.

Khabalygin managed to hoist his hefty bulk to the top of the stairs. Nobody could have walked next to him or passed him on the narrow staircase. After reaching the top he stood still, puffing and blowing. But his expression, always animated and forceful, discouraged any inclination to sympathize with him for the way in which, every time he walked or made a movement, he had to battle his large body, on which the layers of unlovely fat had been skillfully camouflaged by his tailors.

"Shall we go into my office?" Fyodor asked when he reached the top.

"Oh no, there's no point in sitting around," Khabalygin objected. "You go ahead and show us what you've got here. What do you say, comrades?"

The Comrade from the Department pushed back the sleeve of his foreign raincoat, looked at his watch, and said:

"Of course."

Fyodor Mikheyevich sighed. "Honestly, we just don't know where to turn. We have to hold classes in two shifts. There aren't enough places in the laboratories. Different types of experiments have to be carried out in the same room, so that we're always having to put one batch of instruments away to make room for another."

He looked from one to the other, speaking almost in a tone of apology.

"You do make it sound terrible," Khabalygin said, and started to shake with either coughing or laughter—it wasn't clear which. And the rolls of flabby fat hanging from his neck like an ox's dewlap also shook. "It's amazing how you've managed to stand it these seven years!"

Fyodor arched his fair, bushy eyebrows: "But we didn't have so many departments then! And there were fewer students!"

"Oh well, lead on. Let's take a look."

The principal nodded to the dean as a signal that everything should be opened up, and he started to show the visitors around. They followed him without bothering to take off their hats and coats.

They went into a large room with shelves all around the walls, all crammed with equipment. A teacher, a girl lab assistant in a blue smock, and a senior student—it was Chursanov, the boy with the patched collar—were setting up an experiment. The room faced south and was flooded with sunlight.

"Well," Khabalygin said brightly. "What's wrong with this? It's a beautiful room."

"But you must understand," Fyodor said with some annoyance, "that in this one room there are three laboratories, one on top of the other: theory of radio and aerials, transmitters, and receivers.

"Well, so what?" The Comrade from the Ministry turned his large, handsome head and said, also with some annoyance, "Do you think there's more space between the desks in our Ministry after the latest reorganization? On the contrary, there's less than ever."

"These subjects are very closely related, after all." Khabalygin, very pleased with himself at this idea, patted the principal on the shoulder. "Don't act the pauper, comrade. You're not so badly off as all that!"

Fyodor threw him a puzzled look.

From time to time Khabalygin moved his lips and his fleshy jowls, as though he had just had a good meal but hadn't yet had time to remove bits of food stuck between his teeth.

"What are these things for?" The Comrade from the Department was standing before some strange-looking rubber boots with turned-down tops which looked big enough for a giant. He touched them with the sharply pointed toe of his shoe.

"Safety boots," the teacher said quietly.

"What?"

"Safety boots!" Chursanov shouted in the impudent tone of one who has nothing to lose.

"Oh yes, of course," the Comrade from the Department said and followed the others.

The Supervisor from the District Committee, who was the last to leave the room, asked Chursanov: "But what are they for?"

"For when you repair a transmitter," Chursanov replied.

Fyodor had meant to show them all the rooms, but the visitors passed some of them by and went into the lecture hall. On the walls there were charts of English verbs and various visual aids. Geometric models were piled high on the cabinet shelves.

The electronics expert counted the desks (there were thirteen) and, stroking his toothbrush moustache with two fingers, asked:

"How many do you have to a class? About thirty?"

"Yes, on the average . . ."

"That means you have less than three to a desk."

And they continued their tour.

In the small television workshop there were about ten sets of various makes, some brand new and some partly dismantled, standing on the tables.

"Do they work? All of them?" the Comrade from the Department asked, nodding at the sets.

"Those that are supposed to work all right," a young, smartly dressed lab assistant said. He was wearing a sand-colored suit with some kind of badge in his lapel and a loud tie.

Some instruction manuals were lying around on a table. The electronics expert glanced through them, reading out the titles to himself under his breath: *Tuning a Television Set by the Test Table; The Use of the Television Set as an Amplifier; The Structure of Visual Signals.*

"You see, there are no shelves here, but you still manage," Khabalygin commented.

Fyodor grew more puzzled every minute and wondered what the commission was getting at.

"That's because everything is next door in the demonstration room. Show them, Volodya."

"So there's a demonstration room as well? You certainly are well off!"

The door leading into the demonstration room was unusually narrow, more like a closet door. The slim, dapper lab assistant went through it with ease. But when the Comrade from the Ministry tried to follow him, he realized at once that he couldn't make it. The others just poked their heads in, one after the other.

The demonstration room turned out to be a narrow corridor between two sets of shelves from floor to ceiling. With the sweeping gesture of a professional guide, the lab assistant pointed to the shelves and said:

"*This* belongs to the TV lab. *This* to the electricity lab. And *this* is the radio lab's."

Instruments with dials, and black, brown, and yellow boxes cluttered the shelves.

"And what's *that* doing there?" the Comrade from the Ministry asked, pointing to something.

He had noticed that the assistant had managed to keep a little wall space free of instruments, and to this he had affixed a colored pinup—the head and shoulders of a young woman. Without seeing the caption you couldn't tell whether she had been cut out of a Soviet or foreign magazine. But there she was —a beautiful, auburn-haired woman wearing a blouse with red embroidery. With her chin resting on her bare arms and her head tilted to one side, she eyed the young lab assistant and the more worldly-wise Comrade from the Ministry with a look that was anything but a call to duty.

"Well! You say you have no space," the Comrade sputtered, struggling around to get out again, "but just look at the sort of stuff you hang up around the place!"

And, with another quick glance at the lovely creature out of the corner of his eye, he walked away.

The news that some awful commission was around had already spread throughout the school. People kept peering out of doorways and poking their heads into the halls.

Lydia, walking along one of the corridors, bumped into the commission. She stood aside, flattened herself against the wall, and studied them anxiously. She couldn't hear what they were saying, but she could tell from the look on the principal's face that something was wrong.

Fyodor took the Supervisor from the District Committee by the arm and, holding him back a little, asked quietly:

"Tell me, who actually sent this commission? Why is nobody from the Economic Council with you?"

"Knorozov just told me to come along. I don't know what's going on myself."

Khabalygin, standing on the upper landing, cleared his throat, which made the rolls of sallow fat on his neck shake again, and lit a cigaret.

"That's that. I suppose the rest is much the same."

The Comrade from the Department looked at his watch and said: "It all seems pretty clear-cut."

The electronics expert stroked his moustache with two fingers and said nothing.

The Comrade from the Ministry asked: "How many other buildings are there beside this one?"

"Two, but. . . ."

"Really?"

"Yes, but they are quite terrible. Only one story and thoroughly inconvenient. And they're so far apart from each other. Let's go and look at them."

"And there are workshops in them too?"

"But listen, you're aware of the sort of conditions we're working in, aren't you?" Fyodor threw off the restraint imposed on him by the demands of hospitality and by the exalted position of his visitors. He really was worried now: "For one thing, we've got no dormitory. That's what we were going to use this building for. The young people have to live in private rooms all over town where there's sometimes foul language and drunkenness. All our efforts to build their characters are defeated. Where can we do it, on the staircase here?"

"Oh, come now, come now," the members of the commission protested.

"Character building depends on you, not on the premises," the young man from the Department said sternly.

"You can't blame anyone else for that," the District Committee Supervisor added.

"Yes, you really have no excuse," Khabalygin said, spreading his short arms.

Fyodor turned his head sharply and shrugged his shoulders, perhaps in response to this attack on him from all sides, or perhaps to put an end to this relentless interrogation. He could see that if he didn't ask directly he was never going to find out what this was all about. He knitted his bushy, fair brows.

"I'm sorry, but I'd very much like to know on whose authority you are acting and what exactly you are after."

The Comrade from the Ministry took off his hat and wiped his forehead with a handkerchief. He looked even more impressive without a hat. He had a fine head of hair, although it was thinning in spots.

"Haven't you heard yet?" he asked in a tone of mild surprise. "Our Ministry and"— he nodded toward his colleague— "the Department have decided that a research institute of national importance should be set up in this town and accommodated in the buildings originally intended for your school. That's it, isn't it, Khabalygin?"

"Yes, that's it," Khabalygin agreed, nodding his head in its green fedora. "That's the way it is." He eyed the principal somewhat sympathetically and gave him a friendly pat on the shoulder. "I'm sure you can stick it out for another couple of years, and then they'll build you a new school— an even better one! That's how things go, my friend, so don't let it get you down. It can't be helped. It's all for the good of the cause!"

Not very tall to begin with, Fyodor now seemed to become even shorter. He looked stunned, as if he had been hit over the head.

"But how. . . ." Fyodor said the first, but by no means the
most important, thing that came to his mind. "We haven't even
kept this place in good repair." When Fyodor was upset, his
voice, always gruff, dropped even lower and became quite
hoarse.

"Don't worry about that," Khabalygin said. "I bet you painted
it last year."

The Comrade from the Department went down one step on
the stairs.

There were so many things the principal wanted to tell them
that he couldn't make up his mind *what* to say first.

"What have I got to do with your Ministry?" he protested
hoarsely, while blocking the visitors' way. "We come under
the local Economic Council. You need a government order for
a transfer of this sort."

"You're quite right." The commission members pushed him
gently aside, making their way down the stairs. "We're just preparing the necessary papers. We expect the final okay in a
couple of days."

The five men went down the stairs while the principal just
stood there staring blankly after them.

"Fyodor Mikheyevich!" Lydia called out, coming down the
corridor. For some reason or other, she had her hand clasped to
her throat. Her blouse was open at the neck and one could see
how sunburned she had gotten while working on the building
site. "What did they have to say?"

"They are taking the building away from us," he replied in a
flat, almost toneless voice, without raising his eyes.

And with that he went into his study.

"What?" she cried out after a moment. "The new one?
They're taking it away from us?" She hurried after him, her
heels tapping on the floor. In the doorway she bumped into
the bookkeeper. She brushed her aside and rushed in after
the principal.

Fyodor Mikheyevich was walking slowly toward his desk.

"Listen!" Lydia called out in a strained voice. "What is this?
How can they do such a terrible thing? It's not right!" Her
voice was becoming shriller with every word. She was saying
out loud what *he* should have shouted at them. But he was
the principal, not a woman. Tears were now streaming down
her cheeks. "What are we going to tell the kids? That we've
cheated them?"

He couldn't remember ever having seen her cry before. He
slumped into his chair and stared vacantly ahead at his desk.
His forehead was one mass of wrinkles.

The bookkeeper, an elderly, shriveled-up woman, her straggly hair gathered in a bun at the nape of her neck, was standing there holding a checkbook.

She had heard everything. She would have gone away at once and not bothered him, but she had just spoken to the bank and been told that she could cash a check. The check had already been made out, with the amount and date filled in. She therefore had to see the principal, in spite of everything. She put the long, blue-striped book down in front of him and held it flat with her hand.

Fyodor dipped his pen in the ink, grasped his right wrist with his left hand, and raised it to write his signature. But even clutched like this, his hands still shook. He tried to put his signature on the check. The pen started to make some marks, then dug into the paper and sputtered.

Fyodor looked up at the bookkeeper and smiled.

She bit her lip, took the checkbook away from him, and hurried out.

4

Everything had happened so suddenly, and the commission had breezed through with such supreme confidence and so rapidly that Fyodor had not been able to find the words he wanted while they were there, and even after they had gone he was still unable to decide exactly what to do.

He phoned the Education Department of the Economic Council. All they did was listen to his story, voice their indignation, and promise to look into the matter. Another time that might have cheered him up. But now it didn't. He knew the commission hadn't come for a social visit.

He felt so ashamed. He didn't know how he could face the students or the teachers, or anybody else he had gotten to help with the new building on the understanding that it would be theirs. All the plans which for months, even years, he and his colleagues had been making for the new building were now completely ruined. He would gladly exchange his own living quarters for worse ones if only the new building were given to the school.

His mind went blank. He just didn't seem able to think clearly.

Without a word to anyone and without putting on his hat, he went out to try to collect his thoughts.

Leaving the building, he set off in the direction of the railroad. But he wasn't really thinking about where he was going, because in his mind he was turning over the dozens of vitally important things the school was losing along with the new building. The railroad barrier came down just as he got to the crossing.

Fyodor stopped, although he could have slipped through under it. A long freight train appeared in the distance, eventually reached the crossing, and quickly clattered past down the incline. But Fyodor didn't really take any of this in. The barrier was raised and he continued on his way.

He was inside the gates of the new building before he realized where he actually was. His legs had taken him there of their own accord. The main entrance, on which all the glazing and painting were already finished, was locked. So Fyodor went through the grounds which had been marked off and cleared by the students. There was plenty of land, and they had planned to turn it into athletic fields.

One of the builders' trucks stood in the yard, and the plumbers were noisily throwing brackets, piping, and other stuff into it. But Fyodor paid no attention to them.

He went into the building. It made him feel good to hear his footsteps echoing on the stone slabs of the wide lobby. Its two cloakrooms, one on each side, were big enough for a thousand people. The hat- and coat-racks of aluminum tubing shone brightly, and maybe it was this that made Fyodor ask himself a simple question which—because all this time he had been thinking about the school, not its new occupants—had not occurred to him until now: What on earth would the new institute do with such a building? For one thing, they'd probably dismantle these cloakrooms, because the institute wouldn't have even a hundred people. And what about the gymnasium with its wall ladders, rings, horizontal bars, nets, and wire-meshed windows? Was all that going to be pulled down and thrown out? What about the workshops with their specially built concrete foundations under each machine? And the electric wiring? And the whole layout of the building around the lecture halls? And the blackboards? And the main lecture hall, designed like an amphitheater? And the auditorium? And. . . .

At that moment a couple of painters and carpenters walked by him with their tools on the way out of the building.

"Hey! Listen!" Fyodor called to them, pulling himself together. "Comrades!"

But they went on their way.

"Listen, fellows!"

They turned around toward him.

"Where are you off to? It's not quitting time yet."

"We're through," the younger of the carpenters said blithely. The older one continued glumly on his way. "You can stay here and have a smoke. We're off!"

"But where to?"

"We've been taken off this job. Orders from above."

"But how can they take you off it?"

"*How?* Don't you know? They just send us to another job. We've been told to get there right away."

And, knowing the little gray-haired principal to be easy-going, the carpenter came back, tapped him on the hand, and said: "Give us a cigaret, chief."

Fyodor offered him a crumpled pack.

"Where's the foreman of this job?"

"Oh, he's already left. He was the first one to get out."

"What did he say?"

"He said that this has nothing to do with us any more. Another outfit is taking over."

"But who's going to finish here?" Fyodor asked impatiently. "What's so funny? Can't you see how much there's still to be done?" He frowned and looked angry.

"Who cares!" the carpenter shouted, puffing away at his cigaret and hurrying after his comrades. "Don't you know how they handle these things? The Trust will make up a list of what we didn't finish and get it signed when they hand this over, and everything'll be all right."

Fyodor watched as the carpenter walked away lightheartedly in his dirty overalls. And with him went the Economic Council, which had taken on this ill-fated project after three years of paralysis, and which had finished it, right down to the last coat of paint and the last pane of glass.

Although the Council was deserting him, the thought of the innumerable, utterly pointless alterations that would have to be made in the building fired Fyodor's will to resist. He knew that justice was on his side. He hurried across the hallway, his steps echoing on the hard floor.

The room with the only working telephone turned out to be locked, so Fyodor rushed outside. A wind had started to blow, stirring up the sand and scattering it around. The truck with the workers was just going through the gateway. The caretaker was standing next to the gates. Fyodor decided not to go back with him. He felt in his pocket for a coin and walked over to a phone booth.

He called Ivan Grachikov, the Secretary of the town's Party Committee. A secretary told him that Grachikov was in conference. Fyodor gave his name and asked her to find out whether Grachikov would see him and when. In one hour, he was told.

Fyodor continued on his way. While walking, and later, outside Grachikov's office, his mind went over every room on every floor in the new building. He couldn't visualize a single place where the institute wouldn't have either to knock down a wall or put up a new one. So he jotted down what all that would cost in a notebook.

For Fyodor, Grachikov wasn't just the Secretary of the Party Committee. He was also a friend from the war. They had been in the same regiment, though they hadn't served together very long. Fyodor had been in charge of communications. Grachikov had come from a hospital, as a replacement for a battalion commander who had been killed. They discovered that they came from the same part of the country, and on quiet evenings they used to get together or talk on the phone occassionally and reminisce about places they both knew. Then a company commander in Grachikov's battalion was killed, and, as is the practice, all openings were filled with officers from the staff, so Fyodor was assigned to command the company—temporarily. "Temporarily" turned out to be very brief indeed. Two days later he was wounded, and when he got out of the hospital he was sent to a different division.

As he sat there waiting, it occurred to him that unpleasant things always seemed to happen to him in the last days of August. It was on the twenty-ninth of August—that was yesterday's date—that he was wounded for the first time. And when he was wounded again, in 1944, it was on the thirtieth of August. That was today's date.

Some people left Grachikov's office and Fyodor was called in.

"A terrible thing has happened, Ivan," Fyodor said in a flat, hoarse voice as soon as he walked into the room. "Just terrible."

He sat up straight on a chair (Grachikov had got rid of those armchairs into which people sank so deep that their chins barely reached the top of the desk) and began his story. Grachikov rested his head in the palm of his hand and listened.

Nature had given Ivan Grachikov rough-cast features: thick lips, a broad nose, and big ears. But, although he wore his black hair brushed to one side, which gave him a rather forbidding look, his whole appearance was so unmistakably Russian that no matter what foreign clothes or uniform you might put on him, you could never disguise the fact that he was a Russian born and bred.

"Honestly, Ivan," the principal said with feeling, "don't you think it's stupid? I don't mean just for the school, but from the point of view of the state, isn't it plain stupid?"

"Yes, it's stupid," Grachikov said promptly, without shifting in his chair.

"Look, I've jotted down how much all these alterations will come to. The whole building costs four million, right? Well, these changes are sure to cost at least one and a half million, if not two. Look."

From his notebook he read out a list of the various jobs and their probable cost. He was becoming more and more convinced that he had an absolutely airtight case.

Grachikov remained quite still, listening and thinking. He had once told Fyodor that the great thing about this job, compared to the war, was that he no longer had to make decisions by himself and on the spur of the moment, leaving the question of whether they were right or wrong to be settled in the other world. Grachikov much preferred to decide things without rushing—giving himself time to think and letting others have a say. It went against his grain to bring discussions and conferences to an end by simply issuing orders. He tried to argue things out with the people he was dealing with, to get them to say "Yes, that's right" or else have them convince him that *he* was wrong. And even in the face of very stubborn opposition he never lost his restrained, friendly manner. But his way took time. Knorozov, the First Secretary of the District Committee, had been quick to seize on this particular weakness of Grachikov's, and in his laconic fashion that admitted of no argument had once hurled at him: "You're too soft for this job. You don't do things in the Soviet way!" But Grachikov had stood his ground: "What do you mean? On the contrary, I do things the way the Soviets are supposed to: by listening to what other people have to say."

Grachikov had been made Secretary of the Town Committee at the last conference of the local Party organization, following some remarkable achievements on the part of the factory where he was then Party secretary.

"Tell me, Ivan, have you heard anything about this research institute? Whose idea was it?"

"Yes, I've heard about it." Grachikov continued to rest his head in his palm. "There was talk about it back in the spring. Then it got held up."

"I see," Fyodor said in a chagrined tone. "If Khabalygin had signed for the building, we would have moved into it around the twentieth of August, and then they wouldn't have shifted us."

They both remained silent.

During this silence Fyodor began to feel that the firm ground on which he had been standing was slipping out from under him. The prospect of a million and a half rubles' worth of alterations hadn't exactly caused an earthquake. Grachikov hadn't grabbed both of his phones at once, nor had he jumped up and rushed out of the room.

"So what did you hear? Is it a very important institute?"

Fyodor asked dejectedly.

Grachikov sighed: "Once you know that its address is a P.O. box number, you don't ask any questions. With us everything is important."

Fyodor sighed too.

"But, Ivan, what are we going to do? They are planning to get a government decision, and once they do it'll be all over. We've only got a couple of days. There's no time to be lost."

Grachikov was thinking.

Fyodor turned to face him. He leaned on the desk, propping his head on his hands.

"Listen. What about sending a telegram to the Council of Ministers in Moscow? This is just the right moment, when they're talking so much about the need for contact between the schools and real life. . . . I'll sign it. I'm not afraid."

Grachikov studied him closely for a minute. Suddenly all the sternness vanished from his face, giving way to a friendly smile. He began to talk the way he liked to, in a singsong voice, in long, well-rounded sentences which had a tone of genuine warmth.

"My dear Fyodor, how do you picture this being arrived at, this decision by the government? Do you imagine the whole Council sitting at a long table, discussing what to do about your building? Do you think they've got nothing better to do? And then I suppose you think your telegram will be brought in at just the right moment. Is that what you believe? No! A government decision means that one of these days a Deputy Prime Minister will see one of the Ministers. The Minister will have some papers with him to make his report and at some point he will say: 'This research institute, as you know, has top priority. It has been decided to locate it in this town, in which there happens to be a building it can use.' The Deputy Prime Minister will then ask: 'Whom was it built for?' And the Minister will reply: 'For a school. But the school has got rather decent premises for the time being. We sent a commission of experts down and the comrades studied the matter on the spot.' Then, before giving his final okay, the Deputy Prime Minister will ask one more question: 'Does the District Committee have any objections?' Do you get this—the District Committee! Your telegram will be returned right to this place with a notation on it saying: 'Check facts.'" Grachikov pursed his thick lips. "You've got to know how these things work. In this case it's the District Committee that holds the power."

He laid his hand on the telephone but didn't lift the receiver.

"What I don't like about this business is that the District Committee Supervisor was with them and raised no objections.

If Knorozov has already given his okay, then, my friend, you're
in trouble. He never goes back on a decision."

Grachikov was a little scared of Victor Knorozov. But then,
there was hardly anyone in the district who wasn't.

He lifted the receiver.

"Is that Konyevsky? This is Grachikov. Say, is Knorozov there?
When will he be back? I see. . . . Well, if he *does* come back today, tell him I'd be most grateful if he would see me. . . . Even
after I get home this evening. . . ."

He put the receiver down but continued toying with it on
its rest. Then he turned his eyes from the telephone to Fyodor,
who was now holding *his* head in his hands.

"You know, Fyodor," Grachikov said earnestly, "I'm very
fond of technical schools. I really like them. In this country of
ours they're always making such a fuss over the top scientists.
They don't seem to think that anyone with anything less than an
engineering degree has any education at all. But for us in
industry it's the technicians who matter most of all. Yet technical schools get a raw deal—and not just yours alone. Take your
place for example. You accept kids this high"—he held his
hand at desk level, though Fyodor had never accepted anybody
that young—"and in the space of four years you turn them into
first-class specialists. I was there when your kids were taking
their examinations in the spring, remember?"

"I remember." Fyodor nodded unhappily. Seated at his large
desk, to which another covered with a green cloth stood at a
right angle, Ivan Grachikov spoke with such warmth you might
have thought that instead of an inkwell, penholder, calendar,
paperweight, telephones, carafe, filing basket, and ashtray, the
desks were covered with white tablecloths and delicacies, which
the host was offering his guest, even urging him to take some
home with him.

"There was a boy of about nineteen, maybe, who was wearing
a tie for the first time in his life, with a jacket that didn't match
his pants—or is that the fashion now? He hung his diagrams on
the board and set up on the table some regulator or calibrator
or whatever you call it that he had made himself. This thing-
amajig clicked and flashed while the young fellow walked
around waving his pointer at the diagrams and talking away like
nobody's business—I was really envious. The words he used
and the things he knew: what was wrong with existing in-
dicators, the principle on which his thing worked, the power of
the anode current, the meter readings, economic efficiency,
coefficients and goodness knows what else! And he was only a
kid! I sat there and I felt sorry for myself. After all, I thought,
I've been around for fifty years, and what's *my* specialty? That I

once knew how to work a lathe? But the sort of lathe I operated is a thing of the past. That I know the history of the Party and Marxist dialectics? But that's something everybody ought to know. There's nothing special about it. It's high time that every Party official should have some special knowledge or skill. It was boys like him who were running things in my factory when I was Party secretary. Who was I to tell them to increase productivity? I had to learn the ropes as best I could by keeping my eyes and ears open. But if I were a little younger, Fyodor, I'd enroll in your evening classes right away."

And seeing that Fyodor was now thoroughly depressed, he added with a laugh: "In the old building, of course!"

But Fyodor couldn't manage even a smile. He drew his head in, hunched his shoulders, and just sat there with a dazed look.

At this point a secretary came in to remind Grachikov that there were other people waiting for him.

5

Nobody had told the students what was going on. Yet by the next day they already knew all about it.

In the morning the sky was overcast and there was rain in the air.

Those who turned up at the school gathered in groups outside, though it was pretty cold. They were not allowed into the lecture rooms because the students on duty were cleaning them, and the labs were out of the question because apparatus was being set up there. So, as usual, they hung around the stairway in a crowd.

There was a hum of conversation. The girls were moaning and groaning. Everybody was talking about the building, the dormitory, and the furnished rooms. Mishka Zimin, a very strong boy who had broken all records digging ditches at the site, hollered at the top of his voice: "So we put in all that work for nothing, eh? For nothing at all! Well, Igor, how're you going to explain this one?"

Igor, one of the Committee members, was the dark-haired boy in the red-and-brown checked shirt who had drawn up the list of people for moving the labs. He stood on the top landing looking rather sheepish.

"You'll see, it'll all be straightened out."

"But who's going to straighten it out?"

"Well, we will. Maybe we'll write a letter to someone or something."

"That's a good idea," said a prim and serious-looking girl with hair parted in the center. "Let's send a protest to Moscow! They'll surely listen to us."

She was the meekest of them all, but now even she had had
enough and was thinking of quitting. She just couldn't go on
paying seventy rubles a month out of her stipend for a bed.

"All right—let's get going!" another one cried, and slapped
the banister with her hand. She was an attractive girl, with jet-
black, fine, curly hair, and was wearing a loose jacket. "I'm sure
everybody will sign—all nine hundred of us."

"That's right!"

"Sure!"

"You better find out first whether we're allowed to collect
signatures like that," somebody cautioned.

Valka Rogozkin, the school's leading athlete, the best runner
in the 100 and 400 meters, the best jumper, and the loudest
talker was poised on the banister of the staircase. He kept one
foot on the stair, but he had swung over the rail and was lying
face downward on it. His hands were interlocked on top of the
rail and his chin was resting on them. From this awkward
position, ignoring the girls' outcries, he stared up at Igor.
Valka Guguyev, a swarthy, broad-shouldered boy, sat recklessly
in the curve of the banister, apparently unconcerned about the
twenty-foot drop behind him.

"Hey, wait a minute!" cried Valka Rogozkin in a shrill voice.
"That's no good. I've got a better idea. Let's all stay away tomorrow, every single one of us."

"That's it—let's all go to the stadium," others backed
him up.

"Where are you going to get permission?" Igor asked
uneasily.

"Who says we've got to have permission?" Rogozkin burst
out. "Of course they won't give us permission! We'll just stay
away! Don't worry!" His shouts grew louder as he got carried
away by his own words. "In a few days there'll be another
commission. This one will come by plane and they'll give us our
building back and maybe even something else besides!"

But some of them got worried.

"You're sure they won't stop our stipends?"

"They wouldn't do that to us!"

"But they might expel us!"

"That's not the way we do things," Igor shouted above the
noise. "Just forget about it."

Because of all the racket they hadn't noticed old Dusya
coming up the stairs carrying a pail. When she reached
Rogozkin, she switched the pail from one hand to the other
and raised the free one to give him a good smack on the
backside with the flat of her hand. But he saw this just in time
and hopped down from the banister, so that Dusya's hand only

just brushed him.

"Now, Dusya," Rogozkin howled. And he wagged his finger at her in mock anger. "That's not the way we do things! Next time, I'll—"

"The next time you lie down like that," Dusya threatened him with the palm of her hand, "I'll teach you a lesson you won't forget in a hurry! That's not what banisters are for!"

They were all laughing loudly. Everybody at the school liked old Dusya because she was so down-to-earth.

She continued up the stairs, pushing past the students. Her face was wrinkled, but it was full of life, and she had a strong chin. She looked as though she deserved something better than this job.

"Aw, cut it out, Dusya!" Mishka Zimin blocked her way. "Why do you think they've given up the building?"

"Don't you know?" Dusya answered. "There's far too many parquet floors there. I'd go crazy trying to polish them."

And off she went, rattling her bucket.

There was another round of laughter.

"Hey, Valka! Do your stuff!" the boys on the top landing called to Guguyev as they caught sight of another bunch of girls coming into the building. "Lusya's coming!"

Valka Guguyev slipped off the banister, pushed the people next to him out of the way, and stood for a moment studying the rail. Then he gripped it firmly with both hands, swung his body up effortlessly, and calmly did a handstand over the steep drop.

It was a very dangerous stunt.

A hush fell over the staircase. All heads were turned toward him. The boys were impressed. The girls watched with a mixture of admiration and horror.

Lusya, the girl for whose benefit this was being done, was already on the staircase. She now turned and, her blue eyes wide open, looked straight up at Guguyev, who would have crashed right on top of her and on to the stone floor below if he had fallen. But he never did fall! Almost motionless, except for a slight swaying movement, he kept up his handstand over the stairwell and seemed in no hurry to come down. His back was to the drop, and his legs, held tightly together, arched out—on purpose, it seemed—right over the empty space. And his head, too, was strained back, so that he was looking straight down at tiny, slim Lusya, standing there wrapped in a light-colored raincoat with a turned-up collar. She was hatless, which suited her very well, and her short, fair hair was wet from the rain.

But could he really see her? Dark as the stairway was, you

could tell that the young hero's face and neck were purple from
the rush of blood.

Suddenly the others called a warning:

"Look out!"

Guguyev immediately swung off the banister, landed lightly
on his feet, and putting on an innocent look leaned against
the rail.

This performance could easily have cost him his stipend. It
had happened to him once before when he rang the school
bell ten minutes before the end of classes (so they wouldn't be
late for the movies).

Before they'd had time to start their usual din again, Grigory
Lavrentyevich, the gaunt and gloomy dean, started up the stairs.
They made way for him respectfully.

He had heard that warning "Look out," and he realized there
was something odd about the silence that met him. But he had
not seen the cause of it all— particularly since Rogozkin, who
never missed a chance to make trouble, immediately fastened
onto him.

"Sir!" Rogozkin shouted down the stairs. "Why have we
given up the building? After all, *we* built it!"

And he tilted his head to one side inquiringly and put on a
half-witted expression. From his very first day there, he'd
played the fool and made people laugh, especially in class.

They all kept quiet, waiting to hear what the dean would say.

A teacher's life was like this— he was always having to answer
such questions and you never knew what they were going to
ask next.

The dean gave Rogozkin a long, hard look. But Rogozkin
didn't flinch. He kept his head tilted to one side.

"Well, now," the dean said slowly, "when you finish
school here . . . But wait a minute . . . how on earth *will* you
finish school?"

"You mean because of athletics?" Rogozkin came back at him
quickly. (Every spring and autumn he missed any number of
classes because he was competing in either local or national
events. But he always managed to make up for it and he never
had bad marks.) "That's no way to talk. As a matter of fact," and
he tapped his temple comically with a finger, "I already have
some ideas up here about the project for my diploma."

"Really? That's fine. And when you finish school, where will
you look for a job?"

"Wherever I'm needed most," Rogozkin answered with
exaggerated gusto, throwing up his head high and standing at
attention.

"Maybe you'll be given a job at the new building. Or perhaps some of the others will. So all that work you did on it will not have been in vain. It belongs to all of us."

"Oh, how nice! Nothing would please me more. Thank you so much," Rogozkin said, brimming over with mock gratitude.

The dean went on his way. But before he had reached the corridor, Rogozkin reversed his decision in the same flippant manner:

"No, sir, I've changed my mind! I don't really think I want to work in that building!"

"Where do you want to go then?" The dean peered at him.

"I want to go and work on the virgin lands!" Rogozkin said loudly.

"Well, why don't you fill out an application?" the dean suggested with a faint smile.

And he went off down the corridor to the principal's study.

Fyodor himself was not there. He had not managed to get an appointment with Knorozov the day before, so he had gone down to the District Committee again today. But the teachers who were now waiting in the study for a call from the principal were not very hopeful.

A few drops of rain splashed against the windowpanes. The rough, uneven ground right up to the railroad was wet and dark.

The heads of departments were poring over the huge sheets of their schedules. They were passing colored pencils and erasers to each other and coordinating their classes. Yakov Ananyevich, the Secretary of the Party Bureau, was sitting at a little table by the window near the safe with the files of the school's Party group and was sorting papers. Lydia was standing at the same window. In the way women have of changing their looks overnight, she had turned from the happy, brisk, youthful woman of yesterday into the middle-aged, haggard one of today. And she had changed yesterday's blue-green suit for a darker one.

The Party Secretary, short and balding, was dapper and clean-shaven, with a clear, fresh complexion. He was talking without interrupting his work. He handled the papers in their folders as delicately as though they were living things, taking great care not to crease them, and he treated documents written on thin paper with something akin to loving care.

His voice was soft and quiet, but you could hear every word.

"No, comrades, certainly not. There will be no general meeting. Neither will there be any meetings on this subject by departments or by classes. It would mean giving the matter undue attention, and there's no point to it. They will find out all about it sooner or later, without us telling them."

"They already know," the dean said. "But they would like some explanation."

"Well, so what?" Yakov Ananyevich replied calmly, dismissing the problem. "You can explain things to them privately, and that's what you'll have to do. What you should say? What you should say is: This institute is of vital importance to the nation as a whole. It is concerned with the sort of thing we are studying. Today, electronics is the basis of all technical progress, and no one must be allowed to put any obstacles in its way. On the contrary, we must do everything we can to further it."

Nobody said anything. The Party Secretary carefully turned over two or three more papers, but he couldn't find the one he wanted.

"Actually, you don't ever have to go into all that. You can just tell them that this is a state institute and the why's and wherefore's of the matter are none of our business."

He turned over some more papers and found what he wanted. Then he looked up again, turned his clear, calm eyes on them, and said:

"Hold meetings? Make this the subject for a sort of formal debate? No, that would be a political mistake. As a matter of fact, if the students or the Komsomol Committee insist on a meeting, then they must be dissuaded."

"I don't agree!" Lydia turned on him so abruptly that her short, brushed-back hair shook.

The Party Secretary looked at her blandly and asked in his usual punctilious manner:

"But what is there for you to disagree with, Lydia Georgyevna?"

"First of all," and saying this she drew herself up and moved toward him, "first of all . . . well, it's your whole tone! It's not only that you're already reconciled to their taking our building away, but you even seem pleased—yes, actually *pleased!*"

The Party Secretary spread his hands slightly, without moving his arms.

"But, Lydia Georgyevna, if the national interest is involved, how can I be anything *but* pleased?"

"It's your approach I don't like . . . I mean the principle of the thing!" She couldn't keep still any more and started pacing the small room, gesticulating as she spoke. "None of you has as much to do with the young people as I do. After all, I'm with the Komsomol from morning till night. And I know how it'll look to them, the thing you're trying to push down their throats. They'll think we're afraid to tell them the truth—and they'll be right! How will they ever respect us again? Eh? When something *good* happens we let everybody know about it. We plaster it all over the walls and talk about it on the radio. But when there's something *bad* or hard to explain, then they're supposed to find out as best they can and rely on rumor, eh? Is that what you want? It's all wrong!" Her voice rang out, but, unfortunately, for the second time that day she found herself on the verge of tears. "No! You can't do this, especially not to young people! Lenin said that we should never be afraid to bring things into the open. Publicity is a healing sword, he said."

She choked with tears and left the study abruptly so as not to break down in front of everybody.

The Party Secretary watched her go with a pained expression on his face; shutting his eyes, he shook his head sadly.

Lydia went quickly down the dark corridor. Near the store-room with its crates of vacuum tubes, two third-year students called out to her. While cleaning up, they had come across the scale model of the new building and wondered what to do with it. It was the model they had carried, hoisted on four poles, at the head of the school's contingent in the October and May Day parades.

There it was, standing on some boxes. The building, every detail of which they had come to know so well and which meant so much to them, looked almost like the real thing. It was white, with some features in blue and green. There were the two turrets on top of the pilaster. And there were the huge windows of the auditorium and the smaller windows for the rooms— already assigned to somebody or other—on all four floors.

"Maybe we should break it up?" one of the boys asked, avoiding her eyes with a guilty expression. "We may as well. There's no room to turn around here as it is."

6

Ivan Grachikov never told wartime stories. He disliked them because during the War he had had more than his share of trouble and very few pleasures. Every day he had lived and every move he had made in the War were linked in his mind with suffering, the sacrifice, and the death of decent people.

Another thing he didn't like was that almost twenty years after the end of the War, people were still mouthing the same old military expressions, even where they were quite inappropriate. At the factory he had never used—and he had tried to discourage others from using—such phrases as: "Going over to the offensive," "Throwing people into the breach," "Going over the top," "Bringing up reserves." He felt that all such expressions, which introduced a wartime atmosphere into

peacetime conditions, just made people weary. And the
Russian language could manage perfectly well without them.

But today he broke his rule about wartime reminiscences.
He was sitting with the principal in the reception room of the
First Secretary of the Party District Committee and waiting
(while in his own reception room, of course, people were also
sitting, waiting for *him*). Grachikov was very nervous. He
telephoned his secretary a couple of times and smoked two
cigarets. He turned to look at Fyodor, who was sitting there
miserable and all hunched up. Grachikov thought that Fyodor's
hair was much grayer than it had been the day before. Then,
trying to cheer Fyodor up a little, Grachikov started telling him
a funny story about some fellows they had both met during a
brief lull when their division was resting behind the front
line. That was in forty-three, after Fyodor was wounded for the
first time.

But the story fell flat. Fyodor did not laugh. Grachikov
knew that it was better not to revive war memories. But
having started this train of thought, he now recalled what
had happened the following day, when his division was
suddenly ordered to cross the river Sozh and deploy itself on
the other side.

The bridge across the river had been badly damaged. The
engineers had repaired it during the night, and Grachikov was
posted as the officer in charge of the guard on it. He had
instructions that nobody was to be allowed through until the
division had crossed over. It was a narrow bridge—the sides
had collapsed, the surface was very bumpy, and it was important
to keep the traffic moving, because twice already single-engine
Junkers had sneaked up on them from behind the trees and
dive-bombed the bridge, though so far they had missed. The
business of moving the division across, which had begun before
dawn, dragged on into the afternoon. Some other units which
were also anxious to get across had moved up, but they waited
their turn in a small pine woods nearby. Suddenly, six covered
vehicles—they were brand-new and all alike—drove up to the
head of the column and tried to force their way onto the
bridge. "St-o-p!" Grachikov shouted furiously at the first driver
and ran across to head him off, but he kept going. Grachikov
may have reached for his pistol, perhaps he actually did. At
that point a middle-aged officer in a cape opened the door of
the first truck and shouted just as furiously. "Hey you, Major,
come over here!" and with a quick movement of one shoulder
he threw back his cape. And Grachikov saw that he was a
lieutenant general. Grachikov ran up, his heart in his mouth.

"What were you doing with your hand?" the general shouted

ominously. "Do you want to be court-martialed? Let my
vehicles through!"

Until the general ordered his trucks to be let through,
Grachikov had been willing to settle things amicably, without
raising his voice, and he might even have let them through. But
when right and wrong clashed head-on (and wrong is more
brazen by its very nature), Grachikov's legs seemed to become
rooted to the ground and he no longer cared what might
happen to him. He drew himself up, saluted, and announced:

"I shall not let you through, Comrade Lieutenant General!"

"What the hell . . .?" The general's voice rose to a scream
and he stepped down onto the running board. "What's
your name?"

"Major Grachikov, Comrade Lieutenant General. And I'd like
to know yours!"

"You'll be in the stockade by tomorrow!" the general
fumed.

"That may be, but today you take your place in the line!"
Grachikov shot back and then planted himself right in front of
the truck and stood there, knowing that his face and neck were
flushed purple, but quite determined not to give in. The
general choked with rage, thought for a moment, then slammed
the door and turned his six trucks around.

At last some people came out of Knorozov's room; they were
from the District Agricultural Office and the Agricultural Department of the District Party Committee. Konevsky, who
was Knorozov's secretary (though by his manner and the size of
his desk a stranger might well have taken him for Knorozov
himself), went into the office and came right out again.

"Victor Vavilovich will see you alone," he said to Grachikov
in a tone that brooked no argument.

Grachikov winked at Fyodor and went in.

One of the agricultural people, a livestock expert, was still
sitting with Knorozov. His body leaned over the desk as if
his bones were made of rubber, and his head twisted round as
far as it would go, the expert was looking at a large sheet of
paper spread out in front of Knorozov. It was covered with
brightly colored diagrams and figures.

Grachikov said hello.

Knorozov, a tall man with shaven head, didn't bother to turn
toward him, but just threw him a quick glance and said:

"You don't have to worry about agriculture. That's why
you can go around wasting other people's time. Why don't
you relax?"

He was always needling Grachikov like this about agriculture,
as if the town industry, for which Grachikov was responsible,

wasn't earning its keep. Grachikov knew that Knorozov was determined to improve the farm situation and get as much credit as possible in the process.

"Look," Knorozov said to the livestock man, slowly pressing the long fingers of one hand on the large sheet of paper, as though he were putting a massive seal on it. He held himself as straight as a die and didn't lean against the back of the chair. The lines of his body were trim and clean-cut, no matter whether you looked at him from the front or from the side. "Look! I am telling you what you need. What you need is what I'm telling you."

"It's quite clear, Comrade Knorozov," the chief livestock expert said with a bow.

"Take it with you," Knorozov said, letting go of the sheet.

The expert carefully picked up the paper from Knorozov's desk with both hands, rolled it up, and, lowering his head so that his bald patch showed, he strode across the roomy, well-furnished office, which was obviously designed for large conferences.

Thinking that he would be asked to bring in Fyodor almost immediately, Grachikov did not sit down. He just stood leaning against the leather back of the chair in front of him.

Even seated at his desk, Knorozov was a fine figure of a man. His long head made him seem taller, and though he was no longer young, his shaven head, far from aging him, made him look younger. He never seemed to move a muscle without good reason, and he never even changed the expression on his face unless it was necessary. His face seemed cast forever in one mold, never betraying any trivial or momentary emotions. A broad smile would have disarranged his features and destroyed their harmony.

"Victor Vavilovich," Grachikov began, giving every syllable its full value. His singsong manner of speech seemed calculated to put people at their ease. "I won't take long. I've come to see you with the principal about the new building for the electronics school. A commission came down from Moscow and said the building is to be handed over to a research institute. Was this done with your knowledge?"

Knorozov did not look at Grachikov. He kept his eyes fixed straight ahead, looking into a far distance that only he could see. He parted his lips—only as much as was necessary—and said brusquely: "Yes."

Actually, this was the end of the conversation.

"Yes?"

"Yes."

It was Knorozov's boast that he never went back on his word.

As it had once been in Moscow with Stalin's word, so it was still
today with Knorozov's word: It was never changed and never
taken back. And although Stalin was long dead, Knorozov was
still here. He was a leading proponent of the "strong-willed
school of leadership" and he saw in this his greatest virtue. He
could not imagine any other way of running things.

Feeling that he was beginning to get worked up, Grachikov
forced himself to speak in as friendly and affable a manner as
he could.

"But Victor Vavilovich—why don't they build themselves a
place designed for their own needs? In this building they'll have
to make no end of alterations."

"No time!" Knorozov cut him short. "The project is already
under way. They have to have the place immediately."

"But will it pay its way with all these alterations? And"—he
went on quickly, in case Knorozov tried to end the conversation—"and, most important, there's the psychological effect.
The students put in a whole year working on that building,
without pay and with real enthusiasm."

Knorozov turned his head—just his head, not his shoulders—
in Grachikov's direction, and, his voice now beginning to sound
metallic, he said:

"I don't understand you. You are Secretary of the Town
Committee. Do I really have to tell you what's good for the
town? We've never had, and we still don't have, a single research institute here. And it wasn't so easy for us to get it. We
had to jump at it before the Ministry changed its mind. This
puts us into a different class–like Gorky or Sverdlovsk."

He half closed his eyes. Perhaps he was seeing the town
transformed into a Sverdlovsk. Or perhaps in his mind's eye he
was seeing himself in a new, even more important job.

Grachikov was neither convinced nor crushed by Knorozov's
words, which fell like steel girders, and he felt he was coming
to one of those critical moments in his life when his legs were
rooted to the spot and he had to stand his ground.

Because once again it was a clash of right and wrong.

"Victor Vavilovich," he said more harshly and more curtly
than he had intended. "We are not medieval barons, vying with
each other over the grandness of our coats of arms. What we
should be proud of in this town is that these kids built something and took pleasure in doing it. And it's our job to back
them up. But if we take the building from them, they'll never
forget what it means to be cheated. They'll think: If it can
happen once, it can happen again!"

"There's no point in any further discussion!" The steel
girder came down even more heavily than before. "The

decision is final!"

A reddish glint came into Grachikov's eyes. His neck and face turned scarlet with anger.

"Look here! What do we care about most—buildings or people?" he shouted. "Why all the fuss about bricks and mortar?"

Knorozov hoisted up the whole great hulk of his body, and you could see that he was truly made of steel and all of a piece.

"Demagogue!" he thundered, towering over the head of the offender.

And he was so powerful a man that it seemed he had only to stretch out his hand and Grachikov's head would leave his shoulders.

But Grachikov could no longer control himself. He had to keep going.

"Communism has to be built with people, not with bricks, Victor Vavilovich!" he shouted, quite carried away. "That's the hard way, and it takes longer. And even if we finished building Communism tomorrow, but only in bricks, we'd still have a long way to go."

They both fell silent and stood there, stockstill.

Grachikov realized that his fingers hurt. He had dug them into the back of the chair. Now he let go.

"You're not the man for the job," Knorozov said quietly. "We made a mistake."

"All right, I'm not the man for the job. So what?" Grachikov retorted, relieved now that he had spoken his mind. "I can always find work."

"What sort of work?" Knorozov asked suspiciously.

"Any old work! I don't suppose you'll think any the worse of me whatever I do!" Grachikov said at the top of his voice.

He really was sick to death of having to do things without ever being consulted, of always having to take orders from above. He hadn't run things like that back at the factory.

Knorozov made a hissing noise through his clenched teeth. He put his hand on the telephone.

He lifted the receiver.

Then he sat down.

"Sasha, give me Khabalygin."

While the call was being put through not a word was spoken in the office.

"Khabalygin? Tell me, what are you going to do with this building that needs so many alterations?"

(Sounded as though the building was going to Khabalygin.)

"What do you mean—not very many? There's a lot to be done. . . . I know it's urgent. . . . Anyway, for the time being you've got enough on your hands with one building."

(Did Khabalygin own the place or something?)

"No, I won't give you the one next to it. You build yourself something better."

He put the receiver down.

"All right, bring the principal in."

Grachikov went out for Fyodor, pondering the thought: Was Khabalygin going to the research institute or something?

He came back in with the principal.

Fyodor stood there rigidly, staring at the District Secretary. He liked him. He had always admired him, and he enjoyed attending meetings called by Knorozov because he felt invigorated by Knorozov's overwhelming will power and energy. Between meetings he put his heart and soul into the execution of Knorozov's wishes—whether it was a matter of improving the work of the school or getting the students to help with the potato harvest or collecting scrap metal or whatever it might be. What Fyodor most liked about Knorozov was that when he said Yes he meant Yes, and when he said No he meant No. The dialectic was all very well but, like a lot of other people, Fyodor preferred plain and unambiguous language.

So he had not come to argue but simply to learn Knorozov's decision.

"I hear you're having trouble," Knorozov said.

Fyodor smiled wanly.

"Keep your chin up," Knorozov said quietly and firmly. "You're not going to let it get you down, are you?"

"I'm not," Fyodor said hoarsely, and then cleared his throat.

"You've started putting up the dormitory next to the building, haven't you? Once it's up, you'll have a school. Right?"

"Of course, yes," Fyodor agreed.

But this time he didn't feel invigorated by Knorozov's energy. Various thoughts began to go through his mind: Winter was coming, they'd have to stay in the old place for the next year, the new building would have neither an auditorium nor a gymnasium, and there'd be no dormitory adjoining.

"But Comrade Knorozov," Fyodor voiced his worries, "we'll have to alter the whole layout. As they are, the rooms are too small. They're only big enough for four. They'll have to be redesigned for classrooms and labs."

"It's for you to work that out." Knorozov cut him off with an impatient wave of the hand, indicating that the interview was over.

They should have known better than to bother him with such trifling details.

As they walked to the coatrack, Grachikov patted the principal on the shoulder:

It's not as bad as all that. You'll have a new building."

"We'll have to lay a new floor on top of the basement." The principal kept thinking of all the snags. "It'll have to be much stronger to take the weight of the machinery. That means we'll have to pull down what we've already built of the first story."

"I suppose so," Grachikov said. "But look at it this way. You've got a good plot of land in a good location, already excavated and with foundations. And at least you know where you stand. The place'll be ready by spring and you'll move in. I'll help you, and so will the Economic Council. Lucky thing we managed to hold on to the second building."

They left the district office, both wearing dark raincoats and peaked caps. There was a cool but pleasant breeze and a slight, fresh drizzle.

"By the way," Grachikov asked with a frown, "you wouldn't know by any chance how Khabalygin stands with the Ministry?"

"Khabalygin? O-ho! He's really in with them. He once told me that he's got a lot of friends there. Why, do you think he might put in a word for us?" Fyodor's voice reflected a fleeting hope. But he rejected the idea at once: "No. If he could have helped, he would have done so there and then, when he came around with the commission. But he went along with everything."

Grachikov stopped, with his feet planted firmly apart, and stared straight ahead. Then he asked another question:

"What's his special field? Relays?"

"Oh, no, he's not an expert on anything. He ran a transformer plant before this. He's just an experienced executive."

"Why did he come along with that commission? Any idea?"

· "I wonder." The question now formed in Fyodor's mind, which was still dazed from the events of the previous day. "Why indeed?"

"Well, be seeing you," Grachikov said with a sigh, thrust out his hand, and gave Fyodor a firm handshake.

He went home still thinking about Khabalygin. Of course, this kind of research institute was much grander than a mere relay factory. The director's salary and status would be far greater, and there'd be a good chance of wangling a medal into the bargain.

Grachikov had always been of the opinion that it was wrong to wait until a Party member actually broke the law. He believed that the Party should immediately expel anyone who exploited his job, his position, or his contacts to get something for himself—whether it was a new apartment, a house in the country, or anything at all, however trifling. There was no point in just reproving or reprimanding such people. They had to be expelled, because in their case it was not just a matter of a minor offense or a mistake or personal weakness. Their whole outlook was completely alien: they were really capitalists at heart.

The local newspaper had just exposed and pilloried a truck-driver and his wife who had grown flowers in their back garden and sold them on the market.

But how could you expose the Khabalygins?

Fyodor walked slowly because he wanted to get a breath of fresh air. The lack of sleep, the two Nembutals he had taken, and all the things that had been going through his mind for the last day or so had given him a feeling of discomfort, of being somehow poisoned. But the fresh air gradually blew it away.

Oh well, he thought, we'll just have to start all over again. We'll get all nine hundred of them together and tell them frankly: "We haven't got that building any more. We've got to build another. The harder we work, the sooner we'll have it."

It wasn't going to be easy at first.

But they'd soon be just as enthusiastic as ever about it. That's the effect work always has on people.

They would have faith.

And they would build.

All right, they'd put up with the old place for another year.

And now, before he knew where he was, Fyodor found himself at the new building. It shone with metal and glass.

The other one, next to it, still just a mass of earth and clay, had scarcely gotten above ground level.

Grachikov's questions about Khabalygin had set off a train of half-formed, nagging thoughts in Fyodor's unsuspicious mind, and he was now beginning to piece them together: the way Khabalygin had delayed signing for the building in August, and how cheerful he had been with the commission.

Oddly enough, the first person Fyodor saw on the grounds at the back of the site was the man in his thoughts, the man he had just begun to fathom. Vsevolod Khabalygin, wearing his green hat and a good brown overcoat, was striding about the sodden grounds, ignoring the mud he was getting all over his shoes and giving orders to a group of workmen, apparently his own. Two of the men and a driver were unloading stakes from a truck. Some of the stakes were freshly painted, others were rather grubby, as though they had already been in use—you could tell by their points, which had rotted and then been trimmed again. Two other workmen were bending down and doing something under Khabalygin's direction; he gave his orders with rapid movements of his short arms.

Fyodor went closer and saw that they were driving the stakes into the ground. But they were cheating. Instead of placing them in a straight line, they were being crafty and putting them up in a long, sweeping curve, so as to take in as much of the land as possible for the institute and leave as little as possible for the school.

"Listen, Comrade Khabalygin! Be fair! What's all this?" the principal shouted upon seeing this swindle. "Kids of fifteen and sixteen need space to breathe and run around in! Where will they go?"

At that moment, Khabalygin had planted himself at a strategic spot from which the last section of his misbegotten fence would run. Straddling the future boundary, he had already raised his arm to give the signal when he heard Fyodor just behind him. With his hand still poised at eye level, Khabalygin turned (his thick neck didn't make it easy for him to turn his head), bared his teeth slightly, and snarled:

"What? What do you say?"

And without waiting for an answer, he turned away, checked the alignment of his men with the palm of his hand, signaled one of them into line by quick movements of his fingers, and finally cut a swathe through the air with a sweep of his short arm.

It was as though he had sliced not just through the air, but the very ground on which he stood. It was the sort of grand gesture that would accompany the opening up of some great new route. It was the gesture of the warrior of ancient times blazing a trail for his armies. It was the gesture of the first mariner to open up a passage to the North Pole.

And only when his task was done did he turn to Fyodor to say:

"That's the way it has to be, dear comrade."

"Why does it *have* to be?" Fyodor asked angrily, with a shake of his head. "For the good of the cause, I suppose. Is that it? Well, just you wait!" And he clenched his fists. But he could no longer speak. He turned away and strode off quickly toward the road, muttering to himself:

"Just wait, you pig! Just wait, you swine!"

The workmen went on carrying the stakes.

1963

This is not an adventure story. This is a story about how I fought in the war, how they wanted to kill me, and how I made it through all right. I really don't know who to thank for this. Perhaps no one. So don't you worry. I'm alive and well. Some people will be happy to hear this, and then, of course, there will be those who won't like it at all. But I'm alive. There's nothing to be done. After all, you can't please everyone.

Good-bye, Schoolboy!

Bulat Okudzhava

Hayseed

In my childhood I did a lot of crying. As I grew older I cried less. Later, when I was in my teens, I only cried twice. The first time was one evening just before the war. I said to this girl I loved— and I said it with feigned indifference:

"Well then, if that's it, then it's all over."

"If that's it, then it's all over," she agreed with unexpected calmness, and walked away. It was then that I burst out crying because she was leaving me. And I wiped away my tears with the palm of my hand.

I'm crying for the second time right now: here in the Mozdok steppe. I'm carrying a very important message for the regimental commander. Where the hell is this regimental commander? These sandy hills all look the same to me. It's night. It's only my second day at the front. And if you don't carry out orders, they shoot you. And I'm eighteen.

Who said they shoot you? That was Kolya Grinchenko, just before I left. He smiled sweetly when he said it.

"Take care. If you don't, it's the firing squad."

They'll put me up against a wall. But there are no walls here. They'll take me out in the fields—

And I'm wiping away the tears. "Your son showed cowardice and . . ." That's how the telegram will start out. But why did they send me with the message? There's Kolya Grinchenko—he's a real strong, smart fellow. He would have found the place a long time ago. By now he'd be sitting inside the warm headquarters dugout. He'd be drinking tea out of a mug, winking at the girls who operate the radios and smiling pleasantly at them.

Supposing I step on a mine. They'd find me in the morning, and the regimental commander will say to the battery commander, "Lieutenant Burakov, why did you send a green kid? You didn't give him a chance to look around, get used to his place. And it's because of your indifference that we've lost a good man."

"Your son died in action while carrying out a very important mission. . . ." That's how the telegram will start.

"Hey, where are you going?"

That's me they're shouting at. I see a small trench, and someone is waving at me. What the hell do they care where I'm going?

"Halt!" someone shouts behind me.

I stop.

"Over here!"

I go over, and someone pulls me into the trench by the sleeve. "Where are you going?" they ask angrily.

I explain to them.

"Don't you know that there are Germans here! Another thirty yards and. . . ."

They explain it to me. This, it turns out, is our advance observation point.

Then they take me to a dugout. The regimental commander reads the message, looks at me, and I feel small and insignificant. I look at my not terribly venerable, thin legs, all wrapped in leggings, and then at my sturdy army boots. I suppose all this is very funny to them. But no one's laughing. And the beautiful radio operator looks past me. Now, if I wore knee boots and a nice officer's coat. . . . If only they'd give me some tea. I'd like to sit down at the makeshift table and then say something to the beautiful girl that would. . . . Of course, the way I look now—

"Return to the battery," the regimental commander barks. "And tell your commander not to send any more of these reports."

He emphasizes the words "of these."

"Okay," I say, and I hear the quiet laugh of the radio operator. She glances at me and laughs.

"How long have you been in the army?" the colonel asks.

"A month."

"In the army you don't say, 'Okay,' but, 'Yes, sir!' . . . and also, you've got your toes together but your heels apart. . . ."

"A hayseed," says someone in a dark corner behind me.

"I know it," I say and walk out. I'm almost running.

The steppe again. It's snowing, and it's quiet. I can't even believe that this is the front, an advanced post, that there's danger nearby. I won't lose my way this time.

I can imagine how absurd I must have looked to them: feet spread apart, hands in my coat pockets and cap over my ears. While this beautiful girl—They didn't even offer me any tea. When Kolya Grinchenko speaks to officers, he sort of smiles. He salutes smartly and says: "Yes, sir!" But I can hear him saying: "Go ahead and order, I see right through you." And he does see.

My ankle boots are good and strong. That's really fine. A heavy masculine foot. I wish I had a fur cap with earflaps, then I wouldn't look so pitiful. At any rate, I'll be back soon, give my report. I'll drink a lot of tea and then get some sleep.

Now I have a right to it.

I'm carrying a submachine gun across my back, two grenades on one hip and a gas mask on the other. I look real belligerent. Very much so. Someone once said that belligerence is a sign of cowardice. But am I a coward? When I had an argument with Volodka Anilov in the eighth grade, it was me who shouted first: "Let's fight it out!" And I became terrified. But we went behind the school, and our friends stood around us. He hit me first, on the arm.

"So that's it," I shouted and poked him in the shoulder.

Then we kept swearing at each other, neither one wanting to start first.

And suddenly it all seemed very funny to me, and I said to him, "Listen, I'm going to belt you right in the kisser."

"Go ahead," he said, and put up his fists.

"Or you hit me. There'll be blood. Well, what's the difference?"

He suddenly calmed down, and we shook hands according to all the rules. But after that there was no friendship between us.

Am I a coward?

At sunrise yesterday we stopped in these hills.

"Everyone's here," Lieutenant Burakov said.

"Where are we?" someone asked.

"It's the advanced post."

It was his first time at the front, just like the rest of us, and that's why he spoke so solemnly and so proudly.

"But where are the Germans?" someone asked.

"The Germans are over there."

"Over there" we could see small hills, overgrown with patches of withered scrub.

And I thought that I wasn't at all terrified. And I was surprised at how simply the lieutenant had figured out the enemy position.

Nina

"Oh, but you're handsome," says Sashka Zolotaryov.

I'm shaving in front of a broken piece of mirror. There's nothing to shave. It's colder in the trench than outside. My hands are red, my nose is red, and the blood is red. I'm cutting myself to bits. Can I be handsome? Ears set wide apart. Nose like a potato.

Why am I shaving? We've already been at the front lines for three days, and we haven't heard a shot, or seen one German, or had anyone wounded. Then why am I shaving? Yesterday evening that same beautiful girl from headquarters stopped at the entrance to our trench.

"Hello!" she said.

And I looked at her, and I knew I was unshaven. I saw myself in her eyes. It's as though I was reflected in them. She has such large eyes. I forget their color. I nodded to her.

"How's life?" she asked.

"I'm living," I said sullenly.

"Why are you so sullen? Haven't they fed you?"

I took out my cigarets.

"Well," she said, "cigarets."

"What's it to you, haven't you anything better to do?" I said.

"Let's have a smoke," she said and took a cigaret out of the pack by herself.

We smoked and didn't say anything. Then she said, "You know, you're just a small fry."

"What's that?"

"That's a fish that's just been spawned."

I crawled into the trench and could hear her laughing behind me.

"Did Ninka come over?" Kolya Grinchenko asked later.

"Yes. Do you know her?"

"I know everybody," he said.

Now I'm clean-shaven. I still have some cigarets left. I feel that she'll come. I've unbuttoned my shirt collar. So what if I look bad. I've unbuttoned my coat and put my hands in my pockets. And I'm standing behind the shell crates, so that my leggings won't be seen.

Who am I? I'm a soldier. A mortar man. We're the regimental mortar battery. I've risked my life. Maybe it's a miracle that I haven't been wounded yet. Come on, you radio operator you, you headquarters rat. Come on, I'll treat you to some cigarets. Come—perhaps tomorrow I'll be lying with my arms stretched out. . . .

"Oh, but you are real handsome," says Sashka Zolotaryov. I spit and turn away. Maybe he's laughing. But my lips are twisting.

Sashka is scraping the mud off his boots with a stick. Then he smears them with a thick layer of lubrication oil.

Will Nina come or won't she? I'll say, "Hi, small fry. . . ." I'll have a smoke with her. Then it'll be evening. If this is war, why isn't there any shooting? Not a single shot, not a single German or anyone wounded.

"Why aren't there any higher-ups here?" I ask.

"They're in conference," says Sashka.

It's a good thing I'm tall and not fat like Zolotaryov. If only my coat fitted!

Kolya Grinchenko comes over. He smiles winningly and says, "The sergeant's a beast. He makes omelets for himself, but gives me concentrates to eat." Kolya looks at Sashka and me.

"Don't make so much noise," says Sashka.

"This isn't the home front," Kolya continues. "They don't do much talking here. They give it to you in the back of the head, and it's good-bye. They won't even recognize you."

"Why don't you go and tell him that," says Sashka.

The sergeant is standing behind Kolya. He has a grease spot on his chin.

"Okay," he says.

Nobody says anything. He turns around and goes into his trench. Everyone is silent. Sashka's boots shine like the sergeant's greasy chin. My hands are sweating. Kolya Grinchenko smiles sweetly. The smell of fried eggs comes out of the sergeant's trench.

"Fried eggs are good with onions," says Sashka.

Shongin comes over. He's an old soldier. A famous soldier. He has served in all armies and in all wars. In every war he winds up at the front lines, and then he gets diarrhea. He hasn't fired a single shot, nor been in a single attack, nor ever been wounded. He has a wife who has seen him off to all the wars.

Shongin comes over. He's eating a radish and doesn't say anything.

"Where'd you get the radish?"

Shongin shrugs his shoulders.

"Give me a radish," Sashka says.

"It's my last one," says Shongin.

It's a good thing there are no big shots around here. No one is giving any orders or driving you. I really carried that message. The devil only knows why . . . as if they couldn't have sent Kolya Grinchenko. When my father was seventeen, he organized an underground Komsomol, and here I am, round-shouldered, ridiculous-looking, and I haven't done a thing. I just brag about my noble character, which likely doesn't even exist. . . .

Shongin keeps pulling radishes out of his pocket. The red little balls fly into his mouth and make a crunching noise.

"Shongin, give me a radish," I say.

"It's my last one," says Shongin."

I make a wager: if Shongin pulls out another radish, Nina will come. Shongin puts his hand in his pocket and pulls out his tobacco pouch. She won't come. Suddenly Kolya says, "Here's Ninochka."

I turn around. She's coming down a small hillock. With her is another girl I don't know. Nina has a light step. Her coat is buttoned up all the way. She's wearing a fur cap with earflaps. A bit cocked, the cap, and what a cap! Hi, small fry! Everyone looks in her direction. She's coming.

"Aaa!"

That's Shongin screaming.

"Aaa!" and he falls down. Sashka too, and Kolya Grinchenko.
"Down!"

I throw myself face down. Somewhere off in the distance
there's an explosion. A short one. There is some rustling noise,
and then everything is quiet.

Someone's laughing. The sergeant is standing at the trench
entrance.

"That's enough lying around in the dirt, boys."

Silently we get up. Kolya is gone. He's running toward the
hillock where Nina was. From a distance I see her get up from
the dirty snow. The other girl lies there motionless. Face up.

Slowly and silently we go over there. Other soldiers too. That
was our first mine. The first. Ours.

War

I've gotten to know you, war. I've got large welts on the palms of
my hands and a buzzing noise in my head. I want to sleep. Do
you want me to forget everything I've gotten used to? Do you
want to teach me to submit myself unquestioningly? The screams
of the commanding officer—run, do, bellow "Yes, sir!" when
you reply, fall down, crawl, fall asleep on the march. If there's
the sound of a mine—bury yourself in the ground, dig with
your nose, head, feet, your whole body, at the same time not
experiencing fright, or even thinking. A tinful of barley soup—
secrete gastric juice, get ready, grumble, stuff yourself, wipe
your spoon on the grass. If comrades die—dig a grave, cover it
with earth, fire mechanically into the air . . . three times.

I've already learned a great deal. I pretend I'm not hungry. I
pretend I'm not cold. I pretend I'm not sorry for anyone. I only
want to sleep, sleep, sleep.

Like a fool, I've lost my spoon. An ordinary aluminum spoon.
Tarnished, with a jagged edge, but still, a spoon. A very important item. Now I have nothing to eat with—I drink the soup
straight from the tin. And if it's kasha . . . I've adapted a piece of
wood. I eat my kasha with a piece of wood. From whom could I
ask one? Everyone guards his spoon. No one's a fool here. And
me, I have a hunk of wood.

Sashka Zolotaryov makes notches on a stick. One notch for
each casualty.

Kolya Grinchenko smiles crookedly.

"Don't worry, Sashka. There'll be enough dames for
everyone."

Zolotaryov doesn't say anything. I'm silent. The Germans are
silent; today at least.

Lieutenant Burakov goes around unshaven. I'm sure it's for
show. We've not been ordered to open fire. There's some sort
of conference going on. Our commanding officer's making the
rounds of the mortar crews. The mortars are in the trenches, in
a hollow. The trenches have been dug according to all the
regulations. But we don't study the regulations.

The gunner Gavrilov comes over and sits down near me. He
looks at the cigarets I've rolled.

"Why are you smoking so much?"

"What of it?"

"The wind's blowing the sparks all around. It's already dark,
they'll notice it," he says and looks about.

I put out the butt on the sole of my shoe. The sparks start
flying around like fireworks. Suddenly a six-barrel mortar opens
up on the German side. The shells land with a thump somewhere behind us. Gavrilov is crawling in the snow.

"You mother . . ." he suddenly screams. Explosion after explosion. Explosion after explosion. Closer and closer. My comrades are running past me to the mortars. And I'm sitting in the
snow. It's my own fault. . . . How will I ever be able to face them?
Here comes Lieutenant Burakov. He's screaming something.
And the shells keep falling.

Then I get up too, and start running, shouting, "Lieutenant,
Lieutenant!"

The first mortar roars, and suddenly it's more comfortable.
It's as though we found some powerful, quiet friends. Then the
shouting dies down. All four mortars are now firing into the air
from the hollow. Only the telephonist, the young and scrawny
Gurgenidze, shouts, "A hit! A hit!"

I do what I'm supposed to do. I drag the crates with the mortar
shells out of the shelter. How strong I am after all! And I'm not
afraid of anything. I just keep dragging the crates. Rumbling.
Shouting. The sharp smell of explosives. Everything's all mixed
up. Now this is a fight for you. A real battle. Clouds of smoke. . . .
But I'm making it all up. Not one shot has been fired at us.
It's us making all the noise. And I'm at fault. And everyone
knows it. They're all waiting for me to come and say that it was
all my fault.

Now it's getting darker. My back hurts. I barely have time to
grab some snow and swallow it.

"All clear!" Gurgenidze shouts.

I'll tell the company commander everything so they won't
think I'm hiding anything.

"Lieutenant . . ."

He's sitting on the edge of the trench and running his finger
over a map. He looks at me, and I understand; he is waiting for

me to say I was at fault.

"It's my fault. I didn't think. You can do what you want with me. . . ."

"And what am I supposed to do with you?" he asks thoughtfully. "What have you done?"

Is he kidding? Or has he forgotten? I tell him everything. I get it off my chest. He looks surprised. Then he just shrugs his shoulders.

"Listen, go take a rest. What's your cigaret got to do with it? We just launched an offensive. We simply had to do some shooting. Go, go!"

I go away.

"Watch out you don't fall asleep, or you'll freeze to death," the lieutenant calls after me.

In an hour we're on our feet again. We're shooting at the Germans again. An attack. But I can't see it. What kind of an attack is it if we're sitting in one spot? Is this the way it's always going to be? Rumbling. The smell of explosives. Gurgenidze screaming, "It's a hit! It's a miss!" And this damned hollow from which you can't see anything. But there's an attack somewhere else. Tanks rolling, infantry, cavalry, people singing the "International," dying without letting their banners out of their hands.

And when there's a lull, I run over to the observation point. I'll take a look, even if it's out of the corner of my eye, and see what an attack is like. I'll breathe it in. Why, the OP's nothing, just a hilltop, with observers lying on their sides, their heads slightly raised, and battery commander Burakov looking through a stereotelescope. I crawl up the steep hill and raise myself waist high. And I hear birds singing. Birds!

Someone pulls me down by the feet.

"That's enough," says the battery commander. "Back to the battery."

"I just wanted to see," I say.

The observers laugh.

"Where did the birds come from?" I ask.

"Birds?" repeats the commander.

"Birds. . . ."

"What birds?" asks the telephonist Kuzin from the trench.

"Birds," I say, and I no longer understand anything myself.

"Do you think those are birds?" the commander asks wearily.

"Birds. . . ." Kuzin laughs.

I'm beginning to understand what's up. One of the observers puts his hat on a stick and lifts it above him. The birds start singing right away.

"Get it now?" the commander asks.

He's a good man. Anyone else would have started stamping his feet and swearing. Our commander is a good man. I would have been killed if it weren't for him. He was probably the one who pulled me down by the feet.

It's getting darker and darker. A gray dusk is enveloping the hill. I hear a machine gun firing in the distance.

"Machine gun," I shout. No one pays any attention to me.

"They're ours," says commander Burakov. "We'll start any minute now." Then he says to me, "Here, take a look."

I squat down near the telescope and look. I see the steppe. At the extreme edge of the steppe, against a background of gray sky, a settlement stretches out in a line. And there, just like fireworks, multicolored lines of tracer bullets stretch out from one end to the other. And I hear the rattling of machine guns and the staccato of submachine guns. But I don't see the attack. I don't see any people.

"Let's go, let's go!" someone screams behind me.

"Where? Where to?"

And suddenly I see—solitary figures, hunched up, running across the steppe. But only a few of them.

"That's enough," says the battery commander. "Back to the battery."

I roll down the hill. I'm running. A jeep comes toward me. A general is sitting in it. It don't know what to do: run past or march past and salute. . . .

The general is red in the face. He doesn't see me. He's waving his arms. And the jeep is getting closer to the observation point. The commander is already standing at attention. And the men too. And the telescope, also, is standing motionless on its tripod.

The general jumps out of the jeep and runs up to the commander.

"You're firing on your own men, your own men!"

The commander is silent. Only his head moves from side to side.

Then the general looks into the telescope, and the commander explains something to him. The general shakes his hand.

"There are miracles," I think to myself.

"Cease fire!" Kuzin screams into the telephone.

The battery is silent; as though everyone were listening for something. And the mortars, like dogs, sit on their hind legs and are also silent.

"What's the matter with your hands?" asks the sergeant.

My hands are bloody. I don't understand where the blood came from. I shrug my shoulders.

"That's from the shell crates," says Shongin.

They'll bandage them for me in a little while.

The sergeant turns around and goes away. He probably went to get the medical orderly. I stand there with my hands stretched out in front of me. They really must have bled. They'll bandage them, and I'll write home. . . .

"Go wash off your hands," says the sergeant. "We're changing our position now."

The Little Bell— A Gift from Valday

Help me. Save me. I don't want to die. Just a small piece of lead in the heart, or head, and it's all over. And my hot body, will it no longer be hot? I don't mind suffering. Who said I was afraid of suffering? It was at home that I was so afraid. At home. But now I've gotten to know a lot of things. I've tried it all. Isn't this enough for one person to know? I'll be set for life. Help me. You know, it's ridiculous to kill a man who hasn't had time to do something in life. I didn't even finish tenth grade. Help me. I'm not speaking about love. To hell with love. I'm content not to love. When you really come down to it, I've already loved. If you really want to know, I've had enough of that. I have a mother. What's going to happen to her? Do you know how tenderly a mother strokes the head of her child? I haven't had time to get unaccustomed to it yet. I really haven't been anywhere yet. For example, I haven't been to Valday yet. I really must know what this Valday is like. Someone once wrote: "The little bell is a gift from Valday." And I can't even write such lines. Help me. I'll go through everything. To the end. I'll shoot at the Fascists like a sniper, I'll fight tanks single-handed, I won't eat or sleep; I'll suffer. . . .

To whom am I saying all this? Whose help am I seeking? These logs which hold the dugout together maybe? Even they aren't happy about being here. After all, not so long ago they were rustling pine trees. Remember the warm shelter when we left for the front? Of course, I remember. We stood in the open doors and sang some solemn song. We held our heads high. A troop train stood on a siding. Where? At the Kursk railroad station. We didn't get home leave. I only had time to phone home. No one was there. Only an old neighbor, Irina Makarovna. An old witch. Boy, did she get on my nerves! She asked me where the train had stopped.

"Too bad your mother won't be able to see you," she said without feeling.

I hung up and returned to the troop train. An hour later Irina Makarovna turned up at the train and shoved a bundle into my hands. And later, when we were singing, she stood among a group of women spectators. What is she to me? Farewell, Irina Makarovna. Forgive me. How was I supposed to know? I'll never be able to understand it. — Perhaps, you're the very person one should ask for protection? Protect me then. I don't want to die. I'm saying this honestly and without shame.

There were some dried biscuits and sunflower-seed oil in the bundle. I made a vow to save one biscuit as a souvenir. But I ate it. I couldn't even do such a simple thing as that. And wasn't it me who stood in full view when the Heinkel swooped down and everyone took cover?

"Take cover!" they screamed at me.

But I didn't hide. I walked alone and laughed out loud. If they only knew what was going on inside of me! But I can't tremble in view of everyone. No one must know that I'm afraid. But can I myself face the truth? That's what I mean. I'm my own judge . . . I have a right to do this. Me, I'm not Fedka Lyubimov. Remember Fedka Lyubimov? Of course, I do. Fyodor Lavrentyevich Lyubimov. My neighbor. When the war broke out, he'd come out into the kitchen every evening and say: "Those German bastards are really pushing. . . . Everyone should stand up to give protection. Wait and see, as soon as my arm gets better, I'll volunteer."

"You'll be called up anyway, Fedka," they'd say to him.

"It's not a joking matter. Everyone will be called up. When the country is in danger you shouldn't wait. You should join up of yourself."

"Do you love your country?" he would ask me.

"Yes," I said. "I learned that in the first grade."

Once I ran into him in the recruiting office. I was delivering telegrams at the time. He didn't see me. He was speaking to some captain.

"Comrade Captain, I've brought my exemption certificate," he said.

"What exemption?"

"Reserve. As a specialist I've been exempted from the service. They won't release me from my job."

"Go in there and register. If you're exempt, then you're exempt. That's all there is to it," the captain said.

If you're exempt, then you're exempt. That's Fedka for you. What kind of a specialist is he, a watch repairman on the Arbat? And Fedka went in and registered. He passed by me, noticed me, blushed, and stopped.

"Did you see?" he asked me. "That's the way it is. Who wants to die?"

He's probably still exempt. As though he were some well-known engineer or great actor.

We didn't build this shelter. It's a good shelter. True, it's smaller than headquarters, where Nina is, but still, it's not bad. It looks like someone left it in a hurry. Somebody lost a photograph of a woman. A young, unattractive woman smiles at me from the photograph. But someone must love her. Why did he forget to take her picture with him?

"Hey, Sashka, did you get an exemption?" I ask.

"Who's going to give it to me. Not everyone can get one," Sashka replies.

"If you slipped something to the right person, you would have gotten one," says Kolya Grinchenko.

"Probably costs a lot, doesn't it?" Sashka asks.

"Three thousand. You could have sold some stuff to get the money. You could have saved up enough."

"Sure I could. My desk alone is worth three thousand."

"Then you could have given it to them."

"Eh," says Sashka and waves his hand. "Go to hell."

"Why didn't you slip them something and get exempted?" Shongin asks angrily.

"I didn't have any money," laughs Kolya.

"You blabber too much," says Shongin.

Lucky

Our mortars have been at it for eight days now. We have three wounded men. I haven't seen them. When I returned to the battery, they had already been taken away. We keep moving from one place to another, so that not only do we not have any trenches, but we also don't have any communications trenches. There's no time for it. It's an attack. When it began Kolya Grinchenko said: "We're in luck, boys. Now we're in luck. Now we'll eat well. We'll live off captured goods now. We've had enough of canned goods for a while."

At that time we all believed him. But it was in vain. The artillery and we always get there last, when everything is already gone.

It's canned goods again. And it's dried biscuits again. And Kolya Grinchenko says to the sergeant, "Sergeant, this canned goods stuff is crap. Where's our front rations?"

"Do you remember, kid, how you were threatening me?" the sergeant asks.

"Prove it," smiles Grinchenko.

"You'd better shut up," says the sergeant.

Now he has something on Kolya. And I see that Kolya is afraid of him. But sometimes he forgets that he's afraid, and he starts in on him again. This can be very funny.

I remember when we entered the first village—it was the

same one I had seen from the observation point. It was destroyed. The huts, which were already being repaired, were
full of cavalry men; they were dressing, sleeping, playing
harmonicas, and, in one hut, they were even making pancakes. Well, of course, we're late everywhere. Where are we
supposed to go?

"So you're a Cossack!" says Kolya. "Where are you from?"

"What do you want?" the Cossack asks.

"You're a Kalmuk, probably, not a Cossack. A Kalmuk,
right?" And Kolya says to us, "Let's get settled, boys. Oh, you
Kalmuk Cossack!"

And Kolya puts his field pack on the bench. The Kalmuk picks
it up and throws it on the threshold. He stands in front of the tall
Grinchenko; he is so small, with his high cheekbones and wide
shoulders.

"What's the matter? You don't like Kalmuks? Go away!"

"Why, you swine!" Kolya's face turns red.

"Go, go!" the Kalmuk says calmly.

"I've shed blood, and you're throwing me out in the cold?"
Sashka takes Kolya by the arm.

"Don't be cute, Mykola."

"Take your friends with you," the Kalmuk says.

"Please, don't get mad," I say.

"Get going."

Suddenly the door opens, and some Cossacks come in. There
are three of them.

"What's the trouble?" asks one of them.

The Kalmuk doesn't say anything. Sashka and I are silent.
Kolya also keeps quiet. Then Kolya smiles, and asks the Kalmuk,
"Why are you silent, Kalmuk?" and then he says to the Cossacks,
"See that bastard— he lights the stove for himself and sends
Russians out into the cold!"

"What's with them?" the Cossack asks the Kalmuk.

"Come on, boys, take off," says the other Cossack to us.

"Let's go," says Grinchenko.

Sashka Zolotaryov and I follow him. We go into a hut. It's hot
there. The stove is on. The place is empty. Only a Cossack is
there, bent over a frying pan. You can tell he's a Cossack from
his uniform trousers.

"Hi," says Grinchenko from the threshold. "Welcome
some guests."

Kolya really knows how to speak to people. He's really quite
at home with them. He smiles when he speaks. He smiles in
such a way that you can't help but smile back at him. The
Cossack now turns around, and I see a face with high cheekbones and slanting eyes.

And the third one says to the Kalmuk, "Come on, Dzhumak, let's eat."

We leave the hut in silence. Into the cold. It's twilight. If Grinchenko says something now, it'll be sickening. It seems to me that I've insulted a man. Kolya is silent. He "shed blood." He hasn't even got a scratch.

Now we're already beyond this populated point. Fire, mortars, fire! Blow, wind! Pour, you, half-rain, half-snow! Get wet, you back of mine! Hurt, you hands of mine!

What can I do so my feet won't freeze? Boy, do I need a pair of boots! Wide ones. Three sizes too large. So I can really wrap my feet—so my foot will be just like in a nest. I must walk some more. But we almost never walk. We have to change positions all the time. This means get into the trucks and get rolling. It's raining. It's coming down from the sky in a straight line. Now it's snowing. It comes in at a slant. The wind's blowing from all sides. Day and night we get soaked. Toward morning it starts freezing up. You don't feel like moving.

I'm thinking about Nina. And it seems to me that she's somewhere on one of the trucks. The telephonist Kuzin is dead. Caught a bullet right in the mouth. It was a spent bullet, a weak one. But somehow it managed to pierce him, and he died.

Conversations
This is probably the first night that we've been able to sleep normally. We're lying on the floor of an abandoned hut. We're on our coats. It's impossible to cover up. It's hot. Shongin has heated up the stove. We've really crowded into the hut. It's dark. Only the red glow of Shongin's cigaret hovers about slowly and constantly.

"Give me a smoke, Shongin," says Sashka Zolotaryov.

Shongin is silent. The red glow is flying around.

"Give me a smoke, Shongin," I say. We continue the gag, slowly, as we always do.

"He's asleep," says Kolya Grinchenko.

The red glow hangs suspended in the air, pitiful and motionless. I stare into the darkness, and it's as if I can see the smile of Grinchenko's face, and as if I can see Shongin's clenched lips and his blinking eyes.

"I want to smoke," says Sashka. "Should I wake him or not?"

"Don't wake him," says Kolya. "Let the man sleep. Take it yourself. Take as much as you want."

"He's got his tobacco in his gas mask," I say.

"I'll give you 'take it yourself,'" says Shongin. "I'll give you some myself."

"See, you've awakened the man," says Kolya.

You can hear Shongin groaning.

We lie there and assiduously inhale the bitter cigaret smoke.

It's quiet. Then someone says in the darkness, "It'd be nice if Nina would come here. We could talk to her."

Sashka Zolotaryov laughs.

"I like plump girls," he says, "and girls that are taller than me."

"Ninka has a husband," I say.

Sashka laughs.

"I have a wife, too. Maybe Ninka's husband is with my 'dumpling' right now."

"It's war," says Kolya. "Everything has been mixed up. And then, if you want to speak about love, then in that case you can't order—"

Sashka laughs.

"You're a bunch of animals," says Shongin, and he turns over to the other side.

"I wouldn't marry someone like her," someone says in the darkness.

"But I would."

"I had a girl, Katya was her name. What a beauty. Braids down to her waist. Now Ninka, well. . . ."

"No one is forcing her on you," Kolya says angrily.

"If you don't like her," I say, "you don't have to take her. Right, Kolya?"

"Your Katya probably has a nose like a belly button," laughs Sashka. "You like 'em like that. A nose like a belly button and smelling of dough."

"You won't be laughing for long, Zolotaryov," someone threatens from the darkness.

You're still alive, my old girl,
I'm alive too. Regards to you, regards.
Above your roof, let there swirl . . . .

It's Kolya singing.

Suddenly the door opens. The commander's voice cuts into the darkness:

"Who's spreading pessimism here?"

And then it's quiet again.

What will happen tomorrow? Where are we going to wind up? No letters from home. There's no more room for notches on Sashka's stick. If I'm wounded, I'll be put in a hospital. I'll eat my fill. I'll go home on leave. I'll go over to the school. And everyone will see my crutches. I'll have a stripe on my chest. For my wound. And perhaps I'll get a medal, and they'll see that, too. And Zhenya will come out. And she won't be laughing this time. And everyone will look at her, then at me. And I'll say to

her, "Hi, Zhenechka." And I'll walk, walk along the corridor.
And she'll catch up to me. "Why don't you drop over and visit
me at home? I've missed you."

"At home? What do you mean? Why, what do you mean?"

"There's no reason. A lot has changed." And I'll walk along
the corridor. And the girls will tell her quietly: "You fool,
Zhenka. It's your own fault."

"I've got a stomach ache from the pumpkin," says Sashka.

"When I was a civilian, I never even saw one," says someone.

Kolya advises Sashka: "You know, Sashka, you ought to go
and take a load off your mind."

"You fool," says Sashka. "A pumpkin is a good thing, only not
if it's raw."

"And I like borsht," someone says in the darkness. "A thick
one, so that when you put your spoon in it, it'll stand upright.
I don't need any dumplings."

And I don't have a spoon. Being without a spoon is like
being without hands. They laugh at me and my piece of wood.
I'm laughing myself. . . . But I don't have a spoon. . . . And
I don't have boots. If only I had a pair of boots, we'd talk
differently, Nina.

Nina, you're so slim. Look, here we are, you and me, walking
through the city. Here's Zhenya coming towards us. She under-
stands everything. And she's silent. And I'm wearing black slacks
and a white shirt with a turn-down collar, and there's a Leica
across my shoulders. And there's no war.

"And I'd like to eat some sour cream, too," someone says in
the darkness.

Nina

No matter how many times I come to regimental headquarters,
no matter how many times I look at Nina, she doesn't notice me.

But her own people, the ones from headquarters, speak to
her very simply: "Nina, give me the mug . . ."—"What's the
matter, dear, tired? . . ."—"Let's have a smoke . . ."—"Hi,
Ninochka. . . ."—"Good to see you again! . . .," and they
embrace her. And she—she hands them the mug, smiles,
smokes, sitting on the crate, and kisses those who return right
on their unshaven cheeks.

That's because they're "her own." But who are they, these
"her own"? They're headquarters rats, and I come from the
battery. I risk my life. My hands are cut to bits, my coat is
burned, my lips chapped. But they're—"her own."

I crawl into the headquarters dugout. It's warm there. A
joyous, potbellied stove is burning. It smells of bread. There's
no one there. Only Nina is sitting with her earphones near

the receiver.

"Don, Don, this is Moscow. Over. Don, Don, this is Moscow. How do you read me? Over."

"Hi, Nina," I say in an offhand manner.

She nods to me. It's so friendly, so nice. It's so unexpected.

"How do you read me? Is it better now? Over."

She takes off the earphones.

"Sit down, warrior. Rest up."

"No time," I say, and sit down on the boards. And I look at her. She smiles.

"Well, why are you staring?"

"Oh, nothing. It's been long since I've seen a woman smile. There are no women at the battery, you know. Sashka Zolotaryov sometimes smiles and Kolya Grinchenko, but there are no women."

She smiles again.

"Your Kolya comes here often. He keeps telling me about his heroic deeds. I don't like braggarts."

"Come to see us."

"Where?"

"At the battery."

"To drink tea?"

"We'll sit a while, smoke."

"We'll sit a while, smoke." She smiles.

How daring I was when I first walked in. How daring! Even the flame of the lamp trembled. But now it's not moving.

"If you want, I'll give you some tea."

"I don't drink tea," I say ironically.

"Oh, I get it," says Nina. "You've got used to stronger stuff."

"Accustomed or not, I prefer it. We'll get our fill of tea when we're civilians again."

She looks straight at me, not blinking, and smiles.

"You're a strange one. Our reconnaissance men are good kids too, but they don't refuse tea. You're a real strange one. But I'll come to the battery, okay? We'll sit a while, smoke, eh?"

"Really?"

"Yes—you know, you have nice eyes."

White wings sprout on my back. White. White. They make everything light, like a rocket flare at the front. Delirium.

"I still say you're lying about the 'stronger stuff.'"

She says this from afar. I don't see her. Only two large eyes. Round. Gray. Derisive.

Some people come in. They stamp their feet. They speak words. But I hear: "Don, Don . . . you have nice eyes . . . I'm signing off, Roger."

"Are you from Lieutenant Burakov?" they ask me.

"Yes, sir!"

"Here, take this. . . ."

I take a piece of paper, put it in my pocket. I go over to Nina.

"You'll come, then?"

"Where? Oh, the battery? We'll sit a while, smoke. Right?"

"Come."

"But I don't smoke," she smiles. "We'll just sit, okay?"

"Hey, Ninochka, what are you doing, entertaining the handsome soldier boys?" I hear behind my back.

"Everything is calm, quiet, but I feel kind of bad. I have a feeling," says Shongin, "and I'm not happy about this silence. No, I'm not happy about it."

The small, scrawny Gurgenidze stands in front of Lieutenant Burakov. A drop hangs from the tip of his nose. He's waving his arms.

"Let me go home for four days. My house in Kvarely. I bring all kind *purmarili*, food, wine, *khachapuri*, *lobio*. This porridge no good."

The lieutenant laughs.

"And who's going to do the fighting?"

"I will," Gurgenidze bows. "Who will? I will. No war here now."

"And how will you get there?"

"What?"

"How will you go?"

Gurgenidze looks at the lieutenant regretfully.

"Give me leave. I'll get there."

The commander looks at us.

"Well, what do you say, shall we let him go?"

"We'll, you see how it is, Comrade Lieutenant," says Shongin, "it'd be okay to let him go, but supposing it suddenly starts? How are we going to get along without a communications man?"

"You see how it is," says the commander. "We can't get along without you."

"Why not?" Gurgenidze becomes worried. "Sure you can. No fighting four days."

"Listen, Gurgenidze, why don't you go over to the Germans and ask them when they are going to begin. Perhaps you can even go after all," Sashka suggests.

Everyone laughs. They can't hold back. Gurgenidze tries to understand what happened. Then he shrugs his shoulders.

"Eh!" and he himself laughs.

And the drop, no longer being able to hold onto the tip of his nose, falls to the ground.

And the commander says, getting serious, "Rest. All of you.

We'll be working this evening." And he goes away.

In the evening, again, nothing happens. I asked her to come to the battery. Why should she? Why? What is she going to do here? I invited her as though for a walk in the park. If she only saw my hands, covered with scabs and callouses; my hangnails, my hands which are impossible to wash clean, so deep has the dirt eaten into the flesh. . . . I'll say to her, "Listen, why fool around? You see everything, you understand. Well, come on then and let it be simple: you and me. That I might know that you visited *me*. Let everybody see. Come on, what do you say? Listen, we're the same age. It's a lot of nonsense that the man must be older. I've known you for a long, long time. Well, please don't pretend that it's all the same to you. I know that the reason you laugh at me is because you're embarrassed." And when I say this to her, the white moon will come out, and the snow will glisten, and there won't be anyone around us, and my leggings won't be showing.

"Why aren't you resting?" asks Kolya Grinchenko.

What am I going to tell him?

"Yesterday I made a date with Ninochka. She'll come today."

"You're still lying," I say, relieved. "Boy, do you ever lie."

"You'll see," he says. "Wait."

Kolya stands before me. He smells of perfume. He shaved. Shaved? Is she really coming? Why, of course; she smiled, and I. . . .

A white rocket flare goes up over the German trenches. Somewhere in the distance a machine gun rattles, lonely and sadly, and then it falls silent.

Kolya Grinchenko blows cigaret smoke into his cupped hands. He smiles.

"Yes, Ninochka will come, we'll talk."

"But, she's married," I say. "You won't get anywhere with her."

He smiles and continues smoking. Then he walks off. And he doesn't say anything. If he's quiet, it means he's telling the truth. It means she will come. Fool that I was, fool. I asked, begged. One must do it the way Grinchenko said. Yes, that's the way. Embrace her, squeeze her till her bones crack so she can't say a word; so that she feels here's a man! They like that, yes. But conversations, who needs 'em? Oh, you gray-eyed Nina, you! Now I know what to tell you . . .

Beyond the dugout a jeep rumbles. And a female voice is heard. And I see Kolya heading in that direction. She's come. And I hear her voice:

"Hello hello!" What a smile, what a smile. I can't stand it. "See, I came to visit you. Just for a minute. I asked the major to take me with him. Well, how are things? Well, look now, you've even got Germans nearby. Why are you so quiet, Kolya? You even have time to shave. Listen, you have a boy here, a dark-eyed one, where is he?"

"What dark-eyed one?" asks Grinchenko.

I hear her quiet laugh. She laughs well. Should I go over? But why should I? Why must it be me she's talking about? Gurgenidze is dark-eyed, so is the platoon leader Karpov, and so's the battery commander.

Her dark, slim silhouette swims out from beyond the dugout like a dark moon. She has stopped and is rocking back and forth lightly.

"There you are, warrior. We'll sit a while, smoke, right?"

She comes nearer, closer.

"Now that's really something," she says. "I have a date in the middle of the war. Why are you so quiet? Oh, oh, you probably filled yourself with that strong stuff, right?"

"I didn't drink anything. . . ."

"Well, tell me something. . . ."

"Let's go over there, near the shell crates. We can sit."

"Aren't you something! Head for the corner right away."

"Why do you say that?"

"Because everyone wants it. And even more so at the front. What's going to happen tomorrow?"

"I like you, Nina."

"I know."

"You know? You're simply convinced of it?"

"Why, what do you mean? What do you mean, my boy? Grinchenko told me that you speak to me in your sleep."

"He's always lying!"

From beyond the dugout someone shouted: "Nina! Nina Shubnikova, let's go!"

"Well, it's time. You haven't really told me anything. Who you are, what you are, what we're going to do," she says and passes the palm of her hand over my cheek.

"Well, good-bye. It's war. Perhaps we won't see each other."

"I'll come to see you tomorrow. I like you."

"My people like me," she says. "I'm the only one here, you know."

She runs to the car. She runs quickly, and flares go up more and more often above the German trenches.

Oh, Tobacco, Tobacco

Just as thunder roars out of the calm, so unexpected colors appear in a gray morning: red on gray; saffron on gray; black on white. Flames, rusty, warped metal, motionless bodies.

Nina went off with the major to headquarters. The last rocket over the German positions is like the last flower. Nina is probably screaming into the telephone: "Volga, Volga, this is Don, how do you read me? Over!" And I have such a fat, little, peaceful shell in my hands. I'll pass it to the loader. Then the mortar will groan, sitting back on its hind legs.

I know how it's going to be. Boy, am I ever experienced now. And the palms of my hands don't hurt anymore.

And Kolya Grinchenko is sitting on the mortar base plate. He smiles pleasantly. And he sings quietly to himself:

"Oh, tobacco, tobacco. . . ."

"Did you hear? The Germans broke through," says Sashka.

"Infantry?"

"No, tanks."

"Are they heading this way?"

"They're behind us."

"How many?"

"They say about forty."

German bombers are flying high over our position. They don't want us. They'll drop their bombs behind our lines.

"The medics will have plenty of work," Sashka says.

And Kolya sings: "Oh, tobacco, tobacco. . . ."

And then a German shell explodes on the hill, to the right of us. Our mortars send them a friendly answer. All four of them. Then another one. And again.

And behind us red balls of fire burst up. I can feel the hot wind on my back. The back of my head aches. The German artillery keeps pouring it on.

"They're onto us," someone says.

I keep bringing more and more shells. I don't stop to think about anything. Each movement is as automatic as hell. Ten steps back. Pick up a sixteen-kilo, cold suckling pig. Ten steps forward. You can do it with your eyes closed. A couple of round trips. And the fingers themselves unbutton the coat. And they pick up some snow and shove it in the mouth. And suddenly I get a stupid idea: after the battle, I'll take some sugar, mix it with snow, and I'll get ice cream.

Ten steps forward. Ten—back. There are less and less "suckling pigs." How much time has passed? Happy people never notice time pass.

A shock wave hits me in the back. I can't stand up. I fall.

"Aaa, aaaa," someone screams. And then again, but weaker this time, "a-a, a-a-a-a-!"

It's me screaming. I see the backs of my comrades. They're shooting. They don't see me. Thank God, everything is okay. No pain. Why did I scream? Supposing there was a direct attack. . . .

But that's impossible. Why me especially? And why not? And suddenly there is an unusually violent explosion. And there's a scream again. But it's not me, it's someone else this time. The way he screams—you can't bear to look. I see Kolya run up to him, and then he covers his face with his hands and runs back. And before reaching his mortar, he stops and bends over.

Who was on the first mortar? I can't remember anyone. No one. Absolutely no one. And there's no more room for notches on Sashka's stick. The platoon commander Karpov shouts at us to change our position. And everyone's as busy as hell. Quicker, quicker! If we don't get a move on, the Germans will clobber us. The mortars are already hitched to their carriers. And we crawl out of the dugout where our position was. Where will our new position be? What's going to happen? Everybody's quiet. Now I see four spots in the snow and a figure in a long coat approaching us. And I don't want to think about it, but it won't leave me, and I can't get rid of it for anything.

"Number one is gone," says Sashka.

"Gone," I say.

"A lot of the boys are gone," says Sashka.

"Shut up!" says Shongin. He's sitting, hunched over.

The trucks keep moving. And I don't notice the shooting anymore. I only see Kolya's pale face. He is looking somewhere off in the distance and not moving.

"Hey, Kolya!" says Sashka. "Better say good-bye to Ninka. They'll be transferring us to another division."

Kolya doesn't move.

"Shut up!" says Shongin.

"As if it wasn't enough, now they have tanks crawling up our back," says Gavrilov.

We pass some sort of fire. Probably a barn. Burned to the ground. Some logs are still smoldering. Smells terrible. A smell of burning, of burning . . . but that's not the word.

From the new position we can see the firing on the enemy. Three of our mortars keep pouring it on somewhere over the hills. I keep bringing more and more shells.

But it could hit our mortar. Not number one, but ours. And I wouldn't be carrying shells. Maybe I'd be walking slowly along the fields, just barely moving, and then I'd fall. So far it's quiet here. They haven't spotted us yet. There it is again: "Retreat!" And again into the trucks. And into the night, and into the darkness.

We're stamping our feet in the darkness near the trucks. We hitch up the mortars. And somewhere up in the sky the bombers are droning on.

"Ours."

"You never see them in the daytime."

"It's better than nothing."

Second Lieutenant Karpov, our platoon commander, comes over. He's rubbing his hands and cheeks. Our platoon commander is either frozen or he's worried.

"Are we moving again?" Sashka Zolotaryov asks.

"What do you mean," says Karpov. "We're moving up, boys! Enough of this sitting around."

"Sitting around," says Shongin. "Look how many men we've lost."

"That's war," says Karpov quietly. "And what's an old soldier like you, Shongin, talking like this for?"

Everyone is quiet. Words—that's really funny. It really is war. What are you going to do? Is it Karpov's fault? Look at him; young, red-cheeked, energetic. . . . Is it my fault? Kolya's?

We're sitting in the trucks. Miserable road. The truck keeps rocking like a boat. We rock from side to side. It's a good thing we're riding. Otherwise, the road would have become so muddy. You try and pull a truck through the stuff. We're riding. It's half raining, half snowing. We gradually get soaked. At first it's even nice: it's cooling after the heat. And the cold raindrops run down inside your collar comfortably. But now it's no good anymore. Enough. I know, in a minute we'll be shivering. Then try and get warm. And the feet freeze. Quickly and certainly. We're moving to a new battle sector. Already you can clearly hear the explosions and the song of the automatics. And a lit-up sky swims out from beyond the hill.

"And Where Is Your Daughter?"

How well everything is going. Tomorrow I'll write home. I'm alive. What's left of the battery? Two mortars and no more than thirty men. And I'm alive. Didn't even get a scratch. I'll write tomorrow. Home.

"Let's see what's there," says Sashka Zolotaryov.

Night. Some sort of a hut. The windows are dark.

I knock on the shutters. "Lady, would you be so kind as to. . . ." No answer. "Lady, I made it, I'm alive. Oh, if you only knew what it was like!" I knock on the shutters. "The boots— here; the uniform—in the closet; the sword—on the chair. . . ." "Thank you. . . . But where is your daughter?"

"Sleep, sleep, sleep," says Kolya.

I knock on the shutters. "Grouse? Cheese? Wine?" "Oh, thank you. A small piece of cold veal and some rum. I'm a soldier, lady." I knock on the shutters.

"We'll freeze to death."

"Let's go to another one."

"Knock again."

I knock on the shutters. Sashka knocks on the shutters. Kolya knocks on the shutters.

"Here's your room. Good night." "Good night, lady. But where is your daughter? . . ."

"What do you want?"

A woman is standing in the doorway. She's all bundled up.

"We'd like to spend the night here, lady."

"We made it, we're alive," I say.

"So what?" . . ." says the woman. "That's all I needed."

"Can we come in?" asks Kolya.

"It's very cold," says Sashka.

"We'll just stay overnight and then leave," I say.

It's cold in the hallway. Inside it's warm. A lamp is burning and smoking up the place. Someone is tossing and turning on the Russian stove. It's a small room. How are we all going to fit in there?

The woman takes off her kerchief. She's very young.

"Lie down here," she says to Kolya, pointing to the corner. Kolya's got a good place. "And you, over there," she says to Sashka.

Zolotaryov spreads his coat under the table and lies down on it. Kolya undresses silently. She puts me on a bunk near the stove. I can lie only on my side. What the hell—as long as I'm lying down. The woman herself lies on a bed. A folding bed. There's a rag of a blanket on it. She crawls under it without taking off her outer coat.

I put my coat on the bunk. The blue flame of the lamp goes out. A hand strokes my hair.

"Come up here," says a quiet voice from the stove. "It's warm here."

"Who are you?"

"What's the difference. Come on. It's warm here."

"Manka," the woman says indifferently, "watch out."

"Who asked you?" says Manka from the stove. And her hand keeps stroking me, stroking me.

"Come on over here."

"Wait, let me take my shoes off."

"Come on, what's the difference?"

Supposing they hear? "Where's your daughter, lady?" Supposing they hear—now there's a daughter for you. It's warm near Manka. If I just touch her, the whole thing will be shot. Manka—is that really her name?

"What's your name?"

"Marya Andreyevna."

Now there's something for you. How can. . . . She has a hot

flabby stomach and small clutching hands.

"How old are you?"

"Sixteen. . . . Why?"

"Sh . . . !"

"Why? Why?"

"They'll hear us."

"Let 'em . . . come closer."

"Manka," says the woman, "you'd better watch it, Manka."

"Never you mind," says Manka.

Down below, Sashka Zolotaryov coughs, and Kolya says:
"Lady, aren't you cold?"

And Manka wraps herself around me, and I don't know which
is me and which is her. Everything is all mixed up.

"Your heart is really thumping." She laughs right in my ear.
"What's the matter, are you afraid?"

And Kolya asks, "Aren't you cold, lady?"

Is that how simple it is? And will it be the same with Nina?
With everyone?

"What's the matter, are you dead or something?"

"Leave me alone."

"I'm just kidding, silly."

"Let me go, Marya."

"Marya," says the woman. "Hey, Marya, you're not Marya,
you're a tow-headed fool."

"Let go of me, or there'll be trouble."

"Come on, let's just lie here, okay?"

"Let go."

"Go back to your bench if you think it's too crowded here."

The bench is cool. Sashka's coughing.

"Lady, you must be freezing under that rag. Want me to cover
you with my coat?" says Kolya from the corner.

Someone's walking around in the hut. And he's whispering
something. It's a quiet, hurried whisper. I can't make out the
words. It's probably Marya on the stove. And maybe it's the
woman. And perhaps it's not a whisper, but just the stillness.
But someone is sobbing. How difficult it must be in this small
village. And tomorrow I'll be a laughingstock. They'll make fun
of me for sure. . . . Serves me right. She herself asked, begged. . . .
They'll laugh at me. I'll get up early in the morning and go to
another hut, or to headquarters, or to the trucks. She's hot like
fire, that Marya Andreyevna. She'll be the first one to laugh.
Sixteen. . . . Kolya calls them "peaches and cream." But someone really is crying. Or is it outside the window?

"Who is it?" I ask.

"Don't shout," says the woman. "Lie down and sleep."

I must be in a delirium. They'll laugh at me, really laugh at me. And still, someone is crying. Could it be that it's Marya laughing?

In the morning Sashka Zolotaryov says, "Looks like we'll be eating here. The battery commander's eating potatoes. The trucks broke down."

Sashka has already washed. He has an air of cold about him. His cheeks are just like children's cheeks, crimson. He's had time to find out everything. And Kolya is sleeping. And the woman and Marya are gone.

"What's going to happen now?" I ask.

"Nothing," says Sashka. "We'll wait for some new equipment, and then we'll start again."

"And the trucks have broken down?"

"Completely."

"Is the kitchen operating?"

"What kitchen?"

Sashka takes out three packages of powdered peas from his field pack.

"Here's what they gave us. We'll cook it. Better wake Kolya. Get up, Mykola!"

And suddenly the woman comes in. She takes off her kerchief. And I see that she is very young. And beautiful.

"Get up, Mykola," says Sashka. But Kolya sleeps.

"What are you waking him for?" the woman asks. "Let him sleep—he's tired."

She speaks very severely. And she keeps looking at Kolya.

"Give it to me, I'll cook it," she says, taking the powdered peas from Sashka.

We're sitting at the table. We're silent. We're eating the pea soup. With wooden spoons. But I don't have a spoon. As soon as we leave this place, I'll get my piece of wood. . . . For now, I'll use the wooden one. I haven't had a spoon for a long time. . . . We eat the pea soup; there's no bread. Kolya eats slowly. Occasionally he looks up at the woman. She's sitting directly opposite him. And she also looks up at him from time to time. And that's all. And I'm waiting for Marya to start laughing at me. But she won't even look at me. It's only that I haven't really looked at her. She's pug-nosed. And she has a wide face. And a funny lock of hair hangs down her forehead. And she has several large freckles, or birthmarks, on her nose.

"Well now, freckle-face," Sashka says to her, "what's going to happen to us?"

"We'll get along," says Marya.

"It's tasty soup," says Kolya, and he looks at the woman.

"How come you don't look alike?" asks Sashka. "You live together, you're like sisters, but you don't look alike."

"But we're not sisters," says Marya. "We just know each
other and live together."

"You know, the soup's not bad," says Kolya. And he looks at
the woman. But she doesn't say anything.

Suddenly Shongin comes in.

"Here we go again, another one," the woman says loudly.

And Shongin sits down on a stool.

"There are a lot of dead," he says, "and wounded. They've
taken them away." And he takes out his tobacco pouch.

"Are we gonna smoke?" asks Sashka.

"What is there to smoke?" says Shongin. "There's not enough
tobacco for me," and he shows the pouch.

"Where did you sleep, Shongin?" Kolya asks.

"I didn't sleep," says Shongin. "There were a lot of wounded.
By the time we picked them all up, it was morning."

"I'd love a smoke now," says Sashka.

"Here, smoke, smoke," says Shongin, and he takes a drag. He
blows out large clouds of smoke. "I just dropped in to see how
you were," he says.

Meanwhile, the woman is pouring milk into some cups. And
Kolya says, "Listen, Shongin, that powdered stuff wasn't enough.
Would you like some milk?"

"It's goat's milk," says Marya.

"I've eaten," says Shongin. "I've eaten. Gurgenidze was
wounded. I made some soup for both of us."

Poor little Gurgenidze. Just a boy. With an eternal drop hanging from the tip of his nose. "It's a hit—it's a miss."

"Is he bad, Shongin?"

"Nothing much," says Shongin. "He's in the truck. The last
one. They're going to take him away."

I'm running along in the fresh snow. To the truck. Soldiers are
walking around it. Gurgenidze is lying on some straw in the
back of the truck. In a burned coat. He raises his bandaged
head. A drop is hanging from the tip of his nose.

"I got hit," he says with a sad smile.

We weren't even friends. Just knew each other. And his red
eyelids keep flinching.

"Where'd you get it?"

"I got it in the head, the stomach, in the leg. Shongin carry me
on his back."

"It's okay, Gurgenidze. Now you'll rest up. Everything will be
okay."

The motor turns over. Gurgenidze falls back on the straw. His
hands are folded on his chest.

"What's our section?" he asks. "What number?"

"Special mortar battery, friend."

"No, which regiment?"

"The 229th, I think."

"What division?"

"Why do you want to know?"

"They might ask me in the hospital."

The motor is even. The back of the truck shakes.

"What division?"

"Who the hell knows," I shout after him.

The truck rumbles along the fresh snow. Gurgenidze's arm is sticking out from the back of the truck. He's saying good-bye to us. He has left, gone. And I forgot to ask him for his spoon.

"Get them together. It's time. We've rested," the battery commander says to me.

There's no one in the hut. Kolya and the woman are sitting on a log in the back of the hut. She's silent. She's resting her head on her hands. Her eyes are red. Her lips are pouting, just like a little girl's. And Kolya is smoking and is also silent.

"It's time, Kolya," I say. "The battery commander ordered. . . ."

"I know," he says and stands up. And he looks at me.

I wait for him.

"I know," he says.

I go away. Let them say good-bye.

The Road

"Did you see the German trucks?" Kolya asks. "They have tarpaulin covers and all that stuff. They're real comfy, just like at home. But our stuff. . . ."

"I can't feel my feet anymore," says Zolotaryov. "I'd love to have me some boots. Fur-lined ones. To hell with the face, the main thing is the feet. Maybe I've already lost my big toe, eh? If I take off my shoes, it'll probably fall out."

I don't want any fur-lined boots. Just an ordinary pair of boots would do. With wide tops, like boats. If I got into water, nothing would happen. If I got into snow, nothing would happen. Even if I stood there all night. No matter.

Steppe, steppe, steppe. When are we going to stop? Our battery keeps moving from position to position. First we're sent to one section, then to another. Who knows where the regiment to which we were attached is now? And Nina is there. Nina, Nina, you smiled so sweetly to me. And I can't forget you. Who are you, and where are you from? I don't know anything. Where am I going to look for you? Everything in the past has grown dim and hazy. Zhenya is somewhere in a fog, in the distance. There's only you, Nina. And why did you speak so nicely to me?

"Do I talk in my sleep?" I ask Kolya.

"Once, to Ninka Shubnikov."

"What did I say?"

"'Sit next to me, Nina, sit. We'll sit down, have a smoke,' that's what you said. Great fun."

"Did she say anything to you about me?"

And why did I ask? He'll laugh in a minute. Or maybe he'll make up some story.

"No, she didn't," says Kolya with a frown. "What's there to say? She's living with the regimental commander. You remember—that tall major."

I remember. I'd have felt better if he hadn't said anything. If I ever meet her, say, purely by chance—it could happen—I'd say to her. . . .

"When I was serving in the cavalry," says Shongin, "now that was really terrible. I'd come back from a march, and I wouldn't be able to sleep. First I had to unsaddle the horse, then feed it, and then, if there was any time left over, then I could rest."

"The English soldiers have waitresses serving them," says Kolya, "and they get cognac with their dinner."

"You're lying, Grinchenko," Shongin mutters.

The trucks have stopped. A traffic jam. It's getting dark.

"Get down, boys. Warm yourselves."

No letters from home. I wonder what's happening there.

"Shongin, ever get any letters from home?" I ask.

He looks at me attentively.

"Of course, I do," he says, and pulls out his tobacco pouch and offers me a smoke,

"Here, warm up."

If we stay here like this until morning, we'll really catch cold. What eyes that Shongin has. They're tender and kind. Yesterday, when we were cooking the powdered peas, he came over to me and Kolya and put a handful of millet in our mess tins. The millet made the soup thick. He came over himself: "Here, boys, I'll put something extra in."

"Shongin, let's have a smoke," says Sashka.

Shongin is stamping his feet up and down, warming them.

"You'll get along without it," he mumbles.

When it gets dark, you can't see the snow. It feels warmer. The platoon commander, Karpov, comes over. He always has red cheeks. You can even see them in the dark.

He's laughing.

"What's the matter, warriors, you frozen?"

"You'll freeze too," says Kolya. "The sergeant's warm, though—he warms himself on the truck radiator. Maybe we can start a bonfire, Lieutenant, what do you say, eh?"

"No bonfires," says Karpov.

Like a guard, Shongin stomps his feet in the snow and bangs his mess tin with his hand.

Gavrilov comes over and says quietly, "Boys, there are some trucks up ahead, full of groats, and the drivers are asleep."

"So what?" asks Shongin.

"Nothing," says Gavrilov. "I was just saying that the drivers are asleep."

"You know, it wouldn't be so bad if we could get us a potful of groats," says Sashka Zolotaryov.

And he goes off into the darkness, toward where the drivers are asleep. And everyone follows him with their eyes. And everybody is silent.

If it's millet, we can make some thick soup. If it's buckwheat, it's good with milk. If it's pearl-barley, that's nice with onions. Will I last until morning or not? I'm soaked through and through. Supposing I catch pneumonia?

No letters from home. Where are you, military post?

Kids

I'm loading machine-gun magazines. I'm loading, and I'm silent.

"Why so sad, kid?" the sergeant asks.

I can't answer him. What can I tell him?

"Oh, nothing," I say, "just reminiscing about home."

You've got it good, Sergeant. You eat omelets. And we eat cold pea soup. You've got it good, Sergeant. And we don't get any decent sleep for days on end.

You have a pleasant face. And there're less and less of us. And this Mozdok sand screeches in my teeth and in my soul. You ought to give me some boots, Sergeant, or something. The artificial soles on my American knee boots have cracked. When it's cold, I shove my feet into the bonfire. And the knee boots are a beautiful red. But what's left of them?

"You ought to grease those shoes, kid. Just look at them, they're no good."

And what kind of shoes did I wear before I got into the army? I don't remember. Did I have stylish, chocolate-brown shoes with a white edge, like ocean surf? Or did I just dream about it? I probably wore plain black shoes. And in the winter I put on galoshes over them. Yes, yes, galoshes. At the last Komsomol meeting I forgot them at school. I forgot them. I came home without galoshes. And the war had already broken out, and no one noticed my loss. That's the way I left. And they were new galoshes. Shiny ones. Now I don't know—will I ever have another pair like them?

And when we had the last Komsomol meeting, Zhenya was sitting in a corner. While we each took our stand and swore to die for our motherland, she didn't say anything. Then she said, "I'm sorry for you boys. You think it's so simple to fight? Wars need silent, sullen soldiers. Wars don't need noise. I'm sorry for you. And you . . ." she pointed to me. "You still don't know how to do anything except read your books. There's death out there, death—and it loves young people like you."

"And you?" someone shouted.

"I'll go too. But I won't scream and suffer. What for? I'll simply go."

"We'll also go. Why are you lecturing us?"

"You must be mentally prepared."

"Shut up, Zhenka . . ."

"Otherwise, you won't be of any service."

"Shut up!"

"Enough," said the Komsomol organizer. "Why are we shouting like this? Like a bunch of kids?"

And when I kissed you at the gate so that you moaned and embraced me, what was that? Does that mean I don't know how to do anything except read books?

"Tomorrow we'll go get some mortars," says the sergeant. "You can take it easy for another night, kid."

"What mortars?" I ask.

"Don't sleep. We'll be getting some replacements tomorrow. You'll be teaching those babies."

"But how can I?"

"What's the matter, do you need three years of fighting to teach our business to a bunch of schoolboys?"

Our business? My business? Does he mean the mortars? I'll be teaching?

"Okay, I'll teach 'em," I say.

Schoolboys. But I was a schoolboy too. Does this mean I'm no longer a schoolboy? But at that meeting I was a schoolboy. And when everybody made noise, I made noise too. Zhenya said, "You're making noise, just like a schoolboy. You can't do that there. You need severity there."

And she looked at me. I looked at her, too. Someone told me that if a girl loves you, she won't last out a stare. She'll blush and lower her eyes. That means she didn't love me. She didn't love me.

"Let's all go together, the entire class," someone shouted.

"Let's all go!" I shouted.

"Shut up," they told me. "Shut up, you jerk!"

Then the school director came in, and the Komsomol organizer said, "Okay, we'll continue the business of the day."

And on the agenda there was but one question: Komsomol studies.

"When you finish with the machine-gun magazines, come into the smokehouse," says the sergeant and goes away.

And after the meeting we were all walking along the river bank together. And Zhenya was walking with us, but she didn't look at me. It was dark and tense.

"We won't see the tenth of the month, boys," someone said. And a siren suddenly started wailing. And I found myself next to Zhenya.

"So, we're schoolboys?" I asked.

"Of course," she said calmly.

"In other words, we won't make good fighters?"

"Of course."

"To be a good fighter, you have to be broad-shouldered, right?"

"Yes," she laughed.

"And indifferent, right?"

"No," she said, "I didn't say that."

"Let's go over there," I said, pointing to a dark side street.

We were walking along the side street. It was even darker and tenser there. And suddenly a window opened. With a bang. On the third floor. Laughter came out of the window. Then noise. The phonograph was playing an old prewar tango.

"As though nothing ever happened, right?"

"Right." I said.

The window closed. The music died down. And the siren wailed again. . . .

I loaded all the magazines. I'm walking to the smokehouse. It's not a smokehouse, just a simple hut where the sergeant is staying.

The sergeant is warming his hands near the stove. And the platoon commander, Karpov, so pink-cheeked, is shaving near the window. Even through the white, foamy lather, you can see his pink cheeks.

Sashka Zolotaryov is standing at attention in front of the battery commander.

"In other words, you stole someone else's millet?" the battery commander asks.

"I stole it," Sashka says.

"You ate someone else's gruel! When you stole, did you think that someone else would go hungry? Did you?"

"Yes, Comrade Lieutenant!"

"Well?"

"I was hungry, too."

"You know what you can get for this?"

"Of course, I know," Sashka says quietly.

"He gave some to everybody," I say from the threshold.

The battery commander looks at me piercingly. Will he hit me? If he only hit me.

"They're a bunch of hooligans, not a battery," he says.

"They've got out of hand," says Karpov. "Grinchenko is their leader. They're continually talking about love and stuffing their faces."

"Okay, Karpov, go on with your shaving," says the battery commander. "I have other business."

And I want to ask Karpov where he was when we were raw troops, just beyond State Farm No. 3, when we took part in our first battle. He was eating food at school.

"About face!" the battery commander shouts at me.

I walk to my place. Maybe Zhenya really is right. Maybe I really am a schoolboy. The winter will be over soon. Soon we'll be returning to the front lines. Then we'll see what kind of a schoolboy I am . . . and I'll meet Nina again. "Hi, small fry," she'll say. "Haven't seen you for a long time. Let's sit a while, have a smoke, right?"

Conversations

We've been at this destroyed village for four days and nights. There was a state farm here. A big, shredded windmill, like some sad bird, looks down at us from above.

Shabby batteries, battalions drained of blood, regiments thinned out in attack; all of these have gathered here. Depots have sprung up in former dugouts, and tired commissaries, who haven't had enough sleep, distribute, give out and supply us with all kinds of goods.

The roads to the north pass through here. The offensive has gone that way. We can hear the deafening cannonade from there. New units hurry along these roads to the front. In new uniforms. Spic and span. On new trucks. And they look at us with curiosity and respect, with fear and envy.

I haven't seen Nina for a long time now. I'm already forgetting her face. Her voice. How quickly everything happens in war. . . .

Kolya Grinchenko has had a good night's sleep and has cleaned up. He's happy again. Every two hours Sashka Zolotaryov cooks something for himself in addition to the rations. And he sleeps. His eyes are very, very small. His cheeks are even more crimson. I can't tell now whose are more crimson, his or Karpov's. And Second Lieutenant Karpov walks around like a conqueror in his sheepskin coat, cocked hat, and with a twig in his hand. He keeps hitting his boot tops with this twig, just as a calf drives away flies with its tail. His voice has become clearer, more ringing. And for some reason, we clash more with him.

"He's got nothing to do," says Kolya Grinchenko, "so he keeps poking his nose into everything."

"He's a commander," says Shongin.

"Didn't even hear a word out of him at the front," says Sashka, "but he'll start educating us soon."

"He's a commander," says Shongin. "He's got to do it."

"He'll get around to us soon," I say. "See how he keeps looking at Kolya?"

"He doesn't like me," says Kolya. "The battery commander does, but not that one. . . ."

"Now the battery commander, that's something altogether different," says Shongin. "He's not about to walk around with a twig in his hand."

"He's smart," says Sashka Zolotaryov.

Second Lieutenant Karpov comes up. He's hitting his boot tops with his twig.

"Grinchenko, why are you wearing a navy belt buckle? We're in the artillery," he says to Kolya.

"Yes, sir! The artillery," says Kolya and smiles.

"Then take off that buckle and put it away as a memento."

"Yes, sir! Take off that buckle," Kolya salutes and smiles.

"I mean it," Karpov with great restraint. "No joking around on the front."

"Yes, sir!" says Kolya and smiles.

Karpov looks at us. We're not smiling. Sashka looks aside. Shongin stands at attention, but I can't. Both legs just keep buckling under me. Now one, now the other.

"Take it off, and bring it to me," says Karpov. He hits his boot tops with his leafy twig.

Kolya quickly takes off the belt buckle. It's a beautiful buckle with anchors on it.

"But I didn't argue with him," he says. "What got into him?"

"He's a commander," says Shongin, "and you're a jerk. That's why."

Kolya walks off swinging the belt in his hand.

"He'll get it yet," says Sashka Zolotaryov.

Whom does he mean: Kolya or Karpov? I don't know. We also walk away. To our hut. It's warm there.

Kolya's sitting on the bench. He's changing buckles.

"I'll transfer to reconnaissance. They're okay," he says.

We sit and keep quiet. Tired of sitting and being silent— of speaking. No replacements.

"Why don't they send us out a little farther? As it is, we don't do anything," says Sashka. "We'd go into some small town. On leave. An orchestra probably would be playing in the park. Soon the apple trees will begin to bloom."

"Karpov would surely let you have it," says Kolya.

"The apple trees will bloom without you," says Shongin, "and there are no orchestras now. What good are they—now? When I left for the front, there was an orchestra playing."

"That was the last one," I say. "Then everybody became a machine gunner. They all became machine gunners."

"Eh, bull . . . ," says Shongin.

"Yes. No orchestras are playing now. Now they only play when we liberate a city."

. . . And when I left, there was no orchestra playing. It was autumn. It was raining. Seryozhka Gorelov and I were standing at the streetcar stop. We had rucksacks. And we had a packet from the enlistment office. And our orders sending us to separate mortar divisions.

"You'll get there on your own," the head of the second unit told us. "You're not children."

And we left.

No one saw us off. Even Zhenya didn't come. We rode through Moscow in the evening, and we were silent. And at the Kazan railroad terminal it was terribly crowded. And we sat down on the floor. And we liked it. Seryozhka smoked and kept spitting on the floor. We played at being soldiers, and we liked this game. And I kept looking around all the time. Perhaps I'll see Zhenya. No, an orchestra did not play at our farewell. There was just a piano on a raised platform, and some drunken little sailor sat down and played an old waltz. And everyone fell silent and listened. And I listened but kept looking around all the time: maybe Zhenya was coming.

It was some kind of unfamiliar waltz, but you felt that it was old. Even the crying children suddenly stopped crying. And the sailor was rocking on his chair, and his long forelock hung down and touched the piano keys.

"Well, now we're soldiers," Seryozhka whispered to me.

The sailor was playing an old waltz. Everyone listened. Women, children, old men, soldiers, officers. . . . And I was happy that I was sitting on the floor, that next to me I had my rucksack, that I was a soldier, that perhaps tomorrow I'd be given a weapon.

And I was happy that I was with them, that the drunken little sailor was playing the piano. And I wanted very much for Zhenya to come and see us in this world to which we have attached ourselves and which is so unlike our homes, our former life.

And the little sailor kept playing the old waltz. It was stifling in the waiting room. But no one made any noise. Everybody listened to the music. They had all heard music before. And probably better than this. But this music was special. And that's why everybody was silent.

The waltz went on and on. An officer with a red armband and two soldiers from the commandant's patrol were also listening. The officer—sullenly; the soldiers—wide-eyed.

"Well, now we're soldiers," Seryozhka said.

The sailor continued to play. His long forelock kept flopping on the piano keys. Then he suddenly dropped his arms. They slipped down and were just hanging there, his head hit the keys, and the piano gave forth a strange, sad sound.

Everyone was silent. The officer with the red armband walked over to the sailor, saluted, and said something to him. Suddenly, everyone who was close by started to shout at the officer.

"What's all this, boys," said the sailor. "What if the Krauts burned my mother?"

"He sits at home," said Seryozhka. "He ought to be there, then he'd know how to walk around with an armband."

"What's the matter with him?" some women said.

And then I ran over there and shouted at the officer, "You headquarters rat, why don't you leave people alone!"

The officer didn't hear me. One of the patrol soldiers said to me in a tired voice, "Go home, kid!"

The front twilight crawls in through the windows. We don't put on the light.

"When I was in the cavalry," says Shongin, "we'd come back from a march, feed the horses, and then start cooking some thick millet soup."

"And today the sergeant shortchanged us again on the sugar," says Kolya.

"I'm beginning to dream about my wife," says Sashka Zolotaryov. "We won't see any passes, lads."

"When I was in the eighth grade," I say, "we had a very funny math teacher. As soon as he'd turn around, we'd start talking. And he'd give a 'D' for it, but never to the one who did the talking."

The Road

We're setting off for the army base to get some mortars. We—that's Second Lieutenant Karpov, the sergeant, Sashka Zolotaryov, and me.

Karpov gets in front with the driver, while the three of us take our places in the back of our one-and-a-half-ton truck.

And we're off. I'm tired of this stupid sitting around in the

village. It's better to be riding. Everyone's tired of it. Sashka and
I smile and wink at each other.

The sergeant has settled down up front on a soft seat made of
empty American sacks. He leans against the cabin with his hands
on his stomach, his short legs stretched out, and closes his eyes.
"We're off, boys, don't fall off while I'm asleep."

We're moving.

Perhaps I'll meet Nina someplace. Because of the frost, the
truck moves well. It speeds from hill to hill. And up ahead—
more hills. And beyond those—still more. We've got to go
only forty kilometers. Nothing to it. Now I'll see how they live in
the rear.

The road's not empty. Trucks, trucks. . . . Tanks go by, infantry.
They're all on their way to the front.

"The Siberians really took care of the Germans near Moscow," says Sashka. "If it weren't for them, who knows what
might have happened."

"The Siberians are all the same height," I say. "Six feet.
They're specially selected."

"Fools," says the sergeant without opening his eyes. "What's
that got to do with it? It was equipment that did it at Moscow,
equipment."

What's the use of arguing? Let him talk. I know what happened at Moscow. I was told by witnesses. When the Siberians
started moving up, the Germans ran west without stopping. I
know. Because the Siberians stood ready for death. They're all
hunters, bear trappers. They face death from early childhood.
They're used to it. And us? Sashka and me, for instance. Could
we do it? Supposing tanks come at us— we'd just shut our eyes.
And not because we're cowards. We're simply not used to it.
Could I face a tank? No, I couldn't. With mortars, it's simpler.
The front lines are far from here. You can fire away, change
your position. But face to face— it's a good thing we're not
the infantry.

Suddenly the truck stops. Up ahead the road seems empty.
Only far off in the distance a lone soldier stands looking in our
direction. The sergeant is sleeping. Sashka and I jump off the
truck. Second Lieutenant Karpov is asleep in the front. His lower
lip droops like an old man's. The driver has raised the hood.

The soldier is running toward us. A little soldier. You
couldn't imagine a smaller one. He's running toward us and
waving his arms.

"Look, look," says Sashka, "a Siberian."

I laugh. The soldier is really very small. He runs up to us, and
I see that it's a girl. She's wearing a long coat, neatly girded. She
has a sergeant's insignia on her shoulders. Her face is small, and

she has a nose like a button.

"How about a lift, boys. I've been standing here for an hour. All the trucks are heading for the front lines, not a single one the other way. And I'm desperate to get there," she says and gestures by drawing her hand across her throat.

I help her to get into the truck. Sashka and I give her our canvas coats, and she sits on them.

"Where are you boys from?"

We nod toward the front lines.

"Has the fifteenth left yet?"

Sashka and I look at each other and shrug our shoulders.

Our truck finally moves. The sergeant sleeps. He even snores, just a bit.

"That's great," says our traveling companion, and laughs. "He snores as though he were home on the stove."

"He loves to sleep," says Sashka.

When she laughs, her lips turn up at the corners. Like a clown. A sergeant! And I'm only a private! Where is she going, such a tiny one, such a slim young girl? What happened? Everyone has been taken by it, carried away, all mixed up. . . . Schoolboys crawl about in the trenches, they die of wounds, they return home, armless, legless. . . . A girl . . . a sergeant . . . what's happened?

"Day before yesterday, the base was raided by forty Junkers," she says. "It was something. We were swept off our feet."

"And what would you have done at the front?" Sashka asks. "It's even worse there."

"I probably would have cried," she says, and laughs.

What could you expect? Of course, she would have cried. After all, even I almost cried. Before the war, I saw a movie. All the soldiers were like soldiers in this movie: adult, experienced, they knew what was what. But I don't know, Sashka doesn't know, this girl doesn't know. The sergeant's asleep, and Karpov—. But they knew what's what. Yet I don't know, Sashka doesn't know, and our commander, although he's sullen. . . .

"My name's Masha," she says. "I'm a sergeant in the medical corps. In school I beat all the boys."

"And you like to brag a little, eh, sarge?" says Sashka.

The sergeant wakes up. He looks at Masha for a long time.

"And where did you come from?" he asks, using the familiar form.

"May I ask you not to be so informal?" Masha says calmly.

The sergeant's cap slides onto the back of his head.

"Who do you think you're talking to?"

"It's amazing how uneducated a man can be," she says to us.

I want to laugh. The sergeant looks at Masha for a long time, and then he notices her shoulder bars.

"I'm asking you, Comrade Sergeant, where are you from?"

The truck stops again. The driver again raises the hood. Karpov comes out.

"How are things up there?" he asks us.

"While you were asleep, your soldiers froze here," Sashka says.

"Oho," says Karpov. "What a nice passenger. And you, did you freeze?"

And he invites her up front.

She jumps out lightly from the back of the truck. She waves good-bye to us.

How warm it must be up front. Hot air from the radiator, soft seats, the whole road spread out before you.

Karpov climbs in after her.

"No, no," she says, "perhaps I'd better go back, Comrade Second Lieutenant."

"Sit down," Karpov says coldly. He gets into the back of the truck.

"Why have you spread out your legs like that, Zolotaryov?" he says. "Can't you sit like a human being?"

We're riding. It's getting dark already. If we don't get to the base in half an hour, I'll freeze to death. Sashka is all bundled up; only his nose is visible. A big red nose.

"A man needs a bed, not the back of a truck," he grumbles, "and a warm stove, and good food, and love. . . ."

"And who is going to work, kid?" the sergeant asks.

When I return home, I'll study hard. I'll go to sleep at ten. In the winter I'll put on a fur coat, so that nothing can get to me.

We stop a truck. We ask. It turns out that it's still some eighty kilometers to the base.

"What do you mean?" Karpov asks, surprised. "They said forty."

"You should have taken another road," comes the answer from the truck.

"He missed the road, the devil," Sashka hisses.

"We'll freeze," says the sergeant.

Masha comes out of the cabin.

"The first turn off, State Farm No. 7," she says.

"Really?" says Karpov, overjoyed.

"For your information, I always tell the truth."

Not many houses have remained intact at this state farm. Not many. But when you consider it in terms of fingers and lips numb with cold, and legs as though they were made of wood—what's the difference how many houses? There are houses, and they let you in, and it's warm inside, and you can drink some tea.

Karpov picks out a house that's bigger and more nearly intact than the others and invites Masha there.

"You'll be more comfortable there."

And he turns to us.

"And you go there, friends, where the windows are lit up."

"I'll stay with the truck for a while," says the driver. "You can relieve me later."

I can only hold out for another minute. Sashka and I run to the house. A girl opens the door for us. She's wearing felt boots and a kerchief.

"Who's there?" someone asks from the inside.

"They're ours, Mama," says the girl.

The girl's name is Vika. Her mother is also wearing a kerchief and a shawl. She looks like my mother. Very much so. She invites us in. We take off our coats.

"You wouldn't happen to have some tea?" I ask with my frozen lips.

We put our dried biscuits on the table.

"That's all we have, lady," says Sashka. "We'd be glad to. . . ."

"That's okay," she says, "I'll get you some food right away."

"And Karpov has gone off after Masha," says Sashka, "and he's having the sergeant run errands for him."

We're sitting at the table. Vika is also there, and she looks at us with her big eyes. And her mother puts the frying pan on the table. Meat pies are steaming on the frying pan. Gosh, how like my mother she really is. . . .

"The hospital stops here," she says. "They gave me a bottle of vodka. Drink up, boys, warm yourselves."

She has big black-and-blue marks under her eyes. We don't refuse the vodka. I drink my glass and feel that I can't catch my breath. I sit with my mouth open. She laughs.

"You should have exhaled, before swallowing. I completely forgot to warn you. Wash it down with the meat pie."

I eat it. But she really does look very much like my mother. My head is swimming. It's really swimming.

"I made it from your dried biscuits," she says.

"Another one?" asks Sashka.

"Yes, let's belt one more down," I say.

She pours the vodka for us.

"You ought to take one, lady," says Sashka.

She laughs and shakes her head. And my head is swimming, swimming.

"Mama mustn't," says Vika.

"Just a little bit?" Sashka asks.

"Mama mustn't," I say, "why are you so persistent?"

She pats my head and gives me another pie. My head is

swimming. I'm hot. Sashka has moved far off in the distance.
So has Vika . . . and Mama . . . that's so I won't be so hot.

"Are you local?" asks Sashka.

"We're from Leningrad," says Vika.

"How nice," I say, "and I'm from Moscow. What a coincidence. . . . What a meeting . . . at the world's end . . . I'm very
happy, very happy."

"If you go to Leningrad via Moscow, please give me a call at
my home."

Sashka is eating a pie. While he's eating, I'll sleep for a while.
I'll put my head on the table and sleep.

"Wait," says Sashka, "I'll go with you."

He puts on the coat, which he had spread out.

"For some reason, I'm tired," I say.

"Sleep, my boy, sleep," says Mama. She's standing over me.

"Mama," I say, "I'm alive and well. I'll return soon, with the
victory. . . ."

In the morning it's quiet in the room. The driver is sleeping in
Sashka's place. No one home. I put on my coat. I run to the
truck. Sashka is walking around it with an automatic around his
shoulders.

"And me?" I ask. "Why didn't you wake me?"

"You slept so—I couldn't get you up," says Sashka. "You
really drank up last night. You were worn out."

"And you're walking like this? Alone?"

"I've slept enough," says Sashka. "Here, you take it for a
while. I'll go warm up, and then I'll come back."

Me—I'm a scoundrel and a villain. If I were in his place, I
would have tried until I woke him up. I wouldn't do more than I
had to probably. I'm a swine. I ought to be taught a lesson. I'm a
traitor. If anyone came for the truck though, I'd cut his throat in
short order.

The sergeant comes out of the house.

"Well, kid, everything okay?"

I don't answer. He doesn't need it. He gets into the back of
the truck and yawns.

"Go call the boys. We have to go."

"Wait a minute," Vika's mama says to us, "I'll make some
potato pies."

"Thanks, we have to go," I say.

"You and your daughter eat it, eat it to our health,"
Sashka says.

We go over to the truck. Masha is sitting in the truck. She
smiles at us.

"I've got it right now. It's another thirty kilometers to the
base," says the driver.

"That's amazing," says Masha.

"Everybody in?" Karpov pokes his head out of the front seat.

And suddenly I see Vika running from the house. She holds out a bundle. I manage to take it on the move.

"That's the pie," she shouts. "Good-bye!"

"How did you sleep, Masha?" Sashka asks.

"The lady of the house and I slept fine," she laughs, "but I don't think the lieutenant slept."

"He slept," says the sergeant.

"Well, that means you didn't," laughs Masha. "Someone kept waking us up, three times during the night, knocking on the door: 'Masha, I have to speak to you.'"

"I didn't knock," says the sergeant.

Nina

Karpov comes out of the division headquarters. We look at him.

"The replacements have already left," he says. "We missed each other. They didn't wait."

"All the better," says the sergeant. "Fewer worries."

"We'll be getting an American armored car," says Karpov. "That's not a bad deal either. Sergeant, take the boots for the depot, bring up the one-and-a-half-tonner and get going! We'll go in the armored car."

Boots! So there they are. Real boots. Now things will really begin. Boots. The way I am now, I walk around like a cart driver, with rags around my feet. I'm even ashamed. A submachine gun and rags. Now we'll do some fighting!

Karpov goes off to other sections.

"You can wrap all sorts of rags around your feet when you have boots," says Sashka. "No frost can get to you."

"And they won't let any water in," I say.

"It's okay," says Sashka. "Smear them with some lubricating oil and you're all set."

"And you can stick your spoon in the top," I say.

"To put 'em on is just sheer pleasure," Sashka says. "One pull, and you're all set."

"You have to pull 'em by the boot tab," I say.

"Of course, by the boot tab," says Sashka. He goes off to look for some friends. Fellow-townsmen. I'll take a walk too. My submachine gun is getting rusty. I haven't used it once.

"God, where did you come from?" I hear someone say behind me.

It's Nina! She's wearing an athletic shirt. She has an empty mess tin in her hand. It's really Nina.

"Did you come for a visit?"

"I looked for you," I say. "I've been looking since that first time."

She laughs. She's happy. I see it.

"Oh, you darling. . . . There's a real friend. So you didn't forget?"

She's cold standing there. There's a frost, and it's windy.

"Let's go eat. We'll talk, okay?"

She pulls me by the hand. I'm following her, following her.

We sit in the headquarters mess hall. In a barrack. No one around.

"Everyone has eaten already," she says. "I was late. Let's ask Fedya for something."

"Fedya," she says into the window to the cook, "give me some soup, Fedya. I have a friend up from the front lines."

And Fedya pours a full tureen of soup for me. And Nina breaks off a piece of her bread for me.

"Well, we've managed to scrounge up a meal for you," says the black-moustached Fedya from his window.

"It's warm here," I say.

"Well, how are things going there?" she asks. "How's Kolya?"

"Nina," I say, "you know I really did look for you. I thought and thought about you. . . . Why were you silent?"

"Well, we'll eat now, and then have a smoke, right?"

"Why were you silent?"

"If I hadn't gone out to eat, I probably wouldn't have run into you."

"Now I see what color eyes you have. They're green. I tried, but just couldn't remember what color they were. What color were they? Now I finally know."

"Eat! It's going to get cold. Do you have it tough there?"

"You know, I once even imagined how we'd meet after the war. You were wearing a rose-colored jacket, and no hat."

"None at all?"

"We walk along the Arbat."

"Eat. Your soup's probably cold, isn't it?"

"I have to go back soon. If you want, I'll write you a letter."

"And I told the girls here: 'I've got a friend there,' I said. Dark-eyed. He's the only one, all through the war. But they didn't believe me. They laughed. But you remembered me, didn't you?"

"Why the only one? Don't you have any others?"

"With the others it's something else. . . ."

The black-moustached Fedya looks at me attentively. Why is he staring? Maybe he's sorry he gave me the soup. Maybe he's one of those "other ones"?

"Listen, I mean it seriously. I really did think of you. I never thought about anyone like I did about you."

"Well now, you too. . . ." Her lips twisted. "How nice it was then. . . ."

And on the edge of the tureen, a solitary noodle hangs there, just like a tiny worm. A white, sad, little noodle. And Nina has rested her head in her hands and looks past me. And I see the barrack windows in her green eyes. And beyond that, a green twilight approaches.

"You don't even hear any shooting here," says Nina. "We've only been bombed once."

"Listen, Nina," I say. "If you want, I'll write to you, all right? Nothing much. Just how things are. Otherwise I'll lose you. Where am I going to look for you then?"

What a fool she is. Doesn't she understand? What am I, some seducer or something? It's war. It's not Zhenya. Then everything just seemed to be, seemed to be. But this is more real. Doesn't she see? I understand everything now. What a little fool.

"What do you think, that I'm like the others? If you want, I'll prove it to you. If you want, I'll write home about you right now. You can send it off yourself."

Black-moustached Fedya keeps looking at me. Doesn't he have anything else to do?

"Well, we'll have another date, right?"

"And when the war is over, we'll go together."

"Right smack in the middle of the war, we have a date. The only thing that's missing is ice cream. Fedya," she says, "you don't happen to have any ice cream, do you?"

"For you, Ninochka, I have everything," says Fedya, "only, the ice cream is hot, it's almost boiling."

"Before the war, when I used to go for a walk with some boy, he'd always buy ice cream for me. There was one boy who didn't. I got rid of him fast. We had a park in town. . . ."

"Nina, I have to go soon."

"I'm sorry for you," she says. "You shouldn't be fighting. What are you going to get for it? Just don't get angry, don't. I don't mean that you can't fight. Just simply, why do you have to?"

"And you?"

"Well, I'm already used to it. Now, Fedya there, he worked in a restaurant. The Poplavok. Is that right, Fedya? He made salads, cooked chops. . . ."

"I have to go," I say. "Tell me, are you going to write me? It'll make it easier for me."

"I'll write," she says. "I'll write."

We head for the exit. The spoon clatters in the mess tin.

"Listen, Nina, that major, what was he?"

"Major?"

"Yes, that major. . . ."

"Oh, so you noticed him."

We stop again, near the door. She stands next to me. Very close. How really small she is. Frail and thin. How defenseless she is. I'll take her by the shoulders, her little round shoulders. . . . I'll stroke her head with my hand. It's okay if she doesn't explain. I didn't want to ask, I didn't. . . .

"Are you feeling sorry for me, is that it?"

"No, but don't feel sorry for me either, Nina."

"What are you going to do now?"

"I'll wait for your letters."

"Supposing you don't get any? Anything can happen."

"I'll get them. You promised."

"What do you need it for, you dope?"

Boy, I am a dope, a real dope. I said something I shouldn't have. I didn't say what I wanted to.

"You have a bread crumb on your cheek," I say.

She laughs. Wipes off the bread crumb.

"It's time to go. They'll miss you."

"Let 'em miss me," I say. "Let 'em. It's all the same. One problem after another."

"How daring you are," she says with a laugh. And she strokes my head.

We go out into the lobby. I touch her back.

She pushes my hand aside. Very gently.

"Don't," she says. "It's better this way."

And she kisses me on the forehead. And she runs out into the storm, which is just starting.

The armored car is standing near division headquarters. Sashka is walking around it. He looks around.

"We'll be off, right away," he says.

Fun

An armored car is a very convenient vehicle. It's just like a gray beetle. It can go through everything and get out of everything. It's comfortable and warm. The electric heater works. You can even sleep on the go.

I'm not sleeping. I'm just dozing. What's going to happen in the evening, when we catch up to our division? Maybe there'll be a big battle. Maybe we won't find anyone alive. . . . We'll arrive, and I'll wait for Nina's letters. . . . And Sashka is sleeping. Really sleeping. And Karpov is sitting next to the driver; he's either sleeping or staring motionless at the broken road.

And the sergeant has brought the boots. But what if I don't get any?

"Comrade Lieutenant," I say, "If the road was good, we'd probably really move."

But Karpov doesn't answer. Karpov is apparently asleep.

"Fedosev," I say, "now we really have a good vehicle."

"But I'm not Fedosev," he says, "I'm Fedoseyev. Fedoseyev is my name. Everyone mixes me up with someone else. They call me Fedoskin, and all sorts of things. In the war you really can't stop to figure it out: Fedoseyev or Fedosev? No time for it. I was once even called Fedishkin. It's really funny. But I'm really Fedoseyev. I've been Fedoseyev for forty years. From the day I was born, as they say."

We're carrying a barrel of wine. That's for the whole battery. The front-line ration.

"There's a smell of wine here," says Fedoseyev.

He has protruding pink lips, white eyebrows, and his teeth are large and have gaps in them. He speaks in a singsong tone of voice. He probably never loses his temper. He makes you feel comfortable and secure.

"There's a smell of wine here," he says.

It's a big barrel. The opening is closed with a wooden stopper. Very tightly. It can't be knocked out. And even if you could, it's all the same, how would you get the wine out? At the battery they're taking on replacements now. Rookies. Young kids, probably. They're standing around, looking. It's funny. School-boys. Kolya Grinchenko is probably standing around in front of them. The show-off. And Shongin is probably smoking and saying to Kolya, "You just love to talk, don't you, Grinchenko!" The sergeant has brought the boots. Supposing I don't get a pair?

"Fedoseyev, supposing you were to give it the gas, what would happen?" I ask.

"The speed would increase," says Fedoseyev. "An increase in speed. That's if you give it more gas. But you can't here, the road's bad. If I give it the gas, it'll shake."

"Let it then."

"But why?"

"It'd be interesting, when it shakes."

"A pity to ruin the car. And people are sleeping. Let 'em sleep. You and I aren't sleeping. But they are. Let 'em."

What if I don't get any boots? Why shouldn't he feel sorry for me? You ought to drive faster, Fedoseyev. Maybe I'll make it on time yet.

"It smells of wine here," says Fedoseyev.

It really does smell of wine. A sweet aroma comes out of the barrel. And I'm hungry. But we can't drink the wine; it's in the barrel. And the stopper is as big as a fist.

"We could pull out the stopper," Sashka whispers in my ear.
Supposing Karpov hears of it. He'll really let us have it.

"Of course you could," says Karpov, without turning
his head.

"Just say the word, nothing to it," says Fedoseyev.

We turn off the road and stop near a solitary pole. We pull out
the stopper. It's easy. It comes out of its nest, just like out of
butter. And a cloud of wine vapor breaks through the frosty air.
Stronger and stronger.

"Each one take his ration," says Karpov. "No more."

"It'd be nice to have a bite with it," says Sashka.

"We'll grab a bite at the battery," says Karpov.

Fedoseyev does it very simply. He takes a rubber tube used
for siphoning gas, and he puts one end in the barrel.

"Hold out your tins," says Sashka, "so you don't spill any."

The golden wine runs into the tin. Sashka takes aim. We
look at him.

"It stinks of gas," he says.

"That's nothing," says Karpov, "nothing."

He takes a few gulps.

"Pure gas," he says, and spits it out.

"Can't help it," says Fedoseyev. "It's the tube. Here, let
me try it."

We drink up our samples. It's strong wine. You can feel it
right away.

"Don't breathe when you drink," says Sashka.

"Gas fumes are very useful," says Fedoseyev. "They prevent
all sicknesses. You just have to get used to it. It doesn't bother
me. Nothing to it. Here, let's have that tin."

"Well now, pour out the rations in full," says Karpov.

"What is the ration?" I ask.

No one can tell what the ration is.

"As long as we keep drinking," I say.

"Now that sounds like double-talk," says Karpov.

I know what's going to happen. I'll drink, and the fiery liquid
will go through my body. I'll feel hot, weak, and strange.

"Don't drink too much, Fedoseyev," says Karpov. "You have
to drive."

"It's like water," says Karpov. "I could drink two liters full of
this stuff and not bat an eyelash. It's like water."

"Yes," says Sashka. "This isn't vodka, buddy, it's water."

I can't drink anymore. There's still plenty left in my tin, but I
can't anymore. For some reason my lips have become tight. I
can't open my mouth very easily. And Sashka's chin is all
covered with wine. He just manages to catch a breath, and he's
at the tin again. And Karpov holds onto the armored car.

"Damn it, I'm weak from hunger," he says.

"It's time to go," says Fedoseyev and gets into the cab.

"A fine place to stop," says Karpov. "Right smack in the middle of a bumpy field. There's no place to put your foot. There's a more level place over there."

"You've really belted it down," says Sashka to Karpov.

"That's nothing—I can do it with pure vodka," says Karpov.

"What's your first name," asks Sashka.

"Aleksey," says Karpov.

His cheeks are bright red, Sashka's too. They're like brothers. We crawl into the car.

"You want some more, Alyosha?" Sashka asks.

Karpov shakes his head. Sashka sucks the tube. Wine pours into the tin.

"Here, drink." Sashka pushes the tin at Karpov. "Drink, Alyosha. It's like water."

Sashka has short arms. They're like two stumps, and instead of a head he has a barrel. Now there's a head for you.

"But where are you going to put the stopper," I laugh, "not in your mouth?"

Sashka merely shakes his head and doesn't say anything.

"Where's the tube?" Fedoseyev asks.

"In the barrel," says Sashka.

"It's swimming," I say laughingly.

"Swimming?" asks Karpov. "I didn't see it."

"Oh, you Alyosha," I laugh.

He's okay, this Alyosha. I shouldn't have been mad at him. He has such a hurt look on his face. I tickle his neck.

"Hey, Alyosha," I say. "Don't be sad."

Sashka has put his head on the barrel and is sleeping. Let him sleep. He's okay, too. Everybody's okay. And when they give me a pair of boots, I'll really show 'em how to fight.

"Sashka," I say, "close up the barrel. It's sickening."

But Sashka is crying. Large, childish tears flow down his cheeks.

"Where am I going?" he sobs. "What the hell do I have to go with you for! Klava is waiting for me. Where are you, Klava?"

What a sickening smell. A combination of gasoline and wine. Suppose you mix perfume and peaches? It's still bad. And suppose you mix roses and shoe polish. If he just whined quietly and softly, soft like a mosquito, it'd be easier.

"What's the matter, kid," asks Fedoseyev, "you sick?"

But I don't feel sick. It's just that the smell is sickening. And I can't stretch my legs. It's crowded.

"Come and see me. I'll show you my dog," says Karpov.

"Where?"

"Eight Volga Street."

"Funny," says Fedoseyev.

And Sashka is weeping huge tears. He remembers his Klava. And he wipes away his tears. But I don't want to cry. Why cry? And again Sashka has a barrel instead of a head. It whirls and whirls, this barrel. There's no help.

"Because of the Krauts, you'll forget me, Klavochka. . . . Buy a pack of Nord for me as a memento. . . . We'll say farewell on the threshold. Klavochka, buy yourself a bright kerchief," is heard from the barrel, "I'll even give you money. . . ."

But I'm not crying. It'll be better if I just whimper. It's easier to breathe that way. Because this damned smell. . . . Forgive me Nina, so slim, so small, and so strange . . . so unknown . . . forgive me.

"Where are we going?" asks Karpov.

"To the battery," says Fedoseyev. "They're on their way, flying, flying."

"Are you drunk, Fedoseyev? Who's flying? Rockets? Are you driving us to the front lines?"

"That's right. There she is, over there."

"What do I want it for, Fedoseyev?"

"There's nothing to do there for me."

"Better turn off, and let's have a cup of tea at my place."

"I could take a cup myself, but this damned smell. . . ."

I open my eyes. Our armored car has stopped. Firing can be heard distinctly up ahead. My head's all fuzzy. Sashka is asleep. Karpov is asleep. Head thrown back and mouth open. We've been drinking. Repulsive.

"Why have we stopped?"

"We've arrived, but the battery is gone. No one is here," says Fedoseyev. "The front has moved. We have to catch up. . . . You were okay. How did you like it?"

The car moves on. The headlights are out. Very thick snow is falling. It lights up everything around us. It's transparently light. I'm dreaming. Or am I drunk? The offensive is under way, and we got drunk. I'm delirious from the drinking; up ahead there is a white figure. It stands in our way. It has raised its arms. It holds a submachine gun in one hand, and a lantern in the other. The small yellow flame doesn't illuminate anything.

"Fedoseyev, stop!!" I say.

The car stops. Karpov has awakened. He looks at the figure. He reaches for his holster.

"They're ours," says Fedoseyev. "Let's find out what's up."

Supposing they're Germans? Where's my submachine gun? It's gone. It's probably under the barrel, someplace. Under the wine barrel. The figure comes closer and closer. Fedoseyev flings open the doors.

"Boys," the figure shouts, "help us, quick. Some of our friends have been killed. We have to bury them."

The figure comes up to the car. It's a soldier. He is completely covered with snow. One side of his coat is torn off.

"How did they get it?" Karpov asks, and he yawns.

He yawns as though he just got out of bed. He yawns, and our boys are lying there, dead. Karpov is drunk.

"Bullets," I say.

"Mind your own business," says Karpov. "Where are the dead?"

The soldier waves his lantern.

"Over there, over there," he says. "All seven of them. Two of us made it. Help us, boys."

"There's fighting going on," says Karpov. "We can't be late for the battery."

"We're already late," says Fedoseyev.

"We shouldn't have drunk so much," I say, and am surprised at my daring.

But Karpov looks at me and doesn't say anything. He doesn't say anything, because there is nothing to say.

"We got drunk like a bunch of swine, while the fighting was going on," I say loudly. "Let's go, Fedoseyev."

We climb out of the car. Karpov too. Silently. Then the sleepy Sashka. We take the spades and a pick and follow the soldier.

"You've never seen anything like it," he says, and continues walking. "Nothing like it from the very beginning. We pounded each other for six hours. Then we went forward."

We are walking across the bumpy, snow-covered ground. No, it's not a dream. Up ahead the terrible fighting is going on. I can hear it well. Well, Ninochka, your warrior has distinguished himself. Beneath a low hillock, a solitary soldier is hacking away at the frozen ground. And the one who came with us says, "Here, Egorov, I've brought some help. Now we can do it quickly. You go on hacking. We'll all help you in a minute."

A little to the side lie the seven bodies of the dead men. They're all sprinkled with powdery snow. Their coats and faces are white. Seven white men lie there in silence. What dream is this? They're dead men. Ours. And we drank wine.

"Not a bad commander," I say to Sashka. "He got drunk and let us get drunk, too."

"Shut up!" says Sashka.

"Grab the spades," says Karpov.

"Everybody should," I smile ironically.

Sashka and Fedoseyev look at me.

"I'll take one, too," says Karpov calmly. "I also have a spade."

And the seven lie there motionless, as though they had nothing to do with it. We dig in silence. An hour or two. The ground doesn't give very easily. But we manage. We'll be burying the dead in a minute. How will I be able to look at them?

"Put out that lantern," says Karpov.

Egorov puts it out. But nothing changes. It hardly gave off any light anyway. And why did Karpov suddenly think of putting out the light?

It's a deep grave. And the first soldier gets into it.

"Well, come on, Egorov," he says. And I know what he means. And Egorov gives us the sign, and we follow him. Am I really going to pick up dead bodies with my own hands and bring them to the grave? Sashka and Egorov take the first one. They carry him. Fedoseyev bends down for the second one. Karpov looks at me. And why shouldn't I take one? I'll take it by the feet. At least it's not the head. I must. Yes, me. Not Karpov, but me. I pick up the dead man by the feet. We carry him.

"Careful, boys," says the first soldier from the grave. "Don't drop them."

"Certainly not Lenya," says Egorov, going by.

"That's our Lenya," says the first soldier. "Let's have him."

He takes Lenya's body from us and carefully lays it down.

Then we drag over another one, and another.

"Saltykov on top. He was young," says the first soldier. "It'll be easier for him to lie like that."

"Can't you keep quiet?" asks Karpov.

"They don't mind it, Lieutenant," says the soldier," and, naturally, I can keep quiet."

We put them all in. Carefully. They lie there in their coats. All of them have new boots. We work with the spades in silence. We do everything that's necessary. Now even the boots are hidden under a layer of earth. And a helmet is lying on the hillock. Whose—I don't know.

We're off in the same direction again. Toward the firing. We're silent.

Open Score

Who has counted how many times we've changed our position? Who? And how many shells I passed to our loader Zolotaryov? And how my hands ache . . . We don't just change our position. If it were only that. We're going forward. Mozdok is somewhere behind us. Come on! Come on! Now I'll probably get a spoon. I'll have a nice new spoon. And as soon as the fighting is over, the sergeant is going to give me a pair of boots. . . . That is, when it is over. But when is it going to be over? . . . Kolya Grinchenko keeps bending down. He looks through the sights. Then he stands up. He is tall.

"Platoo-oon!" shouts Karpov. He waves his twig. He stands there so pale. "Fire!"

Sashka Zolotaryov has thrown off his coat. The padded jacket has come apart. His lips are white. He just keeps throwing those shells into the mortar barrel. And he groans each time. And the mortar groans, too.

Through the shouting and the explosions, you can hear the German "Vanyusha" mortar begin to snort. And its terrifying shells land somewhere behind our battery.

"I hope they don't close in," says Shongin. He's actually screaming, but he's barely audible. "If they zero in on us, we're goners."

"Retreat!" shouts Karpov.

"Thank God," Sashka laughs pleasantly. "My hands are falling off. Nothing to replace them with."

The trucks come out of their covers. We hitch the mortars. And again we hear the snorting of the Vanyusha and the whistle of the shells overhead and their screech, somewhere behind us. Missed. Missed again. How sickening your own helplessness can be. Am I a rabbit? Do I have to wait until I'm hit? Why doesn't anything depend on me? I stand on a flat piece of land, and suddenly . . . you've had it—it's better in the infantry, really . . . at least there you can go into attack screaming . . . and then it's each man for himself . . . and there's no fear, the enemy is right there. But here, you're fired at, and you cross yourself: maybe, maybe. . . . There it is again. Vanyusha keeps snorting more and more persistently, stubbornly. The shells keep landing more and more frequently, more accurately. Our trucks screech heartrendingly as they get out of the line of fire . . . Hurry up, damn it!

And there's that snorting again. It seems so peaceful. Again and again. And the whistling. . . .

"Get down!"

Behind us, Shongin keeps turning round and round.

"What are you doing, picking mushrooms?" screams Karpov.

"My leggings. . . ."

And he keeps turning and turning. He catches his leggings like a kitten playing with a ball of string.

Something hits me in the side. The end? . . . I hear running. It's to me. No, they go by. I'm alive. My dearest mother . . . alive . . . alive again . . . I live . . . I'm still alive . . . my mouth's full of earth, but I'm alive. . . . It wasn't me they killed. . . .

They all run past me. I get up. I'm okay. My dearest mother . . . I'm okay. Shongin lies not far from me. And Sashka stands

over him. He holds his chin in his hand, and his hand shakes. It's
not Shongin lying there, just remnants of his coat. . . . Where is
Shongin? Can't figure out anything. . . . There's his tin, submachine gun, spoon! Better not look, better not.

"Direct hit," says someone.

Kolya takes me by the shoulder and leads me away.
I follow him.

"Spit out the earth," he says, "you'll choke."

We walk toward the trucks. They're already moving. Several
people remain beside Shongin.

"Come on, come on," says Kolya as he sits me down.

"Everyone okay?" asks Karpov.

"The rest are," says Kolya.

Toward evening we arrive at some kind of village. We stop.
Is it really over? Are we really going to get some sleep? The
kitchen comes up. My stomach is empty, but I don't want to eat.

The three of us are sitting on a log. I drink my soup straight
from the tin.

"The Krauts are putting up a fight," says Sashka.

"It's all over now," says Kolya.

"Now we're even flying in the daytime," I say.

"Is your head all right?" asks Kolya.

"He's got a head like a rock. It can take anything," says
Sashka. He laughs. Quietly. To himself.

"It's tough about Shongin," I say. We finish eating our soup
in silence.

"It's easier for you without a spoon," says Kolya, "you take
a couple of gulps, and it's done. But this way, by the time you
get in the spoon and bring it up to your mouth, you've
spilled half of it."

"I saw some German spoons here," says Sashka, "new ones.
They're all over the place. I should bring you some."

And he gets up and goes off to look for the spoons. I'll have
a spoon too. Of course, it'll be German. But what's the
difference? How long I've gone without a spoon. Now I'll have
one at last.

The spoons are really good ones. A whole bunch of them.

"They're washed," says Sashka. "The Krauts love cleanliness.
Pick any one of them."

The spoons are in my hand.

"They've been washed," says Sashka.

There are a lot of them. Pick any one you want. After eating,
you diligently lick it and put it deep down in your pocket. But
a German has also licked it. He probably had big, wet lips.
And when he licked his spoon clean, his eyes probably
bulged.

"They're washed," says Sashka.

And then he put it in his boot top. His leggings were probably soaked with sweat. And then he dipped it in porridge again and then licked it clean again. On one of the spoons there is a dried piece of food.

"Well, what's the matter?" says Kolya.

I return the spoons to Zolotaryov. I can't eat with them, I don't know why.

We sit and smoke.

"That Heinkel is having a ball for himself," says Kolya and he looks up.

A German reconnaissance plane is flying above us. Our boys shoot at it lazily. But he's high. And it's already twilight. He also shoots at us from time to time. You can just barely hear the machine-gun fire.

"He's getting mad," says Kolya. "That Fascist was probably walking up and down this street yesterday."

And Sashka flips away one spoon after another. He draws back his arm and throws. And suddenly one spoon hits me in the leg. I can't understand how it happened.

"That hurts," I say. "Why are you throwing those spoons around?"

"I'm not aiming at you," says Sashka. And the leg hurts more and more. I want to get up, but my left leg won't straighten.

"What's the matter?" asks Kolya.

"My leg won't straighten for some reason," I say. "It hurts very much."

He looks at the leg.

"Take down your trousers," he orders.

"What's the matter?" I say. "Why?"

I'm not wounded. It didn't even scratch me. But I'm already scared. Somewhere inside, just below the heart, I have a strange, sick feeling.

"Take 'em down, I say, you bastard."

I take down my padded trousers. My left leg is all bloody. There's a small black hole in my white underpants, and blood is pouring out of it . . . my blood . . . and the pain is getting duller . . . and my head is swimming, and I feel slightly sick.

"It wasn't the spoon, was it?" asks Sashka in alarm. "What happened?"

"The Heinkel," says Kolya, "it's a good thing you didn't get it in the head."

I'm wounded! How could it have happened? In battle, nothing. In the still of the evening. I didn't rush any enemy bunker. It wasn't a bayonet charge. Kolya goes off somewhere, comes back and goes off again. The leg won't straighten.

"It hit a vein," says Sashka.

"Why isn't anyone coming?" I say. "I'll bleed to death."

"It's all right, you have enough blood. Lean against this. Lie down for a while."

Kolya comes back. He brings a medic with him. The medic gives me an injection.

"That's so you won't get tetanus."

He bandages me. They put someone's coat on me. Someone comes and goes away. How uninteresting it all is now. I lie there for a long time. I don't feel the cold. I hear Kolya shout: "The man'll freeze to death. He must be sent to the dressing station, but that bastard of a sergeant won't give us a truck."

To whom is he saying this? Oh, that's the battery commander who's coming over to me. He doesn't say anything. He looks at me. Perhaps I ought to tell him to order them to give me a pair of boots? But on the other hand, why do I need them now? . . . The one-and-a-half-tonner drives up. It's carrying empty gasoline barrels.

"You'll have to put him among the barrels," I hear the voice of the battery commander say.

What's the difference where?

They shove some papers into my pocket. I can't figure out who is doing it . . . anyway, what's the difference?

"These are documents," says Kolya. "Hand them over at the dressing station."

They put me in the back of the truck. The empty barrels stand around me like guards.

"Good-bye," says Kolya, "it's not far."

"Good-bye, Kolya."

"Good-bye," says Sashka Zolotaryov, "see you soon."

"Good-bye," I say, "of course, I will!"

And the truck drives off. That's all. While we're traveling the same road we went north on, I sleep. I sleep. Without dreams. It's soft, and I'm warm. The barrels surround me.

I wake up for a few minutes when they carry me into the barrack of the dressing station. They put me on the floor, and I fall asleep again.

It's a large, nice room. And there are windowpanes in the windows. And it's warm. The stove is going. Someone is pulling at me. It's a nurse in a padded jacket worn over her white uniform.

"Let's have the papers, dear," says the nurse. "We have to check you in for the hospital train. They're taking you to the rear."

I take the papers out of my pocket. The spoon falls out. Spoon?

"Don't lose your spoon," says the nurse.

Spoon? . . . Where did I get a spoon? . . . I'll hold it up to my eyes. An old worn-out aluminum spoon, and on the handle is scratched the name "Shongin" . . . When did I have time to pick it up? Shongin, Shongin . . . something to remember you by. Nothing's left except a spoon. Only a spoon. How many battles he had seen, and this was the last one. There's always a last one. And his wife doesn't know anything. Only I know. . . . I'll hide this spoon even farther down. I'll always carry it with me. . . . Forgive me, Shongin, old soldier.

The nurse gives me back my papers.

"Sleep," she says, "sleep. Why are your lips trembling? No need to be afraid now."

No need to be afraid now. What is now? Now I don't need anything. Now I'm completely alone. Supposing Kolya comes in and says: "We're attacking now. Now we'll have some fun, boys. Now we'll drink some cognac. . . ." Or supposing Sashka Zolotaryov suddenly comes in: "My hands are falling off from all this work, and there's nothing to replace them with. . . ." And Shongin will say: "You talk too much, you're a bunch of animals. . . ." But Shongin won't say anything now. Nothing. What kind of a soldier am I? I didn't even fire my submachine gun once. I didn't even see any live fascists. What kind of a soldier am I? I don't have a single ribbon or medal. . . . And other soldiers are lying near me. I hear groans. They're real soldiers. They've gone through everything.

New wounded are brought into the barrack. They put one next to me. He looks at me. The bandage has slipped off his forehead. He puts it on again. He swears.

"Be with you in a minute," the nurse says.

"I'm plenty sick without you," he says. And he looks at me. He has large, malevolent eyes.

"You with the mortar?" he asks.

"Yes," I say, "mortar. Do you know any of our boys?"

"Yes, I know 'em," he says. "I know everybody."

"When did you get it?"

"This morning. Just now. When did you think?"

"And Kolya Grinchenko?"

"Yes, he got it, too."

"And Sashka?"

"Sashka, too. Everybody. Wiped out. I'm the only one left."

"And the battery commander?"

He screams at me: "Everybody, I say, everybody!"

And I scream: "You're lying!"

"He's lying," someone says. "Don't you see his eyes?"

"Don't listen to him," says the nurse. "He's not himself."

"He talks too much," I say. "We're going forward."

And I want to cry. And not because of what he said. But because you can cry for something else besides grief. . . . Just cry, cry. . . . Your wound's not dangerous, kid. You've got a long way to go yet. You'll still be around for a long time, kid.

1961

Promoxys

Bulat Okudzhava

"I do like fresh milk, but I won't have any after all, because, my lovely Nastasya, I don't want to think I care about such things. So why don't we just forget it? Better to look at the sky all above us: isn't that something? Besides, I didn't come here to taste your fresh milk, but to enjoy your loveliness. That's what has brought on this flood of grand words, although I'm a simple sort of fellow as a rule and try to avoid fancy ways of expressing myself. But where I live, downtown Moscow, that is, people have somehow got out of the habit of letting their words free, they say only what's strictly necessary in any situation. So kindly allow me to let the words out as they come and not give a hoot for the impression they make on these distinguished surroundings. I promise you, I shan't say anything off color, because I think only good thoughts; as for the *mode* of expression, let *me* worry about that. So, my lovely, I. . . ."

Just then, however, she came back with a mug of fresh milk, which she held out to him, at the same time turning her head away, so as not to embarrass him probably, while he drank the milk gratefully and forgot the words he had been preparing for her. Well, why say anything, anyway? What was the use? He didn't even know her name. He had simply been passing by, had seen her in the window, and wanted to tease her a little; but then he found himself abashed before her blue gaze and with rather a pathetic air begged her for a glass of fresh milk. Why had he picked on milk? He hardly knew.

He emptied the mug and took his time handing it back to her. As she took it and made as if to leave, he had an awful fear that he would never see her again, though, of course, he had spent thirty years up to now without her and (or so it seemed) had survived.

This fear made him jump up from the steps where he had so strangely seated himself.

In this world where there are butterflies, dragonflies, and all sorts of creatures living all together, trees growing, clouds floating; in this world where people invoke love with kisses, songs, and flowers, where laughter and fear, birth and death rub shoulders, in this world nothing can exist for no reason at all, but every last thing has its grounds for being—there can be nothing strange or redundant in this world, for unto each thing goes its own.

Probably this was what was at the heart of this world's supreme philosophy, and at the heart of this world itself were these steps where—at this very moment—Pavel Sytov was sitting face to face with his destiny.

He was holding a guitar in his left hand. The Sunday was nearing its end and the time had come for him to go back to town, but he went on sitting there trying to work out how things were going to go for him now; she didn't seem to be making a move to go back into the house, either, but stayed on there plaguing him with the sight of her that evoked the elusive image of his stately Marussya.

The devil only knew how it had all happened. As for himself—he was he! He imagined himself going up to strangers, looking them straight in the eye, and saying: "Greetings, I'm Sytov, the guitarist. In the general course of things I'm a screw cutter. But on Sundays I play the guitar, oh, it's an instrument of very old origin, coming from the ancient Greeks, who called it a cithara and played it by pinching the strings. So, greetings, I'm Sytov. If I can be of any service to anyone . . ."

Suddenly he felt her looking at him fixedly. She just stayed there looking, not moving at all. But he wouldn't let himself lift his head to find out just what she *was* doing. Perhaps she was simply looking at the thinning hair on the top of his head and wanted to give him a remedy for baldness?

But when he managed to control his misgivings and force himself to glance in her direction, she had gone.

It was both sad and ridiculous for him to go on sitting there alone on the step. Just behind that door she was tiptoeing about, listening hard to hear if he were going or not. Oh, to the devil with her. And the milk had tasted horrible as well. He ought to have had beer. Well, anyway, was she Nastasya or someone else? And what if he went inside? Not bothering to knock, just went straight in? Here I am, Sytov's my name, the guitarist. Of course, you know, I really don't think it's worth my while coming here again and again just because everyone does it, but let's get on with it, shall we? I've got some qualities, you know, that aren't to be sneezed at. I'm Sytov. Who are you?

But time went by, and it got darker and darker—in fact, the sun had already set, and it was dusk, soon to be night. In August the nights are so dense and dark you lose all hope of morning.

Right away Sytov knew he didn't want to get up off the steps. Can you allow yourself not to get up when you don't want to but you know you must? It's the very last moment of your life, and you ask yourself: So what have you done with your life, brother? And answer, Well, nothing, really. What scared you? How do I know? I was scared, that's all, ashamed, I expect, or perhaps I just couldn't get the hang of it. You don't say! But it's too late now, brother, isn't it? Yes, I suppose it is . . . Really, there is nothing you *can* say. And that's probably why you sometimes have to allow yourself just a little license—let yourself forget all sorts of fiddling rules, that is, as long as you weren't going to murder, plunder, or otherwise offend anyone.

He certainly wasn't going to do any of that, all he wanted was not to get up off these alien steps, just so as to wait for her, or not even that—just to go on sitting there because that was where he was sitting.

It was really worthwhile sitting there: evening, rustling leaves, shining stars (that means fair weather), silence, the guitar snuggling against your back on the warm side. It was a cithara, sure enough! As for the other matter, it is reasonable to assume she has interests of her own. Someone else? Where is he, then? Having a good time somewhere? Or does he sleep at that house? Lying on his back with his mouth open, feeling no need of her at all? But if that was so, there was no reason to put on an act, only wait. . . . Or could this fellow be madly, hopelessly in love with her? Well, and where was he, then? Why wasn't he at his post, sitting here on the steps beside Sytov? Although, come to think of it, why wasn't he, Sytov, sitting on Marussya's steps?

Meanwhile, the evening went on. August is not July: the nights are cold. All was quiet in the house. Perhaps she thought he was gone and that was why she was showing no interest. Why didn't she look outside, then? She could at least come out for a moment. But suppose she thought he was gone, why didn't he strum on the guitar? It would be a reminder for her and a diversion for him.

He touched the steel strings with fingers chilled by the damp of the evening air. At once a window lit up, and the yellow glare fell on Sytov.

No, it's hardly funny, thought Sytov, crouching here with a guitar and all. Another man wouldn't have sat on out here. He would have gone up to the door and knocked.

Sytov plucked the strings again, in despair and in hope. But she didn't come out. Instead, up came Marussya, as if she were standing there before him, warm and vital, looking at him with reproach.

Of course, you could conjure up what and whom you liked, but there was also your conscience to reckon with, and for some reason his seemed to have gone astray.

"All right, step-by-step reasoning now! Marussya is available. So what more do I want? But who can figure out the what's and wherefore's? Why am I sitting on these steps like a fool, in the pure cold night, nursing a guitar? Why won't the one come out of her house and the other get out of my head? It's as good as having her here beside me, standing by that bush. Like seeing her hands clasped in prayer and her eyes full of reproach and her heart . . . What a lot of rubbish can go through a man's head. A complete romantic fabrication. Complete old-fashioned rubbish, you mean!"

Again he touched the cords. Marussya fluttered unsteadily near the bushes. You may well flutter—it's pretty cold! So, "Summer, good-bye. . . ."

Marussya took a step closer to him, then another, and held out her hand.

"Are you out of your mind?"

"No," said Sytov, "well, not so far as I know."

"Sitting on somebody's step like that. You *are*!"

"Don't tell anyone," he said, "it'll pass. I was beginning to feel sorry for the guitar, anyway."

She took the guitar from him and moved away. He followed her, walking or rather prowling along like an Indian—now, he thought, the stag would not come on him unprepared; no sooner did it leap out of the thicket than it would fall dead on the spot. And he raised his gun and fired at the sky, yes, actually fired it. And gone Marussya, gone the stag, gone the gun. The same flight of steps, the same step, the early morning, the dew thick as the foam on beer. It was bitingly cold. There was a motorcycle by the house. And the owner of the motorcycle was knocking on the window. He was wearing boots and a leather jacket with a streak of lightning on it. Tall, broad-shouldered. Sytov wanted to call out to him: no use rapping on the window so early in the morning, but he refrained—the house didn't happen to be his, did it?—the window wasn't his, either, and what's more, the girl behind the window was a stranger. The other went on sharply, insistently rapping, like a wood-pecker on a tree trunk. Sytov decided to take cover: you never knew, he might win yet.

Then the door opened and she came running down the steps, in such haste that she didn't notice him sitting there. She put her arms around the other one in the leather jacket, placed herself behind him on the pillion, and clung to his shoulders.

And away they went, straight across the grass as if Sytov did not even exist, and he wanted to cry out to them, ask them where, I say, where are they off to? Can they really be so happy?

Then he found himself near the station at the level crossing. And just where the ways crossed, there was a beer stand, and just as this stand stood the motorcycle, but no sign of its owner. Pine trees, passengers on the platform, leave-takings, morning air—they all seemed to be mocking Sytov, who was late for work.

Moving quietly up to the stand, he thought, "To hell with all this. I'm for contravention! Look at them all, watching the clock, afraid to be late for work or an appointment, while to me, the screw cutter, the progressive, walking among them, it all comes easily, exquisitely—if you took my photo now, I'd come out enviable, worthy of respect. So respect me! Sytov, the guitarist, lives and walks among you, Sytov, brimming with love and other fine sentiments, loving you all because he's stronger and more beautiful than any of you. And even if this is so for only a moment or a single morning, it is so, and no one can say it isn't.

Just then an attendant came out of the beer stand—a thin little man with a moustache—seized the motorcycle by the handlebars as if they were horns and began laboriously trying to push it inside. The motorcycle opposed itself to this, thrashing about with its horns, refusing to be led inside, but it could not overcome the man.

How is it that anyone can take someone else's object in broad daylight and stow it inside his shop in full view of the passers-by? And where did the other two go, who shot away locked in their own embrace and their own happiness? Sytov hurried onto the platform, looking at the faces. As if especially arranged for him, they were all in pairs, and each couple stood at a distance from the others, their backs turned to the rails, talking quietly.

Here are these people, thought Sytov, happy, minding their own business, waiting for the train to take them somewhere on time, and all the while there's a power in the shape of a clock watching over them, telling them what to do: how is it possible? And how is it possible otherwise? And only he, a screw cutter of an advanced turn of mind, had allowed himself to spend the night on somebody else's steps and then to take his time passing through a forest, wandering around here, leaving his supervisor to imagine that he had got a sore throat or broken his leg. Only he, his August horns thrashing—a bull who would not suffer himself to be put in a stall—he went on meditating on anything and everything, while these other people could only look at one another.

Meanwhile, it was a pleasant thing to contemplate the love all around him running on, like time, without argument or commotion, according to the most high-minded principles. Supposing, he thought, the platform suddenly broke from its moorings and went galloping off, they would hardly be surprised or move, but would stay on it and be carried off who knows where, with every sign of happiness in their faces and gestures. And here he remembered Marussya saying to him: "What is it that makes you go to Klyazma every Sunday and take your guitar? I bet you've got a girl friend over there. Or maybe you're looking for something you lost there once? He goes again and again, the crazy fool. Other people go and visit one another and see movies and walk in the park and think about their future."

And he imagined himself sitting beside her, teasing the curls on her neck, listening to her grumble, and for some unaccountable reason he no longer wanted to shout with the burden of his feelings, break a glass, throw something on the ground, anyway, and catch his happiness in the joyous sound of breaking glass.

After all, he had begun to imagine how he had really wanted to do all this and had actually jumped up and down, shouted, dashed something to the ground, and started to whirl her around and around and run off with her to the throbbing roar of the motorcycle. But it turned out that he was running alone. He had started the wild caper in vain: Marussya always fell back somewhere along the way.

When he saw the women with their long legs, their bright dresses and bracelets, was he envious of the men who walked beside them? Then, so that he might compare, Marussya would fly up before him, ironic, severe, someone to whom all is as self-evident as the nose on your face; it was a useful attitude to mask herself with amid all the confusion of the street.

"I don't see you careening off on a motorcycle with Marussya hugging you from behind, shouting and rejoicing, or leaving the machine near a beer stand, or forgetting about it while you go off somewhere, together with her so you pay no heed to other people."

What else could he have done except get his head broken? Meantime, things were all out of whack at the workshop, or perhaps they weren't—and he was still here. And no one yet had been able to divine that great mystery: to whom goes what?

The electric train charged in impetuously, rather as if it had been creeping along like a thief before them. As he sat down, Sytov suddenly saw those two. Her! They were sitting by the window. He was telling her something. She listened, her lips moving very slightly. She looked as if her hair had been done in a hurry, or not at all, a lock of it fell across her face. But the high forehead above her thin little face was free and it was as if she bore it forward to some distant, unknown place. Her hands lay in her lap like a nun's. She listened. As for the man in the leather jacket, he was not so young, and his arm had disappeared somewhere behind her back.

What could they be saying? It was hard to guess.

Now why had Sytov spent the whole night on that step? So that an overbearing, bold-faced fellow like that one could simply come along and whirl her off on his motorcycle? Ah, Marussya, there's not a place on earth that has any real substance in it. If I'd had some breakfast, yet, but here I sit on an empty stomach. And here I sit looking at her with her hair flopping over her eyes. But, oh Lord, I just can't break away, that's all. There's Old Leather Jacket talking away, and as she's next to him, she has to listen, in fact, she seems to be delighted with what he's telling her.

"Marussya!" cried Sytov inside his soul. "What more could I have wanted?" He let his chin drop forward on his chest. The guitar lay quietly beside him. The train ran on and stopped, ran on farther and stopped again.

It was suddenly as if the strings had stirred abruptly. Sytov snatched up the guitar, but it was silent. But, look in front down there! Leather Jacket was flashing in and out from seat to seat, among the passengers, who shouted at him, "Move on! Move on!" It seemed the impudent fellow was actually crawling on all fours toward the aisle. . . . At that moment Sytov got a glimpse of her blue eyes, her slender little hand stretched forward . . . her elbow . . . shoulder . . . scream. . . .

Somebody in a checked coat would have dashed after the crawling Leather Jacket, but the press of people prevented him. Now a tall fellow in a cap leaped onto the bench as airily as an acrobat, but Leather Jacket let fly with an upper cut . . . and went crawling on; the people drew back against the windows: move on, on. And she—she was standing in front of the man in the checked coat, who was wider than she.

"What's going on?" ripped through the drowsiness in Sytov's brain. "Are those two beating up Leather Jacket because of his bold face? A fight!" He had grasped it now. And tried to make his way nearer. Leather Jacket again lost his footing: over he goes! And the shouting that went on, it was savage, fearful. Sytov drew closer and there before him was a sort of bloody cross on Leather Jacket's forehead. He was coming straight at Sytov with his bloody cross, the boldness gone from his eyes, which blinked and burned like the last burst of gunfire from a hunted man who knows he'll get no quarter. "Lord, I forgot the guitar," thought Sytov unaccountably.

"Sergey! Sergey, darling!" she suddenly cried. "Get up! Get up!"

Wiping his lips, the fellow in the cap seized Leather Jacket and raised his fist with a key in it. "He'll fit it into him!" thought Sytov.

Suddenly again she cried: "Sergey!" her voice trailing, "Look out!"

It was such a cry that Sytov went lurching forward. His fist sent Cap Wearer reeling on top of someone who let out a yell, while the key flew off like a sparrow, no one knew where; then Sytov

grasped Checked Coat and dragged him fiercely close to him:
"Now see here, buster!" And Checked Coat folded like a
man of straw.

Just then Sytov caught the beam of her eye. She was looking
at Leather Jacket, though, not at Sytov, no. "She doesn't
remember," he thought, "she's forgotten."

Look at that, they were already cuddling close to each other
again—she and Leather Jacket, who'd been able to wipe off the
cross and the rest of it. The other two had slipped off toward
the next car.

"Don't let them get away," said Leather Jacket—or Sergey,
if you like.

"Oh, let them go," said Sytov. "They'll be thrown out sooner
or later."

At that moment Cap Wearer turned and shouted at her:
"Just you wait and see, you bitch!"

Sytov hurled himself at the shout, for he had seen the two
blue eyes in her anguished face, while the Cap was bobbing
near the exit in the wake of the Checked Coat.

Well, before the last stop, the two of them had jumped off
the train in despair. Sytov had gone to work with his fists in the
passage between the cars as if he would never stop. He had
gone on for too long, in fact. Now he would be having fits of
nausea for a week. The guitar was unharmed, that was one con-
solation. The old girl was lying on a seat, humming resonantly.
She was a real cithara, that one.

Blue Eyes was already smiling again and went on smiling as
she dabbed at Leather Jacket's forehead with what was probably
her hanky. Then she looked at Sytov and nodded with rather a
vague air. "She doesn't recognize me," he thought, "she
doesn't remember. And that man of hers, such a fine upstand-
ing fellow. The others were tagging on behind her, most likely.
Monday's a heavy day."

Sytov was having quite a pleasant time on the train; Blue Eyes
didn't seem at all sorry for herself, or frightened, or mad. So
could one bet on the other two having cleared off, after they
jumped out? Sytov smiled spitefully and secretly felt the muscle
in his left arm: not at all bad, quite impressive, in fact.

He changed his place—moving closer to them, he felt shy, he
would even have to force himself to do it—. But he simply had
to change his place.

"Thanks," said Leather Jacket, and laughed.

"What did they want to fix you for?" asked Sytov.

"They didn't fix us, we fixed them," said the other with a
chuckle. "We fixed them once and for all, didn't we?"

She nodded affirmatively. Sytov was now sitting facing them.

Her eyes strayed over the guitarist and back to her own Leather
Jacket. "She doesn't recognize me," he thought, "she doesn't
remember."

He wanted to say, "We took care of them all right, eh?" but
he said nothing. He wanted to ask her, "You going to Moscow?"
but did not. Obviously she was going to Moscow. Platitudes—it
all meant nothing to anyone. But then, why had he gone to sit
there? Why hadn't he gone into the next car to think out where
he would take Marussya next Saturday? When you came to
think of it, this girl had long legs, too. Another thing, her hair
wasn't well done. Why couldn't she say something—anything—
so he could shut his eyes in relief, or even if he didn't shut them,
even if he kept them open, look her straight in the face?

Sytov was actually looking at Leather Jacket, whose name was
Sergey, and he didn't see how shamelessly she was stroking her
man's head and shoulder to the surprise of the entire coach.
But the people were surprised because they were ashamed,
nobody knew why. Why be ashamed, anyway? All they needed
to do was grab them and throw them out! But the fact was, they
were ashamed—ashamed of themselves—look how they'd
scattered to the far corners—and ashamed of those two as
well—how could they sit there embracing? "But they don't
pay any attention," thought Sytov, "I'm on my own."

"You fixed them good," said Leather Jacket Sergey, "I thought
I was done for." He laughed.

"Fistwork, that's all it was," said Sytov, amicably. ("Never
mind, he's not so bad.") "They got behind you, took you by
surprise."

"They were annoying this young woman," said a lady.

"Y'ought to have wrung their necks," said Sytov, not looking
at the lady.

"He's not allowed to," piped up Blue Eyes all of a sudden:
she drew into herself, shivering, and went on caressing her
young man. "He's got some very valuable glass things on his
chest." She laughed gently, taking no notice of Sytov.

"But what makes her tick?" he wondered.

Then from under his leather jacket Sergey brought out a
number of test tubes colored sky-blue and pink: inside bubbles
were rushing around and some green species of cricket were
sitting with their legs against their chests and their knees
crossed. They were dead, of course, and it had been in the cause
of their anonymous glory that he had gone crawling down the
aisle with the red cross on his forehead.

He showed his crickets, holding them up to the light, while
she looked at him and nothing else; not at Sytov nor the lady
nor the window, through which a splendid panorama of forest,

half pine, half birch, unfolded.

When you are responsible for the fashioning of a piece of
steel into a spoke or, let's say, a whole wheel, it's an occasion for
hymns of praise and for carrying your head high and proud all
the way through the workshop, through the city, and through
Klyazma. Why, this train and the wheels it was running on,
the whole thing had fallen under the cutter's implement as it
whined and shed its black trail of shavings, but how, as he stood
there grasping his cutting tool like a machine gun, could Sytov
have thought (he knew of them, but would he have thought of
them?) that on that train and swimming in spirits there would be
crickets, or flies, or beetles?

Sergey shook the test tube and the cricket—or whatever it
was—turned a graceful somersault. "Gryllus, that is," said
Sergey, "and this one's a pseudoneuropter." Then something
tumbled down, a little, kind of headless creature—"that's a
stomoxys."

She laughed, looking at Sytov.

"She doesn't remember," thought Sytov, "she's forgotten."
Stomoxys, the family name of this cricket, or fly, or whatever it
was. Stomoxys—like some foreign count. What did this mean
but that she had been staying at home, handing out milk to
Sytov and dreaming all the while of her Sergey here as he ran
about on his motorcycle after all kinds of stomoxys, dropping
them one after another into his test tubes? There they were, in
their own element, sitting in alcohol and demanding love and
admiration (much good might it do them), like your parents,
or someone who invites you to his house. And he—an adult
and no longer very young, in fact, he looked like an airman on a
polar expedition—he carefully picked up the stomoxys between two fingers, so as not to crush them, and brought them
along for her to see. Pure science, was that it? In his own case
there wasn't any science, Sytov supposed. What was there in
him, then? What rotten luck!

"For pity's sake," said Marussya, inside his soul. "Take your
hand away, Pashka! People are looking."

In the evenings, sitting on a bench somewhere in the garden
or on the waterfront, when all was quiet, she would say in his
ear: "Pashka, Pashka, you wicked thing!" in a bold, shameless
whisper. She fluttered in his arms like a bird, uttering no other
words but, "Pashka, Pashka, Pashka."

Later they walked along the waterfront, with no idea where
they were going and, as they went, encountered other couples
strolling like them without knowing where. That's the right way
of doing things from any reasonable standpoint: that's how
people go on. And as long as you do things that way, no one can

touch you or say anything: just exchange kisses, go for walks, take your lunch.

Meanwhile, those two had got involved in this business—everyone else was going to work, you notice, whereas they were showing off the stomoxys and not bothering about anyone. Perhaps this was their own way of overstepping the limits and supporting contravention?

To think of him hurrying to her on his motorcycle—in fact, that was probably why he had the motorcycle, just to hurry to her and then dash boldly with her along the highway.

"Marussya!" he cried inside his soul. "We'll go to Klyazma and walk arm-in-arm over the grass and forget all about everyone. Life is short, and I hardly know you."

"Pashka, you crazy thing," said Marussya, "are you telling me you don't love me any more? Hm. You're like a little child." And then, daringly, she whispered, "Give me your hand. Put it here. What about that? You *are* silly."

"So are you, my dove, d'you know it? Why can't life itself be enough joy for us all?"

"Don't take me right up to the door, my folks'll see us. You're mussing my dress. Pashka! Remember where you are!"

Inside the test tubes the crickets hung suspended with their legs folded under them. She was looking at her young man and could not take her eyes off him. In ancient times, could I have been snatched up by a bolt of lightning and suspended like that in there? Stomoxys. As things are, I'm guilty of unwarranted absence, not because of drinking or sheer foolishness, but I'm guilty all the same. Why? Because I just had to sit here and watch them looking at their stomoxys and at each other. And we'll have to say good-bye. She won't even look at me, because she needs all her eyes for the one with the tubes on his chest.

Oh yes, she has eyes only for him. And she's nothing but a slip of a thing, yet she looked quite plump, even overblown, at the window, or when she put her arms round Sergey on the motorcycle. But now she seems quite slender. Her thin arms are tanned. Her face is tanned. Her cheeks are even rather hollow. And when she smiles at that man of hers, there is a dark place among her white teeth. But what does he care about her faults, looking at her, devouring her with his eyes, not noticing that she's skinny, and her hair's not done, and she's half asleep, and has a black tooth that shows. So go on, smile. Marussya's teeth are a picture, and then she's an athlete, she swims like a fish, and any dress she put on would never be such a crumpled rag as hers. And there she sits holding his shaggy head between her thin little hands, and she even likes his hair all ruffled, with bits of straw in it, and she isn't holding his head to show off

("See how much I love him!") to others, but for her very own delight, she isn't looking around with a self-satisfied smirk on her face.

Then the train stopped. They had arrived without noticing it. Moscow was around them on all sides. And people were breaking into a run.

Sytov tried to get out so as to be able to see—might be for the last time—how they went off together. He got out of the train, thinking over the farewell nod Sergey had given him and the uncaring way in which she had waved good-bye.

There they were, walking along on the double. And he had his hand on her shoulder in the same way as before. What a good thing the guitar was undamaged!

Just then Sytov felt his arm seized in a grip not fierce but demanding. The grip belonged to a lieutenant of the local militia, a red-haired young upstart in a brand new uniform. And he was calling to someone: "Come on, come and get this one as well. They're getting away. Taken off, have they?" he asked Sytov.

"Huh?" said Sytov.

"Your pals, I mean."

"Just let go of my elbow, youngster," said Sytov very softly and deliberately. "And don't address me in that familiar tone."

"That'll do, you!" said the lieutenant. "No wisecracks." But he did let go of his elbow. "Get on and be quick about it."

"Oh, that won't do!" said Sytov, hiding an ironic smile. "It doesn't suit you. You're such a fine young man. Why behave like this?"

"I'm taking you somewhere to sober up," said the lieutenant.

"Look at him swaggering before me!" thought Sytov. "He has to prove his complete power, his complete authority, because he can't be replaced, and if it weren't for him, everything would be inside out and fellows like me'd be treading on people's hands and beating them on the head with my guitar."

They went on to the station.

"It's like a store," thought Sytov on entering the duty officer's room, for the barrier looked like a counter, and the captain behind it like a storekeeper. Sytov wanted to laugh at the whole scene and almost said out loud: "Half a pound of sausages."

Sergey of the leather jacket was there, too, standing near the counter, and the girl with the blue eyes was leaning against that man of hers; his hand was still on her shoulder in exactly the same way.

At that moment Sytov could take in only that her badly crumpled dress was green. Why hadn't he noticed it before?

"How many kinds of devices have they used," thought Sytov,

"just to make sure I don't come out of my little niche and get into someone else's!"

Just then the captain came out.

Sytov collapsed onto the bench, because his empty stomach made it hard for him to sit upright.

"No sitting here!" said the lieutenant, and the guitar reverberated.

Then Sergey winked at Sytov and said to the red-haired, good-looking young officer: "Why are you so, uh, severe with us? We've done nothing."

"Just you hold your tongue and stand up properly," said the lieutenant, and the guitar hummed again.

"What's 'properly'?" asked Sytov, with an air of complete innocence.

"Take your hand off her shoulder. Lovesick—"

"Why act like that?" said Sergey again. "Suppose we're not guilty? How'll you be able to look us in the face?"

"Put that guitar down," the lieutenant ordered Sytov. "What are you strumming it for?"

"I'm not strumming on it," said Sytov.

"You are!" said the lieutenant. "It's sounding off."

"It's sounding off because it's sensitive," said Sytov. "It can't bear to see me roughly treated."

Blue Eyes laughed, and the red-haired officer glared at her. "Well, I couldn't help it," she said.

The lieutenant said nothing as the captain was already there; it occurred to Sytov that this young redhead would now be tame and gentle. Now we'll see if you dance in front of him or not.

Then he began: family name, first name, occupation, address.

"How much have you had to drink?" the captain asked Sytov.

"A mugful," answered Sytov obediently.

"What did you drink?" asked the captain.

"Milk," said Sytov.

"Don't let him tell you that, Comrade Captain," said the lieutenant, showing his white teeth in a grin. "That's enough of your cracks," he said to Sytov.

"All right, all right," the captain told him. To Sytov he said: "You know where you'll be going with your jokes, don't you?"

"But I'm *not* drunk!" said Sytov, astonished.

"And suppose we thought you were?" said the redhead.

Sytov, listening, watched her, how she stood with her shoulders slightly raised as if amazed, whereas it was the questioners who should be amazed at those two standing there so full of love, making no outcry, breaking nothing.

"Monday is a heavy day," thought Sytov. Suddenly he felt relieved and somehow indifferent as he saw how serene they were before this harsh world, which was as it was. Of course, all kinds of stomoxys could go on peaceably kneeling in alcohol and would not be thrown out any which way, together with the broken glass.

"That yours?" the captain asked Sytov, and pointed to the guitar.

"It's a cithara," said Sytov.

Then everything was made clear, oh yes! Two respectable young taxi drivers (one wearing a checked coat, the other a cap) had signed a complaint that they had been on an innocent outing in the suburbs and were just on their way home, sitting quietly in the electric train like anyone else, looking out the window at the environs of Moscow, so dear to us all, when they were suddenly set upon by three toughs, who even used their fists, and that was why those two young drivers had jumped out of a moving train with bloodied faces, whereupon they were seized by a constable of the local militia who just happened to be passing on his way home from his beat. Now they were too ashamed to show up looking like this at their progressive worker's center. Meanwhile, the three toughs had gone on into Moscow as if nothing had occurred. To think that this could happen in a country like ours, where the working class was held in such high esteem!

Sytov burst into loud laughter and said, looking at the captain's sullen face: "Well, that's a twist! You could read it all back to front, and then you'd get it right. A man could write a book!"

"What book?" asked the captain.

"He'll get you all mixed up, Comrade Captain," said the red-haired lieutenant.

But those two weren't laughing. They'd probably realized long since what had happened and were not surprised, as Sytov was, for instance. Truly, who was to say that Sytov wasn't a tough? Or the one in the leather jacket? Or the blue-eyed girl with the crumpled dress and untidy hair?

"I suppose *I'm* the third tough," said she.

The captain pursed his lips, but he asked, "Were you in the fight?"

"Of course I was," she said so defiantly that Sytov quivered and held his breath.

Suddenly it came to him: why were their family names different, and even their addresses? God, she was his mistress, then, just that, and not his legal wife—think how close they'd stood with his hand on her shoulder.

Sytov saw her looking at him now, but as if she were far away, in another sphere. "She doesn't recognize me," he thought, "doesn't recall. . . ."

"All right," said the captain, scratching the back of his head, "I'll be back in a moment. Sit down." And he went off.

Those two exchanged a few words in low tones, God only knows what. Sytov bent his ear to the faint humming of his guitar, "No rest," it hummed, and against the deep bass of the sounding-box the wires rang like bells.

The redhead had already dwindled. (There hadn't been enough to bolster him up for long!) He probably thought he saw now what it was all about, he'd got the hang of it at last! For some time he had stopped shouting and swaggering. His eyes glanced at Sytov, now at the other two, watching for any movement, for him to fix a lock on her forehead, or something. Therefore the redhead was able to say with a broad smile: "Could you use a comb? Be better with a comb."

They made no response, did not even glance in his direction. When Sytov leaned over his guitar to hear whether the strings were now mute, the redhead hastened to say: "It's still twanging. Might be alive."

Sytov didn't look at him either. He said to Sergey: "What I could do to some food! Somebody's played me a rotten trick."

"I hope this joke'll be over soon," said Sergey.

"Just be patient a while longer," said the redhead in a friendly tone. "At least there's no war on to make things more difficult."

But again no one glanced his way.

At that moment the captain came back, and the red-haired officer's eyes darted everywhere. He wanted to hear what the other had been able to make out in order to decide what his own conduct should be.

"Well, now," said the captain, throwing some papers on the table, "it's all been cleared up. What a waste of a day's work! The two who brought charges against you were toughs themselves, it seems." And that was all.

The redhead looked at them, a happy expression in his eyes (and perhaps he really was happy, who can tell?)

"And now," said the captain, "I have to apologize to you. I hope you'll accept my apology. This is a rough neighborhood."

"Well, what d'you say?" said Sergey to the redhead.

"Why, what d'you mean?" he said.

"You can go," said the captain. "I'll have the necessary certificates of absence made out for you to show at work. Excuse me, please."

"Certainly we'll go," said Sergey firmly, "but, before we do, this citizen (indicating the young lieutenant) must personally apologize to my girl friend here."

"What?" shouted the redhead, blustering.

The guitar hummed on several notes in response.

"Get on with it, then," said the captain wearily.

"Why apologize?" said the redhead, lowering his voice. "Arresting them and bringing them here was my job: *you* gave the orders."

"Get on with it," said the captain again.

"Well, all right, I apologize," said the red-haired officer to the blue-eyed girl. "I apologize."

She was standing with her Sergey's arm around her, staring at the red-haired young man as if he were some kind of stomoxys.

"People are always mad at the militia," said the redhead, laughing.

The guitar hummed.

"Oh, why speak like that?" said Sytov to the lieutenant. "Suppose you were working at a beer stand, and somebody gave you flowers to hold, wouldn't you be nicer?"

"What?" The redhead had not caught on and glanced quickly at the captain.

The captain came up to Sytov and said: "About the milk you said just now you drank. Why did you say that? What milk, pal? Anything to make it tough for us, eh?"

"No, I did have some milk, I did," Sytov laughed. "Last evening. She was the one who poured it into the mug and brought it to me. Truly. That's her." And he pointed to the blue-eyed girl. He saw a light come into her eyes, but only for a second, then it went out again.

"She doesn't remember," he thought, "she's forgotten."

They went out into the square. Again Sergey nodded to Sytov, and she waved her little hand, then they plunged into the subway.

Motors were throbbing all around, and the guitar hummed on a trailing note as it rubbed against Sytov's side. Cithara!

Suddenly he remembered Marussya. He had forgotten her while they had been standing at the counter, when Sergey had had his hand on his girl friend's shoulder—she was probably his only girl, too—Sytov was all alone with himself, unless, of course, you counted the guitar.

Then he walked for a long time in the streets. Night fell, but he went on walking. The rain came down, but it didn't matter to him. Even the certificate in his pocket that said he had not been guilty of an unwarranted absence didn't matter.

He stood and rang a long time at the door, soaked to the skin, yet, for some reason suffused with joy. He rang and rang until a man called out in a hoarse voice: "Who is it?"

"A friend of the family," said Sytov.

"Some friend, I must say."

"Where's Marussya?"

"Marussya's gone," said the voice in astonishment.

"Gone?" (She really was gone.) "When?"

"It'll be two years now."

It really was two years. And no letter.

"And who might you be?" asked the voice, still astonished.

"I'm Pavel, Sytov. We were such—"

"What's the use if it's all over and done with?" said the voice. The safety chain rattled, and all was silent.

The rain went on falling as it had two years before, when they still remembered Sytov in that house.

"Stomoxys: that means 'poking chin,'" he said laughing, "I'm Promoxys; that means 'soaking skin.'"

He went on his way, light of heart.

1965

1

Now, they've taken it into their heads he's like a girl! That's just silly. Girls wear dresses and Seryozha hasn't worn one for ages. And when did a girl ever have a slingshot? But Seryozha has one, he can shoot stones with it. Shurik made it for him. And in exchange Seryozha gave Shurik all the old cotton reels he's been collecting his whole life long.

And if his hair's like that, well, it's been cropped with the clipper ever so many times and Seryozha endured it all, he sat quietly till they'd finished, and all the same it grew again, just like it had been before.

But to make up for that, he's very clever for his age, everyone says so. He knows no end of books by heart. If they read him a book two or three times, he can say it all off. He knows his letters, too, but reading things by himself takes such a long time. The books are all thickly daubed with crayons, because Seryozha likes to color the pictures, and if they are already colored he changes them to suit his own taste. Books don't look new for very long, they soon start falling to pieces. Aunt Pasha mends them, she sews in pages and sticks together the ones torn at the edges.

If some page gets lost Seryozha hunts for it and knows no peace until it is found. He loves his books, although in his heart of hearts he does not take everything in them really seriously. Animals can't talk, and the flying carpet can't fly because it hasn't got an engine; you'd have to be very silly not to know that.

Anyway, how can you believe stories when they read you one about a witch and then say: "But there aren't really any witches, Seryozha?"

All the same, he can't bear hearing how the woodcutter and his wife took their children into the forest so that they'd get lost and never come home again. And although Tom Thumb saved them, still, you just can't listen to things like that. He never lets them read that book to him.

Seryozha lives with Mummy, Aunt Pasha and Lukyanych. There are three rooms in their little house. Seryozha and Mummy sleep in one, Lukyanych and Aunt Pasha in another, and the third one is the dining room. They have meals there when visitors come, but when they are alone they eat in the kitchen. They have a veranda and a yard, too. And in the yard there are hens. Onions and radishes grow in two long beds. To keep the hens away from the beds dry prickly branches are pushed into the ground all round, and when Seryozha has to pull up a radish he always scratches his legs.

People say their town is a small one. Seryozha and his friends are quite sure that's all wrong. It's a big town. It's got shops and some water towers and a monument and a cinema. Mummy takes Seryozha to the movies sometimes. And when the lights go down Seryozha says: "Mummy, if you understand anything, tell me."

Cars drive along the road. Timokhin gives the children rides in his truck. But that doesn't happen very often. Only when Timokhin hasn't been drinking vodka. Then he frowns and doesn't talk, smokes, spits and gives them all rides. But if he's looking gay, it's no good even asking—he'll just wave his hand through the window and call out: "Hullo, kids! I can't take you. Wouldn't be right. I've had a drink!"

Seryozha's street is called Far Street. But that's just a name, because really it's close to everything. Vaska says it's only two kilometers to the square, and Vaska says the Bright Shore State Farm's even closer.

There's nothing more important than the Bright Shore Farm. That's where Lukyanych works. Aunt Pasha goes to the shops there to get pickled herrings and cloth. And Mummy's school is on the farm, too. On holidays she takes Seryozha with her to the school parties. That's where he met red-haired Fima. She's big, she's eight years old. Her hair is braided round her ears, with ribbons plaited in and tied in bows. Sometimes the ribbons are black, sometimes blue, or white, or brown. She's got an awful lot of ribbons. Seryozha might not have noticed them, but Fima told him herself: "Have you seen what a lot of ribbons I've got?"

2

She was quite right to tell him, he would like to have noticed it himself, but you just can't take everything in. There are so many things all round. The world is packed with things. How can you possibly notice them all?

Almost all the things are very big. Doors are terribly high, and people (except children) are almost as high as they are. Not to speak of trucks and combines, or of railway engines that whistle so loudly you can't hear anything else at all.

But they aren't really dangerous. People are kind to Seryozha, they bend down to him if he wants them to, and they never tread on him with their great feet. Trucks and combines won't hurt you either if you don't run in front of them. The engines are a long way off, at the station; Seryozha went there once or twice with Timokhin. But in the station yard there lives a terrible creature. It has nasty, angry, suspicious little eyes, a great crop that seems to swell, a chest as round as a cart wheel, and an iron beak. It stands scratching the earth with a horny claw. When it stretches out its neck it's as tall as Seryozha. And some day it may peck Seryozha just like it pecked the silly cockerel from the next yard that flew over to pay a visit. Seryozha always makes a wide circle round that savage creature, trying to look as though he doesn't even see it, and the creature lets its red comb hang down on one side and gobbles something threatening while it follows him with a watchful, malicious eye.

Cocks peck, cats scratch, nettles sting, boys fight, the ground scrapes the skin from your knees when you fall—so Seryozha is always covered with scratches, bumps and bruises. Almost every day something bleeds somewhere. And things are always happening. Vaska climbed the fence and Seryozha wanted to climb up, too, but he fell down and bumped himself. They dug a trench in Lida's garden and all the children began jumping across it, but when Seryozha jumped he fell in. And the first time he got up and went out to play with his ball, the ball flew up on the roof and got itself stuck right behind the chimney, so he had to wait for Vaska to get it down again. And once Seryozha was almost drowned. Lukyanych took the children out on the river in a boat—Seryozha, Vaska, Fima, and a girl called Nadya. But Lukyanych's boat was no good at all; when the children moved it started to rock from side to side and they all fell into the water, all but Lukyanych. The water was frighteningly cold. And it went straight into Seryozha's nose and mouth and ears; he didn't have time to cry out; it even went into his tummy. Seryozha got all wet and heavy, and somebody seemed to be pulling him down. He was terrified as he'd never been before. And it was all dark. And it went on for an unbelievably long time. But then, suddenly, they pulled him up. He opened his eyes and there was the river right by his face, and he could see the bank, and everything was sparkling in the sunshine. All the water that had been inside Seryozha came out again and he breathed air; the bank came closer and closer, and then Seryozha was crouching on all fours on the firm sand, shivering with cold and fright. It was Vaska who'd thought of getting hold of him by the hair and pulling him out. But what if Seryozha hadn't had such long hair, what then?

Fima swam out by herself, she knew how to swim. And Nadya wasn't drowned either, Lukyanych saved her. But while Lukyanych was saving Nadya the boat floated away. Some people on a collective farm down the river found it and telephoned to the office for Lukyanych to come and get it. But Lukyanych never took the children in a boat again. He said: "May I be cursed before I go with you again."

With so much happening and so much to see all day, Seryozha gets very tired. By evening he is quite exhausted, his tongue will hardly move and his eyes roll up like a bird's. They wash his hands and feet and put on his nightshirt and he doesn't even feel it; he has run down like a clock.

He sleeps, his head thrown back, his arms flung wide, one leg stretched out, the other bent as though he were climbing stairs. His soft, light hair falls back in two waves from his forehead, with its stubborn bumps over the eyebrows, like you see on a young bullock. His eyes are shut tight. His mouth is a little open.

He sleeps and you could beat a drum, fire a gun beside him and Seryozha wouldn't wake up; he's saving up strength to go on living.

3

"Seryozha," said Mummy, "you know what? . . . I want us to have a Daddy."

Seryozha looked up at her. He had never thought about that. Some children had Daddies, others hadn't. Seryozha had no Daddy, his had been killed in the war. Seryozha had only seen his photograph. Sometimes Mummy would kiss it, and give it to Seryozha to kiss too. He was quite ready to press his lips to the glass, misty with Mummy's breath, but he did not feel any love. How could he love someone whom he'd seen only on a picture?

Now he stood between Mummy's knees looking inquiringly into her face. It was slowly getting pink—the pink started on her cheeks, and then it spread to her forehead and ears. . . . Mummy gripped Seryozha tight with her knees, put her arms around him and laid her hot cheek on his head. Then all he could see was her arm in a blue sleeve with white dots. "It's bad without a Daddy," she whispered. "Isn't it, Seryozha?"

"Ye-e-es," he answered, also in a whisper.

Actually, he was far from sure of it. He said "yes" simply because she wanted him to say "yes." And he turned it over quickly in his mind—which is better, to have a Daddy or not to have a Daddy? When Timokhin gave them rides in his truck all the children got in the back but Shurik; he sat in front with Timokhin, and they envied him, but no one argued because Timokhin was Shurik's Daddy. But then, if Shurik was naughty, Timokhin gave him the strap, and Shurik went about tear-stained and gloomy, and Seryozha was sorry for him and brought out all his toys to comfort Shurik. . . . But all the same, perhaps it was better if you had a Daddy. When Vaska teased Lida not long ago she told him: "But I've got a Daddy and you haven't, yah!"

"What's that bumping?" Seryozha asked suddenly, noticing

the dull thud thud in Mummy's chest. Mummy laughed, kissed Seryozha and hugged him closer.

"It's my heart."

"And have I got one, too?" he asked, bending his head to listen.

"Yes, you've got one, too."

"No. I can't hear it bumping."

"But it does. It's just that you can't hear it. It has to beat. You couldn't live if it didn't."

"And does it always go like that?"

"Yes, all the time."

"Even when I'm asleep?"

"Yes, even when you're asleep."

"And can you hear it?"

"Yes, I can. And you can feel it with your hand, too."

She took his hand and laid it on his ribs.

"Now can you feel it?"

"Yes. . . . Isn't it banging hard! Is it big?"

"Shut your hand, it's about as big as that."

"Let me go," he said, wriggling out of her embrace, evidently thinking hard.

"Where are you going?" she asked.

"Wait a minute," he said and ran out into the street, his hand pressed against his left side. There he saw Vaska and Zhenka and ran to them.

"Look, would you like to feel? That's my heart. I can feel it with my hand. Would you like to feel, too?"

"Huh, your heart!" scoffed Vaska. "Everyone's got a heart."

But Zhenka said: "No—really?" and put his hand on Seryozha's side.

"Can you feel it?" Seryozha asked.

"M'yes," said Zhenka.

"It's about as big as my fist," said Seryozha.

"How do you know?" asked Vaska.

"Mummy told me," Seryozha said, and suddenly remembering he added: "And I'm going to have a Daddy!"

But Vaska and Zhenka didn't listen, they were too busy with their own affairs. They were taking medicinal herbs to an office that wanted them. There were lists stuck up on the fences saying which kinds were needed, and the boys wanted to earn some pocket money. They had been collecting herbs for two days. Vaska had asked his mother to clean his and sort them out and wrap them in a clean cloth and was taking a big, neat bundle to the office. But Zhenka had no mother, his cousin and aunt were at work, and he couldn't fuss with it all himself; so he was taking his herbs in an old, torn potato sack, together with the roots and even the soil clinging to them. But to make up for that he had a lot— much more than Vaska. When he heaved the sack up on his back he had to bend double to carry it.

"I'm coming with you," cried Seryozha, hurrying after them.

"No, go back home," said Vaska. "We're busy."

"Can't I just walk along with you?" Seryozha begged.

"Go home," ordered Vaska. "This isn't play. There's nothing for kids to do where we're going."

Seryozha stopped. His lip trembled, but he wouldn't cry. Lida was coming and it wasn't wise to cry in front of her. She'd start teasing him: "Cry-baby! Cry-baby!"

"Wouldn't they take you?" she asked. "Too bad!"

"I can get as many herbs as that if I want," said Seryozha, "and I'll heap them up higher than the sky."

"Higher than the sky— nonsense," said Lida. "Nobody can make a heap higher than the sky."

"But I'm going to have a Daddy— he can," said Seryozha.

"That's a story," said Lida. "You're not going to have any Daddy at all. And he couldn't get as much as that anyway. Nobody could."

Seryozha looked up at the sky, his head thrown far back. Could anyone gather enough herbs to reach higher than the sky, or not? While he was still thinking about it, Lida ran home and came back with a colored scarf her mother often wore, sometimes on her head and sometimes round her neck. Lida started to dance, waving it about, throwing out her arms and legs and singing something. Seryozha stood watching her. Lida stopped for a moment.

"Nadka's fibbing, she says they're sending her to the ballet school."

She danced a little more. "In Moscow and Leningrad they have schools where they teach you to be a ballerina."

She saw the admiration in Seryozha's face and said condescendingly: "Well? Do you want to learn? Watch me and do the same as I do."

He started copying her, but without the scarf it was not the same. She told him to sing, but it didn't help.

"Give me the scarf," he begged.

"What next?" she answered. And she didn't give it to him.

Just then a car stopped at Seryozha's gate. A woman was driving, and Aunt Pasha came out through the gate.

"Here you are," said the driver. "Dimitry Korneyevich sent these."

There was a suitcase in the back and a pile of books fastened together with string. And there was something thick and gray, rolled up— it turned out to be an army greatcoat. Aunt Pasha and the driver began carrying the things inside. Mummy looked out of the window and then disappeared.

"Well, that's all the dowry, I'm afraid," said the driver.

"He might at least have bought a new overcoat," said Aunt Pasha mournfully.

"He'll get one," the driver promised. "And in good time. And here's this note, would you give it to her."

She handed over a letter and drove away. Seryozha raced into the house.

"Mummy! Mummy! Korostelev's sent us his soldier's coat!"

Dmitry Korneyevich Korostelev used to visit them. He brought toys for Seryozha and once, in the winter, took him for a sleigh ride. His army coat had no stars on it, it was left over from the war. Seryozha found it difficult to get his tongue round the full name—"Dmitry Korneyevich," so he simply called him Korostelev.

The greatcoat was already hanging on the rack, and Mummy was reading the letter. She did not answer at once; but when she had quite finished reading she said: "I know, Seryozha dear. Korostelev's going to live here with us. He's going to be your Daddy."

Then she started reading the letter all over again; once evidently was not enough to remember what it said.

"Daddy"—that word had made Seryozha think of someone strange, unknown. But Korostelev—why, he was an old friend, Aunt Pasha and Lukyanych call him "Mitya," what had come over Mummy?

"But why?" Seryozha asked.

"Now look here," said Mummy, "are you going to let me read this letter or not?"

So she never answered him. She seemed to have an awful lot of things to do. She took the string off the books and arranged them on the shelves. And she wiped every book with a duster. Then she changed the places of all the things in front of the mirror on the chest of drawers. Then she went into the garden, picked some flowers and arranged them in a vase. Then for some reason she had to wash the floor, although it was quite clean as it was. And then she started baking buns. Aunt Pasha taught her how to make dough. And Seryozha got some dough and jam, too, so he could make a little bun.

When Korostelev arrived Seryozha had forgotten all his puzzlement and cried:

"Korostelev! Look, I've made a bun!"

Korostelev stooped down and kissed him several times. And Seryozha thought: He keeps on kissing me so because he's my Daddy now.

Korostelev unpacked his suitcase, took out Mummy's picture in a frame, got a hammer and nail from the kitchen and hung the picture up in Seryozha's room.

"What's that for," asked Mummy, "when I'm going to be always with you myself?"

Korostelev took her hands, they drew closer—but then they looked at Seryozha and their hands dropped. Mummy went out of the room. Korostelev sat down on a chair and said thoughtfully:

"Well, so here we are, Seryozha. I've come to live with you. You've no objections, I hope?"

"Have you come for always?" asked Seryozha.

"Yes," said Korostelev, "for always."

"And will you give me the strap?"

"Why should I give you the strap?"

"When I'm naughty," Seryozha explained.

"No," Korostelev answered. "I think using a strap that way's stupid. What'd you think?"

"Yes, it *is* stupid," Seryozha agreed. "And it makes children cry."

"We'll manage to settle things as man to man, without any strap, you and I."

"And what room are you going to sleep in?" asked Seryozha.

"It looks as if I'll sleep in this one," Korostelev answered. "Yes, that's what it looks like. And on Sunday we'll go—you know where we'll go?—to the shop where they sell toys. And you shall choose whatever you like. Is that a go?"

"Yes," said Seryozha. "I want a bicycle. Is it long to Sunday?"

"No, it's quite soon."

"How many days?"

"Tomorrow'll be Friday, then comes Saturday, and then Sunday."

"As long as that!" said Seryozha.

There were three for supper—Seryozha, Mummy, and Korostelev. (Aunt Pasha and Lukyanych had gone out somewhere). Seryozha felt sleepy. Gray moths circled round and round the lamp, bumped against it and fell down on the table-cloth with their wings fluttering, and that made him still sleepier. Suddenly he saw Korostelev carrying his bed away somewhere.

"Where are you taking my bed?" asked Seryozha. But Mummy said: "You're almost asleep. Come and wash your feet."

When Seryozha woke up in the morning he could not make out at first where he was. Why were there three windows instead of two, and on the wrong side of his bed? And with different curtains? Then he worked it out, this was Aunt Pasha's

room. It was a pretty room, there were flowers on the windowsills and a peacock's feather tucked in behind the mirror. Aunt
Pasha and Lukyanych had gone already, their bed was made,
with the pillows piled neatly one on top of the other. The early
sunshine was playing in the bushes by the open window.
Seryozha climbed out of bed, took off his long nightshirt, put
on his shorts and went into the dining room. The door of *his*
room was closed. He turned the handle, but it did not open.
And he simply had to get in, all his toys were inside. That new
spade was among them and he suddenly felt he wanted very
much to dig.

"Mummy!" Seryozha called out. "Mummy!" he called again.

The door remained shut. Everything was quiet.

"Mummy!" he yelled with all his lungs.

Aunt Pasha came running in, picked him up and carried him
to the kitchen.

"What's this, what's this!" she whispered. "What d'you want
to scream like that for? You mustn't do that, you're not little any
more. Mummy's asleep, and let her sleep, why d'you want to
wake her?"

"I want my spade," he said excitedly.

"You'll have it, it won't run away. Mummy'll get up and then
you can take it," said Aunt Pasha. "Look, here's your slingshot.
You go and play with that for the present like a good boy. If you
like I'll give you a carrot, you can clean it for yourself and eat it.
But the first thing decent people do is wash."

Kind, sensible talk always quieted Seryozha. He let her wash
him and drank a mug of milk. Then he took his slingshot and
went outside. A sparrow was sitting on the fence across the
street. Seryozha shot a stone at it from his slingshot without
aiming properly and of course missed. He didn't aim on purpose, because however much he aimed he always missed, for
some reason. But if he aimed then Lida would tease him and
now she'd no right to tease him because anyone could see he
hadn't been aiming, he had just been taking a pot shot.

Shurik was beside his own gate.

"Seryozha—come to the woods," he called.

"Oh, shucks with the woods!" said Seryozha.

He sat on the bench by the gate swinging his leg. He felt ruffled and upset again. Passing through the yard he had seen the
shutters closed at his windows. He hadn't paid any attention at
the moment. But now it occurred to him that the shutters were
never closed in summer, only in winter when there was a hard
frost. So his toys were locked in on all sides. And he wanted
them so badly, he could have thrown himself down and howled.
Of course he wouldn't throw himself down and howl, he was

too big for that now, but being too big didn't make him feel any better about it. And Mummy and Korostelev didn't care a bit that he needed his spade this very minute.

As soon as they wake up, thought Seryozha, I'll take every single thing into Aunt Pasha's room. I mustn't forget that building block that rolled under the chest of drawers days ago, it's still there.

Vaska and Zhenka came up and stood in front of Seryozha. Lida came, too, carrying little Victor. They all stood and looked at Seryozha. And he sat swinging his leg and said nothing at all.

"What's the matter with you?" asked Zhenka.

"His mother's got married," Vaska explained.

Another silence.

"Who's she married?" asked Zhenka.

"Korostelev, the director of the Bright Shore," said Vaska. "And didn't he get it in the neck at the last meeting!"

"What for?" asked Zhenka.

"Because he deserved it, I suppose," said Vaska and pulled a crumpled packet of cigarets from his pocket.

"Give me a cig," said Zhenka.

"I'm nearly out of 'em myself," said Vaska, but he gave one to Zhenka all the same, lighted his own and offered Zhenka the burning match. The tiny flame was transparent and invisible in the sunshine. You couldn't see what made the match twist and turn black and smoke rise from the cigaret. The sun was shining on the side of the street where the children had gathered, while the other side was still in shadow, and the leaves of the nettles by the fences, washed by the dew, were wet and dark. And it was the same with the dust in the middle of the street—on the other side it was cool, on this side warm. There were two caterpillar tracks in the dust, someone had driven a tractor down the street.

"Seryozha's in the dumps," Lida told Shurik. "He's got a new father."

"Don't worry about that," Vaska said to Seryozha. "He looks all right. You'll just go on the way you always have. What do you care?"

"He's going to get me a bicycle." Seryozha suddenly remembered last night's talk.

"Has he promised, or do you just think he will?" asked Vaska.

"He promised. We're going to the shop together. On Sunday. Tomorrow'll be Friday, then comes Saturday, and then Sunday."

"A bicycle or a tricycle?" asked Zhenka.

"Don't take a tricycle," Vaska advised him. "What good's that to you? You'll soon be big; what you need's a proper bicycle."

"He's just making it all up," said Lida. "He's not going to get a bicycle at all."

Shurik was frowning. "My Daddy's going to get me a bicycle, too. Next time he's paid he'll get me one."

4

There was a rattle of iron in the garden. Seryozha looked in through the gate—Korostelev was outside, drawing the bolts and opening the shutters. He was in a striped shirt and blue tie, his hair was wet and combed smooth. He opened the shutters, Mummy pushed the window open from inside and said something to Korostelev. He replied, resting his elbows on the windowsill. She reached out and took his head in her hands. They did not see the children watching them from the street.

Seryozha went into the yard.

"Korostelev! I want my spade!"

". . . spade?" Korostelev repeated.

"And all my things," Seryozha added.

"Come in and get what you want," said Mummy.

There was a new smell in Mummy's room—tobacco and strange breath. And strange things lay here and there—clothes, a brush, and cigaret boxes on the table. . . . Mummy was unplaiting her hair. When she loosed the long braids it fell like a lot of little chestnut snakes down below her waist. And then she brushed it till it poured down straight like rain in summer.

"Good morning, Seryozha," said Mummy from behind the chestnut snakes.

He did not answer, he was busy looking at the cigaret boxes. They were fascinatingly new and alike. He picked one up, but it was pasted together and would not open.

"Put that down," said Mummy, who could see everything in the mirror. "I thought you came for your toys?"

The building block under the chest of drawers was right at the back. Seryozha could see it when he crouched down, but he could not reach it, it was too far away.

"What are you puffing and panting about?" asked Mummy.

"I can't get it," Seryozha answered.

Korostelev came in.

"Will you give me those boxes when they're empty?" asked Seryozha. He knew grown-ups only give boxes away to children when what's inside them has been smoked or eaten.

"Here's one to begin with," said Korostelev. He tipped the cigarets out of their box and gave it to Seryozha.

"Would you help him?" asked Mummy. "There's something of his behind the chest of drawers."

Korostelev took hold of the chest of drawers with his big hands—the old chest creaked and moved forward, and

Seryozha got his block without any difficulty at all.

"That's pretty good," he said, looking up approvingly at Korostelev.

Out he went, hugging his box, his block, and as many other toys as he could hold. He took them all into Aunt Pasha's room and dumped them on the floor between his bed and the cupboard.

"You've forgotten your spade," Mummy called after him. "You were in such a hurry for it and now you've left it behind."

Seryozha took his spade in silence and went out into the garden. Somehow, he didn't want to dig any more, it had just occurred to him he'd like to put his collection of colored candy wrappers in the new box, but he had to dig just a little, at least, after Mummy said that.

Under the apple tree the soil was loose and easy. He tried to drive his spade a long way down—to the top of the blade. He worked really hard, panting with the effort, the muscles tensing on his arms and on his bare narrow back, golden with sunburn. Korostelev stood smoking on the veranda, watching him.

Lida came up carrying Victor.

"Let's plant some flowers," she said. "It'll look pretty."

She put Victor down on the ground with his back against the apple tree so he would not fall. But all the same he slumped down sideways.

"Sit up, can't you!" Lida cried, giving him a shake and settling him more firmly. "You silly child! Other babies can sit by themselves at your age!"

She said it all very loudly so that Korostelev should hear it on the veranda and understand how sensible and grown-up she was. With side glances at him, she brought some marigolds and pushed them in the ground where Seryozha had dug it up.

"See how nice that is," she said.

Then she brought some red and white stones from the gutter and arranged them round the marigolds. She smoothed out the ground with her fingers and patted it with her palms, so that her hands became quite black.

"Now, isn't it pretty?" she asked. "Only tell the truth, don't just say it."

"Yes," Seryozha admitted. "It's very pretty."

"There, you see," Lida triumphed. "You can't do a single thing without me!"

At that moment Victor fell down again, this time on his back.

"All right, lie there, if that's all you can do," said Lida.

Victor did not cry, he simply sucked his thumb and gazed with a look of surprise at the leaves stirring overhead.

Lida unwound the rope from her waist where it had been

serving as a belt and started skipping in front of the veranda, counting loudly: "One, two, three. . . ." Korostelev laughed and went inside.

"Look," said Seryozha, "there are ants running over him."

"What an idiot!" cried Lida, irritated; she picked Victor up and started clearing off the ants, smearing dirt over his smock and his bare legs as she did so.

"They wash him and wash him all the time," said Lida, "and he's dirty just the same."

Then Mummy called from the veranda.

"Seryozha! Come and change, we're going visiting."

Seryozha ran in eagerly— he would have gone visiting every day if he could. It was lovely; when you went visiting, people gave you candy and showed you all sorts of toys.

"We're going to Granny Nastya," Mummy told him, although he had not even asked. What did it matter where they were going, if only they went visiting?

Granny Nastya was stern and serious. She always wore a white dotted kerchief on her head, tied beneath her chin. She had a medal which she sometimes wore, and it had a picture of Lenin on it. And she always carried a black bag that fastened with a zipper. She would open the bag and give Seryozha something good to eat. But he had never been to visit her.

They all put on their best clothes— he, and Mummy, and Korostelev, and then set off. Korostelev and Mummy took his hands, but he soon tore himself away, it was much more fun walking by himself. He could stop and look through cracks in fences into yards with terrible dogs on chains and geese waddling about. Or he could run on ahead and back again. He could be a puffing engine. He could pull blades of grass and whistle through them. He could pick up a golden kopeck someone had lost. But when people held his hands, then they just got hot and sticky and there was no fun at all.

They came to a little house with two little windows facing the street. The yard was small, too, and so was the room. They went into the room through the kitchen with a huge brick stove in it, the old-fashioned Russian stove. Granny Nastya came out to meet them.

"All my very best wishes," she said.

So it must be a holiday. Seryozha answered as Aunt Pasha always did: "And the same to you."

He looked round. There were no toys, not even the little figures which people stand here and there for ornaments, only dull things for eating and sleeping.

"Have you any toys?" Seryozha asked. (Perhaps they were put away somewhere.)

"I'm afraid I haven't," answered Granny Nastya. "I've no children here, so I've no toys either. Here's a candy for you."

A blue glass bowl of candies stood in the middle of the table among the plates of cakes and buns. Everybody drew up chairs and sat down. Korostelev pulled the cork from a bottle and poured dark red wine into little glasses.

"None for Seryozha," said Mummy.

It was always like that. They drank themselves, but they wouldn't give him any. As soon as it was something extra good, he mustn't have it.

But Korostelev said: "I'll just give him a drop. So he can drink to us, too."

He poured out a tiny glassful, and Seryozha felt it was going to be all right with Korostelev.

Then they all clinked glasses, and Seryozha clinked glasses as well.

There was another Granny with them. But they told Seryozha she wasn't just a Granny, she was a Great-Granny, and that's what he must call her. Though Korostelev called her just "Granny" without any "Great" at all. Seryozha didn't like her a bit.

She said: "He'll spill it on the cloth."

He actually did spill a drop of wine when they clinked glasses.

Then she said: "There, you see," and sprinkled salt from the saltcellar on the wet spot, breathing heavily, which sounded very cross. And after that she watched Seryozha all the time. She wore glasses. And she was most awfully old. Her hands were brown and wrinkled and knotted; she had a big nose that turned down and a bony chin that turned up.

The wine was sweet and very nice and he drank it at a gulp. They gave him a bun, he began to eat it and dropped crumbs all over himself.

Great-Granny said: "Don't you know how to eat properly?"

He felt uncomfortable on his chair and wriggled.

She said: "Don't you know how to sit properly?"

Then he felt all hot inside and wanted to sing. So he did sing.

She said: "Behave yourself."

But Korostelev took Seryozha's side. "Let him alone. Give the boy a bit of peace."

Great-Granny said ominously: "You wait, you'll see what he'll turn into."

She had drunk wine, too, and her eyes sparkled behind her glasses. But Seryozha shouted boldly: "Go away! I'm not afraid of you!"

"Oh, how awful!" said Mummy.

"Rubbish," said Korostelev. "It'll pass in a minute. He only
had a drop."

"I want some more!" cried Seryozha, holding out his glass
and overturning the empty bottle. There was a crash of dishes.
Mummy gasped. Great-Granny brought her fist down on
the table with a bang and cried: "There you are! A nice state
of affairs.!"

But Seryozha felt he wanted to rock. So he started rocking
from side to side. And the table with the buns rocked in front
of him, and so did Mummy, and Korostelev, and Granny Nastya,
they were talking and rocking as if they were all in rocking
chairs, it was awfully funny and Seryozha had to laugh. Suddenly
he heard someone singing. It was Great-Granny. She held her
eyeglasses in her knotted hand and waved them from side to
side and sang about Katyusha who went down to the shore and
sang a song. And while Great-Granny was singing Seryozha fell
asleep, his head on a piece of bun.

When he woke up Great-Granny was not there, and the
others were drinking tea. They smiled at Seryozha.

"Well, feel all right now?" asked Mummy. "You won't make
any more row?"

Did I really make a row? thought Seryozha.

Mummy took a comb out of her bag and combed his hair.
And Granny Nastya said: "Here's a candy for you."

In the next room, behind a faded colored curtain, someone
was snoring. Seryozha cautiously pushed the curtain aside,
peeped in and saw Great-Granny asleep on the bed. He walked
sedately away from the curtain.

"Let's go home," he said. "I'm tired of visiting."

When they were saying good-bye he heard Korostelev call
Granny Nastya "Mother." Seryozha had never known Korostelev
had a mother, he had thought he and Granny Nastya just
happened to know each other.

Seryozha found the way back very long and very dull.
Korostelev ought to carry me now, he's my Daddy, he thought.
He had seen other fathers carrying their sons on their shoulders.
The sons looked very proud of themselves, and they must be
able to see a long, long way all round. So Seryozha said: "My
legs hurt."

"It's not much further now," said Mummy. "You can
manage it."

But Seryozha ran in front of Korostelev and clutched
his knees.

"A big boy like you asking to be carried," said Mummy. "You
ought to be ashamed of yourself!" But Korostelev picked
Seryozha up and settled him on his shoulders.

Seryozha felt awfully high up. But he wasn't a scrap afraid, because a giant who'd moved a whole chest of drawers like that couldn't possibly drop him. And he could see over the fences, could see everything happening in the yards and even on the roofs. It was wonderful! This interesting view of things kept Seryozha busy all the way home. Proudly he looked down on other boys who had to walk on their own feet. And it was with a feeling of a new, wonderful superiority that he finally arrived home—on his father's shoulders, as a son should.

5

On those same shoulders he set out on Sunday to buy the bicycle.

All of a sudden Sunday was there, much sooner than he had expected, and when he knew it had come, Seryozha was wild with excitement.

"You haven't forgotten, have you?" he asked Korostelev.

"Of course not, I'd never forget an important thing like that. We'll go as soon as I've finished one or two things I have to do."

But that was just a story, about having things to do. He had no things to do at all, he only sat and talked to Mummy. It was stupid talk, and dull, but they seemed to like it because they went on and on. Mummy especially, and she'd keep on saying the same word over and over again for some reason. And Korostelev got it from her. Seryozha hovered round them, too excited to say anything, filled with one single thought, waiting and waiting for them to get tired of their talk and stop.

"You understand everything," said Mummy. "It makes me so happy that you understand everything."

"To tell the truth," Korostelev answered, "I didn't understand very much about things like that till I met you. There was a lot I didn't understand, and I only started to understand when—well, you understand."

Then they took hands as if they were going to play Oranges and Lemons.

"I was just a girl," said Mummy. "I thought I was madly happy. And then I thought I'd die of grief. And now it all seems like a dream. . . ."

She'd got a new word now and kept on and on with it, covering her face with Korostelev's big hands.

"I just dreamed it, you understand? Like a dream you have when you're asleep. It was all a dream. I was dreaming. And now I'm awake and there's—you."

Korostelev interrupted her.

"I love you."

But Mummy didn't believe him.

"Really and truly?"

"I love you," Korostelev insisted. But still she didn't believe him.

"You really love me?"

Seryozha thought: Why doesn't he say "word of honor" or "cross my heart and wish I may die," then she'd believe him.

Korostelev seemed to have got tired of answering, he said nothing and just looked at Mummy. And she looked at him. They went on and on looking at each other maybe for a whole hour. Then Mummy said: "I love you." Like that game where they all say the same thing one after the other.

When will they stop? Seryozha wondered.

Yet short as his life experience was he knew he should not pester the grown-ups when they were taken up with their own talk. That was something they just couldn't stand. They might get really angry and then who knows what they'd do. He could only try to remind them of himself by staying around and sighing noisily now and then.

But the end of his torment came at last.

"I'll have to go out for an hour or so, Maryasha," said Korostelev. "Seryozha and I have something important to do."

He had long legs, Seryozha had hardly time to look round before they were there on the square where the shop stood that sold toys. Here Korostelev set Seryozha down and they went over to the shop.

A doll with round cheeks smiled in the window, her feet in real leather shoes spread wide apart. A family of blue bears sat on a red drum. A bugle gleamed golden. . . . Seryozha was breathless with anticipation. . . . Music came from inside the shop. A man was sitting on a chair holding an accordion. But he wasn't playing it, only pulling it out now and then, so that it gave a mournful wail and then stopped again. The gay music came from somewhere else, from the counter. Some men in Sunday suits and ties were standing listening to it. Behind the counter stood an old shop assistant.

"What do you want to see?" he asked Korostelev.

"A child's bicycle."

The old man leaned over the counter and looked at Seryozha.

"A tricycle?" he asked.

"No, a tricycle's no good to me," cried Seryozha, his voice trembling with anguish.

"Varya!" the old man shouted.

Nobody came, but the old man seemed to forget all about Seryozha, he went over to the men and did something or other. The gay music stopped at once and something slow and sad started instead. To Seryozha's alarm, Korostelev, too, seemed to forget all about why they had come, he went over to the men and they all stood without moving, staring in front of them, never thinking of Seryozha. He couldn't stand it, he pulled Korostelev's coat. Korostelev seemed to wake up; he sighed and said: "That's a grand record."

"Will he give us the bicycle?" Seryozha asked loudly.

"Varya!" the old man shouted again.

Evidently it all depended on Varya whether Seryozha would get his bicycle or not. And at last Varya appeared through a low door between the shelves behind the counter. She had a biscuit in her hand and she was chewing. The old man told her to bring a bicycle from the storeroom. "For this young man," he said. Seryozha liked being called that.

The storeroom must have been at the other end of the world, because it took Varya an age to come back. The man had time to buy his accordion, and Korostelev bought a phonograph. That was a sort of box, you put a black plate on it, then the plate turned round and round and played gay music or sad music or whatever you wanted. It was this box which had been playing on the counter. And Korostelev bought a lot of those plates in paper envelopes as well, and two little boxes of something he called needles.

"That's for Mummy," he told Seryozha. "We'll take her a present."

All the men watched the old man wrap the things up. And then Varya came back from the end of the world, bringing a bicycle. A real bicycle with spokes and a bell and handlebars and pedals and a leather saddle and a tiny red lamp! And it even had a number at the back, black figures on a yellow tin plate!

"You've got something worth having there," said the old man. "Turn the front wheel. Ring the bell. Press on the pedals. Go on, press hard, what's the use of just looking at them? Well? Aye, that's a really good article, not just any sort. You'll thank me for it every day of your life."

Korostelev conscientiously tested the steering, rang the bell and pressed on the pedals, while Seryozha watched in something like terror, mouth open, breathing in little short gasps, hardly daring to believe all this glory was going to be his.

He rode home on his bicycle. That is to say, he sat on the leather saddle, enjoying its springiness, holding the bars with uncertain hands and trying to get his feet on the rebellious, elusive pedals. Korostelev, bent nearly double, pushed the bicycle and kept it from falling. Red and panting he brought Seryozha as far as the gate and leaned him on his bicylce against the bench.

"Now, try by yourself," he said. "I'm just about done in."

He went into the house. Then Zhenka, Lida, and Shurik
came up to Seryozha.

"I've learned just a little already," Seryozha told them.
"Get out of the way or I'll run over you!"

He tried to ride away from the bench and fell off.

"Oh!" he cried, getting out from under the machine and
laughing to show it was nothing much. "I turned the bars the
wrong way. And it's awfully difficult to find the pedals, too."

"Take off your shoes," Zhenka advised. "It's much better
barefoot. You can grip the pedals with your toes. Here, let
me try. Hold it still a minute." He got up on the saddle.
"Hold it firmer."

But though all three held him, he fell off as well, together
with Seryozha, who had been holding him more enthusiastically
than any.

"Me now!" said Lida.

"No, me!" cried Shurik.

"The dust's too thick here," said Zhenka, "you'll never learn
on that. Come to Vaska's Lane."

That was what they called a short blind alley that ran behind
Vaska's garden. On the opposite side was a timber yard with a
high fence. Short, soft, curly grass covered it; it was a wonderful
place to play, with no grown-ups around to interfere. And
although its blind end came up to Timokhin's fence and two
mothers—Vaska's and Shurik's—both threw slops over the
fences on the grass, still nobody ever disputed that the
really important person there was Vaska; and so it was called
Vaska's Lane.

That was where Zhenka wheeled the bicycle. Lida and Shurik
helped him, arguing about who would learn to ride first, while
Seryozha ran behind, trying to catch the wheel.

Zhenka announced he would be first because he was the
oldest. Then came Lida, and after Lida—Shurik. Then they let
Seryozha try but very soon Zhenka said: "That's enough! It's
my turn now!"

Seryozha wanted terribly to go on; he clung to the bicycle
with hands and feet. "I want to ride some more! It's my bicycle!"

But of course Shurik turned on him at once.

"Ugh—stingy!"

And Lida added in a nasty jeering voice: "Stingy-mingy!"

To be stingy-mingy was an awful disgrace. Seryozha got down
without another word and moved away. He went to Timokhin's
fence, turned his back on the children and cried. He cried
because it wasn't fair, because he couldn't stand up for
himself, because there was nothing in all the world he wanted
but that bicycle and they were rough and strong and didn't

understand it.

They paid no attention to him. He could hear their loud squabbles and the metallic clang of the falling bicycle. Nobody called him, nobody said: "Your turn now." They were having their third turn already! And he stood there crying. Then suddenly, Vaska appeared behind his fence.

He was stripped to the waist, in trousers a size too long—to allow for growth—kept up by a tight belt, and a cap with the peak behind—strong, impressive! He looked over the fence and took in the situation at once.

"Hey!" he shouted. "What d'you think you're doing? Whose bicycle is it—yours or his? Come on, Seryozha!"

He vaulted over the fence and took the handlebars with a commanding grasp. Zhenka, Lida, and Shurik fell back respectfully. Seryozha came up, wiping his tears away with his arm. Lida cried squeaking: "You're both stingies!"

"And you're a greedy guts," Vaska answered. He called her some other names, too. "Couldn't wait to let the little chap learn." Then he said to Seryozha: "Get on."

Seryozha got on and rode a long time, and all the children helped him, except Lida; she sat on the grass making a dandelion wreath and pretending she enjoyed that much better than riding a bicycle.

Then Vaska said: "Now I'll try," and Seryozha made way for him willingly, he would have done anything in the world for Vaska. Then Seryozha rode alone, without anyone helping him, and he nearly didn't fall, but the bicycle kept wobbling every way and somehow or other he got his foot in the wheel and four spokes came out. But it didn't matter, the bicycle would still go just the same. Then Seryozha began to be sorry for the other children.

"Let them ride, too," he said. "We'll take turns."

A little later Aunt Pasha came out into the garden and heard Seryozha crying. She opened the gate and saw a procession advancing in single file. First came Seryozha carrying the handlebars. Vaska carried the frame. Zhenka the two wheels, one on each shoulder, Lida the bell and Shurik trotted at the tail with a bundle of spokes.

"Great heavens!" gasped Aunt Pasha.

"He did it all himself," said Shurik in a deep bass. "He got his foot in the wheel."

Korostelev came out and stared.

"Made a thorough job of it," he observed.

Seryozha cried bitterly.

"Cheer up, we'll get it mended," said Korostelev. "We'll take it to the workshop, they'll make it as good as new."

But Seryozha only hung his head and went to cry in Aunt
Pasha's room. Korostelev was just saying it to comfort him. How
could anyone ever put all those pieces together so as to have
that beautiful gleaming bicycle again, just as it had been? To
ride on and ring the bell, with spokes that sparkled in the sunshine? No, it was impossible, quite impossible! It was gone,
gone for ever! . . .

Seryozha mourned all day, he found no joy even in the
phonograph which Korostelev put on specially for him. The
whole street rang with the merry music; Seryozha heard it too,
but did not listen, he was deep in his own sad thoughts and
there was no gleam of brightness in life.

But what do you think? They really did mend the bicycle.
Korostelev hadn't been making it all up after all! The mechanic
at the Bright Shore Farm mended it. Only the bigger children
mustn't ride it, that mechanic said, or it would break again. So
after that only Seryozha and Shurik rode, and Lida when there
were no grown-ups about; but Lida was thin and not so very
heavy, let her ride.

Seryozha learned to ride splendidly, he even learned to
freewheel down a hill with his arms folded, as he had seen
a trick cyclist do. But for some reason he no longer felt that
wonderful joy of possession, the breathtaking delight of those
first blissful hours. . . .

And then he got tired of the bicycle. It stood there in the
kitchen with its red lamp and silver bell, handsome, all in order,
but Seryozha went about his various affairs on foot, indifferent
to its splendor. He was tired of it, that was all, and there was
nothing you could do about it.

6

What a lot of unnecessary words grown-ups used! For instance,
Seryozha happened to upset his tea. And Aunt Pasha said:
"What a careless boy you are! I can never wash tablecloths fast
enough for you! You're not a baby any more!"

All those words were unnecessary, in Seryozha's opinion. In
the first place he had heard them a hundred times already. And
besides he knew himself that he oughtn't to spill his tea; as soon
as it was spilled he knew at once he'd done wrong and felt sorry.
He was so ashamed he only wanted her to take the wet cloth
away as quickly as possible, before anybody saw it. But she kept
on talking and talking.

"You never seem to think that somebody washed that
cloth and starched it and ironed it and that it's all work for
somebody. . . ."

"I didn't mean to do it," Seryozha explained. "The cup sort

of slipped out of my hand."

"The cloth's old," Aunt Pasha went on implacably, "I mended and mended it, a whole evening I sat over it. Look at all the work it was."

Just as though you could spill all you wanted on a new tablecloth.

And Aunt Pasha would end indignantly: "Didn't mean to do it—I should think not, indeed! A pretty thing it would be, if you did it on purpose!"

It was the same thing when Seryozha broke anything. But when they broke glasses or plates themselves, that was quite all right.

And then there was the way Mummy always made him say "please," when the word didn't even mean anything.

"It means you're asking politely," said Mummy. "If you ask me for a pencil, you must say 'please' to show it's a request."

"Why, didn't you understand I was asking for a pencil?" asked Seryozha.

"Yes, I understood, but without 'please' it's not polite, it's not the way well-brought-up little boys talk. What does it sound like—'Give me a pencil!' It's quite different if you say: 'Give me a pencil, please,'—that's polite, and I'm glad to give it to you."

"And if I don't say 'please' will you be sorry to give it to me?"

"I shan't give it to you at all," said Mummy.

All right, "please," Seryozha would give them their "please." Their ideas might be queer, but they were strong, they ruled children, they could give Seryozha a pencil or not give it to him, just as they liked.

Korostelev, now, he didn't bother about little things, never even noticed whether Seryozha said "please" or not.

And when Seryozha was busy in his own corner and mustn't be disturbed, Korostelev never interrupted his play, never said stupid things like "Come here, let me kiss you," as Lukyanych did when he came home from work. Lukyanych would kiss Seryozha, pricking him with his rough beard and then give him a chocolate or an apple. That was very nice, of course, but why did he have to interrupt a person's play, which was much more important than the apple? Seryozha could have eaten the apple afterward.

All sorts of people came to the house, usually to see Korostelev. The one who came the most often was Uncle Tolya. He was young and handsome with long black eyelashes and white teeth and a shy smile. Seryozha looked at him with fascinated respect, because Uncle Tolya could make up poetry. When they asked him to read his latest verses, he would look uncomfortable at first and refuse, then he would get up, go to the other side of the room, and recite.

He'd made up poems about all sorts of things—about war and peace, about the collective farms, about the fascists, about spring, and about some woman with blue eyes whom he waited and waited for and simply couldn't go on waiting for, but all the same she didn't come. Wonderful poems! Just as smooth and musical as the ones in books. Before he began to recite, Uncle Tolya would cough and push his black hair back, then he would recite in a loud voice, looking up at the ceiling. Everybody would praise him and Mummy would pour out tea for him. Then while they were having tea they would talk about sick cows—Uncle Tolya cured the cows at the Bright Shore Farm when there was anything wrong with them.

But it wasn't everybody who was so interesting and so nice. There was Uncle Pyotr, for instance—Seryozha tried to keep out of his way. He had a nasty face and a smooth pink bare head like a celluloid ball. And he had a nasty kind of laugh too—"He-he-he!" Once when he was sitting with Mummy on the veran-da—Korostelev was not there—Uncle Pyotr called Seryozha and gave him a chocolate—a wonderful big chocolate wrapped up in paper. Seryozha politely said: "Thank you," opened the paper, and found there was nothing inside. It was empty. Seryozha felt ashamed—of himself for having believed in it, and of Uncle Pyotr for having deceived him like that. And Seryozha could see Mummy felt ashamed, she had believed it too.

"He-he-he-he!" sniggered Uncle Pyotr.

Then Seryozha said without anger, regretfully: "Uncle Pyotr, you're silly."

He was sure Mummy thought the same. But she cried: "What do you mean by that? Apologize to Uncle Pyotr this very minute!"

Seryozha stared at her in surprise.

"You heard what I said?" asked Mummy.

He did not answer. Then she took his hand and led him into the house.

"Don't you dare come near me," she said. "I don't want to talk to such a rude boy."

She stood a moment, waiting for him to say he was sorry, to ask her to forgive him. But he pressed his lips together and looked away with eyes turned sad and cold. He did not feel he had done wrong. Why should he apologize? He had simply said what he thought.

She went away. He trailed into his room and began turning over his toys, unconsciously trying to forget what had hap-pened. His fingers trembled. As he turned over the pictures cut out of old playing cards, he tore the head off a lady in black. . . .

Why had Mummy stood up for that silly Uncle Pyotr? There she was, talking and laughing with him; but she didn't want to talk to Seryozha. . . .

In the evening he heard her telling Korostelev all about it.

"Well, he was right," said Korostelev. "That's what I call fair criticism."

"But how can you let a child criticize grown-ups?" Mummy objected. "If children start criticizing us, how can we educate them? A child must respect grown-ups."

"But why on earth should he respect that ass?" said Korostelev.

"He must. It shouldn't even occur to him that a grown-up could be an ass. Let him wait till he's Pyotr Ilyich's age before criticizing him."

"To my mind," said Korostelev, "if it's a question of sense, he's a lot brighter than Pyotr Ilyich already. And it can't be right to punish a child for calling a fool—a fool."

About criticism Seryozha didn't understand much, but that remark about a fool he understood splendidly and felt very grateful to Korostelev.

In general, Korostelev was all right, it was queer to think there had been a time when he had not lived with Seryozha, when he had lived with Granny Nastya and Great-Granny, and only came to call on them now and then.

He took Seryozha down to the river to bathe and taught him to swim. Mummy was afraid Seryozha would drown, but Korostelev laughed at her. He took the rails off the sides of Seryozha's bed. Mummy was afraid Seryozha would fall out of bed and hurt himself, but Korostelev said:

"What if he has to go on a long train journey? And sleep on the top berth? Let him learn to sleep like a grown-up."

So now Seryozha did not have to climb over the rail in the mornings and evenings. He undressed sitting on the edge of his bed. And slept like a grown-up.

Once, they told him, he did fall out of bed. It was in the middle of the night, they heard him fall and put him back into bed again. In the morning they told him what had happened. But he couldn't remember it and he wasn't hurt anywhere. And if he wasn't hurt and didn't even remember it, then it didn't count.

Then there was that time he fell down in the yard, scraped the skin of his knees so that it bled, and came home crying. Aunt Pasha threw up her hands and ran for a bandage. But Korostelev said: "Cheer up. You'll be all right in a minute. What if you become a soldier and get wounded some time; what then?"

"When you were wounded, didn't you cry?" asked Seryozha.

"How could I? Everybody would have laughed at me. We're men and that's that."

Seryozha stopped crying and to show his manliness even laughed. And when Aunt Pasha came with the bandage, he said gaily: "Go on, bandage it up, it doesn't hurt a bit."

Korostelev told him about the war. And after that, Seryozha felt proud as he sat beside Korostelev at the table. If there was a war, who would go and fight? Why, he and Korostelev. That was their job in life. And Mummy and Aunt Pasha and Lukyanych would stay at home and wait till they won the war, that was their job.

7

Zhenka was an orphan, he lived with his aunt. The aunt had a daughter, Zhenka's cousin. During the day she went to work and in the evening she ironed her dresses. She would fuss about in the yard with a big charcoal iron. She'd blow on it and spit on it and put the samovar pipe over it to make it burn hotter. And she'd have her hair twisted round bits of metal so it looked as if her head was covered with little sausages.

When she'd finished ironing her dress, she'd put it on and let down her hair and then go to the club to dance. And the next evening she'd start fussing about with the iron all over again.

The aunt worked too. She complained that she was both cleaner and messenger, but they only paid her as cleaner, and the rules said there ought to be a paid messenger. She would stand a long time with her buckets by the water tap at the corner telling the other women how she'd put the manager in his place and what she'd written in the complaint she'd sent in.

Zhenka's aunt was always cross with him because he ate a lot and didn't do anything to help in the house.

But he didn't want to do anything. He got up in the morning, ate what was left out for him, and then went to join the other boys.

He would spend the whole day in the street or with neighbors. Aunt Pasha always gave him something to eat when he came. A little while before his aunt came back from work, Zhenka would go home and sit down to his lessons. He had a lot of holiday homework to do because he was behind the others. He had stayed two years in the second grade and two years in the third, and he was being kept back a second year in the fourth too. When Zhenka first went to school Vaska had been quite small, but now Vaska had caught up with him, although Vaska, too, had doubled the third grade.

And Vaska was even taller than Zhenka now, and stronger, too.

At first the teachers used to worry about Zhenka, they would send for his aunt or go to see her. But she would say: "He's my curse, do what you like with him, he's eaten me out of house and home if you want to know."

Then she would complain to the women: "They tell me to give him a special corner for himself, to do his lessons. It's not a corner he wants, it's the stick, only I'm sorry for him because he's my dead sister's son."

The the teachers stopped coming. And they even praised Zhenka—a very orderly, well-behaved boy, they said; others talked during lessons, but he always sat quietly; only it was a pity he was absent so often and didn't know anything.

They gave Zhenka top marks for conduct and for singing, too. But for everything else his marks were as bad as they could be.

In front of his aunt Zhenka pretended to work at his lessons so that she shouldn't scream at him so much. When she came home he would be sitting at the kitchen table piled high with dirty dishes and greasy rags, writing down figures, doing his arithmetic.

"What d'you think you're doing there, you basilisk?" she'd start, "You haven't brought the water in or fetched the kerosene. How long have I got to put up with you?"

"I've been doing my lessons." said Zhenka.

His aunt would scold, he would sigh reproachfully, put down his pen, and pick up the kerosene can.

"Are you laughing at me or what?" his aunt would scream in a frenzy. "The shop's shut now, and well you know it, you crafty devil."

"All right, it's shut now," Zhenka would agree. "Then why are you shouting?"

"Go and chop the wood!" She would scream with such fury, it sounded as though her throat would burst. "Get out, and don't come back without the wood!"

She would snatch up the buckets from the bench and waving them about furiously, rush off screaming to get the water, while Zhenka went unhurriedly to the shed to chop the wood.

His aunt was not telling the truth when she called him lazy. He wasn't, not at all. If Aunt Pasha asked him to do something, or one of the children, he would do it at once. And if people praised him he tried his very best to do it well. One day he and Vaska together chopped and stacked a whole cubic yard of wood, a huge pile.

He wasn't stupid either, whatever they said. When Seryozha was given a meccano set, Zhenka and Shurik made such a railway signal that the boys came all the way from Kalinin Street to look at it. It had red and green lights. Shurik helped a good bit, of course—he knew a lot about machines, because his father was the truck driver, Timokhin, but it wasn't Shurik who thought of taking colored lamps from Seryozha's New Year Tree and putting them on the signal; that was Zhenka's idea.

Zhenka made little men and animals out of Seryozha's plasticine—they weren't bad, quite lifelike. Seryozha's mother saw them and bought him a box of plasticine for himself. But his aunt said she wouldn't let him waste his time on such rubbish and threw the plasticine in the cesspool.

Zhenka learned to smoke from Vaska. He had no money to buy cigarets, so he smoked Vaska's, and if he saw a cigaret end lying in the street he picked it up and smoked it. Seryozha was sorry for him, so he, too, picked up any ends he saw lying about and gave them to Zhenka.

Zhenka never put on airs with the small kids as Vaska did, he was ready to play with them any time, at anything they liked, soldiers or militiamen or lotto. But because he was the oldest he always wanted to be the general or the chief of militia. And when they played lotto and he won, he was glad; but if he lost, he sulked.

He had a kind face with a big mouth, and big ears that stood out, and tails of hair down his neck because his hair wasn't cut very often.

One day Vaska and Zhenka went to the little wood and took Seryozha with them. There they made a fire to bake potatoes. They had brought the potatoes, some salt, and some spring onions. The fire burned badly, with a lot of acrid smoke.

Vaska said to Zhenka: "Let's talk about what you're going to do."

Zhenka sat hugging his knees; his narrow trousers had slipped up showing his thin legs. He gazed without blinking at the dense column of gray and yellow smoke rising from the fire.

"You've got to finish school, whether you like it or not," Vaska continued; you would have thought from his tone that he had top marks in everything and was at least five grades higher than Zhenka. "What good will you be to anyone without an education?"

"You're quite right," Zhenka agreed. "I'm no good to anyone if I haven't got that."

He picked up a stick and stirred the fire to make it burn more brightly. The damp twigs hissed, the sap oozed out, and they caught fire slowly. Birch, aspen, and alder trees grew thickly round the glade where the boys were sitting. In their games this thicket was always the primeval forest. In the spring there were a lot of lilies of the valley, and in the summer a lot of mosquitoes.

Now most of the mosquitoes had retreated before the smoke, but a few of the bolder ones penetrated through it and bit, and then the boys loudly slapped their legs and faces.

"Put your aunt in her place, that's all," Vaska advised.

"Just you try it," Zhenka said. "Try putting her in her place!"

"Take no notice of her, then."

"I don't. But I'm sick of her. You know yourself, she's always at me."

"And Lyuska—what about her, is she all right?"

"Yes, she's all right. She's going to get herself married."

"Who'll she marry?"

"Oh, somebody or other. She's got an idea she'll marry an officer, but there aren't any here. Maybe she'll go away somewhere where there are officers."

The fire burned up, it conquered the damp and caught a pile of twigs and leaves, mischievously putting out flaming tongues. Something snapped like a shot. The smoke had all gone.

"Go and get some dry twigs to put on the fire," Vaska told Seryozha

Seryozha ran off to do as Vaska said. When he came back, Zhenka was talking, while Vaska listened carefully.

'I'll live like a lord," said Zhenka. "Just think—you come back to the hostel in the evening, there's your bed waiting and a cupboard beside it. You can lie there and listen to the radio or play checkers, and nobody shouts at you. . . . Lecturers come, and entertainers. . . . And they give you supper at eight o'clock."

"Yes," said Vaska, "it sounds fine. But will they take you?"

"I'll send in an application. Why shouldn't they take me? I'm sure they will."

"How old are you?"

"I was fourteen last week."

"Your aunt's not against it?"

"No, she's not against it, only she's afrad if I go away I won't help her later on."

"Oh, to hell with her," said Vaska, and added a few more bad words.

"I'll go away anyway, I guess," said Zhenka.

"You've got to make a decision and act on it," said Vaska. "You keep saying you guess, but the school year'll start soon and then it'll be the same thing all over again."

"Yes, I guess I'll make up my mind and do it," said Zhenka. "You know, Vaska, I often think about it. And when I remember that it'll soon be the beginning of September—ugh, I feel really bad."

"I don't wonder," said Vaska.

They talked about Zhenka's plans until the potatoes were

baked. Then they ate them, burning their fingers, their teeth crunching the juicy stems of the onions, and lay down to sleep. The sun began to sink, the trunks of the birches turned pink, and shadows spread over the glade while the fire still smoldered under the gray ash. The boys had told Seryozha to drive away the mosquitoes, so he sat conscientiously waving a twig over them as they slept, thinking as he did so: will Zhenka really give money to his aunt when he's working? Why, all she does is scream at him! That wouldn't be fair. But soon he, too, fell asleep, snuggled in between Vaska and Zhenka. He dreamed of officers and of Lyuska, Zhenka's cousin.

Zhenka was not particularly resolute by nature, he would sooner daydream than act, but the first of September was near, the redecorating was finished at school and the children were already going there to get their textbooks and exercise books. Lida was boasting about her new uniform. The new school year with all its troubles was just round the corner, and Zhenka made up his mind. If the technical school would not take him, then perhaps a factory school would, he said. Anyway, he was going.

Most people thought he was right and tried to help him. The school gave him a recommendation, and Korostelev and Mummy gave him some money, and even his aunt baked buns for the journey.

The morning he left, his aunt said good-bye to him without screaming and asked him not to forget all she had done for him. He said: "All right, Aunt," and even added: "Thank you." After that she went to the office where she worked, and he started preparing for the journey.

His aunt had given him a wooden suitcase painted green. She had hesitated for a long time, she didn't want to part with it, but all the same she gave it to him in the end, though she said: "It's like cutting off my hand." In that suitcase Zhenka put his shirt, a pair of socks all holes, a worn towel, and the buns. The children watched him pack. Seryozha suddenly rushed off and came back holding the railway signal with the green and red lamps. Everyone had liked it so much; it had not been taken apart; it had stood on the table and had been shown to visitors.

"Take it with you," he told Zhenka. "Take it, I don't want it, it just stands there."

"What'll I do with that?" said Zhenka, looking at the signal. "I'll have fifteen kilograms to carry as it is."

Seryozha rushed away again and came back with a box.

"Take this, then," he said excitedly. "You'll be able to make things there. It's quite light."

Zhenka took the box and opened it. It held pieces of plasticine. Zhenka looked pleased.

"All right," he said, "I'll take it." He put the box in his suitcase.

Timokhin had promised to take Zhenka to the station. It was thirty kilometers away; there was no railway line to the town yet. . . . But just the evening before, Timokhin's truck had gone on strike. There was something wrong with the engine, Shurik said, it was being repaired, and Timokhin was asleep.

"It doesn't matter," said Vaska. "You can get a lift."

"You could go on the bus," said Seryozha.

"Clever, aren't you," Shurik objected. "He'd have to pay for the bus."

"I'll go to the road and get a lift," said Zhenka. "Someone'll take me."

Vaska gave him a packet of cigarets. But he had no matches, so Zhenka took his aunt's. Then they all went out of the house. Zhenka padlocked the door and put the key under the steps. They set off. The suitcase weighed like lead—not because of what was in it, it was heavy in itself. Zhenka carried it first in one hand, then in the other. Vaska carried Zhenka's coat, and Lida carried little Victor. She thrust out her stomach to take part of the weight and kept shaking him, saying: "Be quiet, can't you! What d'you want now?"

It was very windy. They went to the highway that ran past the town. The dust rose in whirling columns and got into their eyes. The grayish grass and faded cornflowers by the roadside were trembling, flattened down by the wind. Round white clouds sailed calmly in the blue sky overhead, not threatening in the least, but further away heavy black ones advanced rapidly, reaching out ragged claws; it was as if the wind came from them, carrying a sharp freshness through the dust. The children stopped, set down the suitcase and waited for a truck. But, as though for spite, they were all going the wrong way, from the station to the town. At last one appeared going the way they wanted. It was loaded with boxes, but there was nobody beside the driver. The children raised their hands. The driver looked out and drove past. Then a black car appeared, almost empty— there was only one man in it besides the driver. But it went past, too.

"Oh, hell!" Shurik swore.

"What d'you all want to put up your hands for," said Vaska. "That's crazy. They think the whole lot want to go! Let Zhenka get in front and put up his hand. Here's another old trundler."

The children did as he said. When it came close nobody put up their hands except Zhenka and Vaska, who went against his own orders. Big boys always do the things they tell the little ones not to do.

The car shot past and then stopped. Zhenka ran after it with his suitcase and Vaska with the coat. The door clicked, Zhenka disappeared inside and Vaska after him. Then a cloud of dust rose and hid everything. When it settled there was neither Zhenka nor Vaska and the car was already a long way off, almost out of sight. So that's what Vaska had had up his sleeve. He'd not told anyone that he was going to the station with Zhenka.

The other children went home. The wind was now at their backs, pushing them forward and slapping strands of Seryozha's long hair stingingly in his face.

"She never made him any clothes," said Lida. "He always wore rags."

"Her manager's an old devil," said Shurik. "He doesn't want to pay her as messenger. And she's a right to it."

But Seryozha thought, as the wind pushed him along—how lucky Zhenka is, he'll ride in a train. Seryozha had never been in a train in all his life. . . . The sky became dark and suddenly a a quick savage flash jabbed across it, then thunder rolled like guns overhead, and the next moment down came the rain. . . . The children ran, slipping in the dust that turned to mud at once, while the rain lashed them till they bent nearly double, the lightning danced over the whole sky and through the rolling, crashing thunder they could hear little Victor's whimpers. . . .

So Zhenka was gone. Soon afterward two letters arrived, one for Vaska and the other for Zhenka's aunt. Vaska told nobody what Zhenka had written and acted as though the letter contained all sorts of secrets between men. But the aunt kept nothing back, she went about telling everyone that Zhenka, God be praised, had been accepted at the technical school. He lived in the hostel. They'd given him a suit. "So I've got him settled after all," said the aunt. "He'll get on now, and who's to thank for it but me!"

Zhenka had never been a leader, and the children soon got used to doing without him. When they remembered him they were glad he was so well off, that he had a cupboard by his bed and entertainers coming to amuse him. If they played soldiers, Shurik and Seryozha took turns at being the general.

8

Great-Granny was ill and they took her to the hospital. For two days everyone said they ought to go and see her, and on the third day, when only Seryozha and Aunt Pasha were at home, Granny Nastya came. She was even straighter and sterner than usual, and she carried her black bag with the zip fastener. After a few words of greeting, Granny Nastya sat down and said: "My mother. She's dead."

Aunt Pasha crossed herself and said: "Peace be on her soul!"

Granny Nastya took a plum from her bag and gave it to Seryozha.

"I took some things for her, and they told me she'd died two hours ago. Eat it, Seryozha, it's washed. They're good plums. Mother was fond of them; she'd put them in her tea, let them get soft and then eat them. Here, you can have them all." She poured the plums out on the table.

"Not all those, keep some for yourself," said Aunt Pasha.

Granny Nastya began to cry.

"I don't want them. I bought them for Mother."

"How old was she?" asked Aunt Pasha.

"Eighty-two. People live longer than that. Some live to ninety."

"Have a glass of milk," said Aunt Pasha. "It's nice and cold, I've just brought it up from the cellar. One has to eat, whatever happens."

"All right, thanks," said Granny Nastya; she blew her nose and began to drink the milk. When she had finished it she said: "I can see her just as if she were standing there. She was so wise, and she'd read so many books, it was amazing . . . the house is empty now. . . . I'll take lodgers."

"Eh, dear me," sighed Aunt Pasha.

Seryozha filled his hands with plums, went out into the yard, into the warm sunshine, and pondered. If Granny Nastya's house was empty, that meant it was Great-Granny who was dead. They had lived together. So Great-Granny had been Granny Nastya's mother. Now, thought Seryozha, there'd be no one to nag and scold him when he went to see Granny Nastya.

He knew what death was. He'd seen a mouse that Zaika the cat had killed; before that the mouse had run about and Zaika had played with it, then suddenly Zaika had made a spring and jumped back again, and the mouse had stopped running, and Zaika had eaten it, lazily shaking his fat face. . . . And Seryozha had seen a dead kitten, like a bit of dirty fur; he had seen butterflies, their wings torn and transparent, with all the dust rubbed off; he had seen dead fish thrown up on the bank, and a dying chicken on the kitchen table. Its neck was long, like a goose's, and there was a black hole with blood dripping from it into a basin. Neither Aunt Pasha nor Mummy could kill chickens, they always asked Lukyanych to do it. He shut himself up with the chicken in the shed, the chicken squawked and Seryozha ran away not to hear it. When he went through the kitchen later he would glance with disgust and involuntary curiosity at the blood dripping down. They told him he needn't be sorry for the chicken any more. Aunt Pasha would pluck it with her large, skillful hands and say comfortingly: "It can't feel anything now."

Seryozha had once touched a dead sparrow. It was so cold that he snatched his hand away, frightened. It was as cold as an icicle, the poor sparrow—lying there with its claws up, under a lilac bush which was warmed by the sun.

Stillness and cold—that was what death must mean.

When they found the sparrow Lida said: "Let's have a funeral!"

She brought a cardboard box, lined it with rags, made a little pillow out of some more scraps, and then put lace round it. Lida really could do a lot of things, you had to admit that. She told Seryozha to dig a hole. Then they lowered the box with the sparrow inside it into the hole, put the lid on and covered it with earth. Linda smoothed over the tiny mound and stuck a twig in it.

"See what a fine funeral we've given him," she crowed. "He never dreamed of having one like this!"

Vaska and Zhenka wouldn't take any part in the funeral. They sat a little way off, smoking, watching morosely. But they didn't laugh at it.

People sometimes died, too. Then they were put in long boxes called coffins and carried along the street. Seryozha had seen it from a distance. But he had never seen a person who was dead.

Aunt Pasha filled a soup plate with boiled rice, white and fluffy, and arranged red candies round the edge. In the middle, on top of the rice, she put some more candies, in a pattern that wasn't quite a flower and wasn't quite a star.

"Is that a star?" Seryozha asked.

"It's a cross," Aunt Pasha answered. "We're going to Great-Granny's funeral."

She washed Seryozha's face, hands and feet, put on his socks and shoes, his sailor suit and sailor cap with the ribbons—an awful lot of things she put on him! She, too, wore something special—her black lace scarf. She tied up the plate of rice in a white napkin. She had a bunch of flowers too, and she gave Seryozha some flowers to carry—two dahlias with thick stems.

Vaska's mother was going for water with buckets on the yoke. Seryozha called out: "Good morning! We're going to Great-Granny's funeral."

Lida stood at the gate holding little Victor. Seryozha called to her too: "I'm going to Great-Granny's funeral!" and she followed them with looks of envy. He knew she wanted to come but felt she couldn't because he was in his best clothes and she was in a dirty frock and barefoot. He was sorry for her, so he turned and called back: "You come as well! It's all right!"

But Lida was too proud; she said nothing and she didn't go with them, she only stood watching them till they turned the corner.

They went along one street, then another. It was very hot. Seryozha got tired of carrying the two heavy flowers.

"You hold them; it'll be better," he said to Aunt Pasha. She took them.

Then he began to stumble. He'd trip and stumble when there weren't any stones at all.

"What's the matter with you?" asked Aunt Pasha.

"It's because I'm so hot," he said. "Take all these off. I want to go in just my trousers."

"Don't be silly," said Aunt Pasha. "Who'd ever let you go to a funeral with only trousers on? We're nearly at the stop, then we'll get on the bus."

That cheered Seryozha and he stepped out more readily along the endless road, past the endless fences with trees hanging over them.

Some cows were coming toward them in a cloud of dust.

"Hold my hand," said Aunt Pasha.

"I want a drink," said Seryozha.

"Don't be silly," said Aunt Pasha. "You don't want a drink at all."

She was wrong, he really did want a drink. But when she said that, he stopped wanting it so badly.

Seryozha and Aunt Pasha took the bus on the square and sat down in the places reserved for children. Seryozha didn't often ride in a bus, so it was a treat for him. He knelt on the seat, looking out of the window and glancing at his neighbor. The neighbor was a fat boy, smaller than Seryozha, and was sucking a sugar cock on a stick. His cheeks were smeared with it. He looked back at Seryozha; that look said: "I've got a sugar cock and you haven't, aha!" Then the conductor came up to them.

"Do I have to pay for the child?" asked Aunt Pasha.

"Come and be measured, little boy," said the conductor.

There was a black mark on the side of the bus for measuring children. If they had grown as high as that mark, they had to be paid for. Seryozha raised himself a little on tiptoe.

"Yes, pay for him," said the conductor.

Seryozha looked triumphantly back at the boy. "They don't take a ticket for you, but they do for me, aha!"—that look said. But the boy came off best in the end, because when it was time for Seryozha and Aunt Pasha to get out, he went on further.

In front of them was a white stone gateway, and beyond it
were long white houses, with young trees round them; and the
tree trunks were painted white, too. People in dark blue dressing gowns were walking about or sitting on benches.

"What's this?" asked Seryozha.

"It's the hospital," Aunt Pasha answered.

They went to the very last house, turned a corner, and
Seryozha saw Korostelev, Mummy, Lukyanych, and Granny
Nastya. They were all standing by a big open door. There were
three old women with kerchiefs on their heads as well.

"We came in the bus!" Seryozha announced.

Nobody answered, but Aunt Pasha said: "Ssssh!" and he
understood, he mustn't talk here. They were talking themselves,
but quietly. Mummy said to Aunt Pasha: "Why on earth did you
bring him?"

Korostelev stood holding his cap in hand, his face quiet and
thoughtful. Seryozha looked into the doorway. There were
steps inside leading down to a cellar, and the darkness below
breathed out a cold dampness. . . . All went slowly forward and
down the stairs, Seryozha with them.

After the daylight it seemed quite dark at first in the cellar.
Then Seryozha saw a broad bench running along the wall, a
white ceiling, and a rough cement floor. High up on trestles
stood a wooden coffin with muslin round the edges. It was cold
and there was a smell of earth. Granny Nastya went with long
steps to the coffin and bent down over it.

"Oh dear, what's this?" said Aunt Pasha under her breath.
"Look how the hands are laid. Dear Lord in Heaven—down by
her sides."

"She wasn't a believer," said Granny Nastya, straightening up.

"That makes no difference," said Aunt Pasha. "She isn't a
soldier to appear before the Lord like that." Turning to the old
women she added: "What were you thinking of!"

The old women sighed. . . . Seryozha could see nothing from
below. He climbed on to the bench, stretched out his neck, and
looked down into the coffin.

He had thought Great-Granny was in the coffin. But it was
something strange that lay there. *It* was a bit like Great-
Granny—the same sunken mouth and bony chin sticking up.
But it wasn't Great-Granny. He didn't know what *it* was. People
never have eyes closed like *that*. Even when they're asleep, their
eyes are closed differently.

It was most awfully long. But Great-Granny had been quite
short. *It* was enveloped in cold, gloom, and quietness, which
made those who stood round speak in whispers. Seryozha felt
frightened. But if *it* had suddenly come to life, that would have

been even more frightening. . . . At the thought of it Seryozha screamed.

He screamed, and as though in answer, from above, from the sunshine, came a sharp, live sound, familiar and gay—a motor horn. . . . Mummy picked Seryozha up and carried him out of the cellar. A truck stood by the door with its side down. Men walked about smoking. Aunt Tosya was at the wheel; she was the driver who had brought Korostelev's things when he came to live with them; she worked at the Bright Shore Farm and sometimes came to fetch Korostelev. Mummy put Seryozha down on the seat beside her and told him to stay there and shut the door.

"So you've come to see Great-Granny buried, have you?" asked Aunt Tosya. "Were you fond of her?"

"No," said Seryozha honestly. "I didn't like her."

"Why've you come, then?" asked Aunt Tosya. "If you didn't like her, then you shouldn't have come."

The light and the voices had dispelled the horror, but Seryozha could not forget it all at once, he wriggled uneasily, looked about him, thought hard, and at last said: "What does it mean—to appear before the Lord?"

Aunt Tosya laughed.

"It's a way of talking."

"But why do they talk that way?"

"Old people talk that way. Don't listen to it. It's silly."

They sat there in silence. Then Aunt Tosya narrowed her green eyes and said: "Yes, we'll all be there some day."

There—where? thought Seryozha. But he felt no desire for more exact information, so he did not ask. When he saw the coffin carried up from the cellar he looked the other way. It was a relief that the lid was on the coffin now. But it was very unpleasant indeed to know that it was on the truck.

At the cemetery they took the coffin off and carried it away. Seryozha and Aunt Tosya did not get out, they stayed in the driver's seat. All round he could see crosses and wooden pillars with red stars on them. Reddish ants kept crawling out of a place where the earth had cracked on a mound nearby. On other mounds weeds grew. . . . Could she have meant the cemetery when she said we'll all be there some day? thought Seryozha. Then the ones who had gone away came back without the coffin and the truck started off.

"Have they covered her with earth?" asked Seryozha.

"Yes, they've covered her up," said Tosya.

When they got home he found Aunt Pasha had stayed at the cemetery with the old women.

"Pasha likes to keep the old funeral customs," said Lukyanych.

"Well, after all, she does the baking."

Granny Nastya took off her kerchief and smoothed her hair. "Well, let them hold their wake if they must."

They were talking in their ordinary voices again, they even smiled.

"Our Aunt Pasha is full of superstitions," said Mummy.

They sat down to table. But Seryozha could not eat. The very thought of it nauseated him. He sat quietly, looking at the faces of the grown-ups. He tried not to remember *it*, but *it* kept coming back to him—long, frightening, enveloped in cold and the smell of earth.

"Why did she say we'll all be there?" he asked.

The grown-ups broke off their talk and turned to him.

"Who said that?" asked Korostelev.

"Aunt Tosya."

"Don't you listen to Aunt Tosya," said Korostelev. "Why d'you want to listen to everything?"

"But shall we all die?"

They looked as uncomfortable as though he'd asked an indecent question. But he looked at them and waited for an answer. Korostelev spoke.

"No. We shan't die. Aunt Tosya can do as she likes, but we shan't die, you especially, that I'll guarantee."

"I won't ever die?" asked Seryozha.

"Never!" Korostelev promised solemnly.

Seryozha at once felt light and happy again. He got quite pink with happiness, then crimson, and started laughing. He suddenly felt most terribly thirsty—after all, he'd wanted a drink a long time ago, and then he'd forgotten. So he drank a lot of water, drank and drank, gasping with enjoyment. He had not the least doubt that Korostelev had told him the truth. How could he live knowing that he would die? And how could he fail to believe the one who told him: "You will not die."

9

They dug holes in the ground, they stood tall posts in them and fastened a wire to the posts. The wire turned and crossed Seryozha's yard, then went in through the wall of the house. And a black telephone appeared on the little table in the dining room, beside the railway signal. It was the first and only telephone on Far Street, and it belonged to Korostelev. It was for Korostelev they had dug holes in the ground, and put up posts, and fastened the wire to them. Because other people could do without a telephone, but Korostelev had to have one.

When you took off the receiver some woman you couldn't see said: "Exchange." Then Korostelev would say—like an officer giving orders: "Bright Shore!" or "Party Committee!"

or "Give me the Regional State Farm Office!" Then he would sit, swinging one long leg, talking into the telephone. And when he was doing that, nobody must disturb him, not even Mummy.

Sometimes the telephone would ring with a silvery trembling voice. Seryozha would run to it, pick it up and say: "Hullo!" Then a voice would ask him to call Korostelev. What a lot of people needed Korostelev! It wasn't often people wanted Lukyanych or Mummy, and Aunt Pasha and Seryozha—never.

Early each morning Korostelev left for the Bright Shore. Aunt Tosya sometimes brought him home for dinner. But usually not. Mummy would ring up the Bright Shore and they would tell her Korostelev had gone to one of the sections and wouldn't be back for a long time.

The Bright Shore Farm was enormous. Seryozha had never thought it could be as big as that till he went with Korostelev and Aunt Tosya one day in the car because Korostelev had some things to see to. They kept on driving and driving and driving. Great wide expanses rushed to meet the car and fell away on either side— great tall haystacks on huge sweeps of autumn meadows reaching out to where the world ended in pale lilac haze, yellow stubble, black velvet ploughland misted with the fresh green of winter crops just coming up in thin lines. Endless roads, like gray ribbons, unrolled and crisscrossed. Trucks and tractors pulling trailers ran along them.

"Where's this?" Seryozha would ask. And he always got the same answer. "The Bright Shore."

Three big groups of farm buildings stood lost in the vastness, a long way from each other— one had a fat silo tower, another big machine sheds. A drill buzzed and a welding lamp hissed in the workshop. Sparks shot up in the dark depths of the smithy and a hammer thudded. And wherever they stopped, people came out to speak to Korostelev, and he looked at everything and asked a lot of questions, gave instructions, then got back into the car and they went on. Seryozha understood now why he was always in such a hurry to go to the Bright Shore—how would they all know what to do if he didn't come and tell them?

There was no end of animals on the various farm sections— pigs, sheep, hens, and geese, but mostly cows. While the weather stayed warm the cows had grazed on the pastures; the makeshift shelters where they had spent the night in bad weather were still standing there. But now they were in the cowsheds. They stood quietly side by side, fastened to a wooden beam with chains round their horns, and they ate out of a long trough, waving their tails. They didn't behave themselves very well; every now and then someone would come and clear away the dung. Seryozha was ashamed to look at them when they

behaved so badly; he walked along the slippery planks through
the cowshed, his hand in Korostelev's, without raising his eyes.
But Korostelev took no notice of the disgrace, he slapped the
cows' spotted flanks and gave instructions.

One woman started arguing about something, but he interrupted her: "All right, that's enough. Get on with it." And the
woman stopped talking and went to do as he had said.

There was another woman in a blue cap with a pompon like
Mummy wore; at her he snapped: "Who's responsible for this?
Do I have to look after little things like that, too?"

She stood there all upset and kept saying: "I don't know how
I forgot it, how I didn't think of it. I just can't understand."

Lukyanych appeared from somewhere holding a paper. He
gave Korostelev a fountain pen and said: "Would you sign
this?" Korostelev hadn't finished scolding the woman; he said:
"All right, afterward." But Lukyanych insisted.

"Afterward is no good, they won't give it to me without your
signature, and people have to get their wages."

Think of that, now, if Korostelev didn't sign that paper, they
wouldn't get their wages!

When Seryozha and Korostelev were picking their way
among the yellow pools to the car, a young man stopped
them—a young man wonderfully clothed in short rubber boots
and a leather jacket with shining buttons.

"Dmitry Korneyevich," he said, "what shall I do now, they
won't give me a place to live, Dmitry Korneyevich!"

"What did you expect?" Korostelev snapped. "A newly built
house all ready waiting for you?"

"It means the end of my married life," the young man pleaded. "Dmitry Korneyevich, please cancel the order!"

"You ought to have thought of that before," snapped Korostelev still more sharply. "You've got a head on your shoulders.
Use it."

"But Dmitry Korneyevich, I'm asking you, as man to man, can't
you understand? I'm new to it, Dmitry Korneyevich, I didn't
understand how one thing depended on another."

"But working on the side—you understood that all right,"
said Korostelev, his face darkening. "Neglecting your own sector, deserting, to earn money on the side—you knew enough
for that!"

He turned to go. But the young man persisted.

"Dmitry Korneyevich! Dmitry Korneyevich! Think of my position. I know I was wrong. I realize it. Give me another chance.
Let me go on working here, Dmitry Korneyevich!"

"Well, all right. But remember," said Korostelev grimly, "if
it ever happens again, even once—!"

"I was a fool ever to bother with them, Dmitry Korneyevich! They only promised me a bed in a hostel, and even that wasn't certain. . . . I've had enough of them, Dmitry Korneyevich!"

"You selfish bastard," said Korostelev, "individualist, son of a bitch! For the last time—get off to your work, and to hell with you!"

"Yes, right away!" cried the young fellow eagerly and turned to go, winking at a girl with a kerchief on her head who stood nearby.

"It's not for your sake I'm doing it, it's for Tanya's. Lucky for you she's in love with you!" Korostelev called after him, and he, too, winked at the girl as he passed. And the girl and the young fellow looked after him, smiling, holding hands.

So that was Korostelev—if he'd wanted, it would have been bad for the young fellow and Tanya. But he didn't want that because he was not only all powerful, but kind too. He arranged things so that they became happy and smiling.

How could Seryozha help being proud that his Korostelev was like that?

It was quite clear, since Korostelev was put in charge of all of them, that he was wiser and better than anybody else.

10

You couldn't see the stars in summer. When Seryozha went to bed and when he woke up it was always light outside. Even if it was cloudy or raining it was still light, because the sun was shining behind the clouds. In a clear sky he could sometimes see, besides the sun, a light transparent patch like a piece of frosted glass. That was the moon, out in the daytime when no one needed it; hung up there and then melted, in the sunshine, melted away and disappeared, and only the sun was left to reign in the great vastness of the sky.

But in winter the days were short. Darkness came early. Long before suppertime Far Street with its quiet snowy gardens and white roofs lay under the stars. There were thousands of them, perhaps millions. There were big ones and little ones. And there was fine star sand heaped together in shiny patches. The big stars shone blue, white, and gold. Sirius had rays like eyelashes. And in the middle of the sky there were big stars and little stars and star dust, all whisked up into a thick, frosty-sparkling mist, a fantastic irregular band flung right across like a bridge over a street—the Milky Way.

Seryozha wanted to know all their names, but Mummy couldn't remember; she had known them once, but she'd forgotten. To make up for that, she showed him the mountains on the moon.

Nearly every day it snowed. People cleared paths, trampled
them hard, and then more snow came down and piled up big
white downy cushions over everything. The fence posts wore
white caps. There were fat white caterpillars on the branches
of the trees and round snowballs where the twigs divided.

Seryozha played with the snow, he built houses and fought
battles with it and went sledging down the hills. Then the
daylight turned lilac and died behind the timber yard. It was
evening, and Seryozha came home pulling his sledge behind
him. He stopped, flung back his head and looked with pleasure
at the familiar stars. The Great Bear had crawled almost to the
middle of the sky, its tail boldly spread out. Mars winked its
red eye.

If Mars is so big there may be people on it, thought Seryozha,
then perhaps there's a boy just like me standing there now with
a sledge just like mine, and perhaps he's called Seryozha,
too. . . . That was a wonderful thought, he wanted to share it, but
not with just anybody; some people wouldn't understand, they
often didn't; they made jokes of things, and Seryozha hated
those jokes, they offended him. So he chose a moment when
nobody else was near and told Korostelev—because Korostelev
never laughed. He didn't laugh this time, either. He thought a
moment and said: "Well, why not?"

Then for some reason he took Seryozha by the shoulders and
looked at him very seriously, almost with a certain fear.

You come home on winter evenings, tired with playing and
cold, and there's the stove burning, puffing with heat; you get
warm, sniffing a bit, while Aunt Pasha puts your trousers and felt
boots on top of it to dry. Then you sit down at the kitchen table
with the grown-ups, you drink hot milk, you listen to their talk,
and you think of how tomorrow you'll go with the others to
besiege the snow fortress that was built today.

Yes, winter's a fine thing, but it lasts too long. You get tired of
heavy clothes and biting winds, you want to run out of the
house in shorts and sandals, to bathe in the river, to lie on the
grass, to go fishing—it doesn't matter that you never catch
anything, it's fun just to be there all together, to dig for worms,
to sit with a rod and line and shout: "Look out, Shurik, you've
got a bite!"

Ugh—another blizzard, and yesterday it was thawing. You're
sick of the beastly winter.

Then tears run zigzag down the window, and instead of snow
in the street there is a thick black mess, with footpaths trodden
through it. Spring! The ice cracks on the river. Seryozha and the
other children go to see it floating down. First come big dirty

chunks, then a gray icy mush. Then the river overflows its banks, and the willows on the far bank stand in water halfway up their trunks. Everything is blue, the water and the sky, and gray and white clouds sail along the sky and along the water.

And when has the grain grown up so tall and thick in the fields beyond Far Street? How did Seryozha miss seeing it? When did the rye manage to flower and form ears? Busy living his life, Seryozha never noticed it, and now the ears have filled, ripened, and they rustle splendidly over his head when he walks along the path. The birds have brought up their fledglings, the mowing machines have gone out into the meadows to cut the flowers that made the far bank so gay. The school holidays have come round, summer is at its height, and Seryozha has forgotten all about the sky and the stars.

Korostelev called Seryozha and stood him between his knees.

"There's a question we've got to discuss," he said. "Which do you think it would be better for us to get—a little boy or a little girl?"

"A little boy," Seryozha answered at once.

"Yes, but look at it this way. Of course, two boys are better than one. But on the other hand, we've got a boy already, so perhaps we ought to get a girl now, what d'you think?"

"All right, if you like," Seryozha agreed without any great eagerness. "We could have a girl. Only a boy would be better for me to play with, you know."

"But a little girl—you'd look after her and stand up for her as her elder brother. See the boys didn't pull her hair."

"Girls pull your hair, too," Seryozha remarked. "And they pull hard." He might have told Korostelev how Lida had pulled his hair not long ago, but he didn't like telling tales. "They pull it so hard they make the boys yell."

"Yes, but ours would be quite tiny," said Korostelev. "She wouldn't pull anybody's hair."

"All the same, you know, let's have a boy," said Seryozha, after thinking it over. "A boy's better."

"Are you sure?"

"Boys don't tease and girls—that's all they ever do, tease you."

"Oh? . . . H'm. That's a point. Look here, we'll discuss it all again, shall we?"

"All right."

Mummy listened, smiling. She was sitting beside them, sewing. She'd made herself an awfully wide dressing gown, Seryozha wondered why it was so wide. But it was true, she'd got fatter. And now she had something very small in her hands, she was sewing lace round it.

"What's that you're making?" asked Seryozha.

"A baby's cap," said Mummy, "for a little boy or a little girl, whichever you both decide to get."

"Will he have a head as little as that?" asked Seryozha examining the doll's cap—that was what it looked like—and thinking: Gosh—give a good tug to hair on a head like that, and you might pull the whole head off!

"At first, yes," said Mummy, "but then he'll grow. You can see how Victor's grown. And the way you grow yourself. He'll grow just the same way."

She put the tiny cap on her hand and looked at it; her face was happy. Korostelev carefully kissed her forehead, just at the place where the soft shining hair started.

They really meant it about getting a little boy or a little girl. They bought a tiny bed and a quilt. They could use Seryozha's old bath for the little boy or girl; it was too small for him, it was a long time since he'd been able to stretch out his legs when he sat in it, but for anyone with a head to fit that cap it would be just right.

He knew where people got babies, of course—they bought them at the hospital. The hospital supplied them. One woman had bought two at once. Though why she had got two just alike he couldn't understand. People said she could only tell them apart by the mole: one had a mole on its neck and the other hadn't. It was queer, why she'd got two just the same. She'd have done better to get them different.

But Korostelev and Mummy delayed for some reason. The bed was there, but no sign of a little boy or a little girl.

"Why don't you go and buy one?" Seryozha asked Mummy.

Mummy laughed—and goodness, how fat she'd got!

"There aren't any just now. But they say they'll have some soon."

Well, that did happen sometimes. You wanted something and it wasn't there in the shop. All right, they could wait, Seryozha wasn't in any hurry.

Babies did grow slowly, whatever Mummy might say. You could see it by Victor. He'd been alive a long, long time, and still he was only eighteen months old. So how long would it take before he could play with the big children? That meant the time when a new little boy or girl would be able to play with Seryozha was so far off that you couldn't even guess at it. And until that time came he, Seryozha, would have to protect the baby and take care of it. Of course that was an honorable occupation, Seryozha knew it, but it wasn't nearly as attractive as Korostelev seemed to think. Lida found it very hard bringing up Victor—carrying him about and amusing him and punishing him. Not long ago her father and mother had gone to a wedding, but Lida had stayed at home and cried. If there hadn't been Victor, she could have gone. But with him it was like being in prison, Lida said.

But—well, all right, Seryozha was ready to help Korostelev and Mummy. They could go to work, and Aunt Pasha could boil and bake, and he, Seryozha, would take care of the helpless creature with a head like a doll's that couldn't do anything if it wasn't looked after. He'd give it gruel and put it to bed. He and Lida would go and visit each other and take the babies, it would be easier to look after them if they were together—while the babies were asleep they could play.

One morning when he got up they told him Mummy had gone to the hospital to buy a baby.

Although he had been expecting it, his heart gave a little jump. After all, it was a big event.

He expected Mummy back soon, he stood by the gate waiting for her to come round the corner with a little boy or a little girl, so he could run to meet her. Aunt Pasha called him.

"Korostelev wants you on the telephone."

He ran into the house and picked up the black receiver lying on the table.

"Hullo?" he called. Korostelev's voice answered, a laughing, delighted voice:

"Seryozha! You've got a brother! You hear me? A brother! With blue eyes! He weighs four kilograms, fine, isn't he? Are you pleased?"

"Yes . . . yes!" cried Seryozha, hesitant, confused. The telephone was silent.

"Blue eyes, takes after his father," said Aunt Pasha, wiping her eyes on her apron. "Well, the Lord be praised! It's a happy hour."

"Will they soon be home?" asked Seryozha. He was amazed and disappointed to hear that it would only be in a week or perhaps even more—because the baby would have to get used to Mummy, and they'd teach him that in the hospital.

Korostelev went to the hospital every day. They wouldn't let him go in and see Mummy, but she sent him notes. "Our boy's a beautiful baby. And unusually clever." She'd quite decided on his name—Aleksey, and they'd call him Lyonya for short. She was very bored, she missed them, she was longing to come home. She sent love and kisses to everyone, especially Seryozha.

A week passed, even more, and then one day when Korostelev left, he told Seryozha: "Wait for me, we're going to fetch Mummy and Lyonya today."

He came back in Aunt Tosya's car, carrying a great bunch of flowers. They drove to the same hospital where Great-Granny had died. They went to the first house near the gates, and suddenly they heard Mummy's voice.

"Mitya! Seryozha!"

She was looking out of an open window and waving to them. Seryozha cried: "Mummy!" She waved again and disappeared. Korostelev said she'd come out in a minute or two. But it was a long time before she came— they had time to walk up and down the path, and look into the door with a spring that screeched, and sit on a bench under a thin young tree that gave hardly any shade. Korostelev got restless, he said the flowers would be wilted before she came. Aunt Tosya left the car outside the gate and joined them. She told Korostelev it always took a long time.

At last the door screeched and Mummy came out, carrying a blue bundle. They ran to meet her and she said: "Careful, careful!"

Korostelev gave her the flowers and took the bundle. He turned back a corner of the lace edging and showed Seryozha a tiny little face, pink and important, with closed eyes. Lyonya, his brother. . . . One eye opened a little, a vague blue something peered out of the crack, then the face twisted. Korostelev said in a kind of weak voice: "Ah—you! . . ." and kissed him.

"Mitya, how can you!" said Mummy sternly.

"Why? Mustn't I?" asked Korostelev.

"He's susceptible to any infection," said Mummy. "They wear muslin masks here whenever they come near him. So please, Mitya."

"All right, I won't do it again," said Korostelev.

When they got home Lyonya was put on Mummy's bed, she unwrapped him and Seryozha could see the whole of him. But why on earth had Mummy said he was beautiful? His tummy was all swollen, and his arms and legs were inhumanly thin and insignificant, and they moved about senselessly. There was no neck to be seen at all. And nothing to show he was clever. He opened an empty toothless mouth and started to cry, a queer, complaining cry, weak and tiresome, and it went on and on.

"Now, now, my little one," said Mummy, "I know what it is, you're hungry, my boy's hungry, that's it. Just a moment, I won't be a moment."

She spoke loudly, moved quickly, and wasn't fat any more, she'd got thin in the hospital. Korostelev and Aunt Pasha tried to help her and ran as fast as they could to do all she asked.

Lyonya's diapers were wet. Mummy put on dry ones, sat down with him on her lap, unfastened her dress, and put Lyonya's mouth to her breast. He gave one last cry, seized the nipple with his lips and began to suck, choking with greed.

What a little pig, thought Seryozha.

Korostelev guessed his thought.

"He's only nine days old," he said softly. "Nine days, that's all, what can you expect of him?"

"Uhuh," Seryozha agreed, shamefaced.

"Later on he'll be a fine chap, you'll see."

But how long will that be, thought Seryozha. And how can I look after him when he's like jelly; even Mummy's careful when she touches him.

Lyonya, well fed, slept on Mummy's bed. The grown-ups sat in the dining room talking about him.

"You'll need a nurse," said Pasha. "I'll not be able to manage alone."

"No, I'll do without," said Mummy. "It's holidays now, I can look after him myself, and then I'll have him in a nursery; there are real nurses there and proper care."

That's fine, let him go to a nursery, thought Seryozha, relieved. Lida was always wishing they'd send Victor to a nursery. . . . Seryozha clambered on to the bed and sat down beside Lyonya, hoping to get a good look at him while he wasn't crying or screwing up his face. It seemed Lyonya had real eyelashes, only very short ones. The skin was soft, like velvet. Seryozha touched it with the tip of his finger.

"What are you doing?" cried Mummy, entering. It was so sudden Seryozha started and snatched away his hand.

"Get down this minute! What d'you mean by touching him with dirty hands?"

"They're clean," said Seryozha, slipping down from the bed in alarm.

"And in general, Seryozha," said Mummy, "keep away from him while he's so small. You might push him off by accident . . . you never know what can happen. And another thing—don't bring children in here; he might pick up something. In fact, let's go out of here." Mummy ended affectionately but firmly.

Seryozha followed obediently. He was very thoughtful. Nothing had turned out the way he had expected. . . . Mummy hung a shawl over the window so the light should not shine on Lyonya, followed Seryozha, and shut the door quietly.

11

Vaska had an uncle. Lida would certainly have liked to say he hadn't any uncle at all, he was making it all up, but she had to keep quiet. For there was an uncle, his photographs stood on the whatnot, between two vases of poppies made of red shavings. Uncle had been taken under a palm tree. He was all in white, and the sunshine was white too, so blindingly white that you couldn't properly see either his face or his clothes. The only things that came out really well were the palm tree and two short black shadows—one from Uncle, the other from the tree.

The face didn't matter, but it was a pity you couldn't make out how Uncle was dressed. He wasn't just Uncle, he was the captain of an oceangoing vessel. It would be interesting to see how captains of ocean vessels dressed. Vaska said the photograph had been taken in Honolulu, on the island of Oahu. Sometimes parcels came from him. Vaska's mother would say: "Kostya's sent me two more lengths."

What she called lengths were just pieces of material. But sometimes there were fine things in the parcels, too. A crocodile in a bottle of alcohol, for instance, tiny as a fish, but still—a crocodile. It could stand there in alcohol for a hundred years and it would never spoil. No wonder Vaska thought a lot of himself. Nothing that the other boys had would compare with that crocodile.

One parcel had a big shell in it, gray outside, rose-colored inside, with rosy edges open like lips; if you put your ear to it you could hear a low, even murmur as though coming from a long way off. When Vaska was feeling kind he let Seryozha listen. And Seryozha would press the shell to his ear, his eyes wide and fixed, holding his breath, listening to the quiet, unceasing murmur that came from the depths of the shell. What was it? Where did it come from? And why did it make him restless, why did he feel he could go on listening and listening?

And that Uncle, that wonderful, amazing Uncle—after seeing Honolulu and all sorts of islands, he was coming to stay with Vaska! Vaska mentioned it when he came out—mentioned it casually, keeping a cigaret in the corner of his mouth and screwing up one eye against the smoke. He mentioned it just as though it were nothing out of the ordinary. And when Shurik, after a silence, asked in a deep voice: "Which uncle? The captain?" Vaska answered: "Who else? I haven't any others."

He said "I haven't" with a kind of emphasis, as much as to say—you may have uncles who aren't captains, but not me. And all admitted that he was right.

"Will he come soon?" asked Seryozha.

"In a week or two," Vaska answered. "Well, I'm off to buy some chalk."

"What d'you need that for?" asked Seryozha.

"Mother's going to whitewash the ceiling."

Of course—with an uncle like that coming you have to have the ceiling freshly whitewashed!

"He's making it up," Lida couldn't keep quiet any longer. "There's nobody coming at all."

She moved hastily back, expecting a slap. But this time Vaska didn't even say "silly ass," he simply walked away, swinging the basket with the bag for chalk inside. And Lida was left looking silly.

They whitewashed the ceiling and papered the walls. Vaska smeared paste over the pieces of wallpaper and passed them up to his mother, and she put them on. The children peeped in from the entry—Vaska told them to keep out of the room.

"You'd get everything mixed up," he said.

Then Vaska's mother washed the floor and laid down runners. They all had to walk on the runners and keep off the floor.

"Sailors are very particular about cleanliness," said Vaska's mother.

The alarm clock was taken into the back room where Uncle was to sleep.

"Sailors do everything by the clock," said Vaska's mother.

Everyone waited for Vaska's Uncle with seething impatience. If a car turned into Far Street they held their breath—was it Uncle coming from the station? But the car would pass by, no Uncle came, and Lida was glad. She had her own peculiar joys which the others could not share.

When Vaska's mother came home from work in the evenings, she would get through her household jobs and then stand by the gate talking to the neighbors, boasting of her brother the captain. And the children would stand nearby listening.

"He's at a health resort just now," said Vaska's mother. "He's taking a cure. His heart's not too good. He was sent to the very best sanatorium, of course. Then, when he's finished his treatment, he'll come here."

"He used to be a wonderful singer," she said another time. "The way he used to sing at the club—better than Kozlovsky! Of course, he's got stout now, and short of breath, and with all the trouble in his family—you don't feel much like singing."

She lowered her voice and said something not for children to hear, "and all of them girls," she went on. "One's fair, the second dark, the third red-haired. Only the eldest's like Kostya. And he goes off to sea and worries all the time. She's got luck, having only girls. It's easier to bring up ten daugthers than one son."

The neighbors looked at Vaska.

"He's my brother, he'll be able to advise me," said Vaska's mother. "Let him decide, he's a man. I'm nearly out of my mind."

"Yes, it's difficult with a boy till you set him on his feet," sighed Zhenka's aunt.

"Depends on the boy," Aunt Pasha objected. "Look at ours. He's ever so affectionate."

"That's only while they're small," said Vaska's mother. "They're all like that when they're little. It's when they get bigger they show what they're like."

Uncle arrived late at night. In the morning the children looked into Vaska's garden and there was Uncle standing on the path, all dressed in white just like in the picture—a white tunic, white trousers with creases in front, and white shoes. And gold on the tunic. He stood there with his hands behind his back, and talked in a soft voice, slightly nasal and a very little bit breathless.

"How really lovely it is here. Beau-tiful. A real rest after the tropics. You don't know how lucky you are, Polya, to live in a place like this."

"Yes, it's not bad," said Vaska's mother.

"Ah, a starlings' box," cried Uncle yearningly. "Starlings on a birch tree! Do you remember our school reader, Polya, there was a picture in it just like this—a birch tree and a box for starlings."

"Vaska put it up," said his mother.

"A splen-did boy!" said Uncle.

Vaska was there, too, well behaved, washed clean, without his cap, his hair sleeked down, as if it were May Day.

"Come to breakfast," said Vaska's mother.

"I want to breathe some more of this air," the captain demurred. But Vaska's mother took him away. He went up the steps, big like a white tower with gold on it, and disappeared into the house. He was stout and handsome, with a kind face and a double chin. The lower part of his face was brown and his forehead white, there was a clear line where the sunburn ended.

Vaska went to the fence, where Seryozha and Shurik had their faces wedged in between the posts.

"Well," he said graciously, "what d'you want, kids?"

They only sniffed.

"He's brought me a watch," said Vaska. Yes, there was a watch on his left wrist, a real watch on a strap. He raised his hand and listened to it ticking, then wound it a bit.

"May we come in?" asked Seryozha.

"All right, come in," Vaska permitted. "But quiet, mind. And when he lies down to rest, and when the family comes, then out with you both at once. There's to be a family council."

"What's that?" asked Seryozha.

"They're going to talk about what's to be done with me," Vaska explained.

He went into the house and the boys followed him in silence and stood by the door of the room where the captain was sitting.

Uncle-captain buttered a piece of bread, put an egg in an egg cup, cracked the top with a teaspoon, carefully cut it off, and sprinkled salt on the egg. He took the salt from the saltcellar with the point of his knife. But there was something missing, he looked about, here and there, and his pale brows were knitted in suffering. At last he asked delicately, in his soft voice: "Excuse me, Polya—may I have a table napkin?"

Vaska's mother hurried away all in a fuss and brought him a clean towel. He thanked her, laid the towel across his knees, and began to eat. He bit off tiny pieces of bread, and you could hardly see at all he was chewing or swallowing. Vaska frowned, and his face expressed contending feelings—chagrin that there had been no table napkins in the house, and pride in his cultured Uncle who couldn't eat his breakfast without one.

Vaska's mother put all kinds of different foods on the table, and Uncle took a little of everything; but all the time it looked as if he was eating nothing, and Vaska's mother kept groaning: "You're not eating, you don't like it!"

"Everything's excellent," said Uncle, "but I have to keep to a diet, so don't be angry, Polya."

He refused vodka.

"I'm not allowed it. Once a day a small liqueur glass of brandy," with a graceful gesture he held up finger and thumb to show the size of the glass, "just before dinner, to assist in expanding the vessels. That's all I can have."

After breakfast he invited Vaska to go for a walk and put on his cap—also white and gold.

"Go home now," Vaska told Seryozha and Shurik.

"Oh, let's take them," said Uncle through his nose. "Splendid little boys! A charming pair of brothers!"

"We aren't brothers," said Shurik in his deep voice.

"They aren't brothers," Vaska upheld him.

"Really?" Uncle was surprised. "I thought they were. They're alike in some way—one fair, the other dark. . . . Well, not brothers, then—it doesn't matter, come for a walk."

Lida saw them going down the street. She would have run after them, but Vaska gave her a look over his shoulder; so she turned and ran with little skips in the other direction.

They walked in the woods and Uncle was enraptured by the trees. They walked through the fields and he was enraptured by the wheat. To tell the truth, they got a bit tired of his raptures.

He'd have done better to tell them about the sea and the
islands. But all the same he was wonderful. It dazzled you to
look at his gold bars and badges glittering in the sunshine. He
walked with Vaska, while Seryozha and Shurik sometimes
followed behind, and sometimes ran on ahead to admire Uncle
from in front. They came to the river. Uncle looked at his watch
and said it would be fine to have a bathe. Vaska looked at his
watch, too, and said—why not? So they undressed on the clean,
warm sand.

Seryozha and Shurik were disappointed to find that Uncle did
not wear a striped sailor's undershirt under his tunic, just an
ordinary white shirt. But when he raised his arms and pulled it
off over his head they stared, thunderstruck.

The whole of Uncle's body, from his neck to his waist, all that
broad, evenly brown body with its fat creases was thickly
covered with blue patterns. Uncle stood up and stretched, and
the boys saw they were not patterns, but pictures and words. On
his chest there was a mermaid with a fishtail and long hair; an
octopus was crawling down to her from the left shoulder, with
twisting tentacles and terrible human eyes; the mermaid
stretched her hands toward him and turned away her face
begging him not to seize her—a terrible picture! On the right
shoulder there was a long inscription, and down the right arm,
too—you might say Uncle was written all over on that side. On
the left arm, above the elbow, two doves were kissing, and over
them were a garland and a crown; below the elbow was a turnip
with an arrow through it, and underneath the name: "Musya"
in big letters.

"Oh, how grand!" Shurik said to Seryozha. "That's really
something," sighed Seryozha.

Uncle went into the water, dove, came up again with wet
hair and a happy face, snorted, and swam up against the stream.
The boys followed him, enchanted.

And how Uncle could swim! He moved through the water
as easily as if he were playing, and just as easily it supported
his massive body. He swam to the bridge, turned on his back,
and floated down again, steering with very small movements
of his feet. And the mermaid on his chest moved under the
water as though she were alive.

Then Uncle lay down to rest on the bank. He lay on the sand
on his stomach, with a blissful smile, while they examined his
back which had a skull and crossbones like the transformer
hut, and the moon and stars, and a woman in a long dress with
bandaged eyes sitting on clouds with her knees apart. Shurik
plucked up courage.

"What's that you've got on your back?" he asked.

Uncle laughed, sat up, and began brushing sand off himself.

"It's to remind me of the time when I was young and foolish," he said. "You see how it is, dear boys, once upon a time I was so foolish, I covered myself with all sorts of silly pictures, and unfortunately, it's forever."

"And what's that written on you?" asked Shurik.

"What does it matter," said Uncle, "what kind of nonsense is written on me? What matters is a man's feelings and his actions, what do you think, Vaska?"

"Yes," said Vaska.

"But the sea?" asked Seryozha. "What's it like?"

"The sea," repeated Uncle. "The sea? Well, what shall I tell you? The sea is the sea. There's nothing more beautiful than the sea. You have to see for yourself."

"And when there's a storm," said Shurik, "is it very terrible?"

"A storm is beautiful," answered Uncle. "At sea everything is beautiful." Shaking his head thoughtfully, he recited:

What does it matter, he said, which is best?
Quietest of all in the water you rest.

Then he began putting on his trousers.

After their walk he lay down to rest, and the children gathered in Vaska's Lane to talk about Uncle's tattooing.

"They do it with gunpowder," said a boy from Kalinin Street. "They make the drawing, and then they rub in the gunpowder. I read about it."

"But where could you get gunpowder?" another boy asked.

"In the shop, of course."

"Can't you see them letting you have it! They don't sell cigarets to anyone under sixteen, let alone gunpowder."

"We could get it from the hunters."

"What a hope—they won't give it to you."

"They might."

"They won't."

Then a third boy chimed in.

"They used powder in the old days. Now they do it with India ink or ordinary ink."

"Will it last if it's done with ink?"

"It will, and how!"

"Better with India ink. It'll last longer."

Seryozha listened and imagined Honolulu on the island of Oahu, where palms grow and the sunshine is blindingly bright. And snow-white captains with gold braid stand under the palm trees to be photographed. . . . And I will, too, some day, thought Seryozha. Like all those boys discussing gunpowder and ink, he believed without the faintest shadow of doubt that every-

thing in all the world was before him—including being a captain
in Honolulu. He believed it, just as he believed that he would
never die. He would try everything, see everything in a life that
would have no ending.

Toward evening he became impatient to see Vaska's uncle
again; but Uncle kept on resting and resting—he had been
traveling all night and hadn't slept. Vaska's mother ran out on
high heels, and told Aunt Pasha as she passed that she was going
for brandy. The lights went on in the house. And there was
nothing to be seen from the street except curtains and geran-
iums. Seryozha was glad when Shurik called him; in Shurik's
garden there was a linden tree, you could see everything if you
climbed it.

"He did exercises when he woke up," said Shurik, trotting
along purposefully beside Seryozha. "And when he shaved he
sprayed perfume on himself through a tube. They've had
supper now. . . . Come through the lane, or Lida'll want
to tag on."

The old linden tree grew close to the fence separating
Timokhin's kitchen garden from Vaska's garden. The fence was
close to Vaska's house, but you couldn't climb it because the
wood was rotten, it cracked and crumbled. The linden had a
hollow in it; one summer hoopoes had lived there, and now
Shurik used it to hide things better kept out of sight of the
grown-ups—cartridge cases and a magnifying glass, which he
used to burn words on fences and wooden seats.

Scraping their legs on the rough, cracked bark, the boys
climbed up and settled themselves on a twisted, knotted branch,
Shurik holding the trunk, and Seryozha holding on to Shurik.

They were up among the silkily rustling, stroking, tickling,
fresh, aromatic leaves. High overhead was the gold of sunset,
down below was the thickening dusk. A branch with dark leaves
swayed in front of Seryozha but did not hide the inside of
Vaska's house. The electric light shone brightly, and there was
Uncle-captain sitting among the family. Seryozha could hear all
they were saying.

Vaska's mother was speaking, moving her hands about.

". . . So they write a receipt for a fine of twenty-five roubles
paid by me for unseemly behavior in the street. . . ."

One woman laughed.

"I don't find it funny," said Vaska's mother. "Then two
months later they send for me to go to the militia station again
and show me a charge, and then they write down that I've paid
fifty roubles for a broken display case at the cinema."

"You tell him," said another woman, "how he had that fight
with the big boys, and how he burnt cigaret holes in the quilt

and nearly set the house on fire."

"And where does he get the money for cigarets?" asked Uncle-captain.

Vaska was sitting there, his elbow on his knee, his chin on his hand, his hair combed so that not a single hair was out of place.

"Worthless brat," said Uncle in his soft voice. "I'm asking you—where do you get the money?"

"Mother gives it to me," said Vaska with a sniff.

"Excuse me, Polya," said Uncle, "but I don't understand."

Vaska's mother broke out sobbing.

"Show me your school report book," Uncle told Vaska. Vaska got up and brought it. Uncle turned page after page, his eyes narrowed. Then he said gently: "You rascal. You good-for-nothing."

He slammed the report book on the table, took out a handkerchief and began to fan himself with it.

"Yes," he said, "it's sad. If you want to make anything of him, you must keep an ab-so-lute-ly firm hand. Look at my Nina. She's brought up my girls beau-tifully. They're well disciplined and they're learning to play the piano. . . . And why? Because she always keeps a firm hand."

"Girls are easier," chorused the relatives. "It's always easier to bring up girls than boys."

"You must remember, Kostya," said the woman who'd told tales about the quilt, "if she doesn't give Vaska money, he takes it himself from her handbag, without asking."

Vaska's mother sobbed more loudly.

"Where else can I take it?" asked Vaska. "From strangers?"

"Get out of here!" cried Uncle through his nose and stood up.

"He'll give him a beating," Shurik whispered. . . . There was a loud crack and the branch on which they were sitting fell down with a determined rustling of leaves. With it fell Seryozha carrying Shurik with him.

"Don't you dare cry!" said Shurik from the ground where he was lying.

They got up, rubbing their bumps. Vaska looked through the fence and understood everything.

"I'll give it to you for spying!" he said.

A white figure rose up behind Vaska glittering with gold in the light cast from the window.

"Give me your cigarets, blockhead," it said.

Limping, Seryozha and Shurik left the garden, but before that they saw Vaska give his uncle a packet of cigarets and they saw Uncle tear them up, break them, crush them to powder, and then take Vaska by the collar and lead him into the house. . . .

The next morning a padlock hung on the door. Lida said they'd all gone away as soon as it was light to relations on the Chkalov Collective Farm. They were away all day. And the morning after that Vaska's mother, sobbing, hung the padlock on the door again and went to work in tears. Vaska had gone away that night with his uncle. He had gone for good. Uncle had taken him to make a man out of him and send him to Nakhimov Naval School. Here was a wonderful thing that had happened to Vaska, and all because he'd taken money from his mother's handbag and broken the display case at the cinema!

"It's all those relations," Vaska's mother told Aunt Pasha. "The way they talked, it sounded as if Vaska was a real criminal. And he isn't such a bad boy, really. Remember how he chopped and stacked a whole meter of wood? And he helped me to put up the wallpaper. And what'll happen to him now, without me?"

She started to cry.

"They don't care, it's not their boy," she sobbed, "and there's never an autumn without he gets boils on his neck, and who'll bother about that now? . . ."

She couldn't see a boy wearing his cap with the peak backward without starting to cry. She'd ask Seryozha and Shurik in and talk to them about Vaska, and what he'd been like when he was small, and show them the photographs her brother the captain had given her. There were pictures of seaports, banana groves, ancient buildings, sailors on the deck, people riding elephants, a motor boat cutting through the waves, a black dancing woman with bracelets on her ankles, black children with thick lips and curly hair—strange things, things you had to ask about to know what they were, and on almost all the pictures there was the sea, stretching out endlessly till it merged with the sky, living, rippling water, with a gleaming mist of foam—and all that unknown world sang a deep, enticing song like the rosy shell when you laid it to your ear.

But Vaska's garden was silent and empty. It became a kind of public garden. You could go in and play all day—nobody shouted, nobody chased you out. The master of the garden had gone into that singing rosy world where Seryozha, too, would go some day.

12

Secret relations had come into being between Kalinin Street and Far Street. There were negotiations. Shurik went back and forth, very busy, and brought Seryozha news. His plump, sunburned legs carried him about quickly, and his black eyes darted quick looks on all sides. That was a way they had—when

Shurik got some new idea in his head his eyes always kept dart-
ing right and left, so everyone knew at once he had a new
idea. His mother worried, and his father, the truck-driver
Timokhin, threatened him with the strap. Because Shurik's
ideas were always of some mischief. So his parents were alarmed
because after all they wanted their son to be alive and well.

But Shurik didn't care a bit about the strap. What did an old
strap matter when the boys on Kalinin Street were going to
tattoo themselves! They made businesslike preparations. And
think of it—they'd got all the details out of Shurik and Seryozha,
every bit of it, what pictures Vaska's uncle had and where,
they'd made their drawings just as Shurik and Seryozha told
them, and now they didn't want to let Shurik and Seryozha in
on it. They said: "That's not for kids"—the devils. Where
was justice?

And you couldn't complain to anyone, either, you'd promised
you wouldn't say a word to anyone in the whole world—that is
to say, on Far Street. Because on Far Street there was a famous
telltale—Lida. She'd go and tell the grown-ups at once, just for
spite—for what good would it do her?—and then they'd make
a fuss, and there'd be trouble at school, you'd be called to
teacher's meetings and parents' meetings, and instead of a
businesslike operation there'd be all sorts of fuss and bother.

So because of that Kalinin Street kept its plans secret from
Far Street. But you couldn't keep much from Shurik. And besides, he'd seen the drawings. Wonderful drawings on cartridge paper and parchment paper.

"They've thought some up for themselves," Shurik told
Seryozha. "They've drawn an airplane and a whale making a
fountain, and they've written slogans. They put the sheet of
paper on you and then prick you with a pin right through it all
along the drawing. It ought to come out fine."

Seryozha shuddered. A pin!

But if Shurik could stand it, Seryozha could, too.

"Yes," he said with assumed carelessness. "It ought to come
out fine."

But the Kalinin Street boys not only refused to give Shurik
and Seryozha a whale, they wouldn't give them even the tiniest
little slogan. Shurik tried them one after the other, argued and
pleaded, but it was all no good. They just said: "Kids like you?
Are you joking? Get out."

Things looked very black indeed until Shurik managed to get
Arsenty on his side.

Arsenty was the kind of boy that all the parents held up as a
model. He always got top marks, he pored over his books, he
was clean and neat, and he was much respected. But what

mattered most was that he understood fair play.

After joking a bit he said: "After all, they do deserve something. Let's make them one letter each. Their initials. What d'you say to that?" he asked Shurik.

"No," said Shurik, "we don't agree to just one letter."

"Get out of here, then," said Valery from the fifth grade. "You won't get anything."

Shurik went, but he'd no choice, he came back again and said—all right, one letter. Only it must be made properly, not just any old how. The whole thing was to be done the next day, at Valery's, because his mother was away.

Shurik and Seryozha came at the appointed time. Lariska, Valery's sister, was sitting by the door with her embroidery. If anybody came to the house she was to say there was nobody at home. The children met in the yard by the bathhouse—boys from the fifth grade and even from the sixth, and one stout, pale girl with a very serious face and a thick, pale, pendulous lower lip. It seemed as though it was this lip that gave her such an earnest, impressive look; if she had pulled it in she wouldn't have looked earnest or impressive at all. . . . This girl—her name was Kapa—was cutting up bandages with a pair of scissors and arranging them on a stool. Kapa was a member of the hygiene commission at her school. Over the stool she had spread a white cloth.

Just inside the door of the small, smoky bathhouse with its dim window under the roof stood a broad low wooden block, and the drawings were on a bench, rolled up into tubes. All the boys picked up these drawings when they arrived, looked at them, argued gaily about them, cursing with satisfaction and choosing which they wanted. There was no quarreling because the same drawing could be used for any number of boys. Shurik and Seryozha admired the drawings from afar, but did not dare take liberties with them—those other boys were so very big and splendid and masterful.

Arsenty came straight from school, still carrying his satchel, because there had been six lessons that day. He asked to be done first because he had a lot of homework—a composition and a big chunk of geography. The others agreed, out of respect for his diligence. He put his satchel neatly on the bench, pulled off his shirt with a smile, and sat down on the block of wood, naked to the waist, his back to the door.

The big boys all surrounded him. Seryozha and Shurik were pushed out into the yard, and however much they jumped they could see nothing. The talk died down, there was a rustling and crackling of paper and a little later Valery's voice:

"Kapa! Go to Lariska and ask her for a towel."

Kapa with her serious face ran past, her lower lip shaking, brought back a towel and threw it to Valery over the intervening heads.

"Why do they want a towel?" asked Seryozha, jumping. "Shurik! What's the towel for?"

"I expect he's bleeding," said Shurik eagerly, trying to push his head in between the boys to see what was going on. A tall boy turned, looked at him sternly, and said with quiet menace: "Now then, stop that fooling!"

The silence went on and on, the uncertainty weighed on them endlessly. Seryozha had time to get tired, to get bored, to catch a grasshopper, and to look at Valery's yard and at Lariska. . . . At last the big boys began to talk, to move, they separated and Arsenty came out—oh! not to be recognized, terrible, purple from neck to waist; where was his white chest, where was his white back? And the towel tied round his waist was spotted with ink and blood! And he was as pale as pale, but all the same he was smiling, that hero Arsenty! He walked firmly to Kapa, took off the towel and said: "Bandage me tightly."

"We'd better let the kids go next, or there'll be trouble with them," said someone. "What about it?"

"Where are you, kids?" asked Valery, coming out of the bathhouse with purple hands. "Not changed your minds? All right, be quick."

How could you say you'd changed your mind? How could you pluck up courage to say it when Arsenty was standing there, all blood and ink, looking at you with a smile. . . ?

One letter won't take long, thought Seryozha.

He followed Shurik into the empty bathhouse. The big boys were all watching Kapa bandage Arsenty. Valery sat down on the block of wood.

"Shall I need a towel?" asked Shurik.

"You'll be all right without," said Valery. "I'll do it on your arm."

He took Shurik's hand and pricked his arm with a pin just below the elbow.

Shurik jumped and said: "Oh! . . ."

"If it's oh, off you go," said Valery and gave another prick. "Just try to think I'm taking out a splinter," he said helpfully, "then it won't hurt."

Shurik set his teeth and did not make another sound, he only jumped from foot to foot and blew his arm where crimson points of blood were appearing one after the other. Then Valery scratched the skin between the points—Shurik jumped again, beat with his heels, and blew with all his lungs, while the blood trickled down. "How brave he is," thought Seryozha, pale and staring at the blood, "he isn't yelling, I won't either, oh-oh-oh— I can't run away, they'd all laugh at me, and Shurik would call me a coward. . . ."

Valery picked up a bottle of ink, dipped a paint brush in it, and painted the blood with ink.

"Finished!" he said. "Next?"

Seryozha marched up and held out his arm.

That was at the end of the summer, when school had only just begun, and the days were warm and golden with sunshine. Now it was autumn, the sky was dirty gray, and Aunt Pasha had put cottonwool and glasses filled with salt between the double windowpanes to prevent the glass from getting steamed and had pasted strips of paper over the cracks to keep out the draughts in winter.

Seryozha was in bed. By the bed were two chairs. One of them was piled up with toys, the other he used for playing on. But it was difficult to play on a chair. There was no room for tanks to turn round properly, and nowhere for enemies to retreat—they'd get as far as the back of the chair and that was all, the battle was over.

The illness started when Seryozha came out of Valery's bath-house, his right hand supporting his left arm—swollen, burning, inky. He came out into the light, and black circles swam before his eyes; he smelt the smoke of someone's cigaret and vomited. He lay down on the grass, his bandaged arm aching and burning. Shurik and another boy took him home. Aunt Pasha did not notice anything because he was wearing a long-sleeved shirt. He went into the house without a word and lay down on his bed.

Soon, however, he started being sick and his temperature went up. Aunt Pasha was frightened and telephoned Mummy at school. Mummy hurried home and the doctor came. They undressed him, took off the bandage, shook their heads and asked him questions. But he answered nothing; he was tormented by dreams, dreadful, sickening dreams of something big, in a red vest, with bare purple arms that smelt horribly of ink, a wooden block and a butcher chopping meat on it, and around him boys cursing and all stained with blood. . . . He talked about the things he saw, unconscious of what he was saying. So the grown-ups did find out all about it.

They were kind and attentive to Seryozha, but they tormented him worse than Valery. Especially the doctor, who kept ruthlessly pouring penicillin into him; and Seryozha, who had not cried for pain, sobbed with humiliation, with helplessness, with offended modesty, with shame. And as if that wasn't enough, the doctor sent a woman in a white overall, a nurse, who pricked his finger with a special instrument and squeezed out drops of blood. And after all the torment, the doctor joked and stroked Seryozha's head—this was real mockery.

Seryozha got tired of playing, he lay back and thought of his sad lot. He wanted to discover the first cause of all his trouble.

"I wouldn't have got ill if I hadn't been tattooed," he thought. "And I wouldn't have got tattooed if I hadn't met Vaska's uncle. And I wouldn't have met him if he hadn't come to stay with Vaska. That's it. If he hadn't thought of coming, nothing would have happened, and I'd be well."

He felt no resentment against Vaska's uncle. It was simply the way one thing led to another, you could never guess where trouble might be coming from.

They tried to find things to amuse him. Mummy gave him an aquarium with little red fish inside. Plants grew in it. You had to feed the fish with powder from a little box.

"He's so fond of pets," said Mummy. "This'll keep him interested."

It was true, he was fond of pets. He was fond of the cat Zaika, and of his tame jackdaw. But fish weren't pets.

Zaika was warm and fluffy, and it had been fun playing with him until he got old and gloomy. The jackdaw was gay and funny, it flew about the room, stole spoons, and came when Seryozha called it. But what could fish do except wag their tails. . . . Why couldn't Mummy understand that!

What Seryozha wanted was the other children, a good game, and a good talk. Most of all he wanted Shurik. Before the double panes had been put in, Shurik came one day and called to him through the open window.

"Seryozha! How are you?"

"Come in," cried Seryozha, jumping up onto his knees. "Come here!"

"They won't let me in," said Shurik. (The top of his head showed over the windowsill.) "Get better and come out."

"What are you doing all the time?" Seryozha asked excitedly.

"Daddy's bought me a satchel. I'm to go to school," said Shurik. "They've got my name down. And Arsenty's ill, too. But none of the others are. And I'm not either. And Valery's been sent to a different school, he's got an awful long way to go now."

All that news!

"Good-bye! Come out quick?" Shurik's voice was already further off, Aunt Pasha must have come out into the yard.

Oh, if only Seryozha could have gone out too. With Shurik! Out into the street! How lovely everything had been before his illness. To think of all he'd had, and all that he had lost.

At last Seryozha was allowed to get up, and then to go out. But they would not let him go far away from the house or to other houses, they were afraid something might happen to him again.

Anyway, they only let him go out in the mornings, when all his friends were at school. Even Shurik was at school, although he was not yet seven. His parents had sent him because of the tattooing, so that somebody should keep an eye on him and see that he was out of mischief. . . . But it was no fun for Seryozha to play with the little ones.

Coming out into the yard one day, he saw a strange man in a worn cap with earflaps, sitting on the logs piled up by the shed. His face was like a brush, his clothes torn. He was smoking a very tiny cigaret, so small it could hardly be seen in his yellowish-black fingers, and the smoke seemed to come straight from them—it was surprising that he didn't burn himself. . . . His other hand was bandaged with a bit of dirty rag. His boots were fastened with string instead of laces. Seryozha took it all in, then asked: "Have you come to see Korostelev?"

"What Korostelev?" the man asked. "I don't know any Korostelev."

"It's Lukyanych you want, then?"

"I don't know Lukyanych either."

"They're not at home, anyway," said Seryozha. "There's only Aunt Pasha and me. . . . Doesn't that hurt?"

"What d'ye mean?"

"You're burning your fingers."

"Ah."

He drew on the tiny end for the last time, dropped it, and put his heel on it.

"And your other hand—did you burn that before?" asked Seryozha.

The man didn't answer, he only looked at Seryozha in a grim way. Why's he looking at me like that? the boy thought.

"How are you off here? All right?" the man asked.

"Yes, quite well, thank you," answered Seryozha.

"Plenty of stuff here?"

"What sort of stuff?"

"Well, what sort of things have you got?"

"I've got a bicycle," said Seryozha, "and I've got toys. All sorts of toys, mechanical toys and ordinary ones. But Lyonya hasn't got very many, only rattles."

"And materials—got much of those put away?" the man asked, then probably thinking Seryozha might not understand, he explained: "You know—stuff for making coats and suits."

"We haven't any here," said Seryozha. "But Vaska's mother

has, she's got a lot."

"Where does she live—Vaska's mother?"

What further talk there might have been it is impossible to say; at that moment the latch of the gate clicked. Lukyanych came into the yard and saw the stranger.

"Who are you? What do you want?" he asked.

The man rose from the logs and stood there looking humble and miserable.

"I'm looking for work, Master," he said.

"Why do you look for it in other people's yards? Where do you live?"

"Nowhere, just now," the man said.

"And where've you been living?"

"Where I used to live—that's gone. A long time ago."

"Just out of prison, is that it?"

"A month ago."

"What were you in for?"

The man shuffled from foot to foot.

"Well, they said it was for carelessness with personal property. But I didn't do it. It was a mistake."

"Well, why didn't you go home when you came out, why are you hanging round?"

"I did go," he said, "but my wife wouldn't have me back. She's got someone else, a counterjumper. . . . Anyway, they won't register you there. Now I'm tramping to where my Ma lives; she's in Chita."

Seryozha listened, openmouthed. So he'd been in prison! . . . In a prison with iron bars and bearded guards armed to the teeth with swords and poleaxes as they are described in storybooks, and his mother was waiting for him in some place called Chita and most likely crying, poor mother! . . . She'd be glad when he came. She'd make him a suit and a coat. And she'd buy laces for his boots.

"Chita, that's a good way," said Lukyanych. "Well, and what now? Are you managing to earn anything—or is it the same as before with personal property?"

The man snuffled.

"Give me your wood to saw, Master."

"All right," said Lukyanych and fetched a saw out of the shed.

Hearing voices, Aunt Pasha had come out and she stood listening on the steps. Then for some reason she called the chickens into the shed, although it was still early for them to go to sleep, and locked the shed. And put the key in her pocket. And told Seryozha quietly: "While you're out here keep an eye on him, so he doesn't go off with the saw."

Seryozha circled round and round the man, staring at him

with curiosity, doubt, pity, and a certain fear. He could not pluck up courage to talk any more, out of respect for the man's strange, mysterious life. And the man said nothing either. He sawed with energy, only stopping now and then to sit down, roll a cigaret and smoke it.

Seryozha was called in to dinner. Korostelev and Mummy were not at home, so there were only the three of them. After dinner Lukyanych told Aunt Pasha: "Give that tramp my old felt boots."

"You could wear them a bit more yourself," said Aunt Pasha. "He's got boots."

"He'll never get to Chita in those," said Lukyanych.

"I'll give him something to eat," said Aunt Pasha. "There's a lot of yesterday's soup left."

After dinner Lukyanych lay down to rest, and Aunt Pasha took the cloth off the table and put it away in the cupboard.

"Why've you taken off the tablecloth?" Seryozha asked.

"Good enough for him without," she answered. "He's filthy dirty."

She heated up the soup, cut some bread, and called the man in a melancholy voice.

"Come and get your dinner."

The man came in and wiped his feet for a long time with a rag. Then Aunt Pasha poured out water and he washed his hands. There were two pieces of soap on the little shelf, one pink, the other gray—washing soap. The man took the gray soap, he didn't know the pink soap was for your hands, or it wasn't proper for him to have it, just as it wasn't proper for him to have a tablecloth or today's soup. In general he seemed shy, and he walked about the kitchen awkwardly, carefully, as though afraid of breaking the floor. Aunt Pasha kept her eye on him all the time. When he sat down, the man crossed himself. Seryozha saw that pleased Aunt Pasha. She filled his soup plate to the very brim and said kindly: "Eat your fill."

The man ate the soup and three huge pieces of bread without a word and all in a minute, working his jaws vigorously and sniffing noisily every now and then. Aunt Pasha gave him some more soup and a very small glass of vodka.

"Now you can have a drink," she said. "It wouldn't do on an empty stomach."

The man raised the glass. "Your health, Auntie, God keep you."

He threw back his head, opened his mouth, and in the twinkling of an eye poured into it all that had been in the glass. Seryozha looked—there was the glass on the table, empty.

He gazed in admiration.

The man ate more slowly now, and he started to talk. He told
Aunt Pasha how he had come home to his wife and she wouldn't
let him in.

"And she wouldn't give me anything either," he said. "And
we'd quite a lot of stuff, a sewing machine and a phonograph
and pots and pans and so on. . . . But she wouldn't give me a
thing. Get back where you came from, she said, you jailbird,
she said, you've spoiled my life. I begged her—give me the
phonograph at least, we bought it together, we both earned the
money for it. But not even that. She'd made a coat and skirt for
herself out of my suit. And she'd sold my overcoat in a commission shop."

"And how did you get on before? Were you happy together?"
asked Aunt Pasha.

"As happy as doves," the man said. "She was crazy about me.
But now she's got that counterjumper there. I saw him, he's
not worth looking at. A shrimp. What took her fancy? Just his
being a shop assistant."

Then he talked about his mother, about the pension she had,
and the parcel she had sent him. Aunt Pasha was completely
melted, she gave him a piece of boiled meat, and tea, and let
him smoke.

"Of course," the man said, "if I had something to go to Ma
with—even the phonograph—that would be better."

Of course it would be better, thought Seryozha. They could
play the records.

"Perhaps you'll manage to get work, then it'll be all right,"
said Aunt Pasha.

"Yes, but they don't much like taking on our sort," the man
answered, and Aunt Pasha sighed and shook her head as though
sympathizing both with the man and with those who didn't like
taking on his sort.

"Yes," said the man. "I could have been a shop assistant,
too. . . . I could have been anything. But somehow I've just
wasted my time."

"Well why did you?" said Aunt Pasha admonishingly. "It
would have been better if you hadn't."

"What's the good of thinking of that now, after all that's happened?" said the man. "Now it's no good talking. Well, thank
you, Auntie. I'll go and finish the sawing."

He went back into the yard, but Aunt Pasha did not let Seryozha go out again because a drizzle had started.

"Why's he like that," said Seryozha, "that man out there?"

"It's because he's been in prison," Aunt Pasha told him. "You
heard what he said."

"But why was he in prison?"

"Because he lived badly, that's why. If he'd lived properly no one would have put him in prison."

Lukyanych had finished his after-dinner nap and was going back to his office. Seryozha asked him:

"If people live badly, are they all put in prison?"

"Well, you see it's this way," said Lukyanych. "He stole other people's things. Suppose, for instance, I work and earn money and buy something with it—and he comes along and steals it. Is that good?"

"No."

"Of course not, it's bad."

"Is he bad, then?"

"Of course he is."

"Then why did you tell Aunt Pasha to give him your felt boots?"

"I was sorry for him."

"Are you sorry for people who are bad?"

"Well, it's this way," said Lukyanych. "It's not because he's bad I was sorry for him, but because his boots were worn out and he'd soon be barefoot. . . . And in general, you don't like seeing a man down and out. . . . Well, and then. . . . Of course I'd have liked giving him the felt boots much better if he were good. . . . Well, I've got to go," said Lukyanych and hurried away.

That's silly, thought Seryozha, I can't understand a word he's said.

He looked at the drizzle outside the window and tried to make sense of Lukyanych's words. . . . The man in the worn cap went down the street carrying the felt boots, one inside the other so that there was a foot at either end. Mummy came home, bringing Lyonya wrapped in a red quilt.

"Mummy," said Seryozha, "you remember when one of the children at school stole an exercise book, did they put him in prison?"

"Of course not," said Mummy.

"But why not?"

"He's a little boy. He's only eight."

"Are little boys allowed to, then?"

"Allowed to—what?"

"Steal."

"No, little boys mustn't steal either," said Mummy. "But I had a good talk with him seriously, and he won't ever steal anything again. Why are you asking?"

Seryozha told her about the man who'd been in prison.

"Yes, there are some people like that, unfortunately," said Mummy. "We'll talk about it again, when you're a little older.

Go and ask Aunt Pasha for my darning mushroom, please."

Seryozha brought the darner.

"Why did he steal?" he asked.

"He didn't want to work, that's why."

"But didn't he know he'd be put in prison?"

"Of course he did."

"And wasn't he frightened? Mummy! Isn't prison frightening?"

"Now, that's enough." Mummy sounded quite cross. "I've told you already, you're not old enough to understand things like that. Think of something else. I don't want to hear another word about it."

Seryozha looked at her frowning face and stopped asking. He went into the kitchen, got some water from the bucket with the dipper, poured it into a glass and tried to drink it all at once, in one swallow. But however much he threw back his head, however wide he opened his mouth, all he did was to get himself wet. Even the back of his collar was wet and water trickled down his spine. But he said nothing about his wet shirt, or they'd have started their fussing and made him change and scolded him. And by the time he had to go to bed the shirt was dry again.

The grown-ups thought he was asleep and talked quite loudly in the dining room.

"What he wants is a plain yes or no," said Korostelev. "If you tell him something in between, he can't understand it."

"I simply ran away," said Lukyanych. "I didn't know what to say."

"Each age has its own difficulties," said Mummy, "and we shouldn't try to answer every question a child asks. Why discuss with him something that's beyond his understanding? What good will that do? It will only confuse him and give him ideas for which he is in no way prepared. It's enough for him to know that the man committed a crime and was punished for it. And I must ask you not to talk to him about these things."

"We don't talk to him about it!" Lukyanych protested. "He does the talking."

"Korostelev!" Seryozha called from the darkened room. Silence fell.

"Yes, here I am," said Korostelev, coming in.

"What's a counterjumper?"

"Now see here, why aren't you asleep?" said Korostelev. "Just you go to sleep this minute."

But Seryozha's eyes were wide open, turned expectantly to him in the dim light. And in a hasty whisper (so that Mummy shouldn't hear and be angry) Korostelev answered his question. . . .

Then he was ill again. For no reason at all he suddenly got ton-
sillitis. Then the doctor said: "Glands." And he thought up a
fresh torment—codliver oil and poultices. And he told them to
take Seryozha's temperature.

They'd smear some stinking black ointment on a rag and put
it on your neck. On top of that they put some stiff paper that
scratched. Then cotton. Then they wound bandages round it,
right up to your ears, so your head was like a nail sticking out of
a board—you couldn't turn it either way. Try living like that.

At least they didn't keep him in bed. And when his temperature was normal and it wasn't raining, they let him go out. But
that didn't happen very often. Almost always it was either raining or else he had a temperature.

They kept the radio on, but not everything interested Seryozha,
far from it.

And grown-ups are so lazy—whenever you asked them to
read to you or tell you a story, they said they were busy. But
when Aunt Pasha was cooking, it's true that her hands were
busy, but her mouth wasn't, she could quite well have told you
a story. Or take Mummy. When she was at her school or changing Lyonya's diapers or correcting exercise books that was one
thing, but when she stood in front of the mirror pinning her
hair first this way, then that, and smiling at herself—was that
being busy?

"Read me a story," Seryozha begged.

"Wait a little, Seryozha," she said. "I'm busy."

"Why are you taking it all down again?" asked Seryozha,
looking at the plaits.

"I want to do my hair differently."

"Why?"

"No special reason."

"Why's there no special reason?"

"Oh, Seryozha dear. Don't get on my nerves."

Why do I get on her nerves, Seryozha wondered. After a
moment's thought he said: "But all the same, read me a story."

"Wait till I come home in the evening," she said. "I'll read to
you then."

But when she came home that evening, she would nurse
Lyonya and talk to Korostelev and correct exercise books. And
again she'd get out of reading.

But here was Aunt Pasha, she'd done all her work and sat
down to rest on the little sofa in her room. She was sitting
quietly, her hands clasped on her lap, there was nobody
at home.

"Now you can tell me a story," said Seryozha, turning off the radio and sitting down beside her.

"Oh dear, oh dear," she said wearily, "what d'you want a story for? You know them all by heart."

"That doesn't matter. Tell me one."

How lazy she was!

"Well," she started with a sigh," once upon a time there lived a Tsar and Tsaritsa. And they had a daughter. And one fine day—"

"Was she beautiful?" Seryozha asked vigilantly.

He knew very well that the daughter was beautiful, everyone knew it. But why did Aunt Pasha leave it out? You mustn't leave out anything when you're telling a story.

"Yes, she was beautiful. Ever so beautiful. . . . Well, one fine day the princess decided to get married. And many suitors came to pay court to her. . . ."

The story followed its familiar course. Seryozha listened attentively, gazing into the dusk with big, serious eyes. He knew every word of it, but the story was none the worse for that. On the contrary.

Just what meaning he put into such words as "suitors" and "pay court" he could not have explained; but he understood everything—in his own way. For instance, "the horse stood rooted to the ground," and then galloped off—well, they'd dug it up by the roots.

The dusk deepened. The windows were blue and the frames black. There was nothing to be heard in all the world but Aunt Pasha's voice telling him about the trials of the suitors who came to pay their court to the princess. Quietness filled the little house on Far Street.

It was dull for Seryozha in all that quietness. The story would soon come to an end, and Aunt Pasha would never agree to tell him another however much he begged or argued. Yawning, sighing, she would go into the kitchen and he would be alone. What could he do? He'd got tired of all his toys while he was ill. He was tired of drawing. You couldn't ride a bicycle indoors, there wasn't room enough.

Boredom took the life out of Seryozha more than illness. It made him languid and dulled his mind. Everything was so tiresome.

Lukyanych came home with a parcel, something he had bought. It was a gray box tied round with string. Seryozha looked at it eagerly, he waited with impatience for Lukyanych to get the string off. Why didn't he just take a knife and cut it? No, Lukyanych stood there breathing hard, undoing the tight knots; the string would come in useful; if he cut it, it would be spoiled.

Seryozha stood on tiptoe, devouring the parcel with his

eyes. . . . But the gray box, big enough for something really interesting and splendid, only contained a pair of big black cloth-topped overshoes with rubber soles.

Seryozha himself had overshoes like that, with the same kind of fastenings, only made of rubber, without any cloth. He hated them, and he wasn't in the least interested in looking at this pair.

"What are those?" he asked wearily, in bored contempt.

"Overshoes," said Lukyanych. "People call them "Farewell to Youth."

"Why?"

"Because young men don't wear this kind."

"Are you old, then?"

"If I'm putting these on, it means I am."

He stamped his foot and said: "That's comfortable!" Then he went to show them to Aunt Pasha.

Seryozha climbed onto a chair in the dining room and switched on the electric light. The fish were swimming about in the aquarium, staring stupidly. Seryozha's shadow fell on them and they came to the top and opened their mouths, expecting to be fed.

I wonder if they'd drink their own sort of oil, thought Seryozha.

He took the cork out of the codliver oil bottle and poured a few drops into the aquarium. The fish stood on their tails with their mouth open, but did not swallow it. Seryozha poured in a few more drops. The fish swam away.

They don't like it, Seryozha thought, without any interest.

It was so dull, so *dull*! Boredom led him into senseless naughtiness. He took a knife and scratched the paint off the doors where it had made blisters. It wasn't that he enjoyed it, it was just something to do. He took the ball of wool with which Aunt Pasha was knitting herself a jumper and unwound it right to the very end, so as to wind it all up again—in which he did not succeed. And every time he knew that he was being naughty, that Aunt Pasha would scold him and he would cry—and she did scold him and he did cry—but all the same he found a certain satisfaction even in that. She had scolded, he had cried—at least *something* had happened.

It was better when Mummy came home and brought Lyonya. The house came to life. Lyonya cried, Mummy nursed him and changed his diapers. Then she'd give him his bath. He was more like a real person than when he was first born, only he was too fat. He could hold a rattle, but that was all he was good for. All day he lived his own life in the nursery, and Seryozha had nothing to do with him.

Korostelev came home late and everyone wanted him for

something. He'd begin talking to Seryozha or agree to read to him, then the telephone would ring. Mummy would interrupt every minute, she always had something she wanted to say, and she couldn't wait till people had finished what they were doing. Lyonya would cry and scream before he went to bed, and Mummy would call Korostelev—it had to be Korostelev and no one else—to walk up and down the room with Lyonya and hum to him. And then Seryozha would get sleepy, and his talk with Korostelev would be put off till some other time, he didn't know when.

There were, however, wonderful evenings, too—not very often, but sometimes—when Lyonya quieted down early, and Mummy was busy correcting exercise books; then Korostelev put Seryozha to bed and told him a story. At first he was bad at stories, he didn't know at all how to tell them. But Seryozha helped him and taught him the proper way, and now Korostelev would start off quite confidently.

"Once upon a time there lived a Tsar and a Tsaritsa. And they had a beautiful daughter, a princess. . . ."

Seryozha would listen and correct him when he went wrong, until he fell asleep.

In those dull days when he didn't know what to do with himself, when he had no energy and could only tease or be naughty, he came to love still more Korostelev's fresh, healthy face, his strong hands, his manly voice. . . . Seryozha would fall asleep glad that he, too, had something of Korostelev, not only Mummy and Lyonya.

15

Holmogory. That was a word Seryozha heard more and more often when Korostelev and Mummy were talking together.

"Have you written to Holmogory?"

"Maybe I shan't be so busy in Holmogory, then I can take my political-economy exam."

"I've had an answer from Holmogory. There's a job in the girls' school."

"They've rung up from the personnel department. It's definitely settled about Holmogory."

"Why take that to Holmogory? It's all worm-eaten." (About the chest of drawers.)

Holmogory, Holmogory.

Holmogory. It must be very high up. Hills and mountains, like in pictures. People climbing from one mountain to another. The girls' school stood on a mountain. Children sliding down the mountain on sledges.

Seryozha drew it all with a red pencil, humming "Holmogory,

Holmogory" to a tune that had come into his head for the occasion.

We must be going to live there, because they talked about the chest of drawers. Grand! The very best thing in the world! Zhenka went away, Vaska went away, now we're going away. That makes us much more important, that we're going somewhere and not staying in the same place all the time.

"Is Holmogory a long way off?" Seryozha asked Aunt Pasha.

"Yes, indeed it is," said Aunt Pasha and sighed. "A very long way."

"And are we going to live there?"

"I don't know, Seryozha dear, I don't know all your arrangements."

"Do you go there by train?"

"Yes, by train."

"Are we going to Holmogory?" Seryozha asked Korostelev and Mummy. They ought to have told him themselves, they must have forgotten.

They looked at each other, and then looked away, and Seryozha tried to meet their eyes and couldn't.

"Are we going? We are, aren't we?" he insisted, puzzled. Why didn't they answer?

Then Mummy said in a careful voice: "Daddy's being transferred to work there."

"And are we going with him?"

That was a plain question and he waited for a plain answer. But Mummy, as always, started talking round and round.

"How could he go all alone? Look how uncomfortable it would be for him. He'd come home and nobody there . . . everything untidy . . . nobody to get him anything to eat . . . nobody to talk to. . . . Poor Daddy would be miserable."

Then at last came the answer.

"So I'm going with him."

"And me?"

Why did Korostelev keep looking at the ceiling? Why did Mummy say nothing and only fondle Seryozha?

"And me?" he cried in panic, stamping his foot.

"First of all, don't stamp," said Mummy, and stopped fondling him. "That's no way to behave. Don't let me ever see you do it again! And second—let's talk it over. How could you go now? You've only just been ill. You're not properly well yet. The least little thing, and your temperature goes up. We don't know what it'll be like out there, how we'll arrange everything. And the climate isn't right for you, either. You'd just go on getting ill again and again and never pick up properly. And who would I leave you with if you were ill? The doctor said you mustn't go there yet."

Long before she had finished he was sobbing, tears streaming down his face. They weren't taking him! They were going, but without him. Sobbing, he hardly heard what else she said.

"Aunt Pasha and Lukyanych will stay here with you. You'll go on living with them, just as you always have."

But he didn't want to go on living as he always had! He wanted to go with Korostelev and Mummy.

"I want to go to Holmogory!" he cried.

"Now listen, darling, stop, hush, don't go on like that," said Mummy.

"What do you want with Holmogory? There's nothing special there."

"There is!"

"Why do you talk to Mummy like that? Mummy always tells you the truth. . . . And you won't stay here all your life, you little silly, now hush, that's enough. . . . You'll only spend the winter here, and then next spring or perhaps next summer Daddy'll come for you, or I will, and we'll take you along, just as soon as you're really well and strong we'll take you, and then we'll all be together again. Just think, how could we leave you for long?"

Yes, but what if he wasn't well by next summer? And was it nothing, to wait throughout the winter? Winter—why, there was no end to it. . . . And how could he bear it that they should go away and leave him behind? They'd live there without him, a long way off, and they didn't care a bit, not a bit! And they'd travel in a train, and he'd have traveled in a train—but they weren't taking him! It all made up one dreadful knot of injury and misery. But he could put it only in the simplest words.

"I want to go to Holmogory! I want to go to Holmogory!"

"Give me a glass of water, Mitya, please," said Mummy. "Here, drink a little. Seryozha, you mustn't get into such a state. . . . However much you shout, it won't help. If the doctor says you mustn't go, that's that. Now hush, now be a sensible little boy, hush, hush now. . . . Seryozha darling, how often have I gone away without you, don't you remember, when I was studying and taking my exams? I went away and came back again, didn't I? And you were quite all right without me here. And you never cried when I went away. Because you were quite happy without me. Don't you remember? Why are you making all this fuss now? Can't you do without us for just a little while, when it's for your own good?"

How could he explain? It had been quite different then. He had been little and silly. When she was not there, he forgot about her, and he had to get used to her again when she came back. And she had gone away alone, now she was taking Korostelev away from him. . . . Then came a new thought, a new suffering: They're sure to take Lyonya. He had to know. In a choked voice, through swollen lips, he asked: "And Lyonya?"

"But he's tiny," said Mummy reproachfully, and got red. "He can't do without me, don't you understand? He has to have me. And he's not ill, he doesn't get temperatures or swollen glands."

Seryozha hung his head and cried again, but now quietly, hopelessly.

He might have borne it if Lyonya had been left behind, too. But it was *only* him that they were leaving. It was *only him* they didn't want.

"Left to my fate," he thought in the words of one of his fairytales.

To his sense of injury against his mother, which would leave a scar however long he lived, there was added the feeling of his own guilt. Of course, it was his fault; he was worse than Lyonya, he had swollen glands; that was why they would take Lyonya and they would not take him.

"Oh," sighed Korostelev and went out of the room. But he came back at once.

"Seryozha, come for a walk. In the woods."

"In this damp! We'll have him in bed again!" cried Mummy. Korostelev shrugged his shoulders.

"He's in bed half the time as it is. Come on, Seryozha."

Still sobbing, Seryozha followed. Korostelev helped him to put on his outdoor things, he only asked Mummy to tie his scarf. Then, hand in hand, they went to the woods.

"You know," said Korostelev, "there's a word—'must.' Do you think I want to go to Holmogory? Or Mummy? We don't. It's upset all our plans, everything. But we must—so we're going. And that's happened to me a lot of times."

"Why?" asked Seryozha.

"That's life," said Korostelev. He spoke seriously, sadly, and Seryozha felt a very little better because Korostelev too was sad.

"When Mummy and I get there, well . . . we must start to work at once a new job. And there'll be Lyonya. We must get him into a créche at once. But suppose the créche is a long way off? Then we must look for a nurse. And that's quite a business too. And I've got exams hanging over my head. I must sit for them if I bust. Wherever you look, everywhere it's a 'must.' But there's only one 'must' for you—to wait here for a while. Why should we make you share all those difficulties with us? You'd only get more ill than ever."

They needn't *make* him. He would be willing, glad, he longed to share all their difficulties. He could do the same as they did. And in spite of the earnest assurance in that voice, Seryozha couldn't rid himself of the thought that they weren't leaving him behind just because he would be too ill, but because if he were, he'd be a nuisance. And his heart knew already that nobody who was really loved could be a nuisance. And his doubt of their love pierced deeper into his heart, which was ripe for understanding.

The woods were empty and sad. The leaves had fallen, the dark nests on the bare boughs looked from below like dishevelled balls of black wool. Seryozha's boots squelched in the wet brown leaves as he walked hand in hand with Korostelev, thinking. At last he said tonelessly: "It's all the same, anyway."

"What's all the same, anyway?" asked Korostelev, bending over him.

Seryozha did not answer.

"It's only till the summer," said Korostelev awkwardly after a pause.

Seryozha would have liked to say: I can think what I like. I can cry as much as I like, it'll be all the same. You grown-ups have the power, you can allow or forbid, you can give presents or punish, and if you say I've got to be left behind you'll leave me behind whatever I do. . . . That is what he would have answered had he had the words. This feeling of helplessness when faced with the tremendous, boundless power of grown-ups crushed him.

From that day he became very quiet. He hardly ever asked: "Why?" He often went off alone; he sat on Aunt Pasha's sofa with his feet tucked under him, whispering to himself. He was still not allowed out very often. The autumn dragged on, damp and unpleasant, and his illness dragged on with it.

Korostelev was hardly ever with them. In the morning he would go away to "hand over." (That was what he always said now: "I'm handing over to Averkiev.") But he didn't forget Seryozha. One day there was a new set of bricks beside his bed when he woke up, another time there was a brown monkey. Seryozha loved this monkey. It was his daughter. She was as beautiful as the princess. He said to her: "Well, old boy." He went to Holmogory and took her with him. Whispering and kissing her cold plastic nose, he put her to bed.

16

Strange men came to the house, they moved about the furniture in the dining room and Mummy's room and packed it in bast matting. Mummy took down the curtains and pictures. The rooms looked dismal and hideous with bits of string littering the floor and with darker patches on the walls. Only Aunt Pasha's room and the kitchen were homely islands amid all this depressing ugliness. Bare electric bulbs shed a harsh light on

bare walls, bare windows, and scraps of reddish bast. Chairs were
stacked one on top of the other, their scratched legs pointed
to the ceiling.

At any other time it would have been good for hide-and-seek.
But not now.

It was late when the men went away. Everyone was tired and
went to bed. Lyonya fell asleep, too, after his usual evening cry.
Lukyanych and Aunt Pasha whispered and blew their noses in
bed for a long time, until at last they too were quiet. Lukyanych
snored loudly and Aunt Pasha thinly, with a nasal whistle. Only
Korostelev sat in the dining room by the bast-covered table,
writing under the bare lamp. Suddenly he heard a sigh behind
him. He looked round, and there stood Seryozha in his nightshirt, barefoot, with his bandaged throat.

"What is it?" whispered Korostelev.

"Please," said Seryozha, "Korostelev, dear Korostelev, take
me with you, please take me too, please, please!"

He broke into heavy sobs, trying to keep quiet in order not to
wake the others.

"Here, old boy," said Korostelev, picking him up in his arms.
"You know you mustn't run about barefoot on this cold floor. . . .
You know how it is, don't you? Haven't we talked it all over and
agreed about it?"

"I want to go to Holmogory!" Seryozha sobbed.

"Your feet are quite cold, you see now," said Korostelev. He
wrapped the bottom of the nightshirt round Seryozha's feet,
and gathered up his thin shaking body. "What can we do
when things turn out this way? You see, you're not well. . . ."

"I won't be ill again!"

". . . but as soon as you're really well—I'll come for you right
away at once."

"Will you really?" asked Seryozha miserably, hugging
his neck.

"I've never lied to you yet, have I?"

No, he hasn't, thought Seryozha, but of course, he does lie
sometimes, they all do sometimes. . . . What if this is the time
when he's lying to me?

He clung to that firm masculine neck, prickly under the chin,
as his last refuge. Here, in this man, was his main hope of protection and love. Korostelev carried him up and down the room
and whispered—all the nighttime conversation was in whispers: "I'll come for you, and then we'll go in the train. The train
goes very quickly. . . . And the coach is full of people. . . . And
before we know where we are we'll see Mummy waiting for
us. . . . The engine will whistle. . . ."

He'll just have no time to come for me, Seryozha agonized,

and Mummy'll have no time, either. Every day people will come to him, or ring them up, and they'll always have to go to work, or take exams, or walk up and down with Lyonya, and I'll go on waiting and waiting forever. . . .

". . . there's real forest where we're going to live, not just little woods like here . . . with mushrooms and berries growing wild. . . ."

"And wolves?"

"That I can't say. I'll find out about the wolves and write you a letter. . . . And there's a river, we'll go bathing. I'll teach you to do the crawl."

Who knows, thought Seryozha with a flicker of hope, weary of doubting. Perhaps it will be like that.

"We'll make fishing rods and go fishing. . . . Look at that now, it's snowing!"

He carried Seryozha to the window. Great white flakes were floating gently down, some of them smashing softly on the glass.

Seryozha looked at them. Quiet, worn out, he pressed his wet, hot cheek to Korostelev's face.

"Here's winter come at last. You'll be able to play out of doors all the time and go sledging. The time'll pass so quickly you won't notice it. . . ."

"Oh, but—" said Seryozha, wearily worried— "the rope on my sledge is very bad, will you put a new one on for me?"

"Right you are, I'll see to it. And you promise me one thing, not to cry any more—right? It's bad for you, and it upsets Mummy. And anyhow, it isn't right for men. I don't like that sort of thing. . . . Now, promise—you won't cry any more, will you?"

"Uhuh," said Seryozha.

"That's a promise? Word of honor?"

"Uhuh. . . ."

"Well, remember. A man always keeps his word!"

He carried Seryozha, exhausted and slumping heavily in his arms, back to Aunt Pasha's room, put him into bed and tucked him up. Seryozha drew one more long quivering sigh and fell asleep at once. Korostelev stood looking at him. In the light from the dining room his face looked very small and pale. Korostelev turned away and went out on tiptoe.

17

Then the day of departure dawned. It was a dull, dreary day, without either sunshine or frost. The snow on the ground had melted in the night, and only a thin layer remained on the roofs The sky was gray. Underfoot it was wet and muddy. Sledging? Why, it was unpleasant even to go out into the yard.

How could you hope for anything in weather like that? How

could there ever be anything good again?

But all the same, Korostelev had put a new rope on the sledge. Seryozha looked into the porch and saw it standing there.

But Korostelev himself had disappeared.

Mummy sat nursing Lyonya. She kept on and on. And she smiled and said to Seryozha: "Look what a funny nose he has."

Seryozha looked. Just an ordinary nose. She likes his nose because she loves him, thought Seryozha. She used to love me, but now she loves him. So he went to Aunt Pasha. She might be full of superstitions, but she would stay with him and she loved him.

"What are you doing?" he asked dully.

"Can't you see?" she said. "I'm making meatballs."

"Why are you making such a lot?"

Raw meat balls wrapped round in breadcrumbs covered the whole kitchen table.

"Because we're having them for dinner and they'll take some for the journey."

"Will they go soon?"

"Not very. Not till the evening."

"How many hours is that?"

"Oh, a lot. It'll be getting dark when they go. As long as it's light they'll still be here."

She went on making meatballs, and he leaned his forehead against the edge of the table, thinking . . . Lukyanych loves me too, and he'll love me more, he'll love me an awful lot. . . . I'll go with Lukyanych in a boat and I'll get drowned. Then they'll bury me in the ground, like Great-Granny. And Korostelev and Mummy'll hear of it, and they'll be so sorry, they'll say—why didn't we take him with us, he was so clever for his age, and such a good boy, he never cried and never got on your nerves. Much better than Lyonya. . . . No, I don't want them to bury me in the ground, I'd be frightened—lying there all alone. . . . We'll have a good time here; Lukyanych'll bring me apples and chocolates, and I'll grow up and be a sea captain, and Mummy and Korostelev will be down-and-out, and they'll come here and say: "Give me your wood to saw," and I'll tell Aunt Pasha: "Let them have yesterday's soup. . . ."

Here Seryozha felt so unhappy, so sorry for Korostelev and Mummy that he began crying. But Aunt Pasha had barely time to say: "Oh, heavens above!" when he remembered he'd given his word to Korostelev.

"I won't do it again," he said quickly.

Granny Nastya came in with her black bag.

"Is Mitya at home?" she asked.

"He's gone about a car," said Aunt Pasha. "Averkiev doesn't

want to give him one. Just think—what a brute!"

"Why a brute?" asked Granny Nastya. "In the first place, he needs the car for the farm. And second, he's lent them a truck. That's better with all that luggage."

"It's better for the luggage, of course," said Aunt Pasha. "But a car would have been better for Maryasha and the baby."

"People are spoilt these days," said Granny Nastya. "In my young days we didn't take children on cars or trucks, and we reared them just the same. She can sit with the baby beside the driver, and they'll be quite all right."

Seryozha listened, blinking slowly. He was filled with the expectation of parting which was now inevitable. It was as though everything in him was tensely prepared to endure the approaching grief. Whether in a car or a truck soon they would go—they would abandon him.

"Why's Mitya gone so long?" said Granny Nastya. "I want to say good-bye to him."

"Aren't you going to see them off?" asked Aunt Pasha.

"I have a conference," said Granny Nastya, and went to Mummy. Then everything was quiet. The day outside became a deeper gray and the wind rose. It made the windowpanes rattle and shake. Thin ice with white lines covered the puddles. The snow started again, whirling in the wind.

"How many hours now?" asked Seryozha.

"Not so many," Aunt Pasha answered. "But still quite a lot."

Granny Nastya and Mummy stood talking in the dining room, among the piled-up furniture.

"Where on earth can he be all this time?" said Granny Nastya. "I want to say good-bye to him. Who knows if I'll ever see him again."

Seryozha thought: She's also afraid that they'll go away and never come back.

Then he saw it was nearly dark: soon they would have to put on the lights.

Lyonya began to cry. Mummy ran to him, almost bumping into Seryozha on the way.

"Why don't you find something to amuse yourself with, Seryozha dear?" she asked kindly.

He would have been glad to amuse himself; he had tried conscientiously to play with his monkey, then with his bricks, but it was no good. It wasn't interesting, nothing seemed to matter. The kitchen door banged, there was a stamping of feet and Korostelev's loud voice.

"Let's have dinner. The truck'll be here in an hour."

"Didn't you get the car then?" asked Granny Nastya.

"No. They can't spare it, they say. What's it matter? We'll manage with the truck."

Out of habit Seryozha cheered up at the sound of Korostelev's voice and nearly jumped up to run and meet him, but he thought: Soon there'll be nothing more of all this—so once more he started moving his bricks aimlessly about on the floor. Korostelev came in, his face red with the snow, and said apologetically: "Well, Seryozha?"

They had a hasty dinner. Granny Nastya went away. It got quite dark. Korostelev went to the telephone and said good-bye to somebody. Seryozha leaned against his knee, hardly moving, and Korostelev drew his long fingers through Seryozha's hair as he talked.

Then Timokhin came in.

"Well? All ready?" he asked. "Give me a spade to clear away the snow, or we won't be able to open the gates."

Lukyanych went with him to open the gates. Mummy picked up Lyonya and started wrapping him in a quilt.

"There's no hurry for that," said Korostelev. "He'll get too hot. There's plenty of time."

He and Timokhin and Lukyanych began carrying out the packed things. The doors kept opening and the rooms grew cold. They all had snow on their boots, nobody wiped his feet, and Aunt Pasha did not scold them: she knew there was no sense in wiping your feet now. Pools of water spread over the floor, it was wet and dirty. There was a smell of snow, straw, and tobacco mixed with animal smell from Timokhin's sheepskin. Aunt Pasha ran about giving advice. Mummy, still holding Lyonya, went up to Seryozha, put one arm round him and pressed him to her. He moved away. Why did she put her arm round him when she wanted to go away without him!

Everything was carried out, the furniture, the suitcases, the basket of provisions, the bundle of Lyonya's diapers. How empty the rooms looked! Nothing left but some scraps of paper and an empty medicine bottle lying on its side. You could see the house was old, the paint on the floor was worn off, it looked new and fresh only where the whatnot and the chest of drawers had stood.

"Here, put this on, it's cold outside," Lukyanych said to Aunt Pasha and handed her a coat. Seryozha jumped in alarm and ran to him.

"I'm going out, too! I'm going, too!"

"Of course, of course, you shall," said Aunt Pasha soothingly, and helped him on with his outdoor things. Mummy and Korostelev were getting theirs on, too. Korostelev put his hands under Seryozha's arms, lifted him up and kissed him hard.

"Good-bye for the present. Get well, and remember what we agreed."

Mummy started kissing Seryozha and crying.

"Seryozha! Say good-bye, darling!"

"Good-bye, good-bye," he said quickly, breathless with haste and agitation, looking at Korostelev. And he had his reward.

"Good boy, Seryozha," said Korostelev.

Mummy was still crying. She said to Aunt Pasha and Lukyanych: "Thank you for everything."

"Nothing to thank us for," said Aunt Pasha mournfully.

"Take care of Seryozha."

"You needn't worry about that," said Aunt Pasha still more mournfully; suddenly she cried: "You've forgotten to sit down! We must all sit down for a minute!"

"But where?" asked Lukyanych, wiping his eyes.

"Oh, heavens above," cried Aunt Pasha, "come into our room, then."

They all went in, sat down here and there, and for some reason waited in silence for a minute. Aunt Pasha was the first to rise.

"Well, God be with you," she said.

They went out and into the porch. It was snowing and everything was white. The gates were wide open. A lantern with a candle inside it hung on the wall of the shed and the snowflakes whirled in its light. The loaded truck stood in the middle of the yard. Timokhin was covering everything with canvas, Shurik was helping him. A good many people were standing about— Vaska's mother, Lida, and a lot more, all come to see Korostelev and Mummy off. Seryozha felt as though he were seeing them all for the first time. Everything round him seemed strange, unknown. Voices sounded different. The yard was not like his own yard. . . . It was as if he had never seen that shed before. . . . As if he had never played with those children.

. . . As if this man had never given him rides on this same truck. . . . As if nothing of it all had ever been *his*, and nothing ever could be, for he was abandoned.

"It's going to be bad driving," said Timokhin in his stranger's voice. "Slippery."

Korostelev put Mummy and Lyonya in the seat next the driver's and wrapped a shawl round them. He loved them more than anyone else, he took care of them, he saw to it that they were warm and comfortable. . . . He himself climbed into the back and stood there, tall as a statue.

"Get under the canvas, Mitya," Aunt Pasha called out. "Under the canvas, or you'll have the snow in your face."

He took no notice.

"Seryozha, move back there a bit," he said, "or we'll run over you."

The truck snorted. Timokhin got in. The truck snorted more

and more loudly, trying to move. . . . There, it gave a jerk, then slipped back; then it went a little forward and back again. Now it would go, the gate would be shut, the lantern would be put out, and it would all be over.

Seryozha stood on one side, under the falling snow. With all his strength he remembered his promise and only sobbed now and then—long, desolate, almost soundless sobs. And one single tear forced its way out and shone in the light of the lantern, a difficult tear, not a baby's tear, but the tear of a boy, a bitter, burning, proud tear.

No, he could not stop there any longer, he turned and walked to the house, bent with grief.

"Stop!" Korostelev called in a desperate voice, and drummed on the back of the driver's cab. "Seryozha! Come on! Quick! Get your things together! You're coming with us!"

He jumped down.

"Hurry up! What've you got there? Clothes, toys, bring them along. Won't take a minute. Come on!"

"Mitya, what are you thinking of! Mitya, think what you're doing! Mitya, you're crazy!" said Aunt Pasha from the door and Mummy from inside the truck. He answered angrily:

"Oh, rubbish. What d'you think this is? Can't you understand? It's like vivisection. Do as you like, but I can't stand it. That's all."

"Oh, heavens above, it'll be the death of him out there!" cried Aunt Pasha.

"Rubbish," said Korostelev again. "I'll take the responsibility, understand? It won't kill him at all. That's all your nonsense. Come on, come on, Seryozha."

He ran into the house.

Seryozha could not move at first. He could not believe it, he was afraid to believe it. . . . His heart beat so loudly he could hear it. Then he dashed inside, ran panting through all the rooms, caught up his monkey as he passed, then had a sudden desperate fear that Korostelev might change his mind, Mummy and Aunt Pasha might talk him round, and rushed back to him. But Korostelev hurried to meet him saying: "Quick, Quick!" And they began collecting Seryozha's things. Aunt Pasha and Lukyanych helped. Lukyanych folded up Seryozha's bed.

"It's right what you're doing, Mitya," he said, "you're absolutely right, good for you!"

Seryozha feverishly scooped up any of his treasures that came to hand tossed them into the box Aunt Pasha gave him. Quick! Quick! or they might go! You could never tell what they might do the next minute. . . . His heart seemed to be beating in his throat, so it was hard to breathe or to hear anything. "Quick! Quick!" he cried while Aunt Pasha bundled him up. He tugged

to get away, looking for Korostelev. But the truck was still standing there, and Korostelev had not even got in. He told Seryozha
to day good-bye to everybody.

Then he picked up Seryozha and pushed him in beside
Mummy and Lyonya, under Mummy's shawl. The truck began
to move, now it was all right.

It was crowded in the driver's cab—one, two, three, four
people, think of that! There was a strong smell of sheepskin.
Timokhin was smoking. Seryozha coughed. He sat wedged in
between Mummy and Timokhin, his cap was down over one
eye, his scarf was too tight round his neck, he could see nothing
but the snow dancing in the light of the headlamps. It was
cramped and uncomfortable, but who cared? We're going,
we're going all together, our Timokhin's taking us, and at the
back there, high up, there's Korostelev, he loves us, he is
responsible for us, he's out there in the snow, but he puts us in
the cab, he'll take us all safely to Holmogory. Oh, heavens
above—we're going to Holmogory, how wonderful it is! What's
there I don't know, but it must be splendid as we're going
there! . . . Timokhin's horn sounded warningly, and the gleaming snow rushed straight toward Seryozha.

1955

Sasha was the only little boy in the backyard of the old two-story house on Metrostroevskaya Street who didn't have a daddy. Actually, he had a daddy, but he had never seen him. All Sasha knew about this mysterious daddy was a vague phrase he overhead from the neighbor women, who said: "He left her for the pretty one." Sasha didn't understand what this meant. The prettiest one in the world was his mama: she was big, fat, and warm. She had a wonderful birthmark with two little black hairs on her cheek, and another birthmark at the corner of her mouth, and still another on her earlobe—and what could be prettier?

A person can't be without a daddy, so Sasha would invent daddies for himself. At one time he considered an old doctor as his daddy; Afanasy Ivanovich had taken care of Sasha when he had the mumps. But last winter Afanasy Ivanovich retired and moved out of town. After all, do daddies retire?

After Afanasy Ivanovich, for a short time his daddy was a young and jolly manager of the stand where Sasha and Fenichka bought tea, sugar, vegetables, and matches. He always joked with Fenichka, and once he bought Sasha an ice cream. But the stand closed unexpectedly, and the jolly daddy disappeared.

Then Sasha's daddy became their next-door neighbor, an artillery subcolonel, Nikolay Sergeich. He was already the daddy of three children: Volodka, who was in the fourth grade, Ninka, who was in the second, and little Pavlik, who went to kindergarten. Nikolay Sergeich took very seriously the fact that Sasha called him Daddy; he would take him along with his children to the theater, the circus, and the Park of Culture. But once Ninka told Sasha that if he was going to call their daddy, "Daddy," they would stop playing with him. So once again Sasha was left without a daddy.

Once, on awakening one hot summer morning, Sasha sensed that in addition to the usual odors of their apartment there was another unfamiliar, strange, and exciting smell. He took a deep breath through his nostrils. He smelled shoe polish, leather, and soap lather. The same wonderful masculine odors filled Nikolay Sergeich's apartment in the morning when Sasha's former daddy shaved, polished his boots, and tightened his creaking leather belt. Sasha quickly put on his shorts and ran into the dining room. Sitting at the table before a small mirror supported by a little leg, dabbing at his freshly shaven face with a hot towel, was a stranger wearing a striped undershirt, wide trousers, and brightly shining shoes. On the stranger's arms, just below the watchband, Sasha noticed a little blue anchor with a chain wrapped around it and a tiny seagull. A sailor's hat with black ribbons lay on the windowsill. In the corner of the room stood a little suitcase, and on it lay a white shirt with a blue collar and two gold stripes on each epaulet.

Noticing Sasha, the stranger took the towel off his face, threw it on the table, arose lightly, braced his broad shoulders, smiled, showing two rows of even white teeth; having clicked his heels, he said: "How do you do, Comrade Admiral!"

"How do you do," said Sasha extending his hand.

The stranger gaily and respectfully shook Sasha's hand with his own, large, warm and rough one.

"Fyodor Baykov, Sergeant Major of the Black Sea Fleet," he said introducing himself.

This was a seaman, and not simply a seaman, but a Black Sea sailor, and he was—as Sasha's instantly warming heart told him—his new daddy.

They quickly became friends. The seaman told Sasha that he was on furlough and was on his way home to the Gorkovskaya region. He said that at home he had a brother named Keshka, who was exactly Sasha's age, and a dog named Gvozdik, and a tame starling that could say the word "Greek." Sasha told the seaman about Afanasy Ivanovich, about the manager of the stand, about the artillery subcolonel, about Ninka, and, as if by accident, he called him "Daddy" several times. At first Baykov didn't seem to notice this strange reference, but then he began laughing and said to Fenichka: "Listen, Fenya, I didn't even know I had a little son here!"

"That's enough out of you!" said Fenichka, brushing him off. "You'd better help me set the table."

"Aye aye, Chief!" he said merrily, and then added somewhat pensively: "Apparently he's longing for something."

It was a pleasure to watch the agile yet firm movements of this new daddy. With just a few motions of the knife he filled the breadbasket with chunks of thick-sliced bread. Several more motions, and the salad bowl was filled with quarters of tomatoes and halves of cucumbers, heavily salted by Baykov, straight from his hand. Then, bending the smoked fish until it broke with a crunch, Baykov raked off its golden scales with two fast movements of his fingernails and sliced it thickly. Sasha noticed Baykov's way of dividing food into large pieces; in their home bread, tomatoes, fish, and everything else was sliced into thin, almost transparent pieces. The food Baykov prepared looked much more appetizing. A warm sense of security and comfort crept over Sasha. Feeling grateful to Fenichka for this new daddy, Sasha decided to do something nice for her.

"Do you know," he said, blushing, "Fenichka isn't a house-keeper at all; she's a college student."

"You don't say!" said the seaman, disappointed. "I thought

you were going to take dressmaking courses?"

"He doesn't understand the difference between courses and college." Fenichka was busy at the buffet and said this without turning to the seaman.

"And besides, she's Mama's niece," added Sasha in a fallen voice.

"Wha-a-t?" the seaman asked in amused surprise. "On whose side?"

Suddenly all the cups and plates in the buffet became very noisy, and perhaps that's why Fenichka didn't hear the question.

"And for whom was this invented?" asked the seaman in a serious voice.

"Don't listen to him!" Fenichka turned around, her face red. "He's talking nonsense!"

Sasha was about to become indignant. Both Fenichka and Mama had told him many times that for Fenichka's friends she was not a housekeeper but a student and Mama's niece. Sasha, ashamed of this lie, would always hide when Fenichka's friends came. And now, when he wholeheartedly wanted to reward Fenichka by using her own invented names, he became a liar. Sasha's feelings were hurt; he was embarrassed and at the same time glad that for this seaman it wasn't at all important that Fenichka be a student and Mama's niece.

Soon Sasha noticed that with Baykov Fenichka behaved quite differently than with her other friends. With them, Fenichka acted as if she had just caught cold: shivering, she would wrap herself in Mama's shawl; now and then she would cough into a handkerchief held tight in her fist. She spoke very little, always turning away from the person with whom she was speaking, and would talk in a strange, false, nasal voice. She completely ignored Sasha as if he didn't exist.

Now Fenichka moved about the room freely and easily in her short, flowered housedress and her soft slippers. She treated Sasha as usual, sometimes sweetly, sometimes curtly. And her speech was simple, free, and perhaps slightly more melodious and pleasant than usual. Even before they sat down to eat breakfast, Sasha learned that Baykov and Fenichka were born in the same village on the Volga; they had been friends since childhood and parted three years ago when Baykov left to join the Navy.

While telling all this, Baykov's narrow gray eyes glanced at Fenichka, and a shy, tender, happy smile would flash on his tanned angular face. And, while Sasha involuntarily took on Baykov's emotions, he saw Fenichka in a new light. Why hadn't he ever noticed that no one else had such blue eyes or such golden curls or such beautiful small ears set close to her head?

They sat down to eat. Fenichka served Baykov a steaming bowl of borscht and he treated even the borscht with sailor's roughness. First he put so much pepper into it that the red beet soup turned gray; then he put almost half a jar of mustard into the bowl. He tasted the borscht and approved it, saying: "We can eat now."

Sasha wanted some borscht too.

"Well!" commented Fenichka. "Since when do you eat soup in the morning?"

"Hot soup in the morning that's a must for seamen!" Baykov pronounced authoritatively, and Sasha received a quarter-filled bowl of borscht.

Fenichka left the room to fetch something, and Sasha also put pepper and mustard into his soup. On tasting the first spoonful, he had a strong sensation of something bursting into flame inside his mouth and singeing his tongue, palate, and throat. Sasha choked, but with a great effort he kept from giving himself away and quickly swallowed a second and third spoonful. A steady little fire began burning inside him; nonetheless, Sasha thought that never in his life had he eaten anything tastier. And the thick-sliced bread was unusually good; for the first time he discovered the true taste of bread.

"Fenichka, how about the sailor's usual drink?" the seaman said rather diffidently, without his usual confidence.

"What's the idea? So early in the morning!" replied Fenichka, grumbling, but nevertheless placing a glass of vodka on the table for him.

Baykov grasped the glass between two fingers, winked at Sasha with a narrowed gray eye, said "Happy meeting," and, tilting back his head, emptied the glass in one swallow, then sniffed a crust of bread and ate a piece of cucumber.

They didn't offer Sasha any vodka. He drank some water in a goblet and also sniffed a crust of bread and ate a piece of cucumber.

After breakfast they discussed where they would go. The theater and the circus were dismissed immediately; since it was too hot, Fenicha wanted to go swimming, so they decided to go out of town.

"Get dressed, Alexander!" ordered the seaman. "And quickly, with a hop and a skip!"

When Sasha was dressed, Baykov twirled him round before him and said: "Your appearance leaves something to be desired: this button's about to fall off, your shoes aren't polished, your hair's shaggy." He pulled a lock of hair at the back of Sasha's head and added disapprovingly, "This little fellow's been neglected!"

Then, after rummaging through his own belongings, he got out a needle and thread and quickly fastened the button to Sasha's suspenders.

Baykov first took Sasha to have his shoes shined and then to the barbershop. This was the first time Sasha had had his shoes polished by a bootblack; it was both interesting and yet a little frightening. The bristles of the polishing brushes pleasantly tickled his toes through the openings of his sandals. And the bootblack's large hooked nose, which appeared to be peppered with gunpowder, seemed to be taking aim as if about to peck at Sasha's feet. When everything was done, Sasha hardly recognized his old sandals; they were transformed into a flaming orange color.

At the barbershop the barber asked Baykov what kind of haircut should he give the boy; did he want a side part, or a crew cut?

"Crew cut!" snapped Baykov decidedly.

The back of Sasha's head felt pleasantly cool, and he now looked like a little Baykov, who also had a crew cut.

"Eau de cologne?" asked the barber.

"White lilac!" snapped Baykov.

A cool, heavy, scented shower splashed on Sasha's head that left him in a pleasant daze for quite a while. Baykov also sprayed some white lilac on himself, and they left the barbershop dispensing fragrance.

Sasha felt that something new, unknown, had happened in his life. He did everything that Baykov did, except he didn't drink any vodka. It wasn't like this with Fenichka or even with Mama; with them Sasha always felt his isolation, and despite their tender care, he stood alone. But now for the first time a grown person shared his everyday life equally with him. Maybe this was what having a daddy meant: to live his everyday masculine life equally with Sasha.

They took a taxi to the railroad station. Sasha sat next to the driver, and Fenichka kept glancing over his shoulder to watch the meter. Then they transferred to the train and got off at the third stop.

Just beyond a settlement of summer homes, the wide, shining river could be seen; its low banks were dense with bushes. At the bend the bushes parted, and there was an expanse of hot, yellow sand spotted with tanned bodies. They chose a little spot on the very edge of the beach which was not so crowded, and Fenichka went into the bushes to change.

Baykov and Sasha changed right on the beach. Sasha watched the seaman with delight; under the brown skin, suntanned almost black, his hard, strong muscles moved. On his broad chest a blue flower was tattooed that seemed to bob its head as the muscles moved. Baykov slapped his sides then did a handstand. He walked around on his hands, and after making a wide circle, he stood first on one hand, then on the other, did a somersault, and landed on his feet. Sasha tried to do a handstand, too, but instead all he did was a hop, his feet jerking. Baykov helped him; grabbing Sasha by the heels, he raised his feet up into the air.

"Use your hands to push your body up!" he said, and gradually he began to let go of Sasha's feet. Then he let go completely, and Sasha tumbled down. Nevertheless, for a fraction of a second he had felt all the weight of his body on his hands, and this meant that he really had done a handstand.

From behind the bushes came Fenichka, barefoot, wearing shorts and a halter, and walking gingerly on the sand. She carried her clothes in her arms. Her skin was so white that it seemed as though the sun had never touched it, and the whiteness of her slender legs had a blue tinge. Sasha felt ashamed of Fenichka in front of Baykov; he was especially ashamed of her bluish frail legs. He tried to shield her, to distract Baykov's attention from her, but Baykov it seemed, was not at all embarrassed by Fenichka's appearance. He took her clothes from her hands, put them on the bank, weighted them down with a flat river rock, took Fenichka's hand and led her to the river. Sasha admired Baykov's manliness but he felt, he himself could not behave that way. She lingered at the edge of the water. She tested the water first with one and then the other foot; she shrieked and pushed away Baykov, who was trying to pull her in from the bank. Sasha couldn't stand this humiliating sight any longer, so he jumped into the water with a splash.

He swam away from the bank and then looked back. Fenichka had waded into the water up to her knees, and Baykov was dumping handfuls of water on her. She was spreading this water over her chest, arms, and stomach; then, holding onto Baykov's finger, with little shrieks, she plunged into the water up to her neck, squealed once more, and plunged in again.

After his swim, Sasha rested on his back for a while. He scared away a green frog sitting on a water lily leaf, and then he caught and let free a dragon fly with dry little mica wings. Baykov was still playing with Fenichka. Now she was pretending to swim: she lay with her stomach on Baykov's hand, slapped the water with the palms of her hands, and jerked her legs in a way that reminded Sasha of the scared frog. Of course Baykov must be very tired of all this; he probably wanted to get into the water himself, to swim around, and he really needed to be rescued.

"Daddy!" Sasha called loudly. "Swim over here!"

Baykov glanced back, waved his free hand, and said something to Fenichka; she floundered on in the water. Then with an easy motion Baykov set her on her feet and with powerful strokes swam over to Sasha.

They got out of the water together. Fenichka sat fully dressed on the bank, combing her hair.

"Have you had enough swimming?" she asked vexedly. "I've hurt my foot on a rock."

"Where?" Baykov asked with concern, squatting.

"Never mind! It's all right now."

"Can you call swimming in a river swimming?" said Baykov disdainfully. "One can swim only in the sea."

"What does the sea look like?" asked Sasha.

"The sea? Haven't you ever seen it?"

"No."

"The sea—well, it's the sea," commented Fenichka.

Sasha had heard such an expression from Fenichka on many occasions, and though it didn't explain anything, somehow it had a consoling effect. However, Baykov didn't agree with Fenichka.

"No," he said pensively, "one can't say that about the sea. It's different. Sometimes it's blue, sometimes green, sometimes white as milk, and other times it's black as night. Sometimes it lies still and smooth as a mirror, sometimes its waves are playful, and other times it seems to turn up its whole depth, throwing up huge waves as big as houses. . . . No, one must see it," he added with conviction.

Sasha listened without noticing how his teeth were chattering with cold.

"Why aren't you getting dressed?" asked Fenichka. "You've turned blue!" and she threw Sasha a towel.

"Stop!" Baykov caught the towel. "The body should dry off by itself. Come on, catch up with me!" He tapped Sasha on the back and ran off.

With a cry of delight Sasha dashed after him. They chased each other all over the beach until the seaman said: "That's enough! Now everything's all right."

And truly both Sasha and his trunks were quite dry.

They put on their clothes and went up the river toward the forest. The path passed through a walnut grove and led them to a wide, calm, blue lake surrounded by a thick forest. Suddenly it started to rain. It was difficult to understand where it came from. The sun was shining as usual, the sky had still the same blue, and light transparent clouds were quickly moving across it; they seemed more like gossamer steam than clouds.

True, the jagged edge of a remote gray cloud was swirling above the other shore of the lake, but that was far away, and Sasha wondered why Baykov suddenly grabbed him and Fenichka by the hand and led them to the forest. They stopped at its edge under some tall elder bushes. From here, through the dense golden mesh of sunlit raindrops, they could easily see the downpour on the other side. There appeared on the lake a white strip that quickly widened and concealed the blue as it approached. The hissing white strip was about to devour the last blue edge of the lake when it suddenly stopped. Just as it seemed the blue would triumph, the seaman quickly bent the elder branches overhead so as to shield them. Just then the blue disappeared, the sky darkened, and with a crash, thunder, and crack, the downpour hit the forest.

The branches Baykov held over their heads provided a good shelter. When the rain wore itself out, stopping as suddenly as it had begun, they discovered that they weren't the least bit wet.

Once again the sun shone, the earth steamed and smelled of freshness, while on the opposite shore, against a background of forest, one end of a steaming rainbow stuck into the ground. And there was heard the piercing cry of a bird which seemed to express a combination of triumph and anxiety.

"A jay," said Baykov. "There it is."

Sasha saw the bird, smaller than a jackdaw but much larger than a sparrow, sitting on the branch of a birch tree which stood apart from the other trees.

At first the bird appeared to be gray, but when it turned around, the sun's rays fell against its feathers, and tiny, bright blue spots flashed on its body.

"It's like a sentinel in the forest— the first to warn of coming danger," said Baykov. "As soon as a hunter or any stranger enters the forest, the little bird signals to all the inhabitants: 'Hey there, look out!' And some creatures hide in a burrow or in the hollow of a tree, while some take to their heels."

As if answering the seaman, the jay again cried sharply and hoarsely, as if coughing, and flew toward the forest.

A narrow, rubber-smooth body swept by close to the ground, and after it landed on the branch of an elm, it appeared to be a pigeon-sized bird with a predatory, hooked beak.

"A little hawk!" said Fenichka.

"Oh no! That's a goatsucker; didn't you recognize it?" Baykov turned to Sasha: "A hawk is destructive, but a goatsucker is a helpful friend: he catches mice even better than a fox does— he destroys the pests in the fields. How I used to love the forest!" he said with joy and wonder. "But now I don't need anything but the sea!"

"Well, you're at it again: the sea, the sea. . . . As far as I'm concerned, there's nothing better than the city," said Fenichka.

"Seamen love the sea, and their wives love the city."

They climbed a hillock and stopped near three old birch trees that had grown together. Behind them was the forest, below them was a meadow covered with bluebells and daisies. To the left, above a grove of nut trees, glimmered a calm, smooth lake. "See how still the lake is!" said Baykov.

They halted here. Baykov lay down on the dry leaves under a cluster of birch trees, Sasha found a place close to him, and Fenichka began pouring tea from a thermos bottle into little yellow plastic cups.

"I like southern towns," commented Baykov. "Moscow isn't so great! Of course it's a big city, but there's no such beauty in it. In Odessa the huge stairway leading from the boulevard down to the water's edge alone is worth admiration! Or the Primbul in Sevastopol!"

"What's the Primbul?" asked Fenichka.

"It's a boulevard by the sea. Seamen always stroll there. Their duck uniforms are white as snow, their buckles shine, and their bell-bottomed pants are so long they sweep the sidewalk. You know, Fenya, when young sailors go to the boulevard they always bleach their collars."

"And what for?"

"So that they look like old seamen. Our worn collars are faded, but their new ones are bright blue."

"And what's the advantage in looking like you?"

"The girls know that the young ones have empty pockets; they can't afford to take girls dancing, to the movies, or for an ice cream. So that's why they disguise themselves."

"Did you disguise yourself, too?"

"I had no reason to." Baykov looked at Fenichka and sighed.

"Sasha, have you finished your drink?" asked Fenichka. "Go run around and play. Why sit here like an old man?"

Sasha would have liked to stay and listen to Baykov's stories about towns, boulevards, and seamen, but he also didn't want to look like an old man to his new daddy.

Sasha went deep into the forest. First he tried to imagine himself as Leather Stocking, then as Otseol, leader of the Seminoles, but somehow he didn't believe his own imagination. He gave a war cry, but his voice sounded cold and uninspiring. He couldn't play Indians today; his favorite heroes from novels faded before the real, live one at the edge of the forest. Sasha didn't try to fight the call of his heart. He ran back to Baykov.

Fenichka and Baykov were sitting on the grass, leaning against a birch tree; he was holding her hand. When Sasha ran up to

them, Baykov jerked his hand away and with a look of anxiety
began winding his watch.

"Daddy, what kind of ships did you travel on?" asked Sasha,
panting.

They sat under a cluster of birches, with Baykov in the middle
and Sasha and Fenichka at his sides. One of Baykov's arms was
around Sasha's shoulders, and the other encircled Fenichka's
waist. Sasha felt the warmth of his body and the gentle weight of
his hand on his shoulders. Baykov sang about the Black Sea,
about seamen in Odessa, about Sevastopol, and about his
friends who had gone to a bloody fight and would never return.

"Vasya, let's sing 'The Moon Turned Crimson,'" asked
Fenichka. Baykov began singing:

The moon turned crimson,
I saw the sea waves rolling. . .

Fenichka joined him in a thin voice:

Let's go for a boat ride, my beauty,
I've been waiting so long just for you!

Sasha thought that Baykov sang better; Fenichka's voice was
shrill, and besides, her little face was straining so hard that it
had turned crimson. But Baykov added more power and fervor
to his voice. Now Sasha really liked the way they sang; a silvery
thread, Fenichka's voice mingled with Baykov's full velvety
basso that carried the tune. They had hardly stopped singing
when Fenichka slapped herself on the forehead, killing a mosquito. "It's time to go home," she said. "Otherwise the mosquitoes will devour us."

Their return home brought Sasha a triumph: Nina, Volodya,
and little Pavlik were playing in the yard, and they saw him
passing, hand in hand with his new father, whom no one in the
world could forbid Sasha from calling "Daddy."

While Fenichka prepared supper, Sasha showed Baykov his
toys. Baykov liked his large fleet of cars, but he was dissatisfied
with Sasha's flotilla consisting of a paddlewheel steamer and a
little boat carved from bark. "You should have a cruiser and at
least a torpedo boat," said Baykov. "As it is, it's completely out-
dated—a Russian fleet of years ago!"

The thing which impressed the seaman most, however, was a
large yellow wool bear with round glass eyes and an oilcloth
nose. When you bent the bear over he would open his pink jaws
and give a long, good-natured, and dwindling growl.

"Devil take you, just like a real one!" marveled Baykov,
bending the bear down over and over again. "Wouldn't Keshka
be surprised to see this!"

Sasha was delighted. He loved this bear. His name was Kuzya,

and Sasha often slept with him. Nevertheless he was afraid that
Baykov might make fun of his toy, but obviously they both agreed about this toy, too.

After supper Fenichka tried sending Sasha to bed. His eyes had been closing for quite a while now, but he really didn't want to part with his new daddy. Baykov looked at his watch.

"It's 10:15," he said, sighing. "I'll have to be going soon."

"Will you come again?" asked Sasha.

"Now it'll have to be on the way back. And I didn't get to meet the lady of the house."

"She's on the night shift today," said Fenichka, and Sasha understood that "the lady of the house" was Mama, and he regretted that his mother would not see Baykov.

"Well, run along, and buck up," Baykov said affectionately.

These masculine words, "buck up," ennobled the vexing, bitter necessity of going to bed, and it made the parting easier for Sasha.

"So long, pal!" and Baykov gripped Sasha's hand to the point of pleasant pain.

"Enough of this fondling!" Fenichka ordered impatiently. "Get to bed!"

Sasha undressed, threw his clothes on a chair, and thought at the same time that Baykov wouldn't like such carelessness. He carefully folded his pants and shirt and hung them on the back of the chair. He was already under the covers, but his overflowing heart prompted him to go to Baykov once more. He just had to take one last—the very last—look at his new daddy. In only his nightshirt, his bare feet thumping on the cold floor, Sasha ran to the door and opened it very quietly. He couldn't understand why Fenichka was so startled and why she scolded him so angrily: "When will you get to sleep, for goodness sake!"

Baykov's eyes were stern, but there was a faint smile in the corners of his mouth, and this was enough for Sasha. He ran back to bed and curled up in a ball. Right away he was overcome by a dream filled with the day's events: here was the river, and the jay crying "Look out!" to the forest creatures, and the goatsucker shining shoes, and the bootblack pecking at mice, and a downpour of white lilac splashing down onto the lake, meadow, and forest, and the song about a solitary sail. And this song awoke Sasha. He opened his eyes and was filled immediately with the warmth of his new love. Baykov was still there, they were separated only by the thin partition of the door nearby. Thinking of Baykov, he suddenly realized that he definitely must give him a gift as a keepsake. The paddlewheel steamer? This was from the Russian fleet of years ago. The little boat? It looked so awkward and puny. One of the cars? He didn't need any. And suddenly an idea dawned on him, and he yielded immediately to it. He had to give Kuzya to Baykov.

"But I don't want to give him up!" said something inside of him, and he felt ashamed at first, then joyful. And that's just why he had to give the bear away: because it was dear to him. The bear would growl, reminding Baykov of Sasha, and later the seaman would give it to Keshka, who would be very surprised!

Sasha got out of bed, mournfully dragged the growling Kuzya from a dark corner of the room, and suddenly thrust open the door. "Daddy!" he shouted in a jubilant voice and became silent immediately.

Fenichka was alone in the room; she was sitting on the arm of the chair, bending over slightly. Had Baykov really gone? But when Fenichka turned around, Sasha saw Baykov. He hadn't left; he was sitting in the armchair, hidden by Fenichka.

"Daddy, take this!"

"The devil take you!" cried Fenichka. "I'm sick and tired of you!"

Sasha's whole body shuddered. He glanced timidly at Fenichka's strange and terrible face, flushed with anger, and he dashed to his room. He dropped the bear on the floor and dug his head into the pillow. For a while he heard nothing but his beating heart, then he heard voices, very quiet and distant, because they came to Sasha through his pain and humiliation, through the unbearable anguish caused by something irreparable.

"Listen," Baykov was saying, "I didn't expect you to be like that."

"Like what?"

"Mean," said Baykov after a short pause.

"You'd be mean, too," replied Fenichka plaintively. "We've met at last, and not a moment of peace!"

"Yes, but you should understand. . . ."

"All right. You understand too much. Sit down."

"He was calling me Daddy!" Baykov smiled.

"Oh, everyone is his daddy. Well, what's the matter with you?"

There was a short silence, then Baykov's voice was heard again: "No. . . . I just can't go on this way . . . it's as if I had a splinter in my heart. . . . Oh, go away, you're no good!"

"So you've become good now? Was it on Sevastopol Boulevard that they made you so good? You should have said so right away!"

"No!" Baykov exclaimed with a ringing sound, and for some reason became formal. "You're wasting your breath. What never happened, never happened—it was just as I wrote you.

I lived and waited for only one thing," and he added very quietly, "You stole from me the person I knew—you stole yourself from me."

"All right! You know what, I've had enough!" snapped Fenichka. "Pick up your junk and get out of here!"

"Yes, it's time I went," muttered Baykov pensively.

A raincoat rustled, the handle of the heavy suitcase clicked, the squeaking boots neared the door to Sasha's room, stopped, and Sasha heard the seaman's cautious breathing. Then the squeaking resumed, now as the footsteps departed.

"Tell the little fellow I'll drop in on my way back."

"You needn't bother."

"That's my business. Any messages for home? All right, good-bye."

Then the front door softly closed.

It was very quiet, so quiet that it seemed no one was left in the apartment except Sasha and his heart. Then came a broken, quick, rushing cry. Between the sobs the words: "I'll run away! Away! Away!"

1959

On the Island

Yury Kazakov

1

The steamer on which Inspector Zabavin had arrived gave a low, tremulous whistle, turned toward starboard with a list and resumed her schedule for remote northern ports. Zabavin didn't spare a glance back at her, he had been so bored for three whole days with this grimy-white ship, with the grinding of her winches at every stop, the din of her engines, her stubby-legged captain and the first mate with his jeering, debauched face, the rude waiters, and the nonstop drinking bout below deck at the bar in third class.

The more Zabavin traveled through the North, the more commonplace and tiresome it became. He had even ceased to notice the beauty of the northern landscape, the dark cliffs, the sea, though at one time he had been very fond of it all. Now here he was in the *karbas*-boat, irritated, angry, and unshaven. The curious contours of the island that crouched like an animal half submerged in the water, the dark green rocks below the surface, the jovial talk around him—all failed to attract his attention. He desired only, and that as quickly as possible, to find himself in a warm room ashore.

When the *karbas* had made its way through swarms of cutters, motorboats, and skiffs and had put in at the wooden wharf, Zabavin was the first to climb ashore; he halted, stretching his arms and legs, feeling the delight of solid ground beneath his feet.

The wharf was piled tightly with huge bales of dried brown and lilac seaweed and barrels of cement; rusting pipes and rails lay stacked along the walls of a squat warehouse. The smell of seaweed was acute and intoxicating with the somewhat weaker scent of fish, rope, oil, lumber, hay, and sea water—in short, all the smells with which seacoast wharves are usually redolent.

Zabavin yawned as he trudged over crushed cinders, past workshops with their quietly running machines, past a boiler shop radiating heat in the cold morning air. All around was the dismal earth, covered by a whitish moss with an outcropping of gray rock here and there. Emaciated horses and cows wandered alone over the moss; they were a melancholy sight, abandoned as they were on this barbarous island, where they were completely superfluous and useless. Zabavin took a deep breath and frowned as he asked some laborers the way to the office. When they pointed it out he walked directly toward it, no longer looking at anything else. His thoughts were focused only on getting to bed as quickly as he could. The last night on ship he had had virtually no sleep at all.

He was assigned to a room, and he slept soundly. On awakening he shaved, wet his hair with cologne, and combed it carefully until it shone. Next he brewed himself some strong, hot tea, which he drank from fine glass, and enjoyed a cigaret. Finally, straightening his tie, he equipped himself with a briefcase full of documents. He took pleasure in the fact that there he was again, comely, neat, and clean and had rid himself at last of the disgusting odor of salt cod with which he had been surfeited aboard ship. Spruced up, brisk and refreshed, fragrant with cologne and good tobacco, he started out for the office to get down to some real work on what he had come for.

All that day and the two following Zabavin spent on routine work, checking thick files of documents which were delivered to his office, making complicated calculations and inspecting vats of agar gelatine, crushing machines, warehouses, and laboratories. During the whole time he was cool, polite, and businesslike.

The director, warmed by this new man, fussed about and chattered, eagerly questioning Zabavin about Archangel as he accompanied him everywhere. He had bulging eyes which showed the underside of his lids, thick sideburns on fleshy, dove-colored cheeks, and he wore a skull cap. Rocking from side to side, he plodded heavily along on his stumps wheezing and sweating. Alongside the enormous director, Zabavin, slim, dark-haired, and wearing narrow slacks, looked like an adolescent.

The director talked about the pension he would soon receive, recited Fet's poetry in a quivering voice as he gazed sadly out to sea, and invited Zabavin to lunch on "what God hath provided," whereupon his eyes brimmed with tears. Zabavin, meanwhile, felt upon himself the young laborers' undisguised looks of envy and became still more cool and polite.

2

One day Zabavin wanted to send a telegram to Archangel. He set out for the weather station, finding it without difficulty by the high antenna from which a wire rigging extended circumferentially to the ground. Zabavin went up onto the porch and knocked on the door. Receiving no response, he opened the door and entered. He found himself in a large room that was clean and warm. No one was there. By the window stood a table and a tall wooden cabinet containing a barometer. A chronometer in a velvet-lined case, a pair of binoculars, and a few half-read magazines lay on the table. Suddenly one of the three or four doors burst open and a boyish radio operator peered out. He was young and self-assured, with a thin neck, a protruding Adam's apple, big ears, and hair combed down over his forehead. No sooner had he caught sight of Zabavin than he assumed a suspicious look.

"And who might you be?" he asked in a scared voice, trying to speak more gruffly and not knowing what to do with his big hands. He didn't let Zabavin finish his answer but, blushing and scowling, blurted out that the chief of the station was not in, that without her he wasn't allowed to accept anything for transmission, and that radio communications with Archangel were scheduled only in the evening.

Zabavin smiled and said he'd come back in the evening. He felt the suspicious, frightened gaze of the radio operator on the back of his head as he went out on the porch.

Rejoicing in the warm weather and in having some free time, he started off on a walk around the island. He climbed up to the white tower of the lighthouse, and as he looked about he noticed first how beautiful the sea was, how it flashed and darkened in the sun. Near the lighthouse he came upon a little boarded-up wooden chapel, and just down the hill from it was an old burial ground. He went down and, drawing a deep breath, began to wander among the scattered mounds and dark gravestones, which were sinking gradually into the ground. On one stone Zabavin deciphered with difficulty:

BENEATH THIS STONE RESTS THE DUST
OF THE SERVANT OF GOD
OF THE SMOLENSK DISTRICT OF THE CITY
OF BELAYA
THE KEEPER AND OVERSEER OF THE LIGHTHOUSE
VASILY IVANOV PRUDNIKOV
HIS LIFE WITHOUT INTERRUPTION MEASURED 56 YEARS
HE SUCCUMBED AFTER A PILGRIMAGE TO THE SOLOVETS MONASTERY
IN THE YEAR 1858, THE 6TH DAY OF SEPTEMBER
LORD RECEIVE HIS SOUL IN PEACE

"M-m-m, yes," mused Zabavin with a touch of sadness. "A hundred years ago. One hundred years." He attempted to read more, but the other stones were even older, completely overgrown with moss and impossible to make out. He sat facing the sea on one of the stones; he remained this way for some time, motionless, surrendering himself to the melancholy fascination of autumn and the forgotten burial ground. Then, deeply but pleasantly bemused, he slowly descended the hill and went home to bed.

But he slept poorly. He suddenly awoke and went to sit by the window. While he had been sleeping, fog had rolled in across the island. The mists were extremely thick so that nothing could

be seen now in any direction. The radio antenna, the lighthouse, the long, dark hillock, the factory workshops and smoke-
stacks, all had become invisible. Some goats stood herded
motionlessly together beneath his window. The life of the island
seemed to have come to a standstill. The mist muffled all sound;
only to the north a foghorn wailed without ceasing, and its
voice was both sad and ominous.

After Zabavin's visit to the burial ground, he began to harbor
a strange feeling toward the island. He found it impossible to
expel from his mind the thought of that lighthouse keeper who
had lived and died a hundred years ago, when the island had
been doubtless even more dismal. He suddenly began to feel
queasy from the mist, the wild moans of the fog horn, and the
specter of the motionless goats. He felt a desire for talk, for
people, for music. He quickly got ready and walked to the
station, peering carefully about. He found his way with difficulty in the fog and the evening darkness, which fell rapidly
in autumn.

The chief of the station was a girl about twenty-five years old
with the unusual name of Augusta. She was petite and had slim
legs. Her hair was cut short, which made her neck seem
unusually delicate and fragile. Her eyes were fringed with long,
thick lashes that gave her face surprising animation. Everybody
on the island nicknamed her simply Gustya. Whenever she
smiled, her cheeks would flame into a warm blush while her
small ears would turn pink. As Zabavin looked at her, he felt
both touched and amused. He felt he wanted to embrace her,
smoothe her short springy hair, and feel her soft warm breath
on his throat.

He gave the radio man the text of his telegram. His warm,
shining eyes looked direct and hard at Gustya, and he asked her
permission to stay awhile and listen to the radio. Gustya, readily
and, as it seemed to Zabavin, happily led him to the one small
room of her apartment. She lit a table lamp and began to set
things for tea.

As she got the cups out, she became more and more agitated.
She placed them on the table, rattling the spoons, and poured
sugar into the sugar bowl. Zabavin sat down. His narrow slacks
rode up, and he gave them a downward tug, crossing one leg
over the other, as was his habit. He turned on the radio.
Illuminated by the garnet-colored twilight, he tuned in on
some nearby Norwegian station and lit a cigaret, his lips set in a
happy expression.

With unaccustomed intensity he examined his amiable
hostess and every detail of her room, with its one window
facing south, the ten or so books in a bookcase, and a carefully

made bed that looked hard. He recalled the unconcealed avidity with which the working women in the factory had looked at him, and to keep from smiling he began to think about the island, the burial ground, and about what was outside the window—darkness and mist. But, strangely, these thoughts failed to upset or depress him now; on the contrary he listened with great pleasure to the glassily transparent music, the snapping of the stove in the large room outside, and surreptitiously watched his hostess.

"Amazing! I didn't dream or even guess that such an evening awaited me!" he exclaimed happily. "You know, you travel and travel and all you have is boiling water, stale gray rolls, and loneliness. Yes, even though you bring your wife! When did anyone ever have such luck as today?"

"Ah!" said Gustya, lowering her eyes. "You're married? Has it been for long?"

"Yes, long!" answered Zabavin with a kind of sadness. "I have two children, too. It's awful! I just can't get used to the fact that I'm married, that I'm thirty-five. Then suddenly somehow it all disappears. When you're traveling alone, or you're sitting in some room for travelers, you keep thinking. How long I have dreamt about love, about happiness—and now nothing. So you knock around the world as an inspector, and you lose contact with your family. But my wife is a fine person; others live worse than I."

Zabavin suddenly intercepted an odd look from Gustya, remembered himself, and blushed.

"Forgive me," he muttered, returning to himself with sudden disgust. "Who do I think I am? This doesn't interest you! But it burst out of me: I haven't talked with anyone for a whole week, and now such a marvelous evening."

"Please, it's nothing!" said Gustya, pouring tea into Zabavin's cup. "Drink up!"

As he lifted his cup, Zabavin began to laugh. They talked, and he soon learned that she had worked here for some time. She had already received a double salary rate on contract; she was bored, and she wanted to go to Archangel or Leningrad. After they had talked about boredom and discussed mutual acquaintances, they began to speak of love and happiness. They both became even more animated.

"You're speaking now of conscious love," Zabavin said suddenly with serious bitterness, even though Gustya hadn't spoken at all of conscious love. "Everyone makes judgments about love; they talk it over and discuss it and judge who should love whom. Writers write about love while their readers get together and argue whether 'he's' worthy of 'her,' or 'she' of

'him,' which is the better, the purer, the more sensitive, and
which more befits the age of socialism. But meanwhile none of
us in our own position can ever comprehend what love is! And
the more I think about it, the surer I am that in love a very small
part is played by such qualities as intelligence, talent, honor,
etc., while the most important thing is something quite
different, something of which you don't speak and which you
can in no way comprehend. And you don't have to go far to find
it! I know a guy who's a lout, a drunk, and a cad. He's a man
without honor or conscience. And, can you imagine, women
are crazy about him, women who are smart and intelligent. And
does he ever know they love him! He borrows money from
them, drinks, treats them like cows, while they weep in shame.
I saw it myself! Why is it?"

"You probably don't see in him what these women do," said
Gustya seriously.

"Bunk! What do they see in him! Intelligence? Talent? Depth
of soul? Not likely! He's a lazy rotten lout. On top of everything
else he even hasn't any looks. He's got a mug like bloated fat.
I'll be damned if I'll ever understand it."

The floor squeaked in the radio room, a key was heard
locking the door, and finally all was quiet except for footsteps
outside the door.

"OK, I've received and sent everything. The radio log is on
the desk," shouted the radio operator as he slammed the outer
door. "Tomorrow is going to be fair. I'm dropping into the
club!" he yelled, already outside. He stomped across the porch,
and the house returned to silence.

Gustya's expression changed at once; she seemed afraid of
something. She gazed steadily at the dark window, looked at
Zabavin, and, blushing, immediately lowered her eyes. To
Zabavin his thirty-five years, his army background, his wife, his
work all seemed never to have existed. He suddenly felt a
poignant, tingling emotion and a dryness in his mouth. It was
exactly as he'd felt in his youth when he would lose his heart to
a girl in school and steal a kiss in the silent, white nights.

"There's still happiness to be had," Zabavin began quietly,
and Gustya understood by his tone that now he was about to
speak of something serious and good. She began to feel calmer.
She smiled up at him, and her beautiful velvet-soft eyes, resting
upon his face, widened.

"Most people hope in the future," continued Zabavin
quickly, sipping his tea. He sensed the darkness beyond the
window and the cold suspiration of the sea. "They hope in the
future while they live fussing in their tiny, uninteresting world.
They live without seeing or noticing anything good around

them. They curse life while being convinced that their day will suddenly come and happiness will be theirs. Everyone's like that. I'm like that, and you're like that. And meanwhile happiness is in everything and everywhere about us. This is happiness, that we are sitting here drinking tea, that I like you and that you know it."

Zabavin faltered, stopping to catch his breath. He smiled as though at himself. Gustya, her face scarlet, couldn't gather the courage to raise her eyes.

"It would be good if someone strong and wise enough to force us all to really look around us were to appear. In fact, the longer and the more we live, the less happy we are. Mankind is always young, but we—we grow old. At this moment I'm thirty-five and you're—"

"Twenty-five," Gustya interrupted in a whisper. She had made up her mind to raise her flaming face and looked straight into Zabavin's eyes.

"Well, there you are! Next year I'll be thirty-six and you'll be twenty-six. Both of us and everybody else will be a year older. Something will go out of us, some particle of eagerness, some amount of our cells will die forever, and then, gradually, from year to year. And most importantly, we'll age not only in body. Not only will we turn gray and bald and succumb to various illnesses that we don't have now, but our spirits will age, little by little, unnoticeably, but they'll age. What kind of happiness is that? No, there's no kind of happiness in that at all. I can't understand these people who live on and on, thinking: 'Summer will soon be here, and I'll be happy'; and when summer comes and they're not happy, they think: 'Winter will soon be here and I'll be happy.' It's not even worth talking about!"

"Then what does happiness consist of?" asked Gustya softly.

"What indeed? I also wonder about that. Take yourself; you want to be rid of the island. You are awaiting something. You think two or three years'll pass and you'll be happy. Absolutely not! Right now you're happy beyond measure, enormously happy, because you're healthy and young, because you have gorgeous eyes, because now that you're twenty-five, to look into your eyes is pure delight. You have meaningful work and the sea and this island. Just think about it!"

"That's easy to say!" said Gustya, smiling uncertainly.

"Sure! Of course the world is wide and there are many lovely places, and what good are islands! Of course Archangel is an immeasurably more interesting place than this island. When you think, and, I confess, even when I now think of Archangel or Moscow or Leningrad, one imagines theaters, lights, museums,

exhibitions, hubbub, traffic, and all that. In a word: Life! Right?
But actually, when I'm there I never notice any of that. I begin
to think about it only when I'm away from it. When I arrive in
Archangel I suddenly learn that my son is ill, that there's a
meeting at work that evening, that they want a report right
away—and you begin to run around like a squirrel in a cage,
completely oblivious to theaters and the like. How can anyone
say I live better than you? On a higher plane, as they say? No,
no, you're much happer than I: you're twenty-five and I'm
thirty-five.

"Of course, you'll get away sooner or later; you'll live in
Leningrad, see the Neva, the bridges and St. Isaac's. But believe
me, after you leave, you won't be able to forget the island, its
people, the sea, the smell of seaweed, the feathery clouds, the
sun, the thunder storms, the northern lights, the hurricanes,
and many years from now you'll realize it was right here that
you were happy."

"I don't know," said Gustya thoughtfully. "Somehow I've
never thought of it in that way."

"Well, it's almost always that way. We miss the past. It looks
better from a distance."

Zabavin felt stirred and, looking at Gustya, he thought against
his will how fine it would be to live a long life with her somewhere. He shook off the thought, realizing that it was out of
place and that he was quite powerless to change anything in
his life. But not to think about it was as impossible for him as it
was for him to leave her now, in spite of the fact that it had
already grown late.

He got up to leave only when the radio operator returned
from the club, began to whistle, and tuned in some jazz. Gustya
went out on the porch with Zabavin. They stood for a while
getting accustomed to the darkness.

"I'll walk you home; the wires are all over here," Gustya said,
and she took his hand. Her hand was rough and hot, and it
trembled.

"My darling," Zabavin said to himself, thanking her in
his thoughts, and he thought of himself immediately and
with sorrow.

The mist had lifted, and the foghorn had long been silent.
Overhead tiny stars shone with sharp intensity. The Milky Way
stretched out brilliantly, but seemingly rent in two. Quickly
mastering the darkness, Gustya went on ahead. Zabavin
followed behind, barely distinguishing her bright kerchief. He
trod uncertainly through the moss as he felt for the stony path.
They walked on in silence for several minutes, and then Gustya
stopped. Zabavin immediately sat down below the few yellow

lights of the settlement.

"Well, here we are," said Gustya. "Now you can go the rest of the way by yourself without getting lost. Good-bye."

"Wait a while longer," begged Zabavin, "while I smoke a cigaret."

"All right," answered Gustya after thinking for a moment. She took his hand once more, continued on a few steps, and stopped by a kind of fence. She leaned against it, turning to face Zabavin. He lit a cigaret and tried to see the expression on her face by the light of the match, but in vain.

Down below them the surf pounded rhythmically with the incoming tide. It had grown cold. The wind bore the uniquely melancholy fragrance of the autumnal sea. And the sea itself was a deep and secretive black.

Zabavin suddenly noticed that Gustya's face was alternately shining palely and then disappearing in the darkness. He turned and in three or four seconds saw the high white window of the lighthouse bathed in brilliance. Its bright beam flashed for a moment into the night and went out again. Soon the window flashed again and went out. It kept on flashing in this way continuously. It was both strange and pleasant to see that momentary, soundless light. Zabavin turned again to Gustya.

"You are a beautiful girl," he whispered softly and sorrow-fully. He felt ashamed, as if looking at himself with another's eyes. He condemned himself as he bent and kissed Gustya hard on her motionless, cold lips. Gustya turned from him without a word. Zabavin took her by her thin shoulders and led her into the darkness, into the rustling bushes and brittle undergrowth with its sharp smell of autumn. To get further away from the lighthouse he led her over the soft moss covering the hard, cold rock. Finally they stopped. Ahead there was silent darkness and the roar of the sea.

"Why?" she asked with sadness. "You don't really know me at all! But besides—why?"

Zabavin kissed her again, but as he did so, his face was sorrowful, his eyes closed, even though he really imagined that perhaps this was that happiness about which they had just been talking.

"Let's not do it. Let's go back," she said softly.

"Don't be angry!" begged Zabavin quietly as he obeyed her.

At the fence where they had first kissed, Gustya paused. With a brief moan she pressed her face to Zabavin's cold raincoat.

"Until tomorrow," she said at last, sighing and wiping away the tears. "Now I won't sleep all night. Why, why all this?"

She pushed him away from her and left almost running

toward home. Suddenly she seemed pitiful to him as he saw her go. Then he stood for some time watching the lighthouse flash and the distant, warm glow of Gustya's window. His face burned, his throat was parched. He kept groaning and frowning, yet he was powerless to leave, and his heart beat slowly and heavily.

3

The ship on which Zabavin intended to leave for Archangel was due at the island in a week. Ahead were seven unusual, happy days! But on the following morning the radio operator from the station came to Zabavin's office and silently handed him a telegram. On the form was written: URGENTLY AWAIT ARCHANGEL STOP DON'T WAIT STEAMSHIP STOP TODAY OR TOMORROW SCHOONER SUVOY ARRIVES ISLAND STOP MAKSIMOV.

Zabavin felt numb as the radio man went out. He tried to continue working, but he didn't understand anything that was said to him, and all the figures were meaningless. Somehow he managed his affairs, signed the final documents, registered the results of his mission with the director and went back to his quarters.

That evening, as Zabavin was getting ready to go to Gustya for the last time, the schooner arrived at the island. The ship appeared all of a sudden, like fate. She made herself known by a short blast of her siren, by her mast lights, one green and one white, and by a radio message that was received first at the lighthouse and then at the station. In agitation Zabavin sent a telegram in answer, and the schooner remained at anchor until morning. Zabavin and Gustya roamed the island until two in the morning. As they walked they frightened some partridges that flew up with a muffled, whirring sound. They sat on cold, rough stones, loving one another with increasing strength and depth, illumined by the schooner's lights, reminders of their fast-approaching separation.

Then they went to the station, and again the radio receiver emitted its garnet twilight. Gay music was playing softly, interspersed by the mumbling of the announcers. Again they drank tea, talked but little—rather they looked at one another, unable to have their fill.

"What is this between us?" asked Gustya. "Is it happiness? Tell me! I don't know. . . ."

"There, there," answered Zabavin lightly, "it's simply a pleasant evening."

"My God!" she said. "How can you? How can you really leave? You're going soon! You've only just appeared, and you're leaving already!"

Give me a ticket
For a farewell gift,
A train ticket
To somewhere. . . .

Zabavin drew out the words.

"What?" Gustya didn't understand. "What kind of ticket?"

"It's a song. . . . "

And I don't care
Where the train goes,
So long as it goes
Somewhere!

"It's a gay sort of song. Don't you know it?"

"You said," Gustya switched on the dial of the radio, "you have a son?"

"I've got two children, two! A boy and a girl. Yes, indeed, my darling."

The pallid dawn broke charily. In the room the window lightened. Zabavin stood up, glancing fleetingly into the mirror. He saw his pale, miserable face. He went to the window and wiped the moisture from it with his hand.

The sky was bright azure, empty as though made of glass; the sea was enormous, bulging and still. Two hundred yards or so from the shore, like a specter, the schooner lay motionless at anchor, and on her masts her pale lights still burned.

Wherever the eye turned, all was frozen in stillness—on the shore and on the water—all was motionless, vacant, dead.

He turned from the window and looked at Gustya. She sat at the table, her hands pressed to her breast. Her eyes were closed, and her pale little face looked as calm as a sleeper's. Zabavin slowly put on his coat.

"Gustya, it's time," he said aloud and lit a cigaret. But somehow he didn't feel the strength of the cigaret.

"What? Already? Wait, I'll—I'll go with you!" Gustya said quickly. Zabavin turned again to the window and leaned on the sill. He heard Gustya's heavy breathing as she walked about the room.

They went out together on the porch. Zabavin breathed the cold, sharp air, he looked at the flaming sunrise, at the moss, gray with frost. They walked side by side, not by the path but directly to the sea. The moss crunched under their feet. It was low tide. The *karbas* on a trailer seemed a long way from the water. They had to push it for quite a while. Their faces became red, they were short of breath, but finally they boarded her and shoved off from shore. Zabavin manned the oars and began to pull away slowly. Gustya sat at the stern. Her face seemed especially dark at this hour as she looked over Zabavin's head as she manned the rudder oar.

The water was extraordinarily transparent. Rocks, sand, seaweed like horses' tails, and fronds of sea cabbage silently swam by beneath them. Every so often Zabavin stopped rowing to look at the dark pink medusae hanging motionless in the water. He wondered that anything could catch his attention at such a moment.

The *karbas* moored quietly alongside the schooner. The skipper, wearing a sleeveless blue jacket and high boots, immediately came up on deck. He was hatless, with tow hair and high cheekbones. His young face was puffy from sleep.

"Comrade Zabavin?" he asked, pronouncing the "o" in "comrade" strongly* as he leaned over from above. "Heave up your line!"

Zabavin passed him his suitcase and heaved up his line. Then he turned to Gustya. Swaying, he took three steps toward the stern. Gustya got up and stood looking at him through tear-filled eyes. They kissed long and hard to the point of pain, then Zabavin, heaving a sigh, turned and climbed aboard the schooner. The skipper looked at them with a serious expression, helped Zabavin, and quickly went below deck in the bow.

In a moment sleepy sailors began to come topside from the lower deck, pulling on their jackets as they came. The schooner sprang to life. The deck, rimmed with frost, became covered with the dark prints of their boots. The diesel engine began to hum as the anchor chain rang. A scarcely noticeable breeze arose, rippling the water. A lock of hair fell over Gustya's forehead. She didn't push it back but sat motionless.

The skipper himself manned the wheel. With a glance at Zabavin, he set sail slowly. The schooner moved, and the *karbas* with Gustya in it began to fall behind. At the schooner's bow stood a tousled-headed sailor. He dropped a plumb line over the side and shouted raucously: "Eight!"

In the depths, the greenish rocks, the dark patches of seaweed, and the medusae were visible as before. Zabavin stood at the rail and watched the shore and the *karbas* receding further and further away. Gustya remained sitting as she was, without moving. The black bow of the *karbas*, riding high, turned slowly toward the shore under the force of the wind. Zabavin heard an empty ringing in his head. He looked at the island, at the *karbas*; his eyes were dry and inflamed. Making her way from dangerous waters into the open sea, the schooner increased her speed. The skipper, passing the wheel to a sailor, left the helm to stand beside Zabavin.

"Tomorrow toward dusk we'll be in Archangel," he said quietly.

* A dialectal trait of northern Russians.

The island had already become a hazy blue strip. Only the white lighthouse was now distinguishable, nothing else. There was a strong swell, the schooner's timbers shivered from the diesel engine. Finally, even the strip of the island disappeared. All around was water, its deep, regular waves stretching as far as the horizon. The sun had come up, but clouds had also gathered in the east, and it seemed quite overcast.

"There'll be a breeze," said the skipper, yawning.

"Now hear this! Batten down! Look alive!" he suddenly shouted.

"Please, won't you join me below?" he invited Zabavin. They went below and sat at a narrow table facing one another. They smoked.

"Would you like a little something?" asked the captain, reaching into a small cupboard. As Zabavin took the drink, his entire body shuddered.

"Now how do you feel?" asked the skipper. "How about a refill?"

"Everything's fine, old man!" said Zabavin. "Thanks!"

"Who was that, your wife?" asked the skipper quietly.

"No," answered Zabavin faintly. His lips began to tremble.

"Lie down and rest," suggested the skipper. "There's a spare bunk over there."

Zabavin obediently undressed and lay on the bunk. It was narrow and hard, with a life jacket at the head. The rising and falling of the deck was hardly noticeable. Beyond the bulkhead the sea rippled.

"So here is happiness," thought Zabavin, and he immediately saw Gustya's face. "This is love! How strange. Love."

Give me a ticket
For a farewell gift.

As he lay there, pressing his lips in sorrow, he kept thinking of Gustya and the island. He kept seeing her face, her eyes, he kept hearing her voice, and he couldn't tell whether it was a dream or reality.

Beyond the ship's hull rippled the sea, and its clamor was the sound of a joyfully coursing, never silent, stream.

1966

Born in Moscow, graduated from the Gorky Literary Institute. He bagan publishing sketches and articles in monthly magazines in 1953. His first volume of short stories, *Manka,* appeared in 1958 in Archangel. Today he lives in Moscow, but travels constantly throughout the country, especially in the North. He is known chiefly as a writer of short stories.

Kazakov, Yury P. (1927–).

His main collections: *On the Bus Stop* (Na polustanke, 1959); *On the Road* (Po doroge, 1961); *An Easy Life* (Legkaya zhizn, 1963); *The Smell of Bread* (Zapakh khleba, 1965); *Two in December* (Dvoe v dekabre, 1966).

Born near Moscow, of an educated family. After studying cinematography at the State Cinema Institute in Moscow, he served during World War II as a political officer and then as a war correspondent. His first story was published in 1940. Today he lives in Moscow, having traveled in France, Finland, Germany, Hungary, and Morocco. Short-story writer.

Nagibin, Yury M. (1920—).

His main collections: *A Man from the Front* (Chelovek s fronta, 1943); *A Big Heart* (Bolshoe serdtse, 1944); *The Grain of Life* (Zerno zhizni, 1948); *Before Holidays* (Pered prazdnikom, 1960); *In the Early Spring* (Ranney vesnoy, 1961); *Clear Creeks* (Chistye prudy, 1962); *Far from War* (Daleko ot voyny, 1964); *The Night Guest* (Nochnoy gost, 1966).

Born in Moscow, of Ossetic origin. In 1942 he volunteered and fought at the front. He graduated from the Tbilisi State University in 1950; for a while taught in a village school. On returning to Moscow, he worked for a time as an editor on literary journals. His first volume (poetry) appeared in 1956. Today he lives in Moscow and is one of the most popular poet-singers in the Soviet Union.

Okudzhava, Bulat S. (1924—).

His main books of poetry: *Lyrics* (Lirika, 1956); *Islands* (Ostrova, 1959); *The Jolly Drummer* (Vesyoly barabnshchik, 1964); *Generous March* (Mart velikodushny, 1967); Prose: Good-bye, Schoolboy! (Bud zdorov, shkolyar!, 1961).

Born in Rostov-on-the-Don, the daughter of a bank clerk. She studied systematically at home and at the local high school, but, for financial reasons, could not finish. She began writing poetry and prose very early; in the 1920s, until 1935, worked on various journals in Rostov. Her first play was published in 1939. During World War II she was assigned to a special ambulance train in order to write a book about it. In 1946 devoted herself totally to writing. In 1960 she visited the United States.

Panova, Vera F. (1905—).

Her main books: *The Fellow Travelers* (Sputniki, also known as *The Train*, 1946); *Kruzhilikha* (1947); *Bright Shore* (Yasny bereg, 1949); *Seasons of a Year* (Vremena goda, also known as *Looking Ahead*, 1954); *Seryozha* (also known as *Time Walked*, 1958); *Evdokiya* (1958); *A Worker's Settlement* (Rabochy poselok, 1966).

Solzhenitsyn, Alexander I. (1918—).

Born in Kislovodsk (Caucasus) into a family of the intelligentsia. Since 1924 lived with his mother (his father died on the front before his son's birth) in Rostov-on-the-Don. Studied at and graduated from the Rostov University, department of physics and mathematics. Later enrolled in the Moscow Institute of Philosophy, Literature and History, where he took courses by correspondence. In 1941, having graduated *cum laude*, he started teaching physics at school, near Rostov; in the same year he was drafted as a simple soldier. Soon, after some training, he was put in charge of the artillery battery, became a captain, and was twice decorated. In 1945 he was arrested and sentenced without trial to eight years of forced labor, to be followed by exile. In 1953, when released from the camp, Solzhenitsyn began his exile in the little village in Kazakstan, where he taught school. While yet in the camp, he was operated on for a tumor; later, in Tashkent, he was treated for cancer. In 1956 settled in Ryazan and continued teaching school till 1962, then devoted himself fully to writing. In 1969 Solzhenitsyn was expelled from the Union of the Soviet Writers, and in 1970 was awarded the Nobel prize for literature.

His main books: *One Day in the Life of Ivan Denisovich* (Odin den Ivana Denisovicha, published in *Novy Mir*, 1962); *The Cancer Ward* (Rakovy korpus, 1968); *The First Circle* (V kruge pervom, 1968); and *August 1914* (Avgust 1914, 1971), published abroad only. His short stories include: "An Incident at Krechetovka Station" (Sluchay na stantsii Krechetovka); "Matryona's Home" (Matryonin dvor); "For the Good of the Cause" (Dlya polzy dela); and "Zakhar Kalita" — all published in *Novy Mir*, 1963–1966.

Yashin, Alexander (1913–).

Born of peasant parents and educated in a pedagogical secondary school. For some time taught in the country. His first book of poems was published in 1934. The following year he entered the Gorky Institute of Literature in Moscow. During World War II served in the navy and published in navy newspapers. He is known as a writer of both poetry and prose.

Born in the Petersburg area of a worker's family, but from the
age of eight until adulthood he was in an orphanage. After
graduating from Leningrad University, faculty of law, 1931,
studied literature and published both articles and essays in
various literary journals. During World War II participated
in the defense of Leningrad and served as a war correspondent.
His first collection of stories was published in 1944.

Zhdanov, Nikolay G.
(1908–).

His main collections: *People of Strong Will* (Lyudi tverdoy
voli, 1944); *The Sea Salt* (Morskaya sol, 1947); *The New Sea*
(Novoe more, 1958); *The Wind of Age* (Veter veka, 1964); and
Goconda (1966).